THE HISTORY OF

LANCASHIRE
COUNTY
CRICKET CLUB

THE CHRISTOPHER HELM COUNTY CRICKET HISTORIES

Series Editors:
Peter Arnold and Peter Wynne-Thomas

DERBYSHIRE
John Shawcroft, with a personal view by Bob Taylor

GLAMORGAN
Andrew Hignell, with a personal view by Tony Lewis

HAMPSHIRE
Peter Wynne-Thomas, with a personal view by John Arlott

KENT
Dudley Moore, with a personal view by Derek Underwood

MIDDLESEX
David Lemmon, with a personal view by Denis Compton

SURREY
David Lemmon, with a personal view by Peter May

WORCESTERSHIRE
David Lemmon, with a personal view by Basil D'Oliveira

THE HISTORY OF

LANCASHIRE
COUNTY
CRICKET CLUB

Peter Wynne-Thomas

With a personal view by
BRIAN STATHAM

CHRISTOPHER HELM

London

© 1989 Peter Wynne-Thomas and J.B. Statham
Christopher Helm (Publishers) Ltd, Imperial House,
21–25 North Street, Bromley, Kent BR1 1SD

ISBN 0–7470–3411–7

A CIP catalogue record for this book is available from the British Library

Phototypeset by Tradespools Ltd., Frome, Somerset.
Printed and bound in Great Britain by Biddles Ltd., Guildford, Surrey

CONTENTS

A PERSONAL VIEW
J. B. Statham CBE

ALMOST 40 YEARS have come and gone since that Saturday in June when I made my debut for Lancashire, in the match against Kent at Old Trafford. The decision to include me in the First Eleven within a few weeks of my joining the groundstaff was made despite the opposition of Harry Makepeace, the old county batsman and head coach. He had seen too many raw recruits summoned to the colours after a handful of useful Second Team performances, only to have their careers set back, or in a few cases ruined by a captain or a committee expecting immediate results.

Nigel Howard, Lancashire's captain, no doubt briefed by Makepeace, allowed me to taste success and acclimatise myself. In the first place he won the toss and decided to bat. We scored 271, of which our senior pro, Cyril Washbrook, made 72. My own contribution – last in the order – made no difference to the total. I provided Colin Page with his only wicket of the innings.

Late in the afternoon, I opened the bowling with Arthur Fagg at the crease. The experienced Test batsman was a cricketer who relished short-pitched deliveries. It was fortunate for me that he tried out his lethal hook shot a little too early in his innings and getting a ball too high up the bat provided Alan Wharton at forward short leg with an easy catch – and me with my first championship wicket.

In the opinion of the captain, I had achieved my goal – dismissing Kent's most prolific run-getter – and he now turned to the spin attack of Bob Berry and Roy Tattersall to capitalise on this breakthrough, a task they performed with such efficiency that on the Monday, Kent followed on 170 runs behind.

The second innings was a repeat of the first, except that I captured the wicket of Fagg's opening partner, Raymond Mays and it was Malcolm Hilton, rather than Tattersall and Berry who bemused the Kent batsmen; only Godfrey Evans, England's wicketkeeper, surviving for long.

So my first match at Old Trafford ended in two days, with an innings victory. This was no isolated win, for Lancashire, having had a modest year in 1949, were enjoying a great revival. There is some truth in the old adage about being in the right place at the right time and, by coincidence, I managed to time my arrival at Old Trafford to a tee.

My serious cricket began as a 16-year-old with Denton West Cricket Club, but as with all those of my generation, National Service arrived all too soon and I found myself playing cricket and taking wickets in various inter-service matches with the RAF. A fellow cricket enthusiast, impressed by my bowling, wrote to Middlesex on my behalf applying for a trial. That county suggested I should first try my native county and this eventually led to a trial and offer of engagement at Old Trafford in the spring of 1950.

The fact that my arrival coincided with the closing of Dick Pollard's county career gave me an opportunity which might not have occurred if I had joined the Middlesex staff instead, for both Alan Moss and John Warr were at the start of successful careers at Lord's. As it was Lancashire needed a fast bowler to replace Pollard and whilst, in Berry, Hilton,

Tattersall and Greenwood, the County had an embarrassment of spinners, fast bowlers were more scarce (how Frank Tyson escaped to go to Northants is another story).

I retained my place in the County side for the rest of the season and Lancashire – mainly due to the spin of Tattersall and Hilton with the batting of Washbrook and Ikin – won 16 of their 28 Championship matches.

Three or four weeks after I had made my debut, the County took the lead at the top of the Championship table and if rain had not come to spoil our last two matches, the title would have been entirely ours. As it was Surrey managed to tie with us on points and therefore shared the honours. The man primarily responsible for the last vital points which Surrey needed was Peter May, who in the match against us hit 92 before I had him caught: Surrey awarded May his county cap for this innings. Like May, I also received my cap in the closing stages of an eventful season.

It is difficult to believe – and it certainly would have been at the time – that Lancashire would not take the Championship title again during my playing career, although we twice came second!

Lancashire may not have obtained many honours, but in my 19 years as a player we played in so many exciting matches and have produced so many notable cricketers that it is impossible in this brief essay to mention more than a few.

Of the players when I first joined the County, Cyril Washbrook was the outstanding figure. He was at the height of his career, having established his Test partnership with Len Hutton and his County partnership with Winston Place. He was the senior professional, and having served his apprenticeship in the 1930s, he was one of the old school. When the County appointed him captain in 1954, he expected the young players to give 100 per cent effort and he demanded the sort of respect he himself had given as a youngster to Eckersley and Lister. Although in those days most other counties had a strong nucleus of pre-war players still, in many cases with several years of cricket left in them in 1950 (I can think of Compton, Edrich, Robertson, Gray and Brown, for example, for Middlesex) Lancashire had only Place apart from Washbrook. Almost the whole of the pre-war regulars – Iddon, Paynter, Oldfield, Nutter, Farrimond, Hopwood – had left Old Trafford.

Harry Makepeace had a set of young players to mould. Jack Ikin, it is true, had played once or twice before the war. Ikin, from Staffordshire, had served with the 'Desert Rats' in the Second World War and had suffered an injury to his back, which recurred from time to time and on more than one occasion deprived him of his England place – in my opinion there have been few cricketers to equal Jack as a fielder close to the wicket. Winston Place was Washbrook's partner and completely imperturbable – an object lesson to those present-day batsmen who become hysterical when given out.

Senior of the players who made their Lancashire debuts after the war was Geoff Edrich, who continued the family tradition for courage, so well displayed by his brother Bill. I remember in particular two brilliant innings by him – one against Freddie Trueman and the second opposed to Frank Tyson. Alan Wharton, the all-rounder, joined Lancashire's First Eleven at the same time as Geoff Edrich. A schoolteacher, Wharton, though he only briefly played for England, proved a very useful county cricketer. He hit the ball hard and could field as well in the slips as in the deep; his bowling included a very deceiving outswinger.

Joining the staff just before me was Ken Grieves, the Australian who took up soccer and kept goal for Bolton Wanderers. I have already mentioned our trio of spinners, Malcolm Hilton, Roy Tattersall (he had, like me, been co-opted on to the 1950–51 MCC team to Australia) and Bob Berry. Peter Greenwood from Todmorden was yet another spinner, but he could also use the seam.

The one ingredient the Lancashire team lacked in 1950 – and in the years which followed – was a top-rate wicket-keeper. This was rather odd, when one thinks that in the 1930s, the County had two, both of whom played for England – Duckworth and Farrimond. Barlow was the regular keeper in my first season, but his hands were easily damaged. Wilson also played; Frank Parr and Jackie Jordan were two others who vied for the post without really establishing themselves.

Lancashire certainly had a great many promising youngsters coming into the side during my first years in the Eleven, but somehow we failed to gain the Championship. In 1956 under Washbrook we came second. We had built on the side of 1950 and added Dyson, Greenhough and C.S. Smith, as well as an oustanding young batsman in Geoff Pullar, but we couldn't quite catch Surrey, who took the title for the fifth year in succession.

In 1960 we again came second. Washbrook had gone, but Pullar was the leading batsman, still with Ken Grieves and Alan Wharton giving support. There was also the new captain, Bob Barber. It was unfortunate that Barber should have been saddled with the captaincy at that stage in his career. He was still in his early twenties and as with most young men he had his own views which did not always fit in with those of the Club's officials – he never seemed very happy at Old Trafford, which was a pity, for the County could ill-afford to lose a player with his talents. He could bowl a useful ball, as well as score runs with relish.

I captained the County for three seasons from 1965 to 1967, a time when the County had a very weak batting side. There seemed to be a shortage of players coming through from the various leagues in the County and it would appear that local club batsmen were none too keen on playing against the famous West Indian fast bowlers who were engaged in the leagues at that time – Charlie Griffith, Wes Hall and Roy Gilchrist for example – on the type of wicket which most league clubs provided. Harry Pilling was almost the only batsman in the Lancashire side who could be relied upon. The County at last solved its wicket-keeping problem by signing the Indian Test player, Engineer, but few of the younger players proved as expert in the close field as Ikin and Grieves had done in the 1940s and 1950s. The one aspect which remained really strong was that of pace bowling, with Ken Higgs and Peter Lever, as well as Ken Shuttleworth.

It was perhaps appropriate that my final appearance for Lancashire should be in the Roses match at Old Trafford – in 1968. The game was for the benefit of Ken Higgs and large crowds, though not quite the size of those in my earliest days, watched a most interesting but low scoring game. Like so many in the past it ended in a draw and in my final innings I was bowled by my old England colleague, Freddie Trueman!

Nineteen years is a long time for a fast bowler to survive in county cricket and certainly by the end of nearly two decades I was pleased to be able to put my feet up, but, for all the hard work, I enjoyed my days as a cricketer at Old Trafford. When I announced my retirement one or two other counties tried to persuade me to join them for a final year or two, but my allegiance to the Red Rose was too strong to allow me to take the offers seriously, even if my feet had been up to the task.

At the present time I am an elected member of the County committee and therefore able to continue to play some part in the life of the County Club and perhaps to guide the footsteps of the young players of today who wish to have a career in cricket at Old Trafford.

AT THE BEGINNING

ON 12 JANUARY 1864 A MEETING WAS HELD at the Queen's Hotel in Manchester at which it was agreed to form a County Cricket Club for Lancashire. The meeting was attended by representatives of the major clubs in the county, namely Manchester, Broughton, Longsight and Western, all in the vicinity of Manchester itself, plus Liverpool, Ashton, Blackburn, Accrington, Oldham, Wigan, Huyton and Northern. It was further agreed that the county side should not be based at one ground, but play at all the major venues in the county. The initial inter-county programme was modest enough with home and away matches arranged against Yorkshire, Shropshire and Warwickshire, resulting in three wins, two losses and a draw; there were also two games against Birkenhead Park, both drawn. All the games were Gentlemen's contests, thus no professionals appeared and the standard was modest in comparison with the major matches of the day. The two major cricket annuals of the day – *Lillywhite's Guide* and *Wisden's Almanack* – both ignored the new County Club.

The early 1860s saw a resurgence of interest in inter-county cricket. The famous wandering Elevens, pioneered by William Clarke in 1846, had staged marvellous 'exhibition' matches throughout the British Isles and whilst after nearly 20 years the novelty of their 'Odds' matches was beginning to wear thin, the standard of cricket – in respect of both the players and the grounds on which they played – had been much enhanced by the exploits of England's major professionals. To be selected to play against the All England Eleven was the pinnacle of ambition for a youngster, for there was always a chance that his performance might lead to an offer of a place in the England side or one of its rivals.

Now, therefore, was the time for county cricket to build on this platform created by Clarke. Together with Lancashire, no less than eight other counties formed, or revived, county cricket clubs in the first few years of the 1860s. Some, like Somerset, Buckinghamshire, Suffolk and Glamorgan, failed to put down strong roots, but Gloucestershire, Middlesex and Yorkshire, with Lancashire, formed the basis for the clubs which are in existence today.

Before this clutch of new county clubs, inter-county cricket, such as it was, revolved around the three great southern counties of Kent, Sussex and Surrey plus the all-powerful Notts team and the occasional Cambridgeshire eleven. The Championship was loosely run on the same lines as the boxing contests – the Champion County held to its title until beaten by a rival. Except at Lord's and the Oval – homes of

MCC and the Surrey Club – there were no places where numbers of cricket professionals were employed, though by 1860 most major clubs had a ground bowler and perhaps a lad to assist him.

Before we follow the progress of the Lancashire County Club, it is necessary to go back to the very beginnings of cricket in the county. G.B. Buckley's 'Fresh Light on 18th Century Cricket' provides the historian with a broad picture of the spread of the game through the British Isles prior to 1800. Mr Buckley gives upwards of 150 places involved in 18th-century cricket in Kent, nearly 100 in Sussex, Hampshire and Surrey, and about 20 in Nottinghamshire and York-shire. Lancashire, however, fails to manage a single reference.

It is clear therefore that cricket was firmly established in Yorkshire and Nottinghamshire before the Napoleonic Wars brought a temporary lull to the game, but Lancashire did not attach much importance to cricket until the second decade of the 19th century. The first match details which have been discovered come from the *Leeds Intelligencer* of 31 August 1812 and report:

August 6 on Newton Race Ground

Rochdale	49 + 5 byes =	54		Liverpool	20 + 1 bye =	21	
	60 + 2	= 62			51 + 2	= 53	
		116				74	

The previous year, a Liverpool newspaper had published a long poem describing the Liverpool Cricket Club, therefore Liverpool would appear to have preceded Manchester in the formation of a cricket club, for the latter town's club claims to have been established in 1816.

In the 1820s the matches between Liverpool and Manchester became the major Lancashire cricket fixtures. The first known mention of a meeting of the two sides came in 1823 with the advertisement of a game to be played on 4 October, but no report of the actual game has survived. In the following season, two matches took place. The first, won by Manchester by two runs, was staged on the ground opposite Salford Crescent, Manchester. The second was at Crabtree Lane, Liverpool, and provided Liverpool with victory by 88 runs. Only the bare scores, with no mention of individual players, are given in the newspaper.

The first full score of a match is dated 1826, when Manchester beat Liverpool at Manchester by 39 runs. Both teams were entirely composed of amateurs and the leading figure for Manchester was Lea Birch, a slow under-arm bowler and father of Scholes Birch, who appeared in the 1840s. The family seat was Loxley Park in Staffordshire. Lea Birch was easily the most effective Manchester bowler at that time and in the 1827 match claimed eight wickets, but was thwarted by Major Labalmondiere, who hit the highest score for Liverpool in each innings, 20 and 30, enabling Liverpool to win by 26 runs. Labalmon-diere later became the Assistant Commissioner of the Metropolitan Police.

In 1832 Manchester won both matches with Liverpool, repeating their double victory of the previous season, and decided the time had come to test their strength against Sheffield, the most powerful Yorkshire club of the day. Despite having twenty-two men against Sheffield's eleven, Manchester were completely outplayed, only two players, one in each innings, reaching double figures and Sheffield won by 6 wickets. Sheffield, however, fielded an all-professional side, whilst Manchester played only amateurs. A match against Leeds in 1836 had a more successful outcome for the Lancashire side, who won by 119 runs, Lea Birch with 59 making easily the highest score for his side; in addition he took six wickets.

Henry Cooke, the honorary secretary of Manchester, and a local mill owner, was instrumental in arranging Manchester's first match at Lord's – against the Gentlemen of MCC in 1842. No doubt he was encouraged to take on the premier club due to the continued success of Manchester over Liverpool and the batting of S.H. Braybrooke, described as a rather stout gentleman, who hit an undefeated 33 out of 66 for Manchester in 1841. Manchester, batting first, were dismissed for 59 and MCC replied with 220 for nine, at which point the visitors conceded the match. Arthur Haygarth appends the following footnote to the score: 'The Manchester bowling was very inferior, being of the old underhand school ... and afforded the MCC Gentlemen much amusement in hitting it away.' It was ten years before Manchester risked opposing MCC a second time.

Manchester did break fresh ground in 1844 with a match against 'Yorkshire' at Moss Lane, Hulme. The Manchester side won by five wickets, their victory being due to John Sherman, the Surrey cricketer, who came to Manchester to work as a calico printer in 1835 and in 1838 began a seven-year engagement as professional to the Manchester club – the first professional of any note to be engaged by the club. Sherman, like Lea Birch, was an underhand bowler, and he took ten wickets in this first match against Yorkshire. Yorkshire fielded a much stronger side in the two matches played the following year and Manchester suffered in consequence, losing the first game by an innings and the second by eight wickets, despite being reinforced by Baldwinson, who hit a fifty for Yorkshire in the first game.

Thomas Hunt, who had played for Yorkshire, moved, like Baldwin-son, to Manchester and the side which opposed Sheffield at Hyde Park, Sheffield, in 1846 contained no fewer than five professionals: Sherman, Baldwinson, Hunt, J. Womack, who was a local player with the Manchester Broughton Club, and Arthur Girling, a native of Burton-on-Trent, who settled in Manchester. Baldwinson hit 73, Hunt 48 and Girling took eight wickets, all of which produced an innings victory for Manchester. Baldwin scored an undefeated 87 in the return fixture, Hunt took eleven wickets and Manchester won again.

In September of the same year was staged the most important game to date in Manchester, when William Clarke's England Eleven opposed Eighteen of Manchester. Hunt, Girling, Womack and Sherman formed the attack for Manchester, but the England team, with Fuller Pilch making 62, totalled 228. Alfred Mynn, Hillyer and Dean then dismissed Manchester for 72, the best batting coming from John Earle, who lasted four hours for just 11 runs. Manchester followed on and lost the game by an innings. This was only the second game ever played by the England Eleven and the fact that Clarke chose Manchester for his opponents must prove that cricket there was very popular – Clarke being a person with an eye to the 'gate' – and he had only one eye!

Manchester further built up their professional strength in 1847 by engaging the Notts bowler, John Buttery. He made all the difference to the match against Clarke's England Eleven that year. This time it was drawn in favour of the Mancunians – England 227 and 125, Manchester 261 and 32 for eight. The England side went from Manchester to Liverpool – another drawn match, but Liverpool were given two leading professionals, Lillywhite and Martingell, and they, between them, took all the England wickets which fell to bowlers.

In 1848 there were nine major matches contested by Manchester – home and away with Sheffield, Liverpool, Leicester and Burton-on-Trent, plus the match with England. On the face of it the results were not too promising, with only three wins, to five losses and a draw. However two losses were against Burton-on-Trent, who had two given men to assist them, and the matches against Liverpool were amateur games. A fairer indication of the growing power of Manchester is that Clarke demanded the odds be reduced from eighteen Manchester players to fifteen, and even so Manchester lost by only three wickets.

A red-letter day in the annals of cricket, and of Lancashire cricket in particular, was 23 July 1849, for on that day began the first ever Lancashire v Yorkshire match – staged on the Hyde Park Ground, Sheffield. The Lancashire team was a combination of Manchester and Liverpool amateurs plus three professionals engaged in the county: Thomas Hunt, John Buttery and George Wigzell, a steady batsman and slow bowler from Sevenoaks. Hunt and G.F. Dallas, the Liverpool opener, made the highest scores for Lancashire and Hunt and Wigzell proved the most effective bowlers, but Yorkshire won by five wickets. The White Rose proved overwhelmingly superior in the return at Manchester, winning with an innings to spare. Another important event of 1849 was the establishment of the Longsight club, whose ground was laid out at the then terminus of horse buses, past Ardwick Green and along the Stockport road, in an area only just starting to succumb to bricks and mortar. The club quickly gained in popularity and by the 1870s had some 300 members.

Aided by three given men, Eighteen of Manchester beat Clarke's England Eleven in 1850, but not without a struggle – Manchester levelled the score, then lost no fewer than five wickets before Birch, coming in at number fifteen, hit the winning run. John Wisden, later of *Almanack* fame, was England's best bowler with ten for 50 in the final innings. A return game was arranged later in the season and England got its revenge, William Clarke's under-arm deliveries picking up 16 wickets. In the following year, the England match was played on the Broughton Ground for the first time. The Broughton club, founded in 1823, had begun its existence in Lower Broughton Lane, but about 1829 moved to an eight-acre site in a pleasant suburb of Higher Broughton. The ground with a line of trees on one side was much more pleasing to the eye than the Manchester club's Old Trafford or Longsight and had a pavilion built rather in the style of a church.

Two Lancashire v Yorkshire matches were played in 1851, and Lancashire, though strengthened by Julius Caesar and Cris Tinley, two of the best professionals of the day, lost both. After this, the fixture was not renewed until the bona fide Lancashire Club was established, though the fault was as much with Yorkshire as Lancashire, since the former's organisation at county level was even more confused than Lancashire's.

The dropping of the Roses match did not inhibit the aspirations of the Manchester club. In 1852 – ten years after the first disastrous experiment – they returned to Lord's to oppose MCC. Aided by John Wisden they lost by only three wickets. They then travelled from London to Canterbury and had the best of a drawn game with a strong local side, which included Fuller Pilch, Edgar Willsher and W.H. Fryer.

Another innovation that summer was the first Gentlemen of the North v Gentlemen of the South match at Lord's. Lancashire's representatives were G.F. Cooke and John Campbell Rowley, the eldest of four cricketing brothers. A solicitor and a hard-hitting batsman, he was killed in a railway accident at Harrow in 1870; another brother, Joseph, was described as a dangerous grub bowler – the grass did not want much mowing after his daisy-cutters had been over it.

The first game between the Manchester club and the Broughton club seems to have taken place in 1853. This was the first major match for a pale, delicate youth, Joseph Makinson of Higher Broughton. Though he failed to score in this match, he developed into one of the best amateur batsmen of the day, being very quick on his feet – he scored a century for the Broughton club against All England in 1860, a very rare feat indeed. His profession – a barrister – prevented him playing regularly in the 1860s. His brother Charles was also a talented cricketer and later played in Australia. Manchester won this contest by 18 runs.

Another cricketer whose career began with the 1853 Broughton club was John Payne, who lived at Heathfield, Broughton, but originated from Knutsford. A slow under-arm bowler he was captain and secretary of the Broughton club for about a decade. Manchester beat Sheffield by an innings in 1853, but only because each side was restricted to one professional and Sheffield's strength lay in their paid players.

Both Preston and Rochdale organised matches against the great England Elevens in 1854. The Preston club, which had been formed in 1845 and played on a ground about one mile north-east of the town, won their match by seven wickets, due in a large part to the bowling of Buttress, the Cambridge pro, whose county career was much curtailed by drink. Buttress took twelve wickets. Rochdale lost their match.

The principal match staged in Lancashire in 1856 was North v South – played on the Broughton ground. Two Lancastrians represented the North, R.T. Bellhouse and J. Makinson. Thomas Hunt's 102 was the feature of a rain-ruined game, his batting against Wisden, Martingell, Dean and John Lillywhite being the equal of any seen that year.

In 1857 the Manchester club moved its ground a hundred or two yards west of its previous location, which was required for the 'Art Treasures' Exhibition'. The new ground, like the old, was still described as 'Old Trafford'.

Bell's Life describes the new ground:

> The new ground is situated to the West of the Exhibition buildings and consists of about eight acres of good, level, sandy land. The pavilion is erected on the north side; and while it is a great ornament to the ground, it is well adapted for the purposes for which it will be used. It consists of a centre compartment (intended for a dining hall) and two wings, a turret surmounting the centre. The dining hall is 36 feet long by 22 feet wide ... Underneath the building is an excellent wine cellar, no unimportant acquisition in a cricket pavilion. The entire front of the dining hall, which commands a view of the whole field, is composed of glass.

The *Sporting Life* correspondent describes his journey to the ground a few years later:

> Starting from the Infirmary, and finding the streets very sloppy and dirty, as usual, we catch one of the 'buses, and turn to the left down the Stretford Road, past villas built more tastefully than ordinarily,

past the Botanical Gardens on the left and Sir H. de Trafford's on the right, we come to the Public and turn down a lane to a somewhat low-lying, dreary-looking, treeless ground, with palings round it. A bowling green is in its immediate vicinity, for that game is much affected in Manchester. Football, pigeon shooting and polo are carried on in the adjoining field. A railway station is close to the ground, which is distant from Manchester by rail about 3 miles. After interviewing some fine Spanish fowls, a mastiff and pointer, we find that civil, obliging cricketer and indefatigable assistant secretary, Frederick Reynolds, in his snuggery by the pavilion.

Appropriately the Manchester v Liverpool match in June was the first staged on the new ground, but the most exciting game in Lancashire that summer took place at the ground of the Western club at Eccles when Manchester, with two given men, John Wisden and John Lillywhite, opposed and beat Surrey by three runs; as Surrey were regarded as the best county that year and this turned out to be their only defeat, this was a major triumph for the Manchester side. The match was a very low-scoring affair, Manchester making 53 and 99, whilst Surrey's totals were 60 and 89. The highest scorer in the home side's first innings was Alexander Rowley, aged 19. Educated at Rossall School, Rowley represented the North v South at Lord's in 1859, when he again realised the highest score for his side. A right-hand batsman, he bowled left-arm slow. His appearances after 1860 were restricted owing to his business commitments as a cotton manufacturer; he was also well-known in yachting circles. Opening the batting for Manchester was a Spaniard, F. Perera, who played for the Broughton club, having a business in the Cottonopolis, and he was later on the Lancashire Committee.

Two games of some historical importance were played either side of this Surrey contest. On 27 and 28 August, the Free Foresters undertook their first 'contest of any note', opposing the Western club at Eccles. Free Foresters won by an innings; then at the end of September Free Foresters went to Old Trafford and beat the Manchester club (including T. Hunt) again by an innings. The Western club was to give much support to the Free Foresters over the next 20 years and it was at the Western club that Free Foresters recorded their famous victory over the united England Eleven in 1861. The Free Foresters fielded an all-amateur Sixteen against the all-professional England side and won by four wickets. It was in this match that, according to legend, an umpire donned a white coat for the first time – Armitstead complained he could not see the bowler's hand against the umpire's dark suit.

The major Lancashire match in 1858 also took place at Eccles. This time Sussex played Manchester. Alexander Rowley scored an excellent

53, but Manchester's given man, William Caffyn of Surrey, was unable to bat in either innings due to illness and Sussex won by an innings. Even the help of W.M.N. Kington, a cavalry officer from the nearby barracks and a noted hitter, failed to save the day.

The amateur talent of Lancashire was, however, improving all the time, as can be judged by the fact that Gentlemen of Lancashire beat the Players at Old Trafford in 1858 by an innings. J. Whittington made 37 for the Gentlemen in this game. Unfortunately the Broughton club had two J. Whittingtons – Joseph and James, both good cricketers – and it is impossible to separate the performances of the two.

One of the Whittingtons appeared in the ranks of the Gentlemen of the North v Gentlemen of the South in 1858, this game taking place on the Broughton ground. Other Lancastrians in the northern side for that game were F. Perera, Alexander Rowley, once more the highest scorer for his side, W.P. Lockart, who was a merchant in Birkenhead, and H.H. Hornby, second cousin of the more famous brothers of the same name. Three of the Southgate Walker brothers appeared for the South in this match and took most of the wickets between them, the South winning fairly easily.

The same fixture was transferred to Liverpool in 1859, but the Walker brothers repeated their success of the previous summer – J. Makinson with an undefeated 63 was one of the few northern batsmen to come out of the match with much credit.

Centre of interest for cricket enthusiasts of 1860 was the meeting of North v South on the Merefield Ground at Rochdale. The Rochdale club showed much enterprise in staging this game and were rewarded by a profit of £113, with about 7,000 spectators attending on the Saturday. The *Rochdale Observer* noted:

> Thanks are due to the Rochdale Club for bringing together the champion Players of England. Everybody seemed satisfied. There was nothing to find fault with. Even the ladies appeared to have been satisfied, especially on the first day when they could get wet through for nothing, while the gentlemen had to pay two shillings for that enviable privilege.

There were no Lancashire players in the northern side, the eleven being all professional. Stephen Leach, uncle of the well-known amateurs of the same name, was President of Rochdale in 1860 and promised a new suit to any batsman who hit 50 in the match – George Anderson and William Caffyn went home looking smarter than when they arrived.

Frederick Reginald Reynolds was engaged by the Manchester Club in 1861 and took up residence in the house in the pavilion at Old Trafford. His tenure of office was to last 48 years, for he did not retire until

December 1908. *Lillywhite's Guide* of 1864 commented on Reynolds: 'This straight and persevering bowler has a permanent situation at the Old Trafford Ground, Manchester, where, by his excellent management and his general good qualities, he is much respected.' Writing much later, W.E. Howard noted: 'He always took a great interest in the ground, and, being rather a pompous man, used to look upon it as a condescension on his part to allow people to play on it.'

Thomas Hunt, who had been at Old Trafford until 1858 as ground bowler, had come to a melancholy end, losing both legs in a railway accident and dying shortly afterwards.

The most popular match of the period – discounting the 'social' events such as Eton v Harrow – was the England Eleven v United Eleven which was the meeting of the cream of professional talent and generally staged at Lord's. In 1861, however, the two sides decided on a second match to be played at Old Trafford and played purely for the benefit of the cricketers taking part. Despite rain washing out nearly all the first day, the players cleared £10 per man. Reynolds umpired the game, but no Lancashire cricketers took part. That the organisers chose Old Trafford demonstrated the interest which the Manchester public was now showing in cricket.

The Broughton ground also staged a major match in 1861, when the North opposed Surrey. Rain seriously interferred with the cricket and the game was drawn. The only amateur in the northern side was the only Lancastrian in the match: E.J. Bousfield, born in Manchester, was a leading member of the Broughton club and a strong defensive batsman, as well as an excellent fielder. He later became a member of the Lancashire Committee. Bousfield represented the North the following season, when the match against the South was arranged for Old Trafford. Rain was the cause of another undecided contest.

When the MCC arranged a match at Lord's against the 'Colts' – professionals who had never played at Lord's or the Oval – in June 1862, Lancashire provided one youngster, a fair-headed 24-year-old. Cornelius Coward was one of the few genuine Lancashire professionals – he was born in Preston – to appear for Lancashire regularly in the early years of the County Club. He later became a well-known umpire.

The North met Surrey for the second successive year in 1862 on the Broughton Ground. This time Bousfield was joined by two more Lancashire amateurs in the North side, E.B. Rowley, a younger brother of Alexander and aged 20, and J.B. Payne. The North won an exciting contest by one wicket. *Lillywhite's Guide* provides an excellent description:

The weather was favourable, the ground in splendid condition, the company good and the cricket fine . . . It was even betting at starting, and the first day (Thursday) was wholly occupied in getting through Surrey's first innings – a fine one of 156; and in a like manner the whole of Friday was devoted to the North's first innings of 183. Then on the Saturday, the 3rd day, it was rare exciting cricket all through. 800 elegantly attired ladies graced the ground; 5,000 spectators formed a compact ring around the pretty Broughton; and the large sloping bank outside was studded with upwards of 1,000 Lancashire lads. Surrey commenced their second innings on a ground dead with the previous night's rain ... Surrey's innings finished up for 83, leaving 57 only for the North to score to win, and the betting 10 to 1 they done it, and they did do it; but the old Surrey form came out so strong, that every man of the North Eleven had to go to the wicket ere it was done.

The upsurge of cricket in Lancashire continued in 1863. Haygarth included eight of what he believed important match cards in *Scores and Biographies* covering 1862, while for 1863 he doubled the number.

The North met the South twice in Lancashire – at a game at Old Trafford sponsored by the Manchester club and at Wavertree Road, Liverpool. These games were in addition to the North v Surrey on Broughton club's ground and the Gentlemen of Manchester v the Gentlemen of Surrey.

The Old Trafford North v South was staged in May and resulted in an easy victory for the North; the Lancashire representative was Edwin Whittaker, who came from Ashton-under-Lyne, and was a useful batsman and wicket-keeper. Many of the leading northern players refused to appear on the Broughton ground for the Surrey match, George Parr having fallen out with Surrey, but the North still won and E.B. Rowley, R. Blackstock, J.B. Payne and F.W. Wright, all local amateurs, appeared for them. Wright was a curate in Broughton, where his father, the Rev Frank Bowcher Wright, was rector of St John's. Wright senior had appeared for Oxford University in 1829. The family were great supporters of the Broughton club over several decades.

The Gentlemen of Surrey side which opposed the Gentlemen of Manchester in August was almost up to 'first-class' county standard, containing as it did three of the Southgate Walkers and E. Dowson, C. Calvert, E.W. Vyse and W. Horner among others. A.B. Rowley took five Surrey wickets in their first innings to give Manchester a lead of 22, but he was unable to bowl during most of the second innings and this misfortune allowed Surrey to win by two wickets. H.W. Barber, the Rossall schoolboy, hit the only fifty of the match, for Manchester.

It is not clear from extant records who was the moving force behind the formation of the County Club in the first month of 1864. Nine matches were played in that season involving no less than 56 players.

The eleven who made more than two appearances were: A.B. Rowley, E.B. Rowley, E.J. Bousfield, B.J. Lawrence, S.H. Swire, F.W. Wright, H.W. Barber, W. Horner, C. Coward, J. Rowley and B. Darbyshire. All of these players have already been mentioned, except Lawrence, a bowler from the Liverpool club, and Darbyshire, who was a member of the Northern club. The officers of the Lancashire Club in its first year were: president, the Earl of Sefton; vice-presidents, Lord Skelmersdale, J.A. Turner, Chas Turner, Mark Phillips and M.P. FitzGerald; treasurer, William Langton of Liverpool; and hon secretary, Frank Glover of Manchester.

TOWARDS THE FIRST CHAMPIONSHIP TITLE

THE 1865 SEASON SAW THE STAGING OF the first 'All-Lancashire' match by the new County Club. The eleven included three professionals, whereas the matches of 1864 had involved only amateurs. The game was against Middlesex at Old Trafford and contained two remarkable features: the scores were tied on first innings and V.E. Walker took all ten wickets (for 104) in Lancashire's second innings. Lancashire won by 62 runs, but in the return on the Cattle Market Ground, Islington, Middlesex had their revenge, winning by ten wickets. It should be stated however that only four of the Lancashire team who turned out at Old Trafford travelled to London and two of the absentees were A.B. Rowley and J. Makinson, who had made the highest scores in the first match. The bowling was in the hands of Reynolds and Iddison in both matches and was therefore not so seriously affected.

Roger Iddison, who took eight wickets at Old Trafford, is described by Caffyn as a 'strong, stout, red-faced, healthy-looking man – a true type of old-fashioned Yorkshire'. He was engaged by the Broughton club for three years and then transferred to the Whalley club, which was his abode for 1865. He had played originally for Yorkshire and was to return to his native county, but from 1865 to 1870 appeared in 16 Lancashire first-class matches. Of the other professionals used by the County, Enoch Storer came from Clay Cross in Derbyshire, but was engaged by the Longsight club and then moved to Bury. A right-arm fast bowler he died aged 32 in 1880. William Perry, a native of Oxfordshire, was the pro to the Liverpool club and his Lancashire appearances were limited to one. J. Smith, who opened the Lancashire batting at Islington, was the professional from Yeadon, who in fact appeared for both Yorkshire and Lancashire in the same season. He was engaged by the East Lancs club at Blackburn from 1863 to 1868. A left-handed batsman, he had played for the Colts at Lord's in 1864. Two amateurs who made fleeting appearances were H.N. Tennent of the well-known Scottish brewing family, who later become involved in the theatre and ran the Empire, Leicester Square, and L.H. Moorsom, who in 1868–69 appeared for Trinidad.

Apart from the two games with Middlesex, there were matches against Yorkshire and Shropshire, but these were purely amateur affairs. The 1866 programme was a trifle more adventurous, the Club tackling Surrey as well as Middlesex. They most probably owed the Surrey fixture to the fact that both Notts and Yorkshire refused to play at the Oval, owing to a dispute. Lancashire failed to win one of their

LANCASHIRE *v.* MIDDLESEX

Played on the Old Trafford Ground, Manchester, 20, 21 and 22 July 1865

LANCASHIRE WON BY 62 RUNS

LANCASHIRE	FIRST INNINGS		SECOND INNINGS	
Mr R. Blackstock	c and b Wilkinson	18	(8) b V. Walker	5
Mr F.J. Crooke	b R. Walker	35	st Morley b V. Walker	20
R. Iddison	b Howitt	20	(4) c and b V. Walker	6
Mr J.F. Leese	c and b Howitt	33	(3) c Haines b V. Walker	0
Mr J Makinson	b T. Hearne	45	(9) st Morley b V. Walker	0
Mr E Whittaker	c Haines b Wilkinson	23	(7) c R Walker b V. Walker	39
Mr. E.J. Bousfield	c V. Walker b. T. Hearne	0	(5) c Wilkinson b V. Walker	15
Mr A.B. Rowley	c Wilkinson b T. Hearne	24	(6) c R. Walker b V. Walker	60
Mr S.H. Swire	not out	18	(1) b V. Walker	16
W. Perry	c Morley b Catling	16	c and b V. Walker	0
F.R. Reynolds	c T. Hearne b Catling	9	not out	13
Extras	b 1, lb 1	2	lb 3, w 1	4
Total		243		178

BOWLING	O	M	R	W		O	M	R	W
T. Hearne	27	11	50	3		8	6	6	0
Wilkinson	24	6	49	2		7	4	6	0
R. Walker	17	5	40	1		2	1	3	0
Howitt	27	8	55	2		36	14	49	0
Mantle	9	3	34	0					
Catling	3	0	13	2	(1 wide)	5	2	6	0
V. Walker						44.2	5	104	10

MIDDLESEX	FIRST INNINGS		SECOND INNINGS	
Mr A.J.A. Wilkinson	c Blackstock b Iddison	59	absent	
Mr J.A. Haines	b Iddison	3	run out	3
B. Roberson	st Perry b Iddison	13	c Reynolds b Iddison	3
Mr R.D. Walker	c Perry b Rowley	84	b Reynolds	28
T. Hearne	c Makinson b Rowley	26	c Bousfield b Iddison	5
Mr V.E. Walker	c and b Reynolds	0	c Perry b Iddison	29
G. Hearne	c Perry b Rowley	14	c Leese b Reynolds	14
W. Catling	b Reynolds	3	not out	0
T.A. Mantle	lbw b Reynolds	0	c Leese b Iddison	4
G. Howitt	run out	23	b Iddison	5
Mr J.H. Morley	not out	6	b Reynolds	19
Extras	b 7, lb 4, w 1	12	b 1, lb 4, w 1	6
Total		243		116

BOWLING	O	M	R	W		O	M	R	W
Reynolds	48.3	15	72	3		32.2	14	38	3
Iddison	20	3	52	3		16	1	45	5
Rowley	43	15	61	3		16	7	27	0
Makinson	5	1	6	0					
Perry	7	0	29	0					
Swire	2	0	11	0					

Lancashire won the toss and batted first.

17

four major fixtures, but *Lillywhite's Companion* makes some encouraging remarks:

> The Lancashire Club includes many well-seasoned gentlemen whose exploits we have in former years had the pleasure of recording, and relying upon their pluck and determination to pull them through, the Committee aspired at once to 'high game', doubtless comforting themselves with the assurance, 'that though in great attempts 'tis glorious to fall', more honour would rebound to their arms if they were defeated by powerful antagonists than in conquering foemen unworthy of their steel.

The Middlesex game at Old Trafford was lost by poor fielding, whilst in the other home match (v Surrey at Liverpool) 'Ben' Griffith, the Surrey all-rounder, won the match on his own, with 11 wickets and 25 and 41 not out. The game at the Oval was a high scoring draw. Surrey made 422 in reply to Lancashire's 195, then Roger Iddison hit 105, the first ever first-class hundred for Lancashire, and with Gideon Holgate (65) enabled Lancashire to bat out time. Holgate was born in Yorkshire, but now lived in Accrington and captained the local club. He played both for Lancashire and his native shire in 1866, but this match was his most outstanding in county cricket, for with 52, he made the highest score in Lancashire's first innings. Lancashire were dismissed for 146 and 142 by Middlesex at Islington, Alec Rowley's 63 not out being the best innings for his side. His brother, E.B. Rowley, hit 125 for Lancashire against Cheshire at Chelford and a 20-year-old from Cheltenham College made 95, in what proved to be his only appearance for Lancashire. But this Cheshire game, like the one at York, v Yorkshire, excluded professionals.

Arthur Appleby, a corn merchant and mill owner in his native Enfield, made his mark in the Lancashire matches of 1867, so much so that he was selected to play for the Gentlemen at Lord's in the same year. *Baily's* makes the following comment:

> It was with good judgment, therefore, that the managers of the match (Gents v Players) secured the services of Mr Appleby – by no means a thoroughly good bowler but one who would be sure to be of use on Lord's ground. And the wicket could not have been prepared more suitable for him. It was hard, bumpy, unsound and untrue.

Appleby was a fast left-hand round-arm bowler and by the 1870s had developed into perhaps the best amateur fast bowler of the day. He was easily the best Lancashire bowler of the year, heading the County averages with 30 wickets at 15 runs apiece, but his only support was from the Derbyshire-born professional, William Hickton, and as the

Lancashire batting failed in nearly every match, the County went through the season without a single victory.

The two counties played in 1867 were Yorkshire and Surrey. The former club had been in disarray for 18 months owing to a dispute with its leading professionals, but all was harmony in 1867 and Yorkshire went through the season undefeated, being proclaimed County Champions as a result. Lancashire had the ill-luck to arrange three fixtures against them and lost all three, two of them by an innings. The first was played at Whalley, when George Freeman and Luke Greenwood bowled unchanged to dismiss Lancashire for 57 and 75. A week later the second game commenced at Old Trafford. Yorkshire had a much weaker side, their best men playing for the All England Eleven at Halifax, but the margin of victory was still 165 runs. A curiosity in this game was that Roger Iddison played for Yorkshire, whilst W.H. Iddison, his brother, represented Lancashire. The away game was played in September in Middlesbrough, another innings defeat, Freeman and Tom Emmett being the destructive bowlers.

Roger Iddison switched his allegiance to Lancashire for the Old Trafford match with Surrey and his batting saved his adopted county, for he made 71 and 64, both not out, and in each case the highest innings for his side. The Oval match with Surrey belonged to James Ricketts. He was very much a nine-day wonder, for on this, his first-class debut, he opened the batting for Lancashire, and was undefeated at the end with 195 out of 429. Ricketts was a tinsmith, living in Deansgate, Manchester, and this sensational start to his career seemed to have an adverse effect on his cricket, for the public expected great things of him each time he went to the crease. He was given a place in the North v South match and the Gentlemen v Players, but failed to achieve much and though he played more than 30 times for Lancashire over the next decade, he never again scored a century. The fact that he was rather slow and careless in the field did not help his career. The *Sporting Life* noted: 'There probably never has been so disappointing a player as Ricketts.'

Directly after the Oval match, Lancashire went across London to Lord's and played MCC for the first time. In a very low-scoring match, Ricketts was dismissed without scoring and *Baily's* was quickly off the mark with:

> Ricketts must indubitably know something of batting to accomplish such a cricketing feat, even against the worn-out Surrey Eleven ... but never think too much of players till you have seen what they can do against Wootton and Grundy at Lord's.

Wootton and Grundy were at that time the major professionals with MCC and Lancashire were all out for 79 and 66, with Wootton bowling unchanged through both innings taking 11 for 63. *Baily's*, however, did note: 'Lancashire is bound in time to produce a strong county eleven, having every requisite for doing so, both in point of men and money.'

The committee, perhaps because of the side's poor showing, decided on only one match against Yorkshire in 1868 and substituted two against Notts. All three were defeats. Freeman and Emmett dismissed Lancashire for 30 and 34 at Holbeck and Wootton and J.C. Shaw were almost as effective for Notts at Trent Bridge, but in the return with Notts Lancashire ought to have won, requiring 70 only when they began the final innings. They were all out for 53. The one success of the year came against Surrey at Old Trafford, when after Surrey had gained a first-innings lead of 49, Roger Iddison and Hickton bowled out the opposition for 42, Hickton's fast bowling taking six for 14, and Lancashire went on to an eight-wicket victory. At the Oval, however, Surrey won by an innings, Harry Jupp hitting 110. The fixture at Lord's was again played directly after the Surrey game and MCC won by four wickets in a match dominated by the bowlers, the best individual score being 37 by Thomas Wall, the Wigan amateur, who came to London with the side as wicket-keeper in the absence of Bousfield. Wall died in 1875, two years before the appearance of his brothers for Lancashire.

Lillywhite's Companion pointed out Lancashire's problems in its review of 1869:

> If the Palatinate could always muster its strongest eleven, the county must be a strong one indeed that can get the upper hand of its eleven; but the amateurs, a very strong division in Lancashire, find it very difficult to travel south for matches in London or at Brighton, whenever the eleven is engaged. In criticising their absence, it must be borne in mind, that with professionals, cricket is business, with the amateurs, pleasure.

The county played home and away with Surrey and Sussex in 1869, winning both matches at Old Trafford and losing both aways, as well as their fixture with MCC. The Rev F.W. Wright and A.N. Hornby, with 120 not out and 61, provided Lancashire with victory by 104 runs over Sussex and Iddison, Cornelius Coward and E.B. Rowley scored the bulk of the runs in the defeat of Surrey.

A.N. Hornby was outstanding among a tribe of Hornbys who were involved in Lancashire cricket. W.H. Hornby, the father of A.N. and C.L., was MP for Blackburn until unseated on a charge of bribery by his agent. The seat was then taken, on an increased majority, by another of his sons, E.K. Lancashire's bowling for 1869 remained very much a two-handed affair – Appleby and Hickton – and they took 24 and 39 wickets respectively, the next most being six by Reynolds.

ALBERT NEILSON HORNBY

A man of great enthusiasm for cricket, his zest transmitted itself to the other players, so that, as a captain – and he led Lancashire for the best part of 20 years – he could get the best out of men under his command. His brilliant example in the field, especially at cover point, inspired the less talented. He is forever associated with R.G. Barlow, the pair being for some years the opening batsmen for Lancashire. Hornby hit the ball tremendously hard and could score all round the wicket. Always ready for a quick single, he sometimes confused his partner even more than the fielders.

His chief flaw was his anxiety to score too fast, but on occasion when his mind was made up he could defend stubbornly.

He went to Australia only once – with Lord Harris's side of 1878–79 and was chosen to play in only two Tests in England – captaining his country in the first Test of the 1884 series, which was drawn.

He was the longest serving president the Lancashire Club have had, being elected in 1894, whilst he was still a player, and staying until 1916. In his later years he was criticised for his handling of certain situations off the field and had particular difficulty with the antics of Walter Brearley. He was also a noted rugby footballer and was capped nine times by England.

A. N. Hornby (NCCC)

Lancashire rather lowered her sights for 1870, deciding to play
Hampshire instead of Sussex. The game at Old Trafford was won by
ten wickets, with A.N. Hornby hitting 132 and Hickton performing
the considerable feat of all ten wickets (for 46) in Hampshire's second
innings. The return at Southampton was won by 40 runs. Surrey lost at
Old Trafford by eight wickets, Hickton taking six for 17 in the second
inngings of a low scoring game, but at the Oval, Surrey proved
victorious by an innings, their new bowler, W.H. Anstead, giving a
brilliant performance on his debut.

Season 1871 saw the debut for Lancashire of a young batsman who
was to represent the County for over 20 years, as well as gain his
England cap. R.G. Barlow in his reminiscences describes how he
became a county cricketer:

> The means of my discovery, and of my being brought to the notice of
> the Lancashire County Committee, was a match in which I was
> playing at Staveley, Derbyshire, in June 1871, against the late Geo.
> Parr's All England XI. W. Hickton, who was at the time engaged on
> the county ground at Manchester, was also playing and hearing that I
> was a Lancashire-born lad, came and had some conversation with
> me. He advised me to write to the Lancashire Committee, and
> promised to back up my application. I therefore wrote to them, and
> at once received a reply asking me to come over to Manchester for a
> trial on the Friday afternoon. I accordingly went, and found a good
> practice wicket ready for me, upon which I was given about half-an-
> hour's batting against the bowling of Hickton and several other
> professionals. This was followed by half-an-hour's bowling and then
> some fielding and catching practice; so taking all round, they gave me
> a very thorough trial. I must have satisfied my attestors, for in a few
> days after my return home, I received a letter from the Lancashire
> Committee, asking me to play against Yorkshire . . .

Barlow carried out his bat for 28 in this match and took a wicket with
his first ball. Lancashire beat Yorkshire for the first time in this game
and by a good margin of ten wickets. The main architect of victory was
Appleby, who hit 99 as well as taking eight wickets. Yorkshire,
however, won the other match by 222 runs. Derbyshire, on paper a
very moderate side, were met for the first time and dismissed
Lancashire for 25, going on to win the match by an innings. It was
rather odd in fact that Lancashire lost one match each to Yorkshire,
Kent and Derbyshire and then won one each against the same
opponents.

Another unusual feature of the season were matches against both
Oxford and Cambridge Universities, again providing one win and one
loss. It was a thoroughly mixed season! Barlow was not the only

notable figure to make his debut that year. A brown, active little fellow described later as the 'Southerton of the North' played in one match. Alexander 'Sandy' Watson came from Coatbridge in Scotland and gained an engagement with the Rushulme Club in 1869. He originally played as a wicket-keeper-batsman, but under the guidance of David Buchanan, he took up slow bowling. Watson noted later: 'It was he who really taught me how to get the twist on the ball with a turn of the wrist.'

This turn of the wrist was later to bring accusations of throwing and his name was linked with Crossland and Nash, who joined Lancashire at the end of the decade. Watson, in fact, was never no-balled and also claimed that he never bowled a wide for the County in 23 years.

Barlow and Watson were just two of no less than 13 players who made their debut for the County in 1871. R.W.D. Hill, Thomas Whatmough and James Unsworth appeared for the County in that season only, whilst George Hartley played just three matches in 1871 and 1872 before emigrating to the United States – his two sons were to make a much bigger impact on first-class cricket 30 years later. Edward Jackson, an amateur wicket-keeper from Huyton, was a useful crick-eter, but the demands of his business meant that he played just 15 times in as many seasons – his brother turned out once for the County in

The Gentlemen of Lancashire v Oxford University in June 1871. Standing: Harris (umpire), J. Leach, R. Walker, R. Stubbs, H.W. Gardner, A. Appleby, J.R. Hillkirk. Seated: W.H. Potter, E.H. Porter, J.F. Leese, J. Makinson. On ground: A.N. Hornby (Lancashire CCC)

1867, before emigrating. James Hillkirk was an estate agent from Beswick, a great athlete who was an expert at wielding the clubs and putting the weight. His father had founded Beswick CC, which in the 1870s was one of the oldest clubs in the Manchester area. In 30 matches for Lancashire, Hillkirk rarely came off, his hard-hitting batsmanship not being up to first-class bowling.

In so far as the County won all four Championship matches in 1872, no one could complain of their lack of success, but it was a pity that the committee reduced the number of fixtures in comparison with 1871 and that two of the four were against Derbyshire. The fact that all fixtures were close to Lancashire, the other opponents being Yorkshire, meant that one or two of the better amateurs played in the away games. Lancashire did, however, bring into the eleven one professional whose bowling considerably strengthened the side. William McIntyre, a right-arm fast bowler, had appeared for his native Nottinghamshire for the last three years, but being engaged by the Bolton club in 1870 he went to live in that town and thus qualified for Lancashire. He was given a trial in a North Lancs v South Lancs match in May 1872, took 12 for 87 and then went straight into the County side with, perhaps the most impressive debut season of any cricketer, before or since.

In the four matches, he took 40 wickets at an average of 5.65, his minimum in any one match being eight. Though not as fast as his successor, Arthur Mold, McIntyre could be effective on all types of wicket and scarcely had an off-day. On six occasions he and Alec Watson bowled unchanged through a completed Lancashire match and together they formed a most formidable pair. McIntyre lost his place in the Lancashire side in 1880 and the following year was given a benefit which is reported to have yielded him about £1,000. Later he seems to have fallen on hard times and he died at Prestwich Asylum in 1892, aged only 48.

The 'gentlemen's agreement' over the qualification of players gave way in 1873 to the first official rulings on the matter. Fortunately both McIntyre and Watson were firmly qualified for Lancashire and their bowling averages for the season make plain the value of these two to their adopted shire: McIntyre 55 wickets at 8 runs each, Watson 48 at 9, all the remaining bowlers 14 wickets between them. The County, after 1872's success, expanded their fixture list, adding matches against Surrey and Kent. Derbyshire were again beaten twice and Surrey suffered a similar fate, but on the other hand Yorkshire reversed the 1872 decisions, beating Lancashire both at Old Trafford and Bramall Lane. Hornby, the Red Rose's best bat, was absent from Sheffield, being at Lord's for the Gentlemen, but at the same time Yorkshire lacked Hill and Pinder. Hornby hit the first Lancashire hundred for three years, off the Surrey attack, but the Surrey fielding was described as poor in the extreme. The most unexpected result of the season was Kent's win at Gravesend, due in the main to the left-arm fast bowler Willsher, who captured 11 wickets.

Of the four new names in the Lancashire eleven in 1873, the only one of more than passing note was Vernon Peter Fanshawe Archer Royle, a 19-year-old, who was in his first year at Brasenose College, Oxford, being then described as 'a neat bat, who bowls with great break-back, but lacks a good pitch'. His outstanding success was as a fieldsman and W.A. Bettesworth, a noted judge of cricketers, stated: 'There have been very many famous cover-points but without doubt the most famous of them all was Mr Royle.' On his debut for Lancashire, Royle forgot to bring his cricket shirt and appeared instead in his multi-coloured harlequin one; this was at Bramall Lane and Royle achieved a couple of brilliant run-outs. The next time Royle fielded at Sheffield, the crowd remembered him and called out to their batsmen: 'Look out for the gent with the shirt' – except they used another word in place of gent.

Royle and Hornby became the first Lancashire cricketers to appear in a Test match, both going with Lord Harris' Team to Australia in 1878–79. The side was a moderate one and easily beaten by Australia. Royle appeared regularly for Lancashire until he became a master at Elstree School, after which his appearances were more or less limited to the summer holidays. The three other debutants of 1873, J. Braddock, E. Moorhouse and A. Ollivant, only managed a total of eight Lancashire matches between them. Braddock, a thick-set little fellow, was the pro at Sefton, Ollivant, son of a Manchester merchant, played for Sale, and Moorhouse was a local amateur wicket-keeper.

Lancashire dropped the Surrey fixture for 1874, but with only six first-class matches they had great difficulty in fielding a regular side. No less than 14 new players were introduced, five of whom were not seen again. The season began with a nine-wicket defeat at the hands of Derbyshire, Lancashire being dismissed for 38 in their first innings. The return at Chesterfield was a rain-ruined draw. The solitary victory was over Yorkshire, due entirely to the unplayable bowling of McIntyre. The reason for the general decline was due to some extent to the absence of A.N. Hornby, who played in one match only. In his absence the most prolific batsman was the newcomer, C.W. Landon, a businessman from Liverpool and a fast scorer. He did not remain long with the Lancashire side, but moved to Yorkshire, becoming a stalwart of the Yorkshire Gentlemen.

Aside from Landon, the best of the other new recruits was W.S. Patterson, the Uppingham schoolboy, who gained his blue at Cambridge in 1875. He lived at Parkside, Mossley Hill. An attractive middle order batsman, business prevented him from appearing in much first-class cricket and he felt that as a Liverpudlian he was rather overlooked when it came to electing Lancashire CCC officials, Mancunians being generally preferred.

With Hornby available more often, 1875 saw an improvement in Lancashire's fortunes. He and Barlow were easily the most effective batsmen; the bowling centred round Watson and McIntyre, with Appleby's fast left-arm deliveries also picking up wickets. Of the county matches five were won and one lost – against Yorkshire at Bramall Lane. An additional game was played against MCC, this registering a second loss. One of the wins came at the expense of Leicestershire, the first time the counties had ever met. In this match W.S. Patterson opened both batting and bowling for Lancashire and

A. Watson, mainstay of the Lancashire attack in the 1880s (NCCC)

returned figures of nine for 74 with his slows. Scoring in general was very low and no Lancashire cricketer hit a century. E.L. Chadwick of the Castleton club made the first of 13 appearances for the County; he had failed to get into the Eleven whilst at Marlborough, but was a good club batsman, and hit 213 in an innings for Castleton in 1877.

Enoch Tranter, a pro with Sefton also made his debut; a fast but erratic bowler, his County matches were restricted to three he later played for Staffordshire.

Though on paper Lancashire did not fare quite so well in 1876, winning five games and losing five, it was clear that, provided the County could field its best eleven, it was the equal of the best sides. *Lillywhite's Annual* summarises the qualities of the County that summer:

> Lancashire appears to combine amateur and professional assistance in precisely the correct degree. Mr Hornby is, of course, the life and soul of the team, as he always must be of any eleven for which he plays. Backed up by D.Q. Steel, Mr Royle, Mr Appleby and a devoted band of supporters, whose useful services are not confined entirely to cricket help, and backed up financially by some of the rich county families, what wonder is it that professionals like Barlow, W. McIntyre and Watson, are found to stand loyally by the county, and that enthusiasm is spread through all ranks of the community. Lancashire was, we think, fortunate in securing W. McIntyre as their professional. He is undoubtedly one of the best fast bowlers in England, bowling a difficult ball without the pace being so fast that it must lead to sacrifice of pitch. Judgment and foresight in singling him out must in fairness be apportioned to the county committee. It is constantly said by spectators that they do not care to see Barlow play, because he is so long in getting runs. To our mind they are thereby paying him a great compliment, for if the onlookers are wearied, what must be the feelings of opposing bowlers, whose physical powers are apt to give way after a certain time? . . . Two better men to go in together than Barlow and Mr Hornby we cannot conceive, and this has been recognised by many an opponent.

McIntyre had an outstanding season, taking 89 wickets at an average of 11.41 each. He was the principal wicket-taker in both the matches against Notts – Lancashire had not met that county since 1868 – and in the first match, at Trent Bridge, Lancashire won by six wickets. The return provided the most exciting finish of any Championship game that season; Notts required six to win when Fred Morley, acknowledged the worst bat in England, came in as last man. Somehow Morley managed five, and William Shrewsbury the other single, so Notts won by one wicket. McIntyre took nine wickets in the game.

For some unexplained reason McIntyre was rarely selected for representative matches and even though he was the bowler of 1876, he did not appear in the Gentlemen v Players match at Lord's. Judging by the result, the Players could have done with him, for A.N. Hornby led the Gentlemen to victory by an innings and 98 runs. The report notes that the match was so utterly one-sided that it was devoid of any interest.

The return match with Notts saw the debut of D.Q. Steel, who celebrated the occasion with a first innings score of 82, the highest of the match. Steel had been in the Uppingham Eleven under the captaincy of W.S. Patterson, and both had benefited from the tuition of the old Surrey pro H.H. Stephenson, who had come to the school as coach in 1872. Steel's best strokes were the square cut and the 'Uppingham' stroke, hitting the ball off the legs firmly along the ground in the mid-wicket area. Steel captained Uppingham in 1874 and 1875, then gained his blue in his first year at Cambridge, hence his inclusion in the Lancashire eleven in July. Although he continued to be a force in local cricket in the Liverpool area until well into his fifties, Steel appeared in only 22 matches for Lancashire and his brief hour of fame was quickly overshadowed by his brother, Allan Gibson Steel, who was to make his debut for Lancashire at the age of 18 in 1877. Two other Steel brothers later appeared for the County.

Another Liverpudlian to make his debut in 1876 was C.L. Jones, an opening right-hand bat. He played for Sefton and with E. Roper (who appeared occasionally for both Yorkshire and Lancashire) he put a hundred on for the first wicket over 30 times. Jones was a regular member of the Liverpool and District team, at the time when they were regarded as a first-class side.

The bowling of Watson and McIntyre continued to play the major role in Lancashire cricket in 1877. The latter's record was almost identical to 1876 and he was again the leading bowler in England, while Watson was only a little behind him. Yorkshire were beaten twice; Sussex suffered two innings defeats and again the Notts matches ended one each. Gloucestershire, under the all-powerful Grace, took the Championship title, winning seven out of eight matches, but they did not play Lancashire. Kent, reviving under Lord Harris, gained two successes at Lancashire's expense, the one at Maidstone proving the best finish of the season. Kent required only five more runs with four wickets in hand when the Lancashire captain put Appleby on and he took three wickets for two runs. However the last pair secured the game. This match marked the first-class debut of Ivo Bligh, who later played his part in creating the Ashes.

Among the cricketers who first appeared for Lancashire during the season were several of note. Richard Pilling was introduced as the County's wicket-keeper in August and immediately secured a permanent place in the side. W.G. Grace noted in his 'Cricket Reminiscences':

> Pilling was one of the most brilliant wicket-keepers the world has ever seen. From 1877 to 1883 he was without a rival as stumper, and his exclusion from a representative Players' team could not be entertained. Quiet and unostentatious though he was, he took the fastest bowling with consummate ease and astonishing quickness. It mattered not whether the bowling was fast or slow, he crouched over the wicket with his nose close to the bails, snapping the ball with unerring certainty, whether it came on the leg or the off side.

The Hon Alfred Lyttelton, who kept wicket for Middlesex and England, was once so impressed by the way Pilling stumped him in a county game, that he not only congratulated him on the feat, which was off the fast bowling of Crossland, but gave him a half-sovereign.

Born in Bedford, Pilling moved to Church in order to qualify for Lancashire and was for some years on the staff at Lord's, before going into business with Alec Watson in Manchester. Following a football match in 1889–90 he was taken ill with inflammation of the lungs and though Lancashire paid for him to spend the next winter in Australia, he died six days after returning home, being aged only 35.

Of the several amateurs who made their debuts in 1877, A.G. Steel, whose details are given separately, was the most accomplished, but S.S. Schultz, the Cambridge blue from Birkenhead, was another product of Stephenson's coaching at Uppingham. A useful all-rounder, he went to Australia with Harris' 1878–79 side and appeared in the single Test. Thus with Hornby and Royle, Lancashire had three members in this international.

Henry and William Wall, brothers of Thomas, who had played in 1868, appeared in a few games without making much impression.

McIntyre's bowling fell away in 1878, but A.G. Steel and an unexpected improvement and Barlow's accurate left-armers meant that Watson still had effective assistance. *Lillywhite's Annual* commented: 'With plenty of bowling, some very dangerous batsmen, and a fielding side superior to any county team of the year, Lancashire was entitled to a foremost position amongst the shires of 1878.'

Five matches were won and three lost, all the latter being away games. In addition the MCC were beaten for the first time, but the Australians, on their first-ever visit to Old Trafford, had the better of a draw, the County being without A.G. Steel. The first appearance of the Australians in Manchester had in fact occurred in mid-June when they were beaten by Eighteen of the Longsight club, but the local victory owed almost everything to young Fred Grace, brother of the Cham-

ALLAN GIBSON STEEL

Although he played for Lancashire from 1877 to 1893, A.G. Steel made only 47 appearances for the county and his best season occurred in his first year at Cambridge, when he took 164 wickets at 9.43 runs each. He bowled slow or slow medium, and could turn the ball both ways. After he left University his bowling powers declined, but he developed into an effective fast scoring batsman.

He captained England in all the three Tests of 1886 and took England to victory in each match, he was not however ever appointed captain of the county. Although he only made eight first-class hundreds in his career, two of these were for England. His most notable innings was his 148 for England at Lord's in 1884. No other England cricketer scored as much as fifty.

Three of his brothers also played for Lancashire and his son appeared in two matches for Middlesex.

Born Liverpool 24 September 1858
Died Hyde Park, London 15 June 1914

A.G. Steel (NCCC)

pion, who scored 42 and 23, only one other double figure innings, and that 11, being recorded by the home side.

In terms of spectator enjoyment 1879 was one of the most miserable seasons on record. *Lillywhite's Companion* recalled:

> As memory runs back to those long months of gloom, visions of sweeping rain-storms, of leaden lowering skies, of grounds converted into quagmires, of elevens disconsolately seated in the pavilion listening to the rain pattering against the window-panes, of matches extending over three days and yet not half finished, rise in endless procession before us.

At Old Trafford, however, all was not gloom, for Lancashire were acclaimed County Champions, jointly with Notts, for the first time. The efforts of those who formed the County Club 15 years before had finally come to fruition.

E.B. Rowley, the sole survivor of Lancashire's first year in county cricket, led the side to this success. Five matches were won and only one, against Yorkshire, lost. The two games against Notts were unfortunately rain-ruined draws.

Hornby easily topped the batting averages and was at the height of his powers:

> Mr Hornby has the most wonderful ability for the game, though it must be granted that his impetuosity sometimes damages his own chances, and has very often cost the patient Barlow his wicket. Mr Hornby has, too, a most useful power in addition to his brilliant talents, for he exercises a sort of fascination over the opposite side, causing them steadily to drop the chances which he has been known at times somewhat liberally to distribute.

Barlow was now almost the most accomplished all-rounder in England, W.G. excepted, for he not only was next to Hornby the best bat, but he also topped the Lancashire bowling table with 34 wickets at 10 runs each. Both Steels had good seasons, but D.Q. played in only four matches and A.G. in three. McIntyre returned to his old form and Vernon Royle's batting produced some useful runs, so the absence of the Steels was not too serious. Appleby played only three times, but three young professionals looked exceedingly worthwhile: George Nash, a 29-year-old from Buckinghamshire, John Crossland, from Nottinghamshire, and Johnny Briggs, also from Notts. Crossland had played in 1878 once or twice and the review of 1879 ominously notes: 'he did not do very much and his fast bowling can hardly be distinguished from throwing'.

Nash, whose delivery was also suspect, was a slow left-arm bowler engaged at Accrington, Crossland was at Enfield and Briggs, whose

JOHN BRIGGS

The only cricketer to score 10,000 runs and take 1,500 wickets for Lancashire – in his full first-class career he took over 2,000 wickets and scored 14,000 runs – John Briggs never achieved the 'double'.

A small man, standing 5 ft 5 in, his county career began at the age of 16 and because of his youthful appearance he was generally known as 'Boy' Briggs. He won a place in the County side due to his exceptional fielding and was retained as a batsman. Not until 1885 was his bowling of great importance.

Most popular amongst his fellow professionals, he went to Australia on five first-class tours and his Test career lasted from his first tour of 1884–85 to 1899, when he had an epileptic attack during the Headingley Test. The attacks increased in frequency and seriousness, and though he played for Lancashire in 1900, he died less than two years later at the early age of 39.

It was in his final season that he recorded the best analysis of his career, taking all ten wickets, at a cost of 55 runs, against Worcestershire at Old Trafford. He was a medium or slow left-arm bowler, who could make the ball turn both ways and his fielding to his own deliveries was particularly expert.

John Briggs (NCCC)

details are noted separately, was engaged at Old Trafford and was only 16 years of age.

The fact that Lancashire had so many prosperous local clubs which lured professionals to the county and thus qualified them by residence, was proving a great advantage. Briggs, for example, had come to live at Widnes, where his father was employed as a professional. Several of the Notts side in fact earned their bread and butter in Lancashire, Bembridge was engaged at Wigan, Martin McIntyre at Todmorden, just in Yorkshire, Tye at Rochdale. Aside from qualifying the professionals for Lancashire, their engagements clearly improved the cricket of local amateurs, who could bat against good class professional bowling each week.

THE GREAT THROWING RUMPUS

IN 1880 A SIGNIFICANT CHANGE TOOK PLACE in the structure of the County Club. It was decided to merge the County with Manchester CC and henceforth the official title was 'Lancashire County and Manchester Cricket Club'.

The Secretary of the new organisation remained S.H. Swire with F.R. Reynolds as his assistant. Dr Royle was briefly honorary treasurer, but by 1881 had resigned in favour of James MacLaren. MacLaren, father of A.C. MacLaren, was a Manchester cotton merchant and the family firm flourished so that James could devote as much time to cricket, and rugby football, as he did to business affairs. He was, however, very hot tempered and it would seem that he and Swire were not compatible, spending much time trying to avoid each other, not, it would seem, the ideal set up for running the County Club. MacLaren remained in office until his death, following a long and painful illness in 1900, aged 54.

The full committee for 1880 was: A.N. Hornby, who also succeeded E.B. Rowley as captain that year, C.G. Hulton, W.E. Openshaw, W. Brierley, J.R. Hay-Gordon, J.R. Hillkirk, E.B. Rowley, Ernest Wolff, Roger Walker, E. Challender, S. Field, Thos T. Bellhouse and Sam Platt. At least eight of these were cricketers of some reputation and this boded well for the new combined Club.

Lancashire however were unable to retain the Championship title they had held with Notts in 1879. Nottinghamshire beat them at Old Trafford by five wickets and in the return by four. Gloucestershire were successful by seven wickets at Clifton College and the game at Manchester was drawn, with the Western county needing 81 to win with eight wickets in hand. Both matches with Yorkshire were also drawn and thus Lancashire's victories, six in all, were achieved against the lesser lights.

As usual it was difficult to persuade the best amateurs to turn out regularly. A.G. Steel played only three times; owing to injury, D.Q. Steel was absent throughout. A.N. Hornby headed the batting, but his average was much boosted by the only Lancashire hundred of the season, 126 at the Oval, when he was dropped early in his innings: Surrey's loose fielding threw away the game. Walter Robinson, engaged at Littleborough, and formerly a Yorkshire county player, was brought into the eleven and proved a great acquisition. A stylish batsman, he punished loose bowling severely and seemed to have a promising future. He played in 11 of the 12 county matches. Barlow's batting fell away, but his bowling, with 42 wickets at 11 runs each, was used more, only Watson being called upon more frequently. McIntyre lost form and was dropped after the first few games, so that Nash was, after Watson and Barlow, the bowler with most wickets.

A note in *Lillywhite's Annual* states: 'Mr R. Wood, an old Carthusian, who would have been very useful, could only figure in one county match.' Subsequently Wood appeared a few more times for Lancashire, but he gained a small piece of fame when he went to live in Australia and was co-opted into the England side for one Test against Australia in 1886–87 – the least known cricketer to represent England in an Ashes match! Wood died in New South Wales in 1915.

Ernest Leese, a brother of J.F. Leese, hit a well-judged 62 on his county debut, but could only play in one other match that season. He had been in the eleven at Cheltenham. Richard Horrocks, a pro from Church, also hit sixty in an innings, but his batting lacked defence and he did not play after 1882.

If the County failed at the very highest level in 1880, they certainly made up the deficiency in 1881. Managing to field an eleven with few changes through the whole season, Hornby welded the the team into a fielding side whose level of brilliance had, according to contemporary accounts, never been seen before, 'the harmony and zeal with which they all worked in the field supplied a striking contrast to the listless and inanimate exhibition of some of the other county teams'. Royle and Briggs in the covers, Watson near the wicket, Robinson in the outfield, Barlow at point were outstanding.

Both the batting and bowling also came off. Hornby, with 1,002 runs, was the first cricketer to hit a thousand in a season for the County. He easily headed the English first-class averages, pushing Grace, for once, into second place. Three of the first five of the county regulars in the bowling averages were Lancashire men, there being little to choose between Barlow, Watson and Nash. A.G. Steel came into the side after the University match and both his bowling and batting added further to Lancashire's strength: in all first-class games Steel hit 848 runs (av 29.24) and took 130 wickets (av 13.41). Crossland played in seven matches, but his bowling was not often required, though when it was it proved fatal to the opposition – at the Oval he took seven for 14, as Surrey were dismissed for 36. In the first few matches the County had preferred another fast bowler, the Uppingham schoolboy, Henry Miller, but he appeared in only four games.

Despite fielding a weak side to the opening game of 1881, Lancashire beat the MCC at Lord's and this started a run of unparalleled success – the County went through the summer undefeated in county matches, winning ten, six by an innings, and having the three remaining games drawn very much in their favour. The one stroke of good fortune was

Lancashire 1881. Standing: A. Watson, J. Crossland, R. Pilling, (unknown), G. Nash or W. Robinson. Seated: (unknown), A.N. Hornby, (unknown), (unknown). On ground: R.G. Barlow, J. Briggs (Lancashire CCC)

that their main rivals, Notts, were badly affected through most of the year by the strike of their principal players, the strike coming into operation just before the first meeting of the two counties at Old Trafford on 2 and 3 June. Lancashire won that game by ten wickets. Rain cut short the return in mid-August.

It may come as a surprise to some that as far back as 1881 cricket statisticians were compiling tables of county records and since the table for 1881 shows quite clearly the supremacy of Lancashire it is worthy of reproduction here.

	P	W	L	D	*Highest Total*	*Lowest Total*	*Runs*	*Wkts*	*Avge*
LA	13	10	0	3	325	78	3,907	166	23.89
YO	16	10	3	3	388	96	4,390	221	19.191
GL	10	4	2	4	483	42	2,683	138	19.61
MX	9	3	3	3	259	77	2,270	137	16.78
NT	12	4	4	4	377	35	2,871	181	15.156
K	10	3	7	0	350	38	2,687	177	15.32
SY	14	4	9	1	310	36	3,936	262	15.6
SX	10	1	8	1	300	56	2,803	189	14.17
D	8	2	5	1	220	48	1,864	142	13.18

There was one blot on Lancashire's record – caused entirely by A.G. Steel. He brought a Cambridge University side to Liverpool in order to open the newly built Aigburth Ground and by taking 11 wickets enabled the students to inflict a defeat on his own county. The match ended before 5.30 on the second day, Cambridge winning by seven wickets, with Steel actually hitting the winning run.

With the argument between the Notts Committee and its players buried, 1882 looked like being an exciting summer for the admirers

R.G. Barlow, the famous stonewaller (NCCC)

of both Notts and Lancashire – and so it proved. The beginning
was deceptive. A programme of 20 matches had been arranged, much
more extensive than in any previous year. The MCC match was lost
in two days by an eight-wicket margin. The County then moved
north to Cambridge and met a second defeat at the hands of the
University. Although they managed to beat Derbyshire with ease
in the third match, the fourth saw yet another reverse, this time at the
hands of the Australians. In the meantime, the born-again Notts
team had easily beaten two major county teams, Yorkshire and
Surrey.

Lancashire managed three successive county wins, against Somerset,
Kent and Derbyshire, all among the weaker counties, before they
arrived at Trent Bridge.

The wicket was made treacherous by rain. Notts scored 116 in the
first innings, but Lancashire could reach only 52 in reply, then Notts
reached a new low, being dismissed for 42. This left Lancashire needing
107 to win. Wilfred Flowers took seven for 35 in 41 overs and Notts
won by 37, but it was not his bowling which hit the headlines. The
magazine *Cricket* reported:

> When I heard of Barlow's extraordinary performance at Nottingham
> on Saturday I hardly knew whether to smile or weep. I have in my
> small way endeavoured to do full justice to a constant succession of
> sensational performances with bat and ball during the last ten
> weeks. But Barlow's last exploit fairly takes my breath away. In
> the second innings of Lancashire he went in first and carried out his
> bat, having been in two hours and a half for five. I think that beats
> the record. Only a week before at the Oval Mr A.P. Lucas was in an
> hour for no runs! When I have my benefit I hope both the
> Amateur and Professional I have just mentioned will be thoroughly
> in practice. If so, we shall be pretty sure of a good Saturday
> afternoon.

Lancashire then played a rain-ruined draw with Surrey, but beat
Middlesex, before going to Aigburth for the return with Notts.
Lancashire batted first and were dismissed for 93, with the incredible
Barlow once more carrying his bat through the completed innings,
though this time he reached 44. In this match, instead of the innings
totals steadily reducing, they increased, Notts scoring 164, then
Lancashire replying with 188. Notts required 118 in the final innings,
but rain had so cut into the match that only 30 minutes playing time
remained and the game was drawn.

At the end of the season, the Championship table as published in
Lillywhite's Annual (*Wisden's Almanack* did not issue any table) read:

	P	W	L	D
Lancashire	16	12	1	3
Notts	12	8	1	3
Yorkshire	16	9	5	2
Middlesex	11	5	5	1
Surrey	14	4	7	3
Gloucestershire	11	3	6	2
Kent	9	2	6	1
Sussex	12	3	8	1
Hampshire	4	2	2	0
Derbyshire	6	1	5	0
Somersetshire	5	1	4	0

Wisden, however, began its review of Lancashire 1882 cricket with:

Which was the Champion County in 1882? Lancashire or Nottinghamshire? That was a subject much debated at the conclusion of the cricket season. In County v County matches each shire had lost but one game, and elaborate statistics were published to prove the post of honour belonged to Lancashire. But the claimants for Notts had one very strong argument in their favour and that was that Nottinghamshire had defeated Lancashire, but Lancashire had not defeated Notts.

The view that generally prevailed in the cricket press was that the title should be shared, and this state of affairs is now generally accepted.

The Lancashire batting in 1882 remained as in 1881 with Barlow, Robinson, Hornby and Royle, and A.G. Steel when available, but there was a marked change in the bowling. Crossland, with 112 wickets in all first-class matches, was the leading bowler in England, though Barlow, Nash and Watson were not too far behind. When the England selectors totally ignored Crossland for the Test match at the Oval, despite the fact that his record was second to none among English fast bowlers at that point in the season, and that the other leading contender, Fred Morley, was unavailable through injury, the newspapers assumed that the selectors judged Crossland's bowling as unfair, though 'no umpire has been found willing to no-ball him'. The question of Crossland's bowling was to grow more heated over the next two seasons.

Returning to the Test match – the only one of 1882 was staged at the Oval – Lancashire had three representatives, Barlow, A.G. Steel and Hornby, the last being the England captain. Barlow took five for 19 to dismiss Australia for 63. The home side managed 101, with Hornby for some reason batting at number ten. Australia reached 122 in their second innings, leaving England requiring 85 – they were brushed aside by the Demon Spofforth and the English defeat evoked the famous obituary of English cricket and the subsequent mission by Ivo Bligh to bring back the Ashes.

A.G. Steel and Barlow went out with Bligh in quest of the Ashes and Steel was the success of the tour, topping both batting and bowling tables. At home it is worth noting the growth of the Liverpool club at its new headquarters. The club employed six professionals in addition to Ubsdell, the groundsman, and income in 1882 was £2,272 18s 3d. No fewer than 60 matches were arranged for 1883, 40 of which were to be played at home. The club in fact was much stronger than all but the most successful county clubs. The membership stood at 792, as against 1,237 for the County Club itself.

The subject of Crossland, linked both with 'throwing' and residential qualification of cricketers, held the public's attention in the April and May of 1883. Nottinghamshire objected to Crossland's qualification for Lancashire and furnished the MCC with 'proof' that Crossland lived in Nottinghamshire. The MCC ruled in favour of Lancashire and Crossland, though stating that Notts were justified in bringing the case to the authorities' attention. The MCC moved in another direction regarding throwing, issuing an edict that umpires should enforce the Law relating to unfair delivery more stringently.

Lancashire began the 1883 season in fine form and with a side little changed from the last summer. When at the beginning of June they completely outplayed Notts – winning at Trent Bridge by nine wickets – it appeared that they would go on to win the Championship. In July they were beaten twice by eight wickets by Yorkshire, then with their confidence in disarray, they suffered defeats at the hands of Kent, Surrey and Gloucestershire. So from being among the leading contenders for the title, the County ended with the also-rans.

A.N. Hornby's form was very variable and this seemed to affect the rest of the team's batting. A.G. Steel was available for only three matches. His brother hit 75 in one of his only two innings, just proving how useful he might have been. Robinson missed a match or two through injury.

Some new amateurs were tried in the eleven. H.B. Steel, another of the brotherhood, was a hard hitting batsman, but in general he did not care for county matches, S.M. Crosfield of the Sefton club was a most reliable run-getter and his career with Lancashire went on until 1899, though for three summers, 1885 to 1887, he elected to play under residential qualification for Cheshire. He was more famous as a shot than on the cricket field, and in one competition at the Manchester Gun Club hit 91 birds out of 100, which was believed at the time to be a record. Another all-round sportsman to appear in 1883 was J.H. Payne, who kept wicket when Pilling was injured and also played as a batsman. He gained a blue at Cambridge as a rugby three-quarter back and then went on to represent both Lancashire and England. His father was J.B.

Payne, who had played cricket in the 1860s. W.M. Massey played in one match with no success; he had previously appeared for Devon and Somerset and soon after playing for Lancashire went off to the United States where he appeared in matches both for Staten Island and Florida. He died in New York in 1899 aged 53.

Lord Harris took up the cause of the abolition of unfair bowling in 1883 and sent a circular to all county clubs. The most effective response he had came from Notts, who refused to continue their fixtures with Lancashire, stating: 'That this committee expresses its entire concurrence with the views expressed by Lord Harris and resolves not to play matches with any county having bowlers with delivery open to suspicion.'

Lancashire sent the following Christmas card to Notts in December 1883:

CRICKETING RULES
Drawn up by the
NOTTS COUNTY CRICKET CLUB 1883–4

Rule 1. That in Playing Lancashire the Lancashire men shall not be allowed to use bats but only broom handles.
Rule 2. That Lancashire shall not be allowed any bowlers, and if so no stumps to be used; and the Notts captain to select the bowler.
Rule 3. That both umpires shall be strictly Notts men.
Rule 4. That in case there is any fear that Notts should lose, even under these rules, the Notts men do leave the field and refuse to finish the game.

Notts retorted with a New Year's card:

LANCASHIRE COUNTY CRICKET

The only rules necessary for players in the County Eleven are that they shall neither be born in, nor reside in, Lancashire. Sutton-in-Ashfield men will have preference.

Both Crossland and Briggs, of course, were born in Sutton-in-Ashfield.

At the 1884 Lancashire AGM, the chairman of the meeting, A.B. Rowley, attacked Nottinghamshire's attitude, saying that it was presumptuous of that county to take over the role of umpire, when the officials themselves had never no-balled a Lancashire bowler. The MCC should deal with all such matters and if that club was incapable then an association of cricketers ought to be set up.

At the same meeting the renewal of the lease of Old Trafford was discussed and it was agreed to pay £2,250 plus £200 per year for 21 years.

Whether by coincidence or design, Nash, whose bowling was

objected to almost as much as Crossland's, was dropped from the Lancashire team for 1884 and due to injury Crossland missed several matches, so that even without the umpires no-balling any of their bowlers, the accusation of 'throwing' could not be levelled at the County to the same extent as the previous year. There is no doubt that the attack was materially weakened and as a result Barlow was much over-used. He took 130 wickets in all first-class matches at a very reasonable cost, but his batting was badly affected and with Hornby not striking form until late in the season, Lancashire had, for them, a poor year.

The executive arranged an extensive programme and home and away games were included against both Cheshire and Leicestershire, as well as two games with Oxford, but indication of Lancashire's problems can be gauged by the fact that Oxford won both matches. In strictly Championship matches the County won seven and lost four, with one drawn. The outstanding success came in mid-July at Bramall Lane when Barlow took 13 wickets for 66, dismissing Yorkshire for 128 and 72. A.G. Steel and Briggs batted well and victory was attained by six wickets.

Immediately prior to this match was staged the first Test ever played at Old Trafford. Following the success of the single Test in 1882, public opinion pressed for three Tests when it was announced in October of 1883 that the Australians would visit England in 1884, and C.W. Alcock managed to arrange a programme which for the first time included Tests at Old Trafford and Lord's as well as the Oval, where he was secretary. The team selected for this historic match at Old Trafford was: A.N. Hornby (capt), W.G. Grace, A.G. Steel, T.C. O'Brien, A.P. Lucas, E. Peate, W. Barnes, G. Ulyett, A. Shrewsbury, R. Pilling, R.G. Barlow or J. Crossland. So the twelve included five Lancashire players, though Crossland was omitted from the final eleven. Lord Harris, it was reported, refused to play in protest at the selection of Crossland.

The first day was totally washed out and though England were dismissed for 95 the Australians were unable to force a win in two days. Shrewsbury with 43 made the highest score of the match and the Australian Boyle was the most destructive bowler.

No fewer than 13 players made their first-class debuts for Lancashire in 1884, eight of whom never appeared again. Most notable of the eight was C.E. de Trafford, whose family owned the freehold of the ground. His biography comments: 'In 1884 he appeared in one match for Lancashire, but as he failed to score and missed two catches was never asked to assist the county again.' He was brother of Sir Humphrey de Trafford and born at Trafford Park, within hailing distance of the county ground in 1864. He qualified by residence for Leicestershire in 1887 and was one of the outstanding cricketers for his adopted shire, his career extending from 1888 to 1920. He captained the county from 1890 to 1906.

Another of the Steel clan played for Lancashire in 1884, E.E. Steel, but he spent many years in India and thus was lost to regular county cricket. Two of the Steel brothers created something of a sensation in Liverpool in 1884, when 388 runs were hit in 138 minutes for Liverpool v Sefton, D.Q. Steel hitting 226 and H.B. 100.

Lyonel Hildyard, like E.E. Steel, made his debut in 1884, but was soon lost to county cricket. He had gained a blue at Oxford, but appeared in only eight Lancashire matches before taking Holy Orders. Frank Ward, a Cumberland man engaged with the Leyland club, was the only one of the newcomers to appear at all often for the County. A stylish middle batsman he played in 47 matches on and off up to 1896.

The acquisition of a Test match seems to have boosted Lancashire's membership figures and in 1884 they stood at 1,684, including 58 life members. A total of 120,000 people paid admission to the Old Trafford ground and income amounted to £11,688 15s 3d. The players were paid £5 per match plus a sovereign for a win at home and an extra £1 for away matches. The Club employed seven professionals, namely A. Watson, J. Briggs, J. Crossland, W. Copeland, Garner, A. Champion and R. Pilling.

The Lancashire committee brought the throwing controversy to a head in May 1885, when they included both Nash, who was scarcely seen in 1884, and Crossland in their eleven to play Kent, captained by Lord Harris. Harris wrote a letter to the Lancashire Club after the match, complaining about the unfair bowling of Nash and Crossland and stating that he was going to suggest to the Kent committee that the return match be cancelled as a protest. The Kent committee endorsed the views of their captain. The Lancashire committee again protested that Lord Harris should not take matters into his own hands, and said that Crossland had in 1884 been selected by the MCC for certain representative matches, Lord's seemed satisfied with his bowling. Further they stated that the reason why Nash had not played much recently was that the wickets did not suit him, not because Lancashire were unhappy with his bowling action.

Nottinghamshire in June repeated their allegation that Crossland was not qualified to play for Lancashire, as his main residence was still in Sutton-in-Ashfield. This time the MCC changed course and agreed with Notts. Crossland was thus banned from Lancashire forthwith and a general meeting of the Notts club agreed that if the Kent committee were also of the same mind, fixtures with Lancashire should be arranged for 1886.

The official communication from Lord's read:

That it having been established to the satisfaction of the committee that Crossland has resided in his native county, Notts, from October 1884 until April 1885, this committee is of opinion that he no longer possesses a residential qualification for Lancashire.

Despite the problems with Nash and Crossland, Lancashire had a better year than in 1884, winning 13 out of 18 matches, though in first-class county matches the record was little changed from the previous year, six wins from eleven games. The reason for the relative success despite the loss of Crossland was the sudden emergence of Briggs as a bowler. From 18 wickets at 22 runs each he increased to 85 at 10 runs each. Good though Briggs' bowling was, it was totally eclipsed by his batting at Aigburth against Surrey.

'Boy' Briggs was 18 not out at the close of the first day with the Lancashire total 186 for eight. When five runs had been added on the second morning, the other overnight batsman, Watson, was caught. Pilling then arrived and with Briggs created a new record by adding 173 for the last wicket. Briggs in 100 minutes had added 100 runs to his score, when just before lunch he was stumped off a lob. Lancashire gained a first innings lead of 247, but rain washed out the last day's play and the match was drawn. A curiosity of this match was that for the first time a Lancashire bowler was no-balled for throwing – G.E. Jowett, who was an amateur making his debut for Lancashire. In later years Jowett played purely for his batting.

The long list of 1885 debutants contained 15 names, most of little more than passing interest. E.C. Hornby, a cousin of the captain, was left-handed both as a batsman and bowler. Mainly connected with Liverpool cricket, he appeared in 13 county games over the next three years. A.T. Kemble, another amateur associated with Liverpool, was to become the regular County wicket-keeper, as illness curtailed Pilling's career. His family were well-known on the stage, but A.T. Kemble qualified as a solicitor in 1891 and later was involved in local politics, being chairman of Garston District Council in 1901 and a member of Liverpool City Council. He usually captained Lancashire in the absence of Hornby and took a team to the Canary Islands in 1899. Excelling on the Rugby field, he represented both Lancashire and England.

Another player better known away from the cricket field also played for the County in 1885. Sir George Kemp, later Lord Rochdale, gained a blue at Cambridge that year as a stylish middle order batsman and played for Lancashire in 18 matches between 1885 and 1892. He represented Cambridge at lawn tennis and athletics, winning the mile at Trinity in 1886. He was elected Liberal MP for the Heywood Division of Lancashire in 1895 and raised to the peerage in 1913. Two more of the Leach family from Rochdale were also in the eleven briefly in 1885:

R.C. Leach and W.E. Leach were brothers of John, who had played in 1886.

The problem of Crossland re-emerged at the County Club's AGM, held at the Albion Hotel, Manchester, on 29 January 1886. A.B. Rowley, from the chair, said Crossland's bowling action was one of the fairest he had seen and that several members of the MCC Committee were incapable of judging the difference between bowling and throwing. It was equally absurd, went on Mr Rowley, that Crossland should be debarred from county cricket after seven or eight years, simply because he had decided to move house.

With regard to the fixtures for 1886, it was agreed to resume matches with Notts and Kent. Alex Watson received £1,101 11s 1d from his benefit match in 1885, a new record sum. The Lancashire Club was flourishing with a surplus of £1,431, and another membership increase to 1,762 plus 60 life members. A total of 106,000 spectators had paid at the gate in 1885.

Another meeting held earlier in the year gives an idea of the progressive nature of the cricket authorities in Lancashire at this time. S.H. Swire, the County secretary, organised a gathering of cricket club secretaries from the Manchester area and over 100 attended. This was to facilitate the arrangement of local club fixtures and was regarded as a great success.

The batting remained Lancashire's weakness in 1886; in County Championship matches, Hornby averaged 30, Barlow 23 and no one else over 20. The side was rescued time and again by the three principal bowlers, Watson, Barlow and Briggs, but they failed to find a fast bowler to replace Crossland. Alfred Teggin, an amateur from the Longsight club, actually topped the bowling table with his slow leg breaks, but he appeared in only six matches, taking 16 wickets at 11 runs each. For some reason he never played again.

George Yates, a pro from Haslingden, engaged at Werneth, appeared regularly and looked a promising all-rounder, but in 92 matches up to 1894, his record is a modest one. A couple of Notts pros were tried, Charles Shore and A.P. Smith. The latter hit a couple of hundreds in a career spanning nine seasons. One oddity was the appearance of R.H. Moss, an Oxford University student, his next outing in inter-county cricket occurring for Worcestershire in 1925!

Lancashire's record for the summer was five wins against five losses. This put the County in third place, behind Notts and Surrey. The first Test was held at Old Trafford. A.N. Hornby, A.G. Steel (despite the fact that he rarely played in Lancashire county matches) and Pilling were the original home selections, but Hornby had to drop out, as did Barnes of Notts, so Barlow and Briggs played instead. Barlow was largely responsible for an England win by four wickets, since he took seven for 44 in the second innings as well as scoring 38 not out and 30, the most runs for England in the match. From a financial standpoint the game was most successful, with 10,000 attending on the first day – the matches were of three-day duration.

. With membership now over 2,000 and the finances continuing to look healthy, it was agreed that a reserve fund be set up in order that the club, at some future date, might buy the Old Trafford ground, or failing that purchase a new ground. Some £1,300 was spent in improvements to the buildings and increasing the seating accommodation in 1886. At the end of the Annual General Meeting in February 1887, the chairman commented:

F.H. Sugg, an attacking batsman for Lancashire and England (NCCC)

> The County were to be congratulated on the position they stood in at
> the end of last season. Considering the amount of amateur talent that
> they had in Lancashire, and considering they were opposed to such
> teams as Notts and Yorkshire, with whom it was rare to find an
> amateur, I think Lancashire has no need to hide its head as to cricket.

What the chairman did not mention was the continued lack of
Lancashire-born professionals, Barlow being of course the outstanding
exception.

The Lancashire Committee had, however, taken steps to reinforce
the professional element of the County Eleven, though in a way which
upset Derbyshire. Frank Sugg, the Derby batsman, had taken a dual
post in Burnley, as pro to both the cricket and football clubs of that
town, in July 1885. He was soon to receive overtures from Lancashire,
and immediately his two year residential qualification was complete he
appeared for his new county, having declined to play for Derbyshire in
the early part of 1887. Sugg, a fast-scoring batsman, was soon making
runs and ended the summer second in the Lancashire batting table with
an average of 33. On the other hand, Lancashire did find some useful
local batting talent, though again an amateur. Joseph Eccles had played
in six Championship matches with modest results in 1886. In 1887 he
played in almost every match and had the highest run aggregate in
Championship games, with 558, average 31. Eccles, born in Accrington, played for Preston, in which town he was a cotton manufacturer.

With these two batsmen giving support to Robinson, who had his
best season since joining the County in 1880, Lancashire challenged
Surrey and Notts for the title. Defeat at the hands of Yorkshire in the
last week of August finally extinguished Lancashire's hopes. Eccles was
unable to play and the bowling failed, but until then Lancashire, like
Surrey, had lost just two matches and there was little to choose between
the two sides. Whilst Lancashire were being defeated by their neigh-
bours, Surrey, in their final match of the summer, had the better of a
draw with Sussex.

Surrey won 12 out of 16 games, Lancashire 10 out of 14 and Notts 8
out of 14. Lancashire could, however, point to one success over Surrey.
Briggs and Barlow dismissed the southern county for 79 and Sugg
justified his place in the Lancashire side by scoring 98 in Lancashire's
second innings, the runs coming in 120 minutes, and this meant Surrey
needed 313 to win, a figure which they never looked like approaching.

If A.G. Steel had been able to play more than two innings during the
season, Lancashire might well have pipped Surrey – Steel scored 32 and
105 in his Championship innings.

Apart from Sugg, Lancashire acquired a second 'foreign' professional
in 1887, G.R. Baker, who was engaged by the Bury club. Brought up

in Malton, Baker was coached by W.E. Bosomworth and made a first appearance for his native Yorkshire in 1884. Like Sugg, he came to live in Lancashire, was quickly noticed by the Lancashire committee and gained a place in the County team very soon after his two-year residential period was completed. A good all-rounder he was to feature in Lancashire's side until 1899.

The wet wickets of 1888 plus the continued failure to find a fast bowler of the calibre of Crossland or McIntyre were the chief factors in Lancashire's failure to challenge Surrey for the Championship title. Neither Hornby nor Barlow found batting easy – the captain's seasonal average fell to 15 and the stonewaller's to 14. Eccles, Briggs and F.H. Sugg were the only three to average above 20. Robinson, who had done so well in 1887, was absent through illness for several weeks and then failed to find his touch. By the middle of July, Surrey had effectively taken the crown. They had won six out of six matches, whilst Lancashire could claim just two from seven, Notts three from seven and Kent, despite the absence of Lord Harris from many matches, had three wins from six. By mid-August Surrey had won all eleven of their first-class county fixtures, including beating Lancashire at Old Trafford in a single day, on 2 August, the home county being dismissed for 35 and 63 in reply to Surrey's first innings total of 123. George Lohmann took 13 for 61.

A fortnight later, Lancashire went to the Oval. Surrey won the toss and on an excellent wicket made 294. By the close Lancashire were 53 for the loss of Barlow. Eccles then played the innings of his life, hitting 184 in 315 minutes, with 19 fours, out of the Lancashire total of 376. At times he was blessed with good fortune, but exhibited some very sound cricket. On the last day, Surrey's batting failed entirely, Briggs and Watson being the successful bowlers and Lancashire made a formality of knocking up the 71 needed for victory. It was to be Surrey's only defeat in 1888 and a performance which Lancashire could regard with pride. The wicket-keeping of Pilling, who conceded only three byes in 446 runs and had four catches and two stumpings, contrasted with Surrey's 33 byes conceded.

The third and final Test of 1888 was staged at Old Trafford and resulted in an innings victory for England; as each side had previously won one game, there was great interest in the match. Lancashire had three representatives in Sugg, Briggs and Pilling. W.G. Grace, captaining England, won the toss, which proved perhaps decisive in a low scoring match. Over 8,000 spectators paid at the turnstiles on the first day, and 7,469 turned up on the second day, though the game was completed by lunch time.

The only notable debutant of 1888 was the Rev J.R. Napier, a fast bowler who created something of a minor sensation by returning an analysis of 3.2–3–0–4 against Yorkshire at Bramall Lane, this proving to be his one and only Championship match. His only other first-class game for Lancashire had come earlier in the season, when, taking 3 for 54 and 4 for 48, he enabled his County to beat the Australians by 23 runs. Injury had prevented him obtaining a blue at Cambridge in 1881 and he was chosen for Lancashire on account of some excellent bowling in local matches in Preston. He was also a very useful batsman, hitting the highest score for Lancashire in the Australian game. He was just the cricketer Lancashire needed, but was unable to spare the time for first-class matches.

In November 1888 a dinner was held in Manchester to honour S.H. Swire and to recognise the service he had done to Lancashire County Cricket Club over the previous 25 years. He was presented with a massive silver tray engraved with a view of Old Trafford Pavilion and his wife received a diamond crescent.

John Briggs also came in for some praise – but in a South African newspaper. He was coaching in Kimberley in 1888–89. The report commented:

A characteristic feature of Briggs in the field is his happy-go-lucky style. He is undoubtedly one of the most popular professional cricketers in England, and the reason is obvious. He is a clever dissembler. Up to all kinds of antics and tricks he raises many a laugh in trying to get rid of a batsman . . . While batting he jumps in and out of his ground, strikes comical attitudes and generally acts as if he were one fourth part a clown. These antics, of course, would not be tolerated in a cricketer of mediocre ability; but Briggs can take liberties which would not be permitted, if attempted, by another man. Besides, when cricket is reduced to an absolute science, it is apt to become monotonous to all but enthusiasts, and at such times the comicalities which the crack professional indulges in are much appreciated by the crowd.

Season 1889 was welcomed as a 'good old-fashioned' one, without an Australian visit and all eyes on the Championship. The preview of the season suggested that both A.G. Steel and J.R. Napier would play for Lancashire – neither in fact did – and that the two professional recruits, Mold and A. Ward, would be distinctly useful. The latter prediction was certainly not optimistic.

When the season closed, the magazine *Cricket* noted of Ward:

There are few instances indeed of such remarkable success as the outcome of a professional's introduction to important matches. It is quite possible that there may have been cases of similar fortune, but of late years we cannot recall to mind one in which a young player has

Albert Ward, a sound opening batsman in the 1890s (NCCC)

reached at the end of a season the highest position in the batting averages of a leading county, as A. Ward can claim in this year of Grace 1889.

Albert Ward learnt his cricket at Rothwell, near Leeds and from there he went on to the Hunslet club. An assistant schoolmaster, Ward gave up his work in the classroom to become a professional with the Lancashire side Darwen, and in 1886 appeared in four matches for

Yorkshire. He moved permanently to Leyland in 1887 and thus in 1889 was qualified for Lancashire. A stylish, undemonstrative opening batsman, Ward played for his adopted county until 1904, completing 1,000 runs nine times and gaining seven England caps.

The second recruit was in a way more vital to Lancashire cricket, since he might possibly fill the vacant fast bowler position. Arthur Mold, a native of Northants, began his cricket with Banbury, but was engaged at Old Trafford in 1887. In that year he also made his county debut for Northants and was very destructive. Though he continued to appear for that county in 1888, it was understood that he was anxious to play for Lancashire as soon as his residential qualifications would allow. The wickets in May 1889 did not suit fast bowlers, but in June Mold quickly proved his worth and in four successive Lancashire matches picked up 33 wickets. Critics regarded him as the fastest bowler in county cricket and his easy action made him seem not as fast as he really was – which fact caused the downfall of quite a number of batsmen up against him for the first time.

The first-class bowling averages for 1889 clearly spell out Lancashire's success and so rare is it to have three bowlers of one county occupying three of the first four places, that the figures deserve reproduction:

	M	O	M	R	W	Avge
W. Attewell (Notts)	26	1364.2	673	1635	149	10.97
J. Briggs (Lancs)	23	1040.3	447	1646	140	11.75
A.W. Mold (Lancs)	18	679	262	1207	102	11.83
A. Watson (Lancs)	18	850.3	438	1139	90	12.65

The battle for the Championship was a thoroughly interesting one. On 8 August, Notts had won 8, lost 1; Surrey won 7, lost 2; and Lancashire won 7, lost 3 – the rest were nowhere. Rain unfortunately meant that all three counties were involved in drawn matches, though Lancashire had further victories against Sussex and Surrey. A new system of deciding the Championship had been invented by Charles Pardon in 1888, awarding one point for a win and half a point for a draw. As the fixtures were scheduled, this meant that with Lancashire and Surrey having completed their games and Notts having one to play, all three counties had 10½ points. Notts made a complete hash of the last match and to the embarrassment of Mr Pardon and his system, the Championship, for the first and last time, ended as a triple tie. The cricket press and others attacked the Pardon system and *Wisden*'s main rival (Pardon being the editor of *Wisden*) *Lillywhite's Annual*, suggested that Notts deserved first place, whilst Lancashire, having defeated Surrey both home and away, ought to be second. In the final analysis

The Lancashire team that played Sussex at Hove in 1889. Standing: W. Clarke (umpire), A.W. Mold, A. Ward, A.G. Paul, F.H. Sugg, W. Draper (umpire). Seated: R. Pilling, R.G. Barlow, A.N. Hornby (capt.), J. Eccles, A. Watson. On ground: G.R. Baker, F. Ward, J. Briggs (Lancashire CCC)

the consensus was that the triple tie should stand, but the whole system be revised for 1890 – and a meeting of the County secretaries did just that.

The success of Ward and Mold has already been discussed, but another reason for Lancashire's high position was that at last they fielded a consistent eleven, only 15 players being called upon for Championship matches. The bowling was completely in the capable hands of Mold, Watson and Briggs – of the 249 wickets which fell to bowlers in Championship matches, the triumvirate accounted for 241. Sugg, the batting find of 1888, continued to make runs, as did Eccles, whilst Barlow, having been given a rest from bowling, was also among the major batsmen once more. A.G. Paul was a third important 1889 debutant. He was not the usual professional recruit, for his father was a colonel and he was educated at Victoria College, Isle of Man, where his father had been appointed Chief Constable. He first came to public notice with the Gentlemen of Notts and Notts Castle CC, but then seemed to prefer rugby, being a very good full back and touring Australia with the 1888 English footballers. He was training to be a civil engineer when he decided instead to become a professional cricketer with Nelson, hence his connection with Lancashire. He developed into a useful county batsman, playing regularly until 1896, but an operation in 1900 ended his first-class cricket completely.

ENTER THE NOBLEST ROMAN

'THERE NEVER WAS A CRICKETER with more than the grandeur of A.C. MacLaren. When I think of his play now, years after it all happened, the emotions that stir in me afresh, and all my impressions of it, are mingled with emotions and impressions I have had from other and greater arts than bat and ball.'

That was how Neville Cardus commenced his essay on the eldest son of the Lancashire Treasurer. A.C. MacLaren captained Harrow against Eton at Lord's in July 1890, scoring 76 out of Harrow's all-out total of 133 – the report noted: 'as he has defence as well as hit, he should train on'. A few weeks later he made his Championship debut for Lancashire at Hove and made 108, virtually saving the County from collapse, the side being all out for 248. He was at the wicket for 130 minutes and gave no chance, indeed hardly played a faulty stroke. MacLaren through his batting and his leadership was to supersede A.N. Hornby as the dominant figure in Lancashire cricket from the middle 1890s through to the First World War. He was a great stylist and a master of all the textbook strokes; more importantly, he refused to allow the bowling to have the ascendency. As a captain, MacLaren was a brilliant general on the field, but when leading England he tended to be at loggerheads with the selectors, which was the cause of problems over the years.

The arrival of MacLaren thus coincided with the new system of deciding the Championship, wins being deducted from losses and draws ignored. Of the dozens of changes in the Championship system, this first remains the simplest and perhaps one day will be revived.

Although Lancashire began their 1890 Championship campaign with an easy win over Kent, Mold taking seven for 21 in Kent's second innings and Ward hitting his highest score to date – 145 in 195 minutes – there followed two successive defeats. The first was at the hands of Surrey at Old Trafford, the southern county almost repeating their one-day win of 1888, the match ending at 1.30 on the second day, with Lohmann taking 13 for 54 and not a single Lancastrian reaching 20 in either innings. Then at Lord's Middlesex caused a major upset. Following on with a deficit of 129, Middlesex seemed in an entirely hopeless position, but lapses in the field allowed A.J. Webbe to score freely and his century took Middlesex to 311. The task of hitting 183 in the final innings was too much for Lancashire, and they lost by 73 runs.

These two defeats meant that Lancashire were almost out of the running in terms of the title chase before the season was half over. As it was, they suffered only one more defeat – again at the hands of Surrey,

ARCHIBALD CAMPBELL MacLAREN

At the age of 23 A.C. Maclaren eclipsed the immortal W.G. Grace by creating a new English first-class record score: 424 v Somerset at Taunton in 1895. At the age of 49 he came out of retirement to inflict defeat on the all-conquering 1921 Australian touring team, employing an eccentric collection of part-time players to do the foul deed. In between times he captained Lancashire to the County Championship. He was believed by some to be the greatest Test captain England ever had, but he lost all four of the series against Australia when he was England's leader.

Tactically there have been few cricketers better qualified to captain England, but he had unorthodox views when it came to the selection of teams. Sometimes, as in the case of S.F. Barnes, MacLaren's ideas were sound, at others they caused embarrassment. According to Hubert Preston, Mac-Laren also lacked the 'buoyant optimistic temperament' needed for success on the cricket field.

As a batsman, however, he had few peers and in Australia, where the dry weather suited him, he played some of the greatest of his innings. He came either top or second in the first-class batting table on each of his three major tours 'down under'.

A.C. MacLaren (NCCC)

with Lohmann once more the architect. If Lancashire had performed a miracle and beaten Surrey, the title would have gone north; as it was Lancashire came a creditable second, having seven victories out of 14 matches, against ten in 1889.

Aside from the introduction of MacLaren during August, the major change in the eleven was the absence of Pilling. Illness laid him low in the early months of the year and though he recovered, he was not strong enough to play three-day cricket. At the end of the summer the Lancashire Club paid for him to spend the winter in Australia – hopes were that the wicket-keeper would be able to return to the side in 1891, but it was not to be. In his absence the amateur, Kemble, kept very efficiently and when he was unable to play, Whiteside took his place.

The batting was consistent, rather than brilliant, with eight players averaging between 20 and 30. Due to his 145, F. Ward headed the table, but Briggs hit most runs. Briggs topped the first-class bowling averages, as well as those for Lancashire. He was chosen for all three Tests, but failed to play in any, which might constitute something of a record. Briggs withdrew at both Lord's and the Oval due to a slight strain, then the third match at Old Trafford was completely washed out by rain, giving Manchester an unwanted accolade. More unfortunate than Manchester or Briggs, was his colleague Mold, who was in the England twelve at Old Trafford but had to wait until 1893 to make his Test debut.

Cecil Holden, the Birkenhead Park amateur, played in his one and only Championship game for Lancashire in 1890. He was a hard-hitting batsman and useful medium-pace bowler, but could not spare the time for first-class cricket and played instead for Cheshire, as well as captaining Birkenhead for 20 years.

The pattern of 1890 repeated itself in the year which followed. Lancashire were beaten in the early matches by both Surrey and Middlesex; they also had the misfortune to have another two games ruined by rain – the match at Liverpool against Kent was abandoned without a ball being bowled, whilst Sussex at Old Trafford escaped from certain defeat, but the wicket was badly affected by the weather that Lancashire scarcely deserved to win.

Perhaps the Lancashire cricketers felt out of sorts early on, for Pilling had returned from Australia only to die just a week after his return, consumption having gone too far to be arrested.

A.N. Hornby was beginning to feel his age, the runs no longer came so freely from his bat and as the summer wore on he dropped himself from the eleven, allowing S.M. Crosfield to take the reins.

Watson's slow medium bowling was also beginning to lose its bite and in 11 Championship matches he could claim only 29 wickets. Mold and Briggs, however, remained most effective and claimed second and third places in the first-class averages, only Lockwood of Surrey having a fractionally better set of figures.

MacLaren topped the Lancashire batting, but could turn out in only five Championship games; it was therefore fortunate that the committee discovered a new batsman who had just qualified by residence. Arthur Smith had appeared once or twice for his native Nottinghamshire, but had taken a post with Oldham CC and moved to Lancashire. His chief asset as a batsman was his defence and it was appropriate that Lancashire should find him at the moment when their arch-stonewaller, Barlow, had decided to retire; 1891 was his final summer of Championship cricket and his value to the side had been enormous. The strange aspect of his career was that right through he remained the only Lancashire-born professional to reach the top of his trade.

In the magazine *Cricket*, the Rev R.S. Holmes, who states he lived in Lancashire for many years, wrote an article in May 1892 extolling the virtue of home-grown players in county teams. When coming to Lancashire, he stated that the reason for the lack of Lancashire-born professionals was that the working class could not afford the two guineas subscription demanded by the many top rate cricket clubs in the Liverpool and Manchester areas – he cites Sefton, Huyton, Northern, Dingle, Broughton, Sale, Rusholme, Longsight and Manchester as leading examples. In both Yorkshire and Nottinghamshire the subscription rates were half a guinea or even less. Another factor was that the Lancashire clubs allowed their professional to play in first team matches, which of course helps the batsmen, but does not encourage amateur bowlers.

What the Rev Holmes did not mention was that the relatively high subscriptions enabled the Lancashire clubs to attract the better professionals, which allowed the County Club the pick for Championship matches, provided the necessary residential rules were complied with. Also, 1892 saw the foundation of the Lancashire League, which for the reasons noted has been regarded in many quarters as the premier league in the British Isles.

As now seemed usual, Lancashire made an unsatisfactory beginning in the season. This time they were beaten by Yorkshire. The White Rose county required only 61 to win in the final innings, but so well did Watson and Briggs bowl that six wickets fell for 33. Wainwright and Tunnicliffe then got set and for some reason Hornby declined to change the bowling and bring on Mold. Yorkshire won without losing another wicket.

By the halfway stage – in 1892 all counties played 16 matches, home and away against all, there being now nine first-class counties since the elevation of Somerset in 1891 – Notts and Surrey were fighting for the title, with Yorkshire and Middlesex third and fourth and the rest, including Lancashire, which county had only two wins in eight games, well to the rear.

The bright spots of the second half of the season were MacLaren's hundred on the Aigburth Ground – at the time rated the best in Lancashire – against Gloucestershire and in the following match the record attendance at Old Trafford, where 20,000 turned up on the Bank Holiday to view the battle of the Roses. Lancashire, due to hundreds by Arthur Smith and Albert Ward, beat Yorkshire by an innings, as they had in the previous game beaten Gloucestershire. They then beat Somerset by eight wickets, Briggs taking 12 for 83, and the three wins pushed Lancashire into third place. Lancashire's summer ended with their best result of the year, when Notts were conquered at Old Trafford, Mold being irresistible and bowling unchanged in the second innings for seven for 29.

Uncertainty with regard to the captaincy possibly played its part in Lancashire's uneven record – Hornby remained official leader, but appeared in only nine of the 24 matches undertaken by the First Eleven. S.M. Crosfield led the side in most of the other matches. Smith, the previous year's outstanding debutant continued to impress, topping Lancashire's batting. F.H. Sugg, Albert Ward, G.R. Baker and Crosfield all played useful innings, but Briggs shone only spasmodically and G.M. Kemp reappeared with no success. The bowling remained in the hands of Briggs, Mold and Watson, the last named seemingly evergreen.

It was estimated that 25,000 people watched the Bank Holiday match at Old Trafford against Yorkshire in 1893 – a record 22,554 paid at the turnstiles – and the reason was that for the first time Lancashire and Yorkshire were the two main contestants in the Championship battle. It was a grim struggle. Lancashire, batting first, lasted 135 minutes for 64, with Albert Ward being at the crease two hours for 19. Yorkshire were then dismissed by Briggs and Mold for 58 and when play ended on the first day Lancashire were 7 without loss in their second innings. About 10,000 arrived on the second day to see Lancashire removed for just 50 in 90 minutes. Yorkshire wanted only 57 to win and their openers hit off 24 in 16 minutes. The game seemed over. F.S. Jackson was then run out and the side collapsed, Lancashire winning by five runs.

The County won nine and lost five matches during the year and runs came more easily on wickets that were drier than those of the last year or two. Albert Ward, F.H. Sugg and A.C. MacLaren headed the batting table. Briggs, Crosfield and, for the first time, A. Tinsley, made useful contributions. Alfred Tinsley was yet another in the line of imported professionals. Born in Yorkshire, he had played briefly for his native county and then taken a post as professional with Leyland, hence his residential qualification for Lancashire – his brother also played

The Old Trafford Pavilion in 1890 (Lancashire CCC)

occasionally for both counties, whilst a third brother was the well-known jockey, G.A. Tinsley.

Lancashire were most fortunate that Briggs and Mold went through the year without serious injury, for, with Watson finally retired, they were in effect the entire attack. Briggs and Mold took 225 wickets between them, the rest obtained 46, spread among six also-rans. One fresh face was William Oakley, a medium-slow left-arm bowler engaged at Longsight – it is repetitious to add that he was not a native of the county, being born in Shrewsbury and had in fact played with success for Shropshire in 1892.

Credit for Lancashire's success must also be given to the fielding – no county's fielders supported their bowlers so keenly. The regular wicket-keeper remained A.T. Kemble, but Charles Smith, another Yorkshireman qualified for Lancashire, stood in several matches, but without Kemble's flair.

The third Test was staged at Old Trafford in August. England was not fully represented because Yorkshire refused to release certain players, but three Lancastrians, Albert Ward, Briggs and Mold, played and saw England have the better of a draw.

'Everyone would be glad to know the why and the wherefore of the constant failures that in late years have afflicted Lancashire during the early part of the season. At the annual meeting of the club, "faint-heartness" was urged as an explanation of the mystery.' So noted *The Cricket Handbook* of 1895, in its review of 1894. For 1894 had followed the same well-trodden path. This time one victory and six defeats were the sum total of the first seven matches.

Matters improved sharply in the second half and Lancashire ended with seven wins, plus a tie, but this left them in the middle of the field.

The most curious factor relating to the tied match was that it took place at the Oval and the previous five first-class ties in England had all taken place on the same ground, stretching back to Surrey v Kent in 1847. In the present instance, Lancashire, batting in the final innings, required 75 to win. Seven wickets went down for 26, and the situation appeared hopeless for the visitors. The wicket-keeper, C. Smith, then joined Tinsley and the pair added 39, forcing the first bowling change, with Hayward replacing Richardson. Smith was immediately caught. Bardswell then hit eight of the ten required for victory, only to be caught by the wicket-keeper, standing back. Mold arrived, a half chance to Brockwell provided the run which brought the scores level, then Mold was caught behind. Tinsley played with great nerve and judgement, to be 19 not out.

Though both Hornby and Crosfield continued to play occasionally, the Lancashire committee resolved the leadership question by appointing the 22-year-old MacLaren. *Wisden* commented: 'although very young for so important a post, he acquitted himself satisfactorily and with increased experience of both the cricket field and the world at large may be expected to justify his selection'.

Season 1894 was that in which it was decided to grant first-class status to Warwickshire, Derbyshire, Leicestershire and Essex, but not include them in the Championship. By organising home and away games with Derbyshire and Leicestershire therefore, Lancashire increased their first-class programme by four matches, and with home and away games with Oxford University, plus a match at Lord's v MCC, the total first-class Lancashire programme amounted to 23 matches. This put a tremendous strain on Mold and Briggs, for they remained the only bowlers of any credibility in the side. Their records for 1894 for Lancashire are worthy of note:

	M	O	M	R	W	Avge
A.W. Mold	23	1099.2	390	2171	187	11.60
J. Briggs	21	1027.4	367	1896	137	13.83

Next on the list came Baker with 13 victims. Briggs was given the Bank Holiday match against Yorkshire for his benefit and despite the game being over in two days – Lancashire lost by an innings – Briggs realised in all about £1,000. The tremendous amount of work done by 'Boy' Briggs forced him to drop out of the final games of the season due to a strain. In the last game Ellis, a slow bowler who had been tried before, was brought in for Briggs and completely baffled the Leicestershire batsmen, taking eight for 21. It was to prove the only worthwhile first-class performance of his career.

Earlier in the summer Lancashire had given a trial to G.E. Wharmby, the former Notts all-rounder, but he did little. In later years he became a mainstay of the Bedfordshire eleven.

A more outstanding cricketer to make his debut was G.R. Bardswell. Five years in the Uppingham Eleven, he had been captain in 1892 and 1893. He obtained his blue as a freshman at Oxford and after the term ended was drafted into the Lancashire side. He had much to do with Lancashire's win over Middlesex at Lord's. An accurate bowler who could vary his pace and a useful batsman, Bardswell came from Liverpool. He looked set for a long career in county cricket, but business prevented him playing as often as was hoped, though he captained the side with MacLaren in 1899. He died in New Orleans in 1906, aged 33, following an operation from which it appeared he had entirely recovered.

The Championship competition expanded from nine to fourteen for 1895. One feat alone however formed the talking point of the year and this was the innings of 424 which MacLaren played against Somerset at Taunton in mid-July. MacLaren had been out in Australia for the winter of 1894–95 with Stoddart's Team and, though only succeeding in one Test, had come second in the first-class batting averages. He dallied on the way back from the Antipodes and did not appear in the Lancashire side until the last week of May. He played twice and then announced he had accepted a post as an assistant master at a prep school in Harrow and would not therefore be available for Lancashire until the term end.

When he returned on 15 July, Lancashire were third in the Championship with seven wins out of ten matches, one point behind Yorkshire, but four behind Surrey. Lancashire batted first against Somerset and MacLaren, opening the innings with Albert Ward, batted all through the first day and 2¼ hours into the second, making 7 hours 50 minutes in all for his 424. The previous first-class record score, Grace's 344, had stood since 1876. The Lancashire total of 801 was also a record for Championship matches, but had been exceeded once in English first-class cricket. A.G. Paul was MacLaren's major support. The Irishman hit 177 and added 363 (or 368 in another report) for the second wicket.

Lancashire were then most unlucky to have four of the next five matches drawn due to rain, including the return with Somerset, in which not a ball could be bowled. It appeared that they then had no chance of catching Surrey, but the whole matter was thrown open in mid-August when Lancashire won two games, while Surrey lost two, the vital fixture being the clash between the two at the Oval – this game had of course been a tie in 1894.

K.J. Key, the Surrey captain, took the unusual step of inviting Lancashire to bat first, and seven wickets went down for 37. MacLaren

SOMERSET *v.* LANCASHIRE

Played on the County Ground, Taunton, 15, 16 and 17 July, 1895

LANCASHIRE WON BY AN INNINGS AND 452 RUNS

LANCASHIRE — FIRST INNINGS

*Mr A.C. MacLaren	c Fowler b Gamlin	424
A. Ward	c R.C.N. Palairet b Tyler	64
A.G. Paul	c Gamlin b L.C.H. Palairet	177
A.W. Hallam	c Fowler b L.C.H. Palairet	6
Mr C.H. Benton	c and b Fowler	43
F.H. Sugg	c Wickham b Woods	41
A. Tinsley	c Gamlin b Woods	0
G.R. Baker	st Wickham b L.C.H. Palairet	23
J. Briggs	not out	9
†C. Smith	c Trask b L.C.H. Palairet	0
A.W. Mold	c R.C.N. Palairet b Gamlin	0
Extras	b 9, lb 4, w 1	14
Total		801

Fall: 1-141 2-504 3-530 4-637 5-732 6-738 7-792 8-792 9-798

BOWLING	O	M	R	W
Tyler	59	5	212	1
Woods	46	5	163	2
L.C.H. Palairet	44	10	133	4
Gamlin	26	8	100	2
Fowler	23	5	97	1
R.C.N. Palairet	11	3	41	0
Trask	2	0	9	0
Porch	5	3	16	0
Bartlett	6	0	16	0

SOMERSET

	FIRST INNINGS			SECOND INNINGS	
Mr L.C.H. Palairet	b Briggs	30		b Mold	4
Mr G. Fowler	c sub b Hallam	39	(6)	c MacLaren b Mold	46
Mr R.C.N. Palairet	c Hallam b Mold	2	(4)	st Smith b Briggs	7
Mr H.T. Stanley	c Smith b Briggs	8	(3)	c Smith b Mold	12
Mr R.B. Porch	run out	18	(7)	c MacLaren b Mold	1
*Mr S.M.J. Woods	c Smith b Mold	11	(5)	b Briggs	55
Dr J.E. Trask	c Ward b Mold	11	(8)	c and b Mold	26
†Rev A.P. Wickham	b Mold	3	(10)	not out	0
E.J. Tyler	not out	15	(2)	b Briggs	41
Mr E.W. Bartlett	b Briggs	4	(9)	c Mold b Briggs	6
H.T. Gamlin	st Smith b Briggs	0		hit wkt b Briggs	0
Extras	leg byes	2		b 4, lb 4	8
Total		143			206

Fall: 1st inns: 1-71 2-73 3-73 4-94 5-107 6-121 7-122 8-132 9-137
2nd inns: 1-5 2-61 3-61 4-83 5-150 6-151 7-187 8-206 9-206

BOWLING	O	M	R	W	O	M	R	W
Briggs	37.3	15	59	4	37	17	78	5
Mold	35	15	75	4	33	11	76	5
Hallam	2	1	7	1	8	2	19	0
Baker					5	2	25	0

Umpires: J. Wickens and G. Hay.

Lancashire won the toss. Close of play: 1st day: Lancashire 555-3 (MacLaren 289*, Benton 6*); 2nd day: Somerset (2) 58-1 (Tyler 38*, Stanley 12*).

* Captain; † Wicket-keeper

and Charles Smith then added 84 for the eighth wicket, MacLaren's 52 being, the state of the wicket considered, the best he played all year. Key had expected the pitch to improve, but it steadily deteriorated and each successive innings reduced in size, Lancashire winning by 44 runs.

The Lancashire challenge for the Championship was then thrown away by an unexpected defeat at the hands of Derbyshire, so that victories in the last three matches of the summer did no more than hold Lancashire in second place. The matches enabled MacLaren to close the year in a blaze of glory, since, batting once in each match, he hit three successive hundreds – another new Championship record. MacLaren however was not alone in compiling records, for Briggs and Mold bowled unchanged through two successive matches, a feat without parallel in Championship cricket up to that time.

It need hardly be added that MacLaren topped the Lancashire batting averages by a wide margin, scoring 1,162 runs at 58 per innings, and Mold and Briggs again captured over 300 Championship wickets between them.

Three or four players were seen fairly regularly in the Lancashire team for the first time in 1895. A. Lancaster, a slow left-arm bowler from Enfield, took 27 Championship wickets and A.W. Hallam, engaged on the staff at Old Trafford, but a native of Notts, took 28 with his medium right-arm deliveries. Hallam proved useful for a few seasons and was later of even more use to Notts, but Lancaster made only occasional appearances until 1899.

Of most importance was the first of the Tyldesleys – J.T. or John Tommy – he hit 152 not out in his second match for Lancashire. Tyldesley, who played for Little Lever and lived at Roe Green, Worsley, was to develop into both the most popular and the most prolific Lancashire batsman of his day.

He became one of Neville Cardus' heroes:

Tyldesley was certainly not an artist in a deliberate, proud, selfish way. Remember his dourness as he stood over his bat ready for the bowler's attack. He was the image of antagonism, vigilant and shrewd. Tyldesley never seemed, even in his most sparkling innings, to be toying with the bowlers in the manner of the virtuoso, merely to amuse himself and us; he most plainly was checkmating them by courage and opportunism. If he was audacious that was because audacity paid – offence was his best means of defence.

Nineteen times he exceeded 1,000 runs in a season and his 2,633 in 1901 remains the Lancashire record; he was the first batsman to complete 30,000 runs for the County, indeed, the only other one was his younger brother, Ernest, whose career began a decade later. J.T. Tyldesley retired in 1923 and died in 1930, aged 57 – he was putting on

JOHN THOMAS TYLDESLEY

Coming in first wicket down, Tyldesley established himself in the England side at the turn of the century and played Test cricket for a little over ten years. His outstanding series was the 1905 games in the England, when he hit hundreds at Headingley and the Oval.

An attractive batsman, he played the cut and off-drive with textbook precision, but could also hook the ball and execute attacking shots all round the wicket. His defence was mostly off the back foot and he was equally at home either going for the runs or holding the fort.

He was one of the few batsmen to master the art of scoring runs on a sticky Australian wicket and though nowhere near his highest innings the two scores of 97 and 62, which he made in the Melbourne Test of 1903–04, were perhaps the best of his long career – in the second innings the individual score nearest his 62 was only 10 and England were dismissed for 103.

Having a quiet sense of humour and a most pleasant personality, Tyldesley was one of the most popular cricketers of his day. His last few years were marred by ill-health, though he remained at Old Trafford until the year before his death in 1930, acting as head coach.

J.T. Tyldesley (NCCC)

his boots prior to leaving home for work when he collapsed and died.

C.H. Benton, a civil engineer who had been in the Harrow eleven of 1885, played quite a few times as a batsman, but never really came off. He committed suicide in 1918, at the age of 49, his death coming as a great shock to his friends and acquaintances.

For several years discussions had taken place with regard to the building of a new pavilion – the membership had increased so much that accommodation in the old building was now totally inadequate. Several architects were invited during 1894 to submit designs and finally the one entered by Thomas Muirhead of Manchester was accepted. The old pavilion was demolished as soon as the 1894 season was ended and it was planned to have the new edifice ready for 20 May 1895 – the first county match of the summer.

Reynolds, the assistant secretary, lived in the old pavilion and W.E. Howard in his reminiscences tells how reluctant the old retainer was to move. In the end, he arrived back at his home to find the workman in the process of taking the roof off and apparently enjoying a bottle of his whisky as demolition proceeded.

According to Howard faults in the design began to emerge as the new building went up. The dressing rooms were not large enough; the bathrooms attached to them not plumbed in properly; too many pillars obscured the views of the ground; the caterers were dissatisfied with the cellars. When Reynolds came to inspect his new quarters, he complained the rooms were too small and in the end one wall of his house was taken down and rebuilt to increase the size.

The same architect was later commissioned to build the pavilion at the Oval – Howard suggested that it would have been better if Mr Muirhead had built the latter first and thus found all the faults in the design before he reached Old Trafford.

The cost of the new pavilion was about £12,000, as against £990 for the old one. Severe weather and a strike of plasterers – plus presumably the alterations – meant that the building was not ready for 20 May.

At the Annual General Meeting in January 1896, MacLaren was made a life member of the Club in recognition of his 424. The members had risen to 2,370 and, more remarkable, the attendance figures compared with 1894 had risen by 51,000 to 97,230. The financial statement showed that the Club had a balance in hand of £2,299 9s 5d. The gate receipts were £5,251, compared with £8,596 at the Oval, but only £1,273 at Trent Bridge and £663 at Derby.

The Australians re-appeared in 1896. The second Test was staged at Old Trafford and the main criticism of the England side was the inclusion of MacLaren, who had scarcely played serious cricket in 1896. He failed, scoring 0 and 15. England were saved from embarrassment by Ranjitsinhji, who made 62 out of 231 and 154 not out, out of 305.

The New Pavilion at Old Trafford, built in 1895, as it looked in 1914 (NCCC)

Australia won by three wickets. Briggs was the other Lancashire representative.

Owing to a dispute with Yorkshire, the annual Roses match at Old Trafford for 1896 was arranged as the first match commencing 4 May, rather than at Whitsuntide, but even this early in the season 8,000 spectators turned out to watch the first day. MacLaren, the official captain, was still engaged in schoolmastering and therefore Hornby led the side, which contained one face new to Lancashire, if not Yorkshire. Willis Cuttell, son of the old Yorkshire player, had played a couple of games for his native Yorkshire in 1890, but like so many others came as a professional to Lancashire and was engaged by Nelson. As a slow-medium leg-break bowler and useful batsman he gained a regular place in the Lancashire side in 1897 and appeared successfully for a decade. However, he achieved little in his first match, Briggs and Mold monopolising the bowling in a low-scoring game which Yorkshire won by two wickets.

Contrary to 'tradition', Lancashire then had a run of victories in Championship matches: Sussex, Kent, Leicestershire, Derbyshire, Warwickshire, Surrey, Somerset and Gloucestershire. This placed the County, on 27 June, second to Yorkshire. A new system was in vogue for 1896 for deciding the championship whereby draws were ignored and losses deducted from wins, then the position determined by percentage of points gained to matches finished.

Middlesex defeated Lancashire in the final match of June and more crucially Yorkshire won in the return at Headingley; this meant that barring a sudden decline Yorkshire would take the title, which they duly did. Surrey, also among the front runners for the first half of the way, fell right away and left Lancashire the second spot.

As to the individual performances, MacLaren was the dominant batsman from the moment he joined the side in mid-July, and averaged over 50. Frank Sugg was the only batsman to complete 1,000 runs in Championship matches and with a double century against Gloucester, came second to MacLaren. Baker and Ward had good seasons and Ernest Rowley, the son of E.B. Rowley, looked promising, but his fielding was weak. Rowley was to live on until 1962, dying at the age of 92, the oldest Lancashire player at the date of his death.

The bowling was mostly in the hands of Mold and Briggs, but Hallam, until he was injured, did well, taking 58 Championship wickets at 17 runs each. John I'Anson, another Yorkshireman in Lancashire club cricket – with Leyland – bowled some useful fast stuff early on, but then faded, but would turn out like Cuttell to be of use.

The Championship of 1897, until the end of July, looked as if it might make the authorities at Lord's the object of ridicule, for Notts had by then played 11 matches and won just two, but topped the table, because the remainder of their games had been drawn. Gloucester then beat Notts and the Championship race was more open than ever before, with Lancashire, Yorkshire, Essex, Surrey, Notts and more remotely Gloucestershire still in the running. By mid-August however the match between Lancashire and Surrey at the Oval was being billed as the game to decide the Championship. About 15,000 turned out on the first day, and the report in *Cricket* commences: 'Although it was not absolutely certain that the result of this match would determine which side should be Champion County for the ensuing year, there can be no question that the meeting of the two counties was considered by most people as a sort of final tie.'

Lancashire decided to bat first and had reached 140 by lunch with Sugg undefeated on fifty, After the interval Lees and Richardson swept through the side, the all-out total only being 154. Surrey gained a first-innings lead of 62, but Lancashire seemed to be coming back into the game when a ball from Richardson broke Sugg's finger – he retired hurt for 37 and Surrey required 90 to win in the final innings, a task they achieved for the loss of four wickets.

It appeared that this decided the Championship. As it happened, however, Lancashire could still win if they beat Notts and Surrey lost to Somerset. Although the former was quite likely, the latter seemed improbable, Somerset being one of the weakest counties. Both matches commenced on 26 August and luck went Lancashire's way. They had first use of the wicket, scored 284 and then rain followed by sunshine forced Notts to struggle on a wicket suited to Briggs and Cuttell – Lancashire won at half past five on the second day by an innings.

All attention now turned to Taunton. No play had been possible on the first day. Somerset batted first on Friday morning and were quickly reduced to 19 for five. Robson however then played some wonderful cricket, scoring 48 and aided by the tail taking the total to 110. Surrey began even more poorly than their rivals, six wickets going down for 19. Lees then hit out, and making 41 pushed the total to 93, a deficit of 17. Somerset did much better the second time round and left Surrey needing 211 with most of Saturday afternoon remaining. The visitors never really looked like achieving the target and with Hayward unable to bat due to an injured hand, Somerset won the match by 66 runs and thus gave the title to Lancashire. Considering the harsh way in which Lancashire had dealt with Somerset over the last few summers, there were perhaps mixed feelings in Taunton at the result!

So Lancashire were outright winners of the title for the first time since 1881, and for the first time in many years they had a balanced attack, rather than having to rely on two bowlers. In the overall first-class averages all four of the main bowlers came in the top ten and their records in purely Championship games read:

	M	O	M	R	W	Avge
J. Briggs	26	1149	340	2294	140	16.54
W.R. Cuttell	25	1039.2	418	1813	102	17.70
A.W. Mold	20	759.2	261	1571	88	17.75
A.W. Hallam	26	952.4	421	1651	90	18.31

The great surprise was the record of Cuttell. His best delivery was the one which went with his arm and he used it with great skill – the fact that he was selected as one of *Wisden's* Cricketers of the Year in what was virtually his first season clearly demonstrates the opinions formed about his bowling. The unfortunate thing was that he was already 32 years old and that Lancashire, or indeed Yorkshire, had not given him an extended trial before now. Apart from his bowling he was a useful hard-hitting batsman and a very good field.

Hallam continued to improve. An accurate bowler, his one failing was a tendency not to vary his deliveries, so that the batsman, once he had accustomed himself to the wicket, was in no danger unless by his own hand.

Briggs bowled better than he had for some years and he was rewarded with a place in Stoddart's side to Australia; Mold suffered several injuries and did not bowl with such a keen edge as in the last few years.

Sugg, Tyldesley, Baker, Ward and MacLaren all averaged over 30 with the bat – MacLaren concentrated more on hitting, and so while his runs came at an even faster pace than previously, his was an easier wicket to take. Paul lost his place in the eleven and neither of the amateurs, Bardswell and Rowley, turned out in Championship games. The wicket-keeping was in the hands of the capable Charles Smith until injury removed him in August, then the committee discovered Lees Radcliffe of Rochdale, whose style was reminiscent of Pilling, and so there was no weakness behind the stumps.

Apart from Radcliffe, the only cricketer to make his debut was C.R. Hartley. Son of George Hartley, who had played in three matches in the 1870s, he was born in New Orleans, but came back to Cheshire and not only appeared for Lancashire as a batsman for a dozen or so years, but also played rugby for Cheshire, as well as appearing for the North v South. Demands of business reduced his first-class cricket after 1900, but afterwards his brother played with some success for Lancashire.

Misfortune came not as single spies for Lancashire cricket in 1898, as *Lillywhite's Annual* put it. Serious illnesses prevented Hallam from making a single appearance all summer; Mold was compelled to miss a match in July and then broke down in August, being unavailable for three weeks; Briggs, who had failed entirely whilst in Australia, his nine Test wickets costing 53 runs each, was nothing like as accurate for Lancashire in 1898 as in the previous year. In fact of the four bowlers who won the Championship in 1897, only Cuttell could be depended upon, and with his batting improving he was one of the leading all-rounders in the country.

The falling-off in the bowling might not have had such an effect if the batting had been more stable. As it was, however, MacLaren could play in only six Championship games and even then his form was poor, his average being less than half that of 1897. Ward's untiring patience still wore out the opposition and Tyldesley demonstrated his ability by scoring 1,900 first-class runs, a figure exceeded only by Surrey's Abel. The fact that Tyldesley was not picked for the Players – the highest honour which could be bestowed on a professional in a non-Test Match season – brought adverse comment from the press. Sugg was left out of several matches due to lack of form, but Baker retained his skill in the middle order. The Yorkshire match was given to him for his benefit.

Until the middle of July, Lancashire, though always behind Yorkshire, were well placed in the table and if Yorkshire had slipped and Lancashire continued to win they might have retained the title, but as Mold was injured and the expected boost from MacLaren's bat never materialised, the side was beaten successively by Essex, Yorkshire and Sussex and finished the season in sixth place. They won nine matches out of 26: Yorkshire won 16 from the same number.

Season 1899 proved to be the end of an era. A.N. Hornby played his final game for the County. Appropriately he scored 53 in his last innings, but now he was batting at number nine or ten. Francis Thompson was soon to pen his famous poem of which the final five lines run:

> For the field is full of shades as I near the shadowy coast,
> And a ghostly batsman plays to the bowling of a ghost;
> And I look through my tears on a soundless clapping host
> As the run-stealers flicker to and fro, to and fro.
> O my Hornby and my Barlow long ago.

The fact that Hornby had to turn out at the age of 52 to captain the team in three matches gives an idea of the major problem faced by the County that summer. Bardswell had been appointed captain for the season, but then turned out in only four Championship matches, so MacLaren, Eccles and Hornby filled in the gaps as necessary. The contrast between the four captains was too much for the players: the pugnacious Hornby, who according to legend whipped a misguided reporter who dared to turn up at Old Trafford after having criticised Hornby's tactics in the field; MacLaren, the pessimistic optimist; Eccles, the Oxford blue, who was feeling his way in county cricket; and the official leader, Bardswell, whose post as managing director of G and J Greenall took up more time than he anticipated.

The bowling caused almost as much concern as the leadership, though like the latter it seemed in order when the season opened. Briggs looked something like his old self and Hallam bowled very well in the match v MCC, but in the next game, Hallam seized up in the middle of an over and had to be carried from the field: he did not reappear in 1899 and the general opinion was that he would never take part in county cricket again.

The following month an even more serious event ended Briggs' cricket for the summer. He had bowled so well in the early matches that he was chosen in preference to Rhodes for England's side for the third Test at Headingley. He bowled England into a good position on the first day of the match, but was taken ill overnight and was then detained in Cheadle Asylum, where he remained for the rest of the season. He had suffered from a form of epilepsy for some years and the attacks were becoming more acute.

Despite this catalogue of misfortune, Lancashire finished the year in fourth place and only Yorkshire, who played three more matches, gained more victories. In mid-August Lancashire were actually in second place, just marginally behind Yorkshire. Three matches in succession were then lost and all by decisive margins. At Lord's, Middlesex hit 406, Lancashire were routed by Trott – he who hit the ball over the Lord's pavilion – and were forced to follow on. One Lancastrian batsman stood out when everyone else failed; R.H. Spooner

REGINALD HERBERT SPOONER

A tall elegant figure, R.H. Spooner was the epitome of the Edwardian amateur county cricketer. His stylish batting, which contained a full repertoire of classical strokes, was used as a model for many an aspiring youngster.

He made his name at Marlborough and twice in Schools matches at Lord's scored hundreds. Only 18 when he made his debut for Lancashire in 1899, he was quickly lost to the County through serving in the Boer War.

Even after the war he was unable to give his full attention to county cricket and his appearances in some seasons were very restricted. He appeared in ten Tests for England and hit a century against South Africa in 1912. Although asked to join MCC teams on overseas tours he was unable to find the time to do so.

A noted three-quarter, he represented Liverpool and England on the rugby field.

R.H. Spooner, Lancashire's elegant batsman
(NCCC)

scored 44 and in the second innings, he made 83, which was the highest score of the match on either side, but again with only Ward supporting him, Lancashire lost by ten wickets.

Travelling on to Hove, the side met defeat by an innings, the feature being a hundred by Ranjitsinhji, which enabled him to break the record for most runs in a season in English first-class cricket. One unusual incident of the game was the retirement of Painter, the umpire, suffering from sunstroke – an ex-Sussex cricketer took his place in the final stages of the game.

Back in London, the Lancashire side went to the Oval where Surrey administered the final *coup de grâce*, another innings defeat, with Surrey knocking up an invincible 556, Abel making 178, Lockwood 131 and D.L.A. Jephson 100. Of the Lancashire side only Tyldesley in either innings made a fifty.

These matches had not only pushed Lancashire down to fourth place, but enabled Surrey and Middlesex to move into first and second places, which situation remained constant until the season's close.

The player who caught the headlines in the last month was R.H. Spooner, mentioned above. He was an 18-year-old schoolboy from Marlborough and had gained a place in the Lancashire team at Lord's on account of some extraordinary batting on the same ground earlier in the month. For Marlborough against Rugby he hit 69 and 198, the latter innings lasting only 210 minutes. He followed this with 158 for Lancashire Second Eleven v Surrey Second Eleven. 'His career will certainly be followed with more than ordinary interest' commented F.S. Ashley-Cooper on 10 August, and how right he was.

'Reggie' Spooner won the heart of Neville Cardus, the writer as a schoolboy even trying to style his hair to match Spooner's. When Spooner failed to score, Cardus says that he wandered the streets, sad and inconsolable. In his later years, Cardus wrote:

R.H. Spooner was one of the rarest of stylists among batsmen of any or all time. His strokes would have honoured the lawns of a royal palace. But I must be careful – nowadays – in my use of the almost obsolete word 'style'. To most cricketers of this most unstylish epoch of 1963, style in batsmanship of Spooner's period is associated with an automatic push forward at the ball, left foot well out of the crease, the right grounded behind it – elegant strokes on the offside but unbalanced against spin, especially from leg. As a fact, Spooner was a superb back player. He could force a four off his pads past and to the left of the square-leg umpire. His wrists were as strong as they were supple. He was incapable of awkwardness of physical (or mental) poise. His drives past cover, made without perceptible muscular effort, rippled rather than scorched the grass. There was nothing ferocious or brutal in Spooner's batsmanship. It was all courtesy and breeding.

He became to be regarded as the supreme example of the 'amateur' batsman of the so-called Golden Age. His statistics are not all that impressive, but this is largely because he chose to serve during the Boer War and then both in 1903 and 1907 he declined invitations to tour Australia with the England side. He had only four summers of regular first-class county cricket: 1903 to 1906, after which business commitments rarely allowed him to play.

The need in 1899 was more for bowlers than batsmen and Lancashire found a useful man in the guise of the Everton footballer, Jack Sharp, who hit 57 on his debut against Surrey coming in at number nine and then as a right-arm fast-medium bowler picked up 29 wickets at a reasonable cost over the next few weeks. While Lancashire were being humiliated at the end of August, Sharp was absent being recalled to the football field. An outside right, he is one of the handful of players to be capped by England at both soccer and cricket. His career was to last until 1925 and he played in over 500 matches for his adopted county – yet another professional import!

Before Sharp made his debut, Lancashire found another cricketer in rather an odd way. Jerry Ainsworth had been invited by Pelham Warner to go with his band of amateurs for a short visit to the United States in the late summer of 1898. 'Cub' Ainsworth, as he was known in America, was perhaps one of the few first-class cricketers to appear with his initials embroidered in large letters on his sweater. His slow left-arm bowling picked up 75 wickets at six runs apiece on the American trip. These figures might seem somewhat deceptive, but he easily out-bowled both V.T. Hill and Bosanquet. His cricket in England had been confined to club matches, largely with the Old Marlburians. Ainsworth captured seven wickets on his Lancashire debut, in the first game of the season, but after bringing the total to 18 in four matches, left county cricket for higher things. Pelham Warner thought Ainsworth good enough to represent the Gentleman at Lord's, but it was not to be.

One amateur who could spare the time for cricket was A.N. Hornby's son, A.H., who had the unusual honour of playing for Lancashire in the same eleven as his father. A dashing batsman in the mould of his great parent, he never really hit the headlines, content to bat low in the order, but he later became an astute captain of the County.

Two or three others briefly appeared in 1899, but will be better described in other seasons, but the Middlesex professional, Sidney Webb, did make some impact immediately. He qualified by residence in mid-season, having appeared for Middlesex in 1898, and taking six for 50 helped dismiss Somerset for 85. He was to have a great year in 1901, but his county cricket ended two years later.

THE GOLDEN AGE

AN ANNOUNCEMENT IN MARCH 1900 SOLVED the problem which had bedevilled Lancashire cricket for several years. A.C. MacLaren was appointed assistant secretary to the County Club. His duties were largely confined to captaining the county team and his remuneration enabled him to resign his teaching position and devote his summers entirely to cricket. Before the season began MacLaren suffered a tragic personal loss when his father died, still in early middle age. James MacLaren had held the post of hon treasurer to the County Club for exactly twenty years. The post was taken over by James Horner, the secretary of Stockport CC.

The Club began the new summer in great form – the first six matches, true all except Middlesex against the lesser counties, were easy victories. Then came two draws, before the Whitsun meeting with Yorkshire at Park Avenue, Bradford. Yorkshire, like Lancashire, had an unbeaten record. It was to the visitors' great disadvantage that neither Briggs (who had made a remarkable recovery from his illness and only a few days before taken all ten wickets in an innings) or Mold could play. On a damp wicket Yorkshire, batting first, made a creditable 230; Lancashire could do nothing with the left-arm bowling of Rhodes and were all out for 96. Some careful batting by Sharp at number nine thankfully avoided the follow-on. Yorkshire in their second innings could do little and Lord Hawke, captain of the home side, declared setting Lancashire 199 in two hours. The rain, which had already seriously reduced the playing time, then returned and probably saved Lancashire.

With draws being ignored and only wins and losses counting in the Championship, Yorkshire and Lancashire went on through the weeks both undefeated and therefore both with 100.00 per cent at the head of the table. Sussex, by dint of their incredible batting, drew game after game, but in mid-July they met their match at Bramall Lane, Rhodes bowling Yorkshire to an innings victory and Sussex's percentage tumbled.

On 26 July, Gloucestershire came to Old Trafford – for the first season since the Western county began in county cricket they were without W.G. Grace at the helm. In his place was the great Gilbert Jessop, he of the hurricane innings, and he chose this match to prove that his talents were not only in making runs. In the first stages of the match Lancashire could be well pleased. Ward played a characteristic innings of 107, the total reached a quite reasonable 338. Gloucestershire replied with 318, of which Jessop hit up 66 in an hour, and Lancashire were 110 for four at the close of the second day. Owing to rain play could not resume until half past one on the last day, a draw therefore looked certain, but Jessop caused a complete collapse, the last six wickets going down for 34 runs, Jessop returning figures of six for 25. It remained to be seen if Gloucester on such a tricky surface could make the 166 required for victory. Jessop came in to make 47 in about half an hour and Gloucestershire brought Lancashire to earth by a margin of three wickets. Lancashire now had to sit and wait to see if anyone could defeat Yorkshire. It was a fruitless vigil and whilst it took place, Lancashire lost a second match, this time at the hands of Surrey at the Oval. Lancashire did well on the first morning, reducing Surrey to 119 for five, but later V.F.S. Crawford and D.L.A. Jephson joined forces, both hitting hundreds, and Surrey totalled 463. Good bowling by Surrey removed Lancashire cheaply twice and an innings defeat was the result.

Aside from these two reverses, Lancashire had a fine summer and their record of 15 wins and two losses out of 28 games would in many years have taken the title. Ward, MacLaren, J.T. Tyldesley and C.R. Hartley all made over 1,000 championship runs at an average above 30; their attack was versatile – five bowlers captured 50 wickets, with Briggs and Cuttell topping the hundred. Briggs' recovery was quite miraculous; only the two Yorkshiremen, Rhodes and Haigh, his colleague, Mold, and W. Mead of Essex had better records in 1900. Hallam, who had also recovered from his illness, was unable to get a place in the side, even though in the four matches in which he did play his ten wickets cost only 13.80 runs each.

The one cloud came at Trent Bridge in June, when umpire Phillips, standing at square leg, no-balled Mold for throwing, the first time in eleven years of county cricket that Mold had been penalised. The Editor of *Wisden*, commenting on Phillips' action, stated that he felt Mold had been very fortunate not to be no-balled before. He praised Phillips for making a stand against illegal bowling and no doubt as a result the county captains agreed to act to ban any bowlers with doubtful actions; MacLaren made a half-hearted attempt to defend Mold in a newspaper article, but Mold was again no-balled in 1901 and this brought his career to an abrupt end.

Charles Smith remained the regular wicket-keeper, but he was dropped for a few matches and Harry Pennington, the Notts County footballer, played in four Championship games in his place, earning the following ambiguous comment from *Wisden*: '... acquitted himself fairly well, but he possesses some mannerisms which are hardly likely to strengthen his position in county cricket.'

John Stanning, who had made a splash in 1894 when he hit 152 for Rugby v Marlborough at Lord's, had proceeded to Cambridge and gained his blue in 1900, and he was tried in the Lancashire side in a few games over the next four years, but with little success. He then went out to Kenya, where he was killed in a motor accident in 1929; his brother later played for the County, the two coming from Leyland. Their father was a keen supporter of Lancashire cricket and a member of the County committee until his death, which like that of John junior occurred in rather unusual circumstances – he died of malaria in Egypt in 1905 aged 65.

The renewed attack on 'throwing' filled the pages of the sporting press over the winter months of 1900–01. The County captains actually issued a list of bowlers who ought to be banned – the list included Mold. Certain counties opposed to the blacklist then said that they would ignore it since it was not issued by the MCC. Of equal interest to Lancashire supporters was the sad news that Briggs had had a relapse and was unlikely to play in 1901. Hallam, finding his services more or less ignored by Lancashire in 1900, decided to approach Nottinghamshire, his native county, and was accepted.

Lancashire, despite the objections, decided to continue with Mold, and in the first Championship game of the season he was in fine form, taking six for 69 and enabling Lancashire to open their fixtures with an eight-wicket win. Early in the season, G.R. Bardswell showed he could still score runs by hitting 119 for Formby, whilst the rest of the batsmen

The Lancashire team which played Sussex at Hove in 1901. Standing: Lunt (scorer), A.W. Mold, J. Sharp, W.R. Cuttell, S Webb, J.J. Broughton, W.J. Hibbert. Seated: A. Ward, H.G. Garnett, A.C. MacLaren, A. Priestley, J. Hallows. On ground: J.T. Tyldesley, C. Smith (Lancashire CCC)

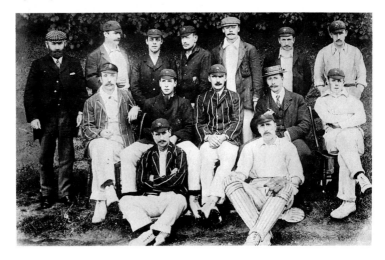

managed only 20 between them, but this innings did not lead to his return to Championship cricket.

As in 1900, both Lancashire and Yorkshire were undefeated when they met at Whitsuntide. Naturally there was a tremendous interest in the game. The report in *Cricket* commented:

It used to be said that it was more difficult to make runs in Yorkshire v Notts than in any other match, partly because the competition between the teams was so exceedingly keen that nine out of ten of the batsmen were bound to be nervous, partly because the bowlers worked as they worked in no other match – and the bowlers were of the best – and partly because the fielding was so good. In the University match there is the same tension, which makes good batsmen fail; but when once a man has broken through the spell he may have a beanfeast if he is lucky. But in Yorkshire v Notts he never found the bowling become loose, and every run had to be fought for. The position so long held by Notts in these annual encounters has of late been taken by Lancashire, and at least as much enthusiasm is now shown in the North over the Lancashire-Yorkshire match as in the old days over Notts v Yorkshire. In the South of England there is nothing to correspond to this match ... every man in the two counties feels that he has a personal interest in the result, and he discusses the chances of victory or defeat with a vigour which is decidedly refreshing.

It was thus hardly surprising that some 25,000 spectators were at Old Trafford on Bank Holiday Monday. MacLaren won the toss, but the wicket was fiery and Rhodes and Hirst dismissed Lancashire for 133. Yorkshire could do no better and were dismissed for 134 by Sharp, Mold and Webb. Lancashire, however, capitulated completely in their second innings, Hirst taking seven for 23 and Lancashire being all out for 44; Yorkshire strolled to an easy win by nine wickets on the second afternoon. A week later the Lancashire bowling was completely mastered by Warwickshire, who ran up a total of 532 before declaring with only four wickets down. The midland county won by an innings and it put an end to Lancashire's faint hope of overhauling Yorkshire – Yorkshire were in fact beaten quite unexpectedly by Somerset in mid-July, but by then the White Rose county was so far in advance that it made no difference to the Championship title.

Despite this foregone conclusion, the August Bank Holiday game at Headingley attracted even greater numbers than in the past. A total of 30,891 people passed through the turnstiles on the first day, many more than expected, and the boundary ropes were moved inward to accommodate them. At lunch time so many people strolled on to the playing area that the resumption of play was delayed by about 30 minutes until the police finally cleared the area. Yorkshire batted the whole of the day, making 319, but MacLaren and Ward both hit hundreds in the Lancashire reply and the match was a draw.

The chief reason why Lancashire's record of eleven wins, five losses and 12 draws did not bear comparison with 1900 was the decline in the bowling strength. Mold was again no-balled and this virtually ended his career in mid-season; Cuttell broke a bone in his hand, missed 11 Championship games and was out of form even when he played; Briggs, as forecast at the start of the summer, was unable to play. This left Sharp and Webb to shoulder the main burden. The Old Trafford wicket was exceedingly lively during May and Sharp, bowling at a good pace, made the ball leap and rear as he took full advantage of the conditions – he picked up 38 wickets in the first five home games. Webb took 104 Championship wickets, but came in for much adverse comment because of his poor fielding.

The surprise of the summer was the appearance of E.E. Steel, who had not been seen regularly in county cricket for many years. He played for Liverpool against the South Africans in late June, was then invited to appear against the tourists for the County a week later and, opening the batting hit the highest score. He played in the Championship game v Somerset on 11 and 12 July, when the newspapers were covered with reports of Mold being no-balled 18 times, so the fact that Steel's slow bowling took ten wickets and won the game got rather lost. His record of 44 Championship wickets placed him in the top ten in the season's bowling table, but he could not afford the time to play in more than seven games. Like his brother, A.G., he was another cricketer lost to the county game.

Another amateur sprang a pleasant surprise in the Lancashire batting. H.G. Garnett had played once or twice prior to 1901, but this season he made himself available for all Championship games and played so consistently that he came second to Tyldesley in the averages, being considered by some critics to be the best left-hand batsman in England, or at least the equal of Kinneir of Warwickshire. Whilst Kinneir came in the category of 'steady', Garnett was quite in the 'dashing' class. The best match of the year for him was against Sussex when he made 110 and 89; he generally opened the batting, with MacLaren, Ward, or E.E. Steel. MacLaren was so impressed that he invited Garnett to go to Australia with the England side during the winter. Garnett failed totally on the tour, but MacLaren's other protégé, also selected with little experience in county cricket, went with him 'down under' and until he was injured took Australia by storm. The player in question was S.F. Barnes. He had played on the odd occasion for Lancashire prior to 1901 and had qualified by residence through being engaged with Burnley. Picked for the last Lancashire match, v Leicestershire, he took six for 70

S.F. Barnes, the protégé of MacLaren (NCCC)

and in mid-September Barnes was given the 14th and final place in MacLaren's Team for Australia. Barnes' knee gave way in the third Test, but his record by then was 19 wickets for 17.00 runs each and he was top of the Test averages. Barnes had originally tried county cricket with Warwickshire, but he was a cold, aloof character and did not enjoy life at Edgbaston. For the same reasons his connection with Lancashire did not last beyond 1903 and he returned to the leagues and minor county cricket where he was a giant among minnows.

MacLaren had a very mixed year, but towards the end batted very well so that his overall record was quite respectable. Three days before MacLaren boarded the Orient steamer *Omrah* at Tilbury with his Australian-bound cricketers, he dropped a quiet bombshell in the lap of Mr Swire:

> Dear Mr Swire,
>
> It is with the greatest reluctance that a combination of circumstances causes me to resign not only the assistant secretaryship of the club, but also my connection with Lancashire cricket. My wife's health is such that it is no longer possible for me to leave her for any length of time. She is very delicate and her doctor has advised me not to leave her. Her only sister lives at Woking, and my wife is most anxious to be near her. She is only just able to get about after a long illness, which I hear will leave its mark. For these private reasons, and no other, do I feel bound to relinquish my connection with Lancashire cricket. Last year the worry and anxiety of illness at home quite prevented me at time from concentrating my whole thoughts on the game. The kindness received at your hands, and others of the committee, will always be treasured by me, no captain ever getting better treatment than I did. Happiness of home comes before my county, and as it is my wife's wish for me to be near her, I have decided to take this step and am notifying the Hampshire committee to the effect that I will play for them next season.
>
> Yours sincerely,
> Archie MacLaren

At the Annual General Meeting of the County Club in December 1901, Mr J. Stanning moved that 'in view of the heavy indebtedness of the Club, due to the purchase of the ground, every member of the Club, excepting life members, shall from January next pay an annual subscription of 26s'. This was carried unanimously. The Club had paid £24,082 for the freehold of the ground in 1899, after a great deal of debate. A.N. Hornby was the chief advocate of the proposed purchase, which included about 18 acres, with the two cricket grounds and other vacant spaces. Mr Swire, the honorary secretary, was against the purchase believing the price asked was too high, but Hornby was supported by James MacLaren and the purchase went through.

In 1899 the Club had reached a membership of 3,000 for the first time and the Test receipts that year – the first in which five matches were played in England – showed that Old Trafford brought in £3,737, the Oval £2,441, Headingley £2,315, Lord's £1,868 and Trent Bridge

£2,211, so that in those terms Manchester was the most popular venue, though the weather and circumstances of each match had their effects.

In view of MacLaren's resignation, the committee appointed Alex Eccles as captain for 1902, but as soon as MacLaren arrived back in England he announced that Australia had done his wife's health a great deal of good and that he wished to remain with Lancashire, rather than transferring to Hampshire. Mr Eccles gallantly stood down and MacLaren therefore continued as captain.

The 1902 Championship was totally overshadowed by the visiting Australians – the fact that Yorkshire once more were all but invincible made the domestic competition a one-horse race anyway. Fortunately for Old Trafford, one of the two most exciting Tests of the year was staged there, and Lancashire fans had some compensation for the rather indifferent performance of the county side. The first two Tests were rain ruined draws, the third was won fairly easily by Australia.

In the fourth match at Old Trafford Australia scored 299, with Trumper and Duff putting on 135 for the first wicket in 80 minutes, after which the bowling of Lockwood and Rhodes gradually gained control. The England innings owed all to F.S. Jackson and Len Braund who added 115 for the sixth wicket, and the home side reached 262. Lockwood bowled quite splendidly in Australia's second innings, taking five for 28 as Australia were dismissed for 86, leaving England needing 123 to win. Things went England's way and with six wickets still in hand just 32 runs were needed. Saunders and Trumble, however, saw to it that none of the remaining batsmen could get set and when rain drove the players in eight runs were needed and one wicket to fall. After 45 minutes the match resumed, and Fred Tate, the number eleven, hit a leg side four off the first ball, but with no further addition he was bowled by the fourth delivery, giving Australia victory.

Turning to the Championship, Lancashire's record of seven wins against five losses placed them fifth, lower than in the last few years, though still respectable. The batting was largely in the hands of Tyldesley and MacLaren, the once reliable Ward not striking form until well on into the season. H.G. Garnett, the find of 1901, played in only three Championship games. James Hallows, who after playing for Little Lever, had joined the groundstaff at Manchester in 1897, gained a regular first-team place, batting at number four and scoring over 700 runs as well as taking 49 wickets. He superseded Sharp as the County's leading all-rounder. Like Briggs (the famous England cricketer had died in the winter of 1901–2) he was left-handed and also subject to epileptic fits. If his health had been better Hallows might have gone on to play for England. As it was he dropped out of the side in 1907 and died at Farnworth in 1910 aged 34.

The most important regular recruit was S.F. Barnes, but to the surprise of many he did not return any astonishing figures in his first full year of first-class cricket, partly because the slow sticky wickets produced by the overabundance of rain told against his style of bowling. Webb easily headed the Lancashire bowling table, but was dropped from the side after a handful of matches – no reason was published, but perhaps his fielding was too dreadful for the rest of the attack to suffer.

The main bowling was shared by I'Anson, E.E. Steel and Cuttell, as well as Barnes and Hallows. Charles Smith retired from his wicket-keeping post, but with no obvious successor the job was passed from Thomas to Lees Radcliffe to W. Findlay. The last named was the Oxford University 'keeper. He played until 1906, when he was appointed secretary to Surrey CCC. In 1919 he became assistant secretary at Lord's and from 1926 to 1936 Secretary of the MCC. On retiring he headed the Findlay Commission of 1937 which tried to solve the problems of county cricket. A man of great diplomacy, his temperament was ideal for the tasks which he undertook. He came back to Lancashire CCC as President in 1947 and 1948.

Geoffrey MacLaren, brother of Archie, played twice for Lancashire and in contrast to Archie, made a duck on his debut – he had opened the batting for Harrow earlier in the summer, making 41 v Eton at Lord's. He did not reappear in county cricket in 1903, having joined the South African Police. From South Africa he went to Egypt, where he was in business until the First World War, and after serving with distinction in the Army he later became a Governor of Jenin Sub-district in Palestine.

Another Oxford blue to appear occasionally for the County was Sir Frank Hollins. He was one of three brothers from Preston all of whom were noted on the sports field. The eldest, A.M., gained his blue for cricket at Oxford in 1899, but never played for Lancashire, the youngest, J.C.H.L., played for the County in 1914. The father of the trio was a long standing supporter of Lancashire cricket, a member of the committee and later president. He was one of the people who put up the money to buy Old Trafford.

Financially the club fared well in 1902 and was able to repay £2,000 of the loan raised for the ground. The main grumble of members was the catering arrangements, which the committee promised to improve in 1903; the scorers had a moan regarding the position of the scorebox, which was behind the cheap seats. This meant that the scorers' attentions were continually being distracted by the antics of the crowd immediately in front of them.

With the ending of the Boer War came the good news that R.H. Spooner had returned from South Africa and had taken a business appointment in Manchester with permission to be released for county matches. MacLaren had also secured a job which allowed him time off for county cricket. With no Test matches arranged for 1903, interest in the Championship was bound to revive, and for once Yorkshire did not have everything their own way.

Yorkshire in fact lost four matches by the end of June, a circumstance not seen for some seasons. Lancashire in the same period had lost only two, but the dark horse Middlesex put the northern counties firmly in their places, by going through until August without a single reverse. Yorkshire fought back and towards the end the title was between that county and Middlesex, Lancashire not being near enough to have a bearing on the final outcome.

The star of the Red Rose side was Sidney Barnes. He improved greatly on his modest showing of 1902 and on his good days, making the ball go away with his arm, as well as come quickly off the wicket, he was considered the best right-arm bowler in England. He did, however, have bad days and Lancashire were in need of a consistent bowler. *Wisden* noted that it was a pity that Barnes did not possess the temperament and the enthusiasm for county cricket to the same degree as Barlow or Briggs.

To support Barnes, Cuttell (awarded a joint benefit with C. Smith) bowled better than for some time, his 70 Championship wickets costing 19.72 runs each. The only other bowler to deliver more than 400 overs was the amateur Walter Brearley, who had made a few appearances in 1902.

Brearley, with a rolling gait and body swing, delivered the ball in a style similar to Mold and was nearly as fast. He had about an eight-yard run, four of which he walked, and his great strength plus the swing of his body produced the necessary speed. The new bowler was a character of the Hornby variety. When two members walked over the wicket at Old Trafford, Brearley shouted at them from the pavilion. When that had no effect, he rushed out and attempted to frog-march one, whilst the other attacked Brearley with an umbrella. On another occasion, when playing against Gloucestershire, Brearley lost his temper with Jessop and ended by bowling fast full pitchers at Jessop's head! According to Laurence Meynell the reporters remembered the way Hornby dealt with those who wrote articles against him, and thus no one described the incident in the press.

In the early weeks of 1903, Brearley took full advantage of the hard wickets, but as the rain dominated most of June, July and August, he was not so effective. Barnes took 131 Championship wickets, Cuttell, as noted, 70 and Brearley 69. No one else reached 30. Hallows and E.E. Steel did not play a great deal; Sharp lost his bowling entirely. Littlewood, whose father had played three matches for Lancashire in 1885, bowled slow left-arm quite respectably, but was not selected very often.

Much was expected of Spooner. He scored 247 against Notts at the beginning of July on a batsman's wicket at Trent Bridge and 168 against Gloucester at Liverpool, when he and MacLaren created a new Lancashire first-wicket record stand of 368. Like most other batsmen he found runs harder to obtain in the rain, and therefore his average of just under 30 was good considering he had been away from county cricket since 1899. His talent was recognised when he was chosen to tour Australia at the end of the summer, though his business commitments meant he had to decline. MacLaren had been asked to lead a team, chosen by himself, but failed to persuade several leading players to accompany him. The arrangements for the tour were eventually taken over by the MCC – their first such to Australia – and they ignored MacLaren, selecting Warner instead as captain. MacLaren apparently decided it was against his principles to go under the captaincy of Warner and the press made much of this. Even in those days the popular press were not above misquotation and announced that MacLaren had said that, out of his three visits to Australia he had not made a halfpenny, and this cut him to the quick. What he actually said was that it cut him to the quick when people accused him of making money out of the trips!

With MacLaren and Spooner not going, the MCC had one Lancashire player only in their party, J.T. Tyldesley, who played in the Tests and in all first-class matches hit 670 runs, average 33.50, being effectively the third best batsman of the tour, behind Hayward and R.E. Foster.

Tyldesley's winter in Australia had a beneficial effect on his batting in 1904. Batting at number three for the County he put together a string of high scores and by the summer's end had 2,237 runs at an average of 69.90 in Championship matches. He hit eight centuries of which the most valuable was against Yorkshire at Leeds and his powerful stroke play was as brilliant as ever. Spooner was also seen at his best. He was now firmly established as the most stylish batsman in England, though curiously he was not seen at his best in the matches at Lord's or the Oval. In a side full of excellent fieldsmen, his displays at cover-point were quite outstanding.

Lancashire began the fixtures with wins over Leicestershire and Warwickshire. The match against Yorkshire came third on the list and it ought to have been played at Leeds, but in deference to Hirst, who wanted the August Bank Holiday match as his benefit, the Whitsun game was staged at Old Trafford. This was unfortunate, as it turned out, since rain washed away the third day when the match was evenly poised. Spooner's hundred was the major event of the game.

Kenty, Surrey, Somerset and Gloucestershire were then all beaten, three by an innings and one by ten wickets. So in mid-June the magazine *Cricket* noted:

On Monday last Lancashire alone among the counties had an unbeaten record for the season, while Hampshire was the only county which could not claim a single victory. Lancashire seems destined to win the Championship, and undoubtedly its team is stronger than it has been for many years, but a great many curious things may happen before the end of the season.

The game at Edgbaston, played immediately after the above comment, saw Lancashire in deep trouble; Warwickshire made 426, whilst the Lancastrians collapsed to be all out for 156, and were invited to follow on. Cuttell was sent in first with Spooner and the veteran all-rounder, now in his 40th year, batted quite in the manner of former days, hitting 128 and saving the game. A high scoring draw against Sussex was followed by wins over Surrey, Kent and Somerset, so that July was reached without a single reverse.

The match at Trent Bridge during the first week of July brought forth some adverse comment from MacLaren, writing his column in the *Daily Chronicle*:

Jones (the Notts captain) commenced bowling wide on the leg side, and after Tyldesley and myself had driven him to deep mid-off, that isolated fieldsman was moved to the on-side, leaving not a single man on the off. The bowling naturally was then wider still outside the legs, the fieldsmen waiting for catches with their mouths open –like birds in a nest. Tyldesley was eventually easily caught at short mid-on ... and after his dismissal the wide balls on the leg side were served up with wonderful consistency. Both batsmen refused to hit to leg, the bat being shouldered over after over.

Jones's reasoning was that Notts must avoid losing at all costs – the system of, in effect, deducting a point for a loss, made captains anxious to force a draw if a win was not possible.

Six successive wins after the drawn farce at Trent Bridge took Lancashire to the Bank Holiday game at Headingley. Lancashire, although still undefeated, had not obtained at this stage a commanding lead in the Championship, because Yorkshire had met with only a single defeat, and therefore if they could overcome Lancashire the title chase would be wide open.

No fewer than 78,681 people paid to watch this holiday game. MacLaren won the toss, putting Yorkshire in on a wicket which ought to have suited Hallows and Cuttell. The bowlers squandered their opportunities and Yorkshire reached 403. Hirst then demonstrated what could be done, dismissing Spooner, MacLaren and Tyldesley for 0, 4 and 0 in three overs. A.H. Hornby saved a complete debacle, but Lancashire still followed on 230 in arrears. MacLaren then remained

75 minutes for five, but Tyldesley stole the show and the match was saved.

Warwickshire then surprised cricket followers by defeating Yorkshire – the first time this had happened in Championship matches – and this meant Lancashire could afford to lose two games and the title would still be theirs. As it was they went through the programme undefeated and thus thoroughly deserved their season of success.

The attainments of Spooner and Tyldesley in 1904 were much as one might expect, so the surprise of the year was the all-round cricket of Hallows. In 1903, the presence of Barnes had much restricted his appearances, but the Staffordshire player's decision to quit county cricket provided Hallows with an opportunity which he exploited to the full. By the end of the year he had not only achieved the 'double', but was top of Lancashire's Championship bowling table with 108 wickets at 18 runs each and third, behind Tyldesley and Spooner, in the batting, with 1,058 runs, average 40.09. Cuttell was the only other player to complete 100 wickets, but Brearley did well until he dropped out of the eleven after the August Bank Holiday match. Being of the same character as A.N. Hornby, the president, it was not surprising that these two volatile personalities would clash, and this happened in mid-season. When at the end of the year Brearley was not invited to play for Lancashire against the Rest of England, the fast bowler announced his retirement from the Lancashire Club. At the AGM in December, members studying the Club's annual report found Brearley's name conspicuous by its absence and demanded to know the reason. A.N. Hornby stated:

> As long as I am president of this Club I will not tolerate bad behaviour on or off the cricket ground by any player, be he amateur or professional. The press have been much against me in this matter of Brearley and Lancashire, and they (the press) should be really more careful in what they say, and ought not to try and injure any player against his committee. In the middle of July Mr Brearley and I shook hands and agreed to let bygones be bygones. Mr Brearley and myself are the best of friends, and that gentleman has since been my guest at my club.

Lancashire had two Australians as regular members of the 1904 side and both played a part in winning the title. Alexander Kermode had been discovered by MacLaren on the 1901–02 tour of Australia. A fast bowler from Sydney, he had been encouraged by the Lancashire captain to emigrate to England and take up a post as a cricket professional in Lancashire with the idea of qualifying for the County, following the example of Trott, who had qualified for Middlesex.

Kermode's qualification period was completed during June and this turned out a stroke of luck, since not only was Brearley at loggerheads with the committee, but Hallows injured a knee in July. Kermode, a big man with a heavy frame, managed to vary his pace deceptively as well as make the ball move off the pitch. At times he was somewhat expensive, but he did take 65 Championship wickets at a vital time.

The other Australian also came from New South Wales and made his debut on 2 June against Surrey and with 55, hit the highest score of the match. The batsman was L.O.S. Poidevin, who had also been spotted by MacLaren, but had come to England to qualify as a doctor. He had played for W.G. Grace's side at Crystal Palace since 1902 and made some useful scores. A stylish player with an excellent defence, he scored 865 runs, average 34.60 in the 1904 Championship and thoroughly justified MacLaren's faith in him.

Lancashire broke with tradition in 1904 and for the first time appointed a paid secretary. S.H. Swire's health had been giving cause for concern for several years and the office, which was situated in the middle of Manchester at 26 Barton Arcade, was run by Tom Irving, as assistant secretary, with Mr Swire coming in twice a week to keep an eye on things. Irving was a useful cricketer, a left-arm bowler, and turned out in matches for Manchester. Irving left the Club at the end of 1900, and a former journalist on the *Manchester Courier*, Tom Matthews, was taken on as his replacement. Matthews was elevated to secretary in the middle of 1904, when it became plain that Mr Swire was unable to continue on a day-to-day basis.

To an extent the Test matches of 1905 decided the destiny of that year's Championship. The complaints that Australian tours put the Championship in the background had grown with each visit. The second Test was staged at Lord's when Yorkshire were challenging for the title. England deprived them of four men – Jackson, Haig, Rhodes and twelfth man Hirst – and as a result Yorkshire were defeated by Derbyshire. Later in the season Lancashire, then at the head of the table, were deprived of MacLaren, Spooner, Brearley and Tyldesley for the Oval Test and were beaten by Gloucestershire. As it turned out both Yorkshire and Lancashire each lost two other matches and the two matches in which they played each other were of vital importance. On Whit Bank Holiday Monday 24,461 spectators paid for admission to Old Trafford and saw a brilliant second wicket stand of 253 between Tyldesley and Spooner, made in 160 minutes. Tyldesley was dropped in the slips when he had made 14 and Spooner had a piece of luck when 37, for the ball hit the wicket without dislodging a bail, but those two blemishes aside the partnership was flawless and won the match for the home side. No one else reached 50 for Lancashire. Then Yorkshire disintegrated before Brearley in their first innings, and before Kermode in the second, Lancashire's margin of success being an innings and 52 runs.

LANCASHIRE *v.* SOMERSET

Played on the Old Trafford Ground, Manchester on 3 and 4 July 1905

LANCASHIRE WON BY AN INNINGS AND 150 RUNS

SOMERSET	FIRST INNINGS		SECOND INNINGS	
†Mr H. Martyn	c Spooner b Brearley	6	b Brearley	0
L.C. Braund	b Brearley	1	c Hornby b Brearley	16
F.P. Hardy	b Brearley	1	b Brearley	0
E. Robson	not out	15	c Sharp b Hallows	61
*Mr S.M.J. Woods	b Brearley	10	c Garnett b Brearley	1
Mr E.S.M. Poyntz	b Heap	21	b Poidevin	32
Mr M.A.S. Sturt	b Brearley	4	c Garnett b Brearley	35
Mr C.E. Brown	b Brearley	0	c Findlay b Brearley	53
A.S. Sellick	c Cuttell b Brearley	2	c Cuttell b Brearley	0
B. Cranfield	b Brearley	2	c Findlay b Brearley	13
J. Bucknell	b Brearley	0	not out	5
Extras	b 2, lb 1	3	b 6, lb 3, nb 2	11
Total		65		227

BOWLING	O	M	R	W	O	M	R	W
Brearley	12.4	2	47	9	23	5	90	8
Heap	12	6	15	1	3	0	12	0
Sharp					9	1	35	0
Hallows					6	0	35	1
Poidevin					10	0	44	1

LANCASHIRE	FIRST INNINGS	
Mr R.H. Spooner	c Robson b Braund	80
W.R. Cuttell	b Robson	45
J. Hallows	c Cranfield b Braund	47
Mr L.O.S. Poidevin	st Martyn b Robson	17
Mr H.G. Garnett	c Poyntz b Braund	12
J. Sharp	c Martyn b Bucknell	34
J.S. Heap	c Sturt b Braund	52
Mr A. Eccles	c Martyn b Bucknell	6
*Mr A.H. Hornby	c Brown b Robson	106
†Mr W. Findlay	not out	31
Mr W. Brearley	c Woods b Braund	0
Extras	b 8, lb 4	12
Total		442

BOWLING	O	M	R	W
Cranfield	5	0	40	0
Braund	40.2	2	227	5
Robson	32	6	94	3
Bucknell	16	4	69	2

Umpires: Wm. Attewell and A. Pike

In the August meeting it seemed as if Brearley again had Yorkshire on their knees. He took seven for 35, as the Tykes were dismissed for 76. Lancashire replied with 177. David Denton, F.S. Jackson and Wilfred Rhodes fought back for Yorkshire in the second innings, leaving Lancashire with 185 to score for victory. They made 50 for the loss of two wickets on the second evening and so had the whole of the last day to make 135. The pitch was at its worst and the light poor. Rhodes and Haigh bowled Lancashire out and therefore Yorkshire evened the score.

The weather in the last half of August was equally unkind to both counties, each having their final three games ending as rain-affected draws. Yorkshire carried off the title with 18 wins from 28 matches; Lancashire had 12 wins from 25.

Poidevin topped the batting averages; Hallows, Tyldesley, Spooner and MacLaren followed not far behind and with Sharp and A.H. Hornby also among the runs, there was little at fault with the batting. Brearley and Kermode formed as good a pair of fast bowlers as any in the country, both taking over 100 wickets, though towards the end of the summer Kermode looked stale and became somewhat wayward. The slow bowling, however, was the side's weak point. Both Hallows and the veteran Cuttell took a few wickets and those they obtained were very expensive. Poidevin tried his googlies, but they came off only once. Sharp also had one great match as a bowler.

Billy Cook, the Preston professional, took Kermode's place in the match against Gloucestershire at Old Trafford and took eleven wickets with his fast deliveries, but his connection with Championship cricket was even briefer than S.F. Barnes', and despite 51 wickets at 18 runs each in 11 matches, he preferred League cricket. In later years he helped Burnley to carry off the Lancashire League title in three successive years. He was also a notable soccer player with Preston and Oldham.

T.A. Higson played the first of five first-class games for Lancashire in 1905 – he represented the County in a Blackpool Festival game against An England XI. Tommy Higson had been born in Stockport in 1873. He gained a place in the Rossall School Eleven and whilst at school appeared for Cheshire. In 1899 he turned out for Derbyshire, acting as captain for several matches, but he failed to obtain a blue at Oxford. After his debut for Lancashire in 1905, he appeared in the odd match until 1923, but he rapidly became better known as a cricket administrator. A Manchester solicitor, he gained a place on the Lancashire committee and was later hon treasurer of the Club, his philosophy being to build a strong team round a sound balance sheet. In the 1930s he was a Test selector and helped to pick the 1932–33 team to Australia, though he later condemned bodyline bowling and on that account persuaded Lancashire to stop playing matches with Notts.

Higson usually got his own way and Lancashire were fortunate to have a man of his character on the committee. He was largely responsible for obtaining the services of the Australian fast bowler McDonald after the war and many benefited from his acts of spontaneous generosity. Two of his sons later also played for Lancashire.

Within a few months of Higson's debut for Lancashire came the news of the death of S.H. Swire, the first and to this date only honorary secretary of the County Club. Ill-health had finally taken its toll. With his death the post of hon seccretary was abandoned, T.J. Matthews assuming all duties.

The fact that Brearley played in only five Championship matches made a large difference to the strength of Lancashire's bowling in 1906. *Wisden* rather teasingly notes: '. . . for some reason with which we are imperfectly acquainted the fast bowler dropped out of the eleven.'

Cuttell, however, returned to his best form and as in the previous year Kermode did well until August. At the end of the year Cuttell announced his retirement and accepted a coaching position at Rugby school. Huddleston, who was engaged with the Lancashire League side Church, could only play in mid-week matches, but he topped the bowling table with 50 wickets at 12 runs each.

With only the West Indian side touring, the Championship took centre stage and the tussle for the title was keener than for many years. In the early days it seemed to be a battle between Surrey and Yorkshire, with Lancashire running third, but through July and into August Kent began to overhaul the front runners and at the last gasp snatched the lead from Yorkshire. Lancashire, with 15 wins from 26 matches, but with six losses, had to settle for fourth place. The improvement in the Kent side can be clearly seen from the fact that Lancashire in June beat the hop county by 10 wickets, Tyldesley taking the opportunity to score a career best 295 not out, but at Canterbury in August, Kent won the return fixture by an innings. On the first day Kent made 409 for three, Hutchings and Mason hitting 201 in 110 minutes. For Lancashire no one reached fifty and totals of 169 and 115 meant defeat by an innings and 195 runs.

Although Lancashire had little hope of the Championship by the time the August Bank Holiday fixture took place at Old Trafford, over £2,000 was taken at the gate, the game being given to Tyldesley as his benefit. Yorkshire won both this and the Whitsun meeting, due to the collapse of Lancashire's batting. Although the County's batting line up was not dissimilar to 1905, the fortunes of the individuals were considerably altered. Only Tyldesley and Sharp could point to averages over 30. MacLaren's highest innings was just 61 and Poidevin's 79; Spooner's 1,122 aggregate owed much too much to the 240 he scored against Somerset at Bath, opposing a very moderate attack. However,

in *Cricket* of 2 August 1906 under 'Pavilion Gossip' appeared the
following paragraph:

In H. Makepeace Lancashire have found a batsman who ought to
develop into a fine player. He bats in a pleasing style and does not
seem at all nervous, and with more experience seems likely to score
fairly quickly. He is at present better known as one of the Everton
half-backs, who was injured early in the match between England and
Scotland this year.

Makepeace had just made his debut against Essex at Leyton and
scored 49, opening the innings with MacLaren. He was a 24-year-old
Yorkshireman from Middlesbrough. He quickly joined Tyldesley and
Spooner as one of the idols of young Neville Cardus:

What a foil the dour Makepeace then had! MacLaren and Makepeace
going into the field for Lancashire were as Don Quixote and Sancho
Panza among cricketers – MacLaren ready to tilt at windmills, his bat
a chivalrous lance, and Makepeace stubborn and canny, with no
romantic nonsense about him – a shrewd fellow, biding his time,
confident that patience and diligent service will bring him at last a
batsman's kingdom. He has been in the Lancashire side, has
Makepeace, for even more years than the records show – only his
name was Barlow at one moment and Albert Ward at another.

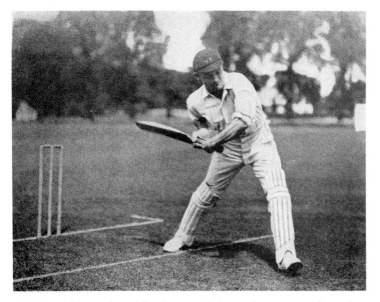

*J.W.H. Makepeace, the Yorkshire batsman, who became the cornerstone of Lancashire
cricket* (NCCC)

Through him, as through Barlow and Ward, a tradition has been expressing itself – the great stonewall tradition. You must see to it that you have one man at least on your side with a cool head and a wide bat. And no cricketer in our time has so completely given you the image of the authentic stonewaller as Makepeace.

Makepeace's career with Lancashire was to span almost the rest of his life. He played in 487 matches and the final one did not take place until 1930 – then he became the Lancashire coach, retiring in 1951 and dying the following year. In contrast to Makepeace another professional made his debut for the County on the same day – W.R. Gregson. He looked a useful fast bowler, though with a tendency to drop the ball too short. In the next game, the first Championship match ever staged at Blackpool, Gregson returned a first innings analysis of 9.3-6-8-5, which included the hat-trick, his victims being V.F.S. Crawford, R.T. Crawford and C.E. de Trafford. He finished the game with nine for 76, but though he was engaged at Old Trafford in 1907 his entire first-class career was confined to five matches in 1906.

The Lancashire Club had a deficit of £423 on the year, but the reasons for this were that Tyldesley had been given the Yorkshire match for his benefit and that there was no Australian tour.

Lancashire opened the 1907 season with an eight-wicket win over Leicester, but the victorious side had an unfamiliar look about it. MacLaren was in India with Ranjitsinhji, having gone there for the winter and remaining there until June. He had written to the Lancashire committee stating that he would not be able to play regularly, but the committee decided to retain him as official captain. Spooner had also gone abroad for the winter and was able to turn out for only four matches in 1907. W. Findlay, the main wicket-keeper in 1906, had accepted the post of Surrey secretary, which had become vacant on the death of C.W. Alcock. Findlay's connections with Lancashire's Championship side thus came to an end. Brearley seemed to have broken entirely with the County committee and was not seen in the side at all in the season. Cuttell, as noted, had gone off coaching and therefore half the 'first-choice' players of the 1906 side were absent. Though the team began with an impressive win it was not long before their weaknesses began to show and in the first weeks of the summer they lost to Cambridge University (by an innings), Essex and Worcestershire. The last-mentioned was the most remarkable. Cuffe, Worcestershire's Australian left-arm spinner, dismissed Lancashire for 138, but Worcestershire fared much worse, being all out for 87. Lancashire's second innings amounted to 118, Burrows and Cuffe continuing to extract assistance from the wicket. Worcester needed 170 in their final innings and few gave them a chance. H.K. Foster and Bowley opened the batting and actually hit off the runs in two hours without being parted. Worcester were to go on and surprise several more of the 'senior' counties and ended the year tying for second place with Yorkshire.

Aside from these early reverses, Lancashire with their weakened side had quite a few days of success in the first half of the season, but the fielding went completely adrift in August and they lost five out of six matches in a row. Victories in the final two games of the season moved them two places further up the table and they finished sixth, with 11 wins against seven losses. The match against Middlesex at Lord's was one of the talking points of the summer. On the first day rain meant that only 25 overs could be bowled, Lancashire scoring 57 for one. The second day was fine and a number of would-be spectators paid admission, but it was agreed that the pitch was unfit for play. When this was announced several of the spectators gave vent to their feelings on the wicket. A crowd gathered in front of the pavilion and the MCC Secretary eventually dispersed them by issuing free passes for the next day. MacLaren and MacGregor (the Middlesex captain) then went out to look at the pitch and on returning to the pavilion, MacLaren issued the following statement: 'Owing to the pitch having been deliberately torn up by the public, I, as captain of the Lancashire eleven, cannot see my way to continue the game, the groundsman bearing me out that the wicket could not be again put right.'

The Middlesex captain did not associate himself with MacLaren's remark and made no statement. As Lancashire gave up the match, the question arose as to whether Middlesex should count the game as a win. Middlesex should have arrived on the third morning and claimed the game in the absence of their opponents. They did not do this and the match went down as 'Abandoned' and therefore did not count in the Championship.

Harry Dean came to the fore as Lancashire's bowler of 1907 with 98 Championship wickets, 23 more than his nearest rival. A left-arm bowler with an easy delivery and a fair pace, he was able to swing the ball effectively and he could also bowl a slower ball, which as his career developed he used more frequently. In all matches in 1907 he took 100 wickets, a feat he was to repeat in each of the next six seasons. Another bowler who was to be of use to the County for some years to come was 'Lol' Cook, brother of Billy. Right-arm medium, his best years were those immediately following the First World War.

M.C. Bird was the outstanding schoolboy cricketer of the year. For Harrow against Eton at Lord's in July he hit a century in each innings, a feat never previously accomplished in this historic match. As he captained Harrow to victory and also captured five wickets, young Bird seemed to have a very bright cricketing future. Born in Toxteth Park, Liverpool, he came from a cricketing family, his father playing for

Lancashire in 1880. He played in five Championship games during the school holidays, but did not have much success. In 1909 he played for Surrey under residential qualification and later for England.

Illegal bowling reappeared in Lancashire's ranks in 1908. The County introduced a young all-rounder, Ralph Whitehead from Ashton-under-Lyne. His first game was at Old Trafford against Notts at the end of June. Umpire Brown at square leg no-balled Whitehead when he attempted to deliver his extra-fast ball, Notts batting first. Whitehead went in at number eight for Lancashire and had the satisfaction of scoring 131 not out in his first innings for the County. The fact that he was also no-balled produced an unusual statistic – the only player to be no-balled as well as score a hundred on his debut. He was to be the last bowler thus penalised in England first-class cricket until the 1950s.

The first talking point of the 1908 season with regard to Lancashire's bowling was not however the misfortune which befell Whitehead, but this piece in 'Pavilion Gossip' of May 7:

> It is good to hear that a reconciliation has been effected between Walter Brearley and the Lancashire authorities, and the famous bowler will resume his place in the County Eleven ... The estrangement has lasted rather more than eighteen months, and I cannot help feeling that with a little tact the misunderstanding might have been done away with long ago.

Brearley took eleven wickets on his re-appearance, enabling the County to beat Somerset at Bath by an innings. He repeated the eleven wickets in the second Championshp game as Northants were also beaten by an innings. In the third match, of which the second day was almost rained off, Brearley captured a further eight of the fourteen Derbyshire wickets which fell. The fourth game produced Lancashire's first defeat of the summer, but Brearley captured yet another eleven wickets and was badly let down by the batsmen, only A.H. Hornby hitting a fifty for the losing side. So, including six wickets against Cambridge, Brearley had taken 47 wickets by the end of May. A further eight wickets came his way in the first match of June, when he sank the Champion County, Notts, without trace – all out 111 and 79 – and Lancashire won by nine wickets. It has, however, to be mentioned that Brearley severely injured Notts' leading bowler, Wass. Wass was forced to retire hurt and was unable to bowl at all for his side.

In all first-class matches, Brearley took 163 wickets and came fourth in the averages after Haigh, Hirst and Rhodes. There was another side to this success and it came to the attention of the general public through a salvo from the *Athletic News*, which commented on the wickets now provided at Old Trafford:

A sporting wicket is not to be condemned, but cricketers ought not to be under fire at one end for most of the time that they are trying to get runs. There were as many as three balls in an over buzzing about the faces of players. That both sides suffer equally has nothing to do with the case. This may or may not be so, but we feel that the wickets now obtained are prejudicial to Lancashire cricket ... The players have complained for some time, and we include both amateurs and professionals. Ordinary stroke play on stereo-typed lines, is at a discount.

The Lancashire committee were not slow to react to this criticism and within a few months, Reynolds, who had been 'ground manager' as well as his other appointments, was prevailed upon to retire. For some time he had had to put up with adverse comments about the wickets he prepared and William Howard tells how Reynolds found he was invariably in the wrong. If he used the heavy roller it ought to have been the medium, if the medium, then the light one should have been applied. On one occasion he used all three so that no-one could complain! Perhaps the last straw for the Lancashire committee was when a ball from Brearley badly injured the wicket-keeper.

The following advertisement appeared in the press: 'Wanted a Ground Manager for the County Ground, Old Trafford. Salary £200 per year, with house, gas, coal, etc.'

Over three hundred applications were received, most totally unqualified for the post, which eventually went to R.G. Barlow. The famous stonewaller did not last long. He found the worries of the job and the number of bosses who gave him instructions too much with which to contend, and though he had signed a contract initially for one year, the committee agreed to release him after nine months.

Apart from Brearley only Dean had any great success bowling for Lancashire in 1908 and after many years of having a balanced attack, the County were suddenly reduced to two really effective bowlers. Dean took 124 Championship wickets. F. Harry, who had promised a great deal, played in eight Championship games, took 23 wickets and at the close of the season resigned, taking a coaching post in Scotland. Kermode, the Australian, was seen in only two Championship games and this signalled the end of his cricket with Lancashire. K.G. MacLeod, the Cambridge blue, a brilliant fieldsman in the deep, came in the side in the vacation, but was more use as a batsman than a bowler. Although born in Liverpool he was educated at Fettes and went on to play for Scotland as a wing-threequarter.

Partially due to the wickets, the Lancashire batting had a poor time in 1908. Only J.T. Tyldesley and Sharp could look back on a good summer. MacLaren rarely played – he was not seen at all until nearly the end of June and on his re-apparance a brief biography was published about him which related a rather amusing incident. MacLaren was fielding on the boundary in a Test match at Sydney, when the ball was hit at a great height in his direction. The crowd went suddenly quiet as they waited for the catch, but a small supporter of Australia piped up: 'Miss it Archie, and I'll let you kiss my sister.' MacLaren caught the ball!

The Championship battle was initially between Yorkshire and Surrey, but the former soon left all rivals behind and by August they had only to avoid defeat to take the title. Lancashire at the end of June were in sixth place and by the close of the contest had dropped to seventh.

At the Annual General Meeting of Lancashire in December, Reynolds was awarded an annual pension of £100 and he and his wife were made life members of the Club.

The first news of major importance in connection with the 1909 Lancashire season was the announcement, even before the County had played its first match, that A.C. MacLaren was selected as captain of England for the forthcoming series against Australia; F.S. Jackson had been approached first, but declined the post. It was an unusual appointment, though it demonstrated the standing of MacLaren in the cricket world and was generally applauded. F.S. Ashley-Cooper, in his weekly column, simply noted: 'When F.S. Jackson declined the honour, the Selection Committee naturally turned to the Lancashire ex-captain as the person best qualified for the position.'

On the domestic front, Lancashire, captained by A.H. Hornby, expected few if any changes in their eleven and thus it seemed unlikely they would be among the contenders for the Championship – in fact their most promising youngster, Whitehead, was struck down with scarlet fever and was ruled out of the side for at least the first half of the summer.

When Yorkshire arrived at Old Trafford for the Whitsun match, Lancashire could reflect on a productive first month, having won four out of five games, the other, at Leicester, being a rain-ruined draw. Although Brearley had been largely responsible for two victories, Huddleston and Dean had proved that the County could win without the controversial amateur when they bowled unchanged against Essex, dismissing that side for 83 and 130, even though the report notes that their analyses owed something to the feebleness of the Essex batting.

Directly before the Bank Holiday match, MacLaren led England to a ten-wicket victory at Edgbaston and it is interesting to note that 4,000 spectators turned up for the first day of the Test, whereas four days later 12,000 arrived to watch Lancashire play Yorkshire. Brearley was at his best in the latter match, and bowling unchanged took nine for 80 as

Yorkshire crashed to 133 all out. Haigh soon had the measure of the Lancashire batsmen and included the hat-trick in his figures of seven for 25, Lancashire being dismissed for 89. Not to be outdone, Huddleston returned an analysis of eight for 24, as Yorkshire went down for 78, leaving Lancashire 128 to win. The opening of the final innings was quite sensational, with five wickets down for six runs, and though A.H. Hornby then fought back, Yorkshire won by 65.

At this stage of the year, Yorkshire were in the doldrums and Surrey were making the running with eight wins from eleven matches. Nominally Middlesex topped the table, though with only two wins, simply because they were yet to be beaten.

The doings of England's selectors occupied much space in the press in the first days of June. There was a great outcry when it was learnt that Brearley was not chosen for the second Test at Lord's and that cry became quite deafening when England were totally outplayed. Mac-Laren, writing in *Country Life*, told the world that he had asked Brearley ON THE MORNING OF THE MATCH to join the England side. Brearley, whose quarrels with the Lancashire authorities were public knowledge, had already taken umbrage at not being in the originally selected team, and declined to change his plans simply to accommodate the muddled thinking of the selectors. His response was given in no uncertain terms a week later when he took 12 Kent wickets, enabling Lancashire to win at Tonbridge by 312 runs.

Not only was Brearley chosen for the third Test, but Jack Sharp was selected for the first time, Lancashire having four players – MacLaren and Tyldesley being the other two – in the 14 names from which the side would be picked. On the morning of the match it was announced that S.F. Barnes had been added to the England squad. When the final side took the field it was found that for the first time five Lancashire players (including Barnes) were present. Sharp hit the highest score for England – 61 – the only other fifty coming from Tyldesley, as England's batting failed twice. Barnes was the most successful England bowler.

Lancashire had no match during the Lord's Test, but immediately before and after they had very conflicting results, being beaten by Notts by an innings, then inflicting defeat by the same margin on Surrey. Surrey, after a great start to the season, were suddenly ripped apart by internal strife.

Old Trafford was the scene for the fourth Test. Spooner, who had made his first appearance of the season for Lancashire on 5 July and immediately hit top form with two hundreds within the space of ten days, was chosen for England, so although Brearley was omitted, Lancashire still had five representatives. Rain meant the match was drawn, but 16,000 attended on the first day and 17,000 on the second. The receipts at Manchester were £3,153 6s – £400 more than at Lord's.

In the meantime, the Championship, though taking a backseat to the Test problems, was building up to an interesting climax. On 29 July, Lancashire and Kent were tied at the top, each having eleven wins and two losses from 17 matches; Yorkshire having recovered from their poor start were third with nine wins and two losses.

With the race for the title so tight, Lancashire went to Bradford for the August Bank Holiday game. Yorkshire accomplished the double, winning by 100 runs, with the Lancashire batsmen unable to cope with Rhodes' left-arm deliveries: at the same time Kent beat Middlesex by an innings and thus took a twin step forward under the prevailing system of deducting points for losses. Not only did Kent leap ahead, but Yorkshire moved into second place in front of Lancashire.

The Lancashire fixture with Worcestershire clashed with the fifth Test at the Oval; so while Jack Sharp was hitting his maiden Test hundred and saving England, his County struggled and eventually lost by seven wickets.

The Australians moved to Blackpool where they met an England XI. None of the home side came from Lancashire and the County therefore had a strong team to oppose Middlesex on the same days. They won relatively easily, the only real spark from the opposition being 50 in 38 minutes from Albert Trott. Another win – at Chesterfield – put Lancashire back into second place. Kent, however, were all but certain of the title and Lancashire's two-day win in their last match did the Red Rose cause no good, since Kent ended the summer with two more victories. All in all, however, Lancashire could be more than satisfied with their second place. Just as the season was ending the Club found a replacement for the disgruntled Barlow in Albert Ward.

The averages show the reason for Lancashire's rise: Brearley in Championship matches took 115 wickets at 15 runs each and four batsmen averaged 30, plus Spooner, but he played in only six games. The main support for Brearley came from Huddleston and Dean. The former managed to smash the myth that he was ineffective on firm wickets and he captured 82 wickets at 16 runs each.

MacLeod joined the team after the University match, but he did little, apart from his hundred against Somerset at Bath. His fielding was his outstanding asset – Lancashire's weakness was in the wicket-keeping department. Worsley was a great trier, but was injured several times and his reserve was Blomley from Oldham. One new player made his first-class debut during the year, Ernest Tyldesley. The brother of J.T., he was 20 at the time of his first match, and over the course of the next 25 years he was to prove an even more successful batsman than his elder brother. Their styles differed, as did their temperaments. Whilst J.T.

GEORGE ERNEST TYLDESLEY

G.E. was the younger brother of J.T. Tyldesley, the latter having been in the Lancashire side for 14 years when Ernest (as he was known) made his debut. Despite the fact that he amassed 102 centuries in his career, unlike his brother he never obtained a regular place in the England side. On his one Australian tour, 1928–29, he was chosen only for one Test, and in international matches his best results were against South Africa.

Ernest lacked the sharp edge of J.T.'s batsmanship and never dominated the bowling in quite the same way, but he had a very powerful hook shot. He flourished more against the slower bowlers, the fast men always seeming to have a chance against him, especially early in an innings.

His record of 34,222 runs for Lancashire remains a record aggregate and in all first-class matches he exceeded 1,000 runs in a season 18 times. He usually batted at number three and in 1928 helped F.B. Watson in a stand of 371 for the second wicket.

He served on the Lancashire committee after retiring, but his eyesight became very poor in later years.

G.E. Tyldesley (NCCC)

was a ruthless slayer of bowlers, never happy until he had mastered the bowling, Ernest had more patience, generally waiting for the runs to come.

The County Club was financially healthy, with 117,745 people paying admission to matches during 1909, receipts amounting to £4,897. Of the loan of £20,000 for the purchase of the ground, £7,000 had been repaid. Not all counties were so flourishing and C.E. de Trafford presided at an extraordinary meeting of the Leicestershire club called to consider the worsening financial situation of the club.

In the winter of 1909–10 various counties put forward suggestions to improve the method of deciding the Championship title. The one which won the approval of the MCC Committee was proposed by Lancashire: 'that draws and losses be ignored and only matches won count in the percentage of matches played'. This Lancashire system was adopted for 1910. After the traumas of the 1909 Ashes failure, 1910 was a season when the Championship came back into its own.

Kent took an early lead in the season's title race and by the halfway stage were comfortably ahead of their rivals with ten wins from 13 matches; Middlesex were second with six wins out of ten and Lancashire bracketed third with Sussex.

Undefeated until mid-June, the County then suffered two two-day defeats, the first at the Oval, where Surrey won by seven wickets and the second at Trent Bridge, where Notts gained victory by an innings. Lancashire were weakened by an injury to Brearley, which together with his other commitments meant that he played in only three Championship games all summer. Defeats of course under the new system were not so serious as in the past, but Lancashire also suffered most with drawn matches through rain. The last four games of the season were all home fixtures more or less washed out – three of which were against the weaker counties and if won would have placed Lancashire second to Kent in the table, rather than in the fourth position they eventually occupied.

The most satisfactory match of the damp summer was the August Bank Holiday game at Old Trafford. Brearley reappeared after an absence of ten weeks and took nine wickets. Spooner, another irregular, took the opportunity to hit an unbeaten 200, Hornby declaring the innings closed at 395 for five, when Spooner reached exactly that landmark. Lancashire went on to win by an innings. The match was awarded to Sharp for his benefit and 33,874 spectators passed through the turnstiles.

Lancashire's outstanding bowler was Dean. His 133 Championship wickets at 15.21 was the best of his career to date and he topped Lancashire's bowling table. He bowled both fast-medium left-arm and in the slower style of Hirst. His most effective partner was Huddleston,

LANCASHIRE *v.* YORKSHIRE

Played on the Old Trafford Ground, Manchester, on 1, 2 and 3 August 1910

LANCASHIRE WON BY AN INNINGS AND 111 RUNS

YORKSHIRE	FIRST INNINGS		SECOND INNINGS	
W. Rhodes	b Brearley	4	c Tyldesley b Heap	34
B.B. Wilson	c Worsley b Dean	1	c Tyldesley b Brearley	31
W.E. Bates	b Brearley	5	c Hornby b Brearley	0
M.W. Booth	b Dean	0	c Spooner b Cook	24
G.H. Hirst	b Heap	46	b Dean	11
H. Myers	run out	0	c Tyldesley b Brearley	33
E. Oldroyd	c Worsley b Brearley	4	c Worsley b Dean	1
A. Drake	b Brearley	1	b Dean	4
S. Haigh	b Dean	15	c Makepeace b Brearley	27
*Mr E.J. Radcliffe	not out	13	b Dean	2
†A Dolphin	c Worsley b Brearley	0	not out	1
Extras	b 5, lb 9	14	b 9, lb 1, nb 3	13
Total		103		181

Fall: 1st inns: 1-5 2-7 3-7 4-27 5-34 6-38 7-40 8-63 9-94
  2nd inns: 1-69 2-69 3-71 4-95 5-119 6-128 7-147 8-151 9-158

BOWLING	O	M	R	W	O	M	R	W
Brearley	13.1	2	50	5	28.2	10	80	4
Dean	18	10	25	3	25	11	46	4
Cook	6	1	14	0	10	1	23	1
Heap	1	1	0	1	7	3	12	1
Makepeace					4	1	7	0

LANCASHIRE	FIRST INNINGS	
Mr R.H. Spooner	not out	200
Mr A. Hartley	b Booth	0
J.T. Tyldesley	b Drake	32
J. Sharp	c Rhodes b Booth	51
J.W.H. Makepeace	c Dolphin b Hirst	27
J.S. Heap	b Rhodes	10
*Mr A.H. Hornby	not out	60
Mr W. Brearley		
H. Dean		
L.W. Cook		
†W. Worsley		
Extras	b 2, lb 11, nb 2	15
Total	(5 wkts dec)	395

Fall: 1-13 2-75 3-174 4-237 5-272

BOWLING	O	M	R	W
Hirst	36	6	98	1
Booth	28	4	81	2
Myers	19	4	68	0
Drake	11	2	26	1
Haigh	18	5	43	0
Rhodes	24	5	56	1
Oldroyd	2	1	5	0
Radcliffe	1	0	3	0

Umpires: W. Flowers and J. Blake

*Captain; †Wicket-keeper

R.H. Spooner became the first Lancastrian to score a double century in a Roses match.

but Heap and L. Cook also took more than 50 wickets each. Whitehead played in about half the matches and, having recovered from his initial no-balls picked up 44 wickets at 22 runs apiece.

J.T. Tyldesley stood out from the rest of the batsmen, having an excellent season and exceeding 2,000 runs in all first-class matches. Spooner nominally came second in the averages, but owed everything to his double hundred. Third in the list was Alfred Hartley, whose aggregate included 234 against Somerset. He won a place in the Gentlemen's side at Lord's and in a low scoring game scored more runs than anyone else. Sharp's record was similar to Hartley's, and he also played in the premier match at Lord's. MacLaren had ten Championship innings, totalling 305 runs, of which 227 came in two innings, at the expense of the weak attacks of Warwickshire and Worcestershire.

Yet another Tyldesley made his debut in 1910. James Tyldesley, brother of William, who had begun in 1908, was a useful all-rounder, who gained a regular place in the side in 1912. They were not related to J.T. or Ernest.

R.V. Bardsley, the Shrewsbury schoolboy, who played in the Oxford freshmen's match of 1910, taking five for 37, turned out once for Lancashire, but he was not to spend much time in county cricket, though obtaining his blue in 1911, 1912 and 1913.

The weather had an adverse effect on Lancashire's accounts, and they also had the additional expense of a new wall along the Warwick Road. There was an appeal for an additional 1,000 members – such an increase would make the club independent of gate receipts.

First of the 1911 fixtures at Old Trafford was the match against Warwickshire. In view of the course which the remainder of the season took for the midland county it is interesting to note the following comment made directly after the match: 'Many will say that Lancashire didn't try to win against the Midlanders last weekend or else they took matters too easily.' Warwickshire won by the margin of 137 runs, the Lancashire bowling in the second innings, Dean apart, being thoroughly mastered.

Two more defeats came in May, the first at the hands of Derbyshire by two runs (the Peak county had not beaten Lancashire since 1895), the second, much more decisive, by an innings against Middlesex at Lord's. It was unfortunate for Lancashire that J.T. Tyldesley injured his shoulder and was unable to play, but H.G. Garnett, who had been absent in the Argentine for six years, made a welcome re-entry into county cricket and scored 77 against Derbyshire.

By some odd twist of fate, J.T. Tyldesley, whilst still off injured, was asked by a reporter how he managed to keep so fit. He ascribed his general fitness to the dance floor: 'Well, I think that social life is developing. There are far more whist drives and dances than there used

The Lancashire team which played Sussex at Hove in 1911. Standing: L.W. Cook, W.J. Tyldesley, R. Whitehead, H. Dean, J.W.H. Makepeace, J.T. Tyldesley. Seated: A. Hartley, K.G. McLeod, A.H. Hornby, H.G. Garnett, R.H. Spooner. On ground: J. Sharp, J.S. Heap (Lancashire CCC)

to be years ago – even ten years ago. I have done my share of whirling buxom Lancashire lasses round a room ... Dancing has helped to keep me fit and it is much more fascinating than using skipping ropes.'

Lancashire were still without J.T. Tyldesley when the Whitsun match was played at the end of the first week in June. They also lacked their captain, who had had the misfortune to knock himself out whilst tripping over a net in the previous match. When Yorkshire batted first however, Brearley took seven wickets and with Makepeace playing a steady role, Lancashire gained a first innings lead. A brilliant innings by Hirst – 156 in 225 minutes – put Yorkshire back in the game and Alonzo Drake finished off Lancashire to provide the Tykes with victory by 159 runs. There followed immediately a second home defeat – Kent, set 222 in 180 minutes, winning with two minutes to spare by three wickets.

On 20 June, Lancashire had won five games and lost five and were standing eleventh in the Championship table, probably the lowest position they had ever occupied at this stage of the season.

Three successive innings victories at the expense of Worcestershire, Hampshire and Derbyshire moved Lancashire back into the top half of the Championship. The most remarkable of these wins was against Hampshire. Spooner, Sharp and MacLeod all made hundreds and J.T. Tyldesley 98, in a total of 676 for seven declared. Dean then took ten wickets and Cook six, as poor Hampshire lost by an innings and 455 runs. It was the largest victory ever obtained by Lancashire. In the Derbyshire match, the Tyldesleys, J.T. and William, scored 152 and 125, adding 252 for the second wicket.

Despite the poor results overall, Lancashire did have some say in the destination of the title, for they defeated the leaders, Kent, on 12 August by nine wickets Brearley removing 12 Kent batsmen, and when the final table for the year appeared, Kent finished second to Warwickshire – one more victory for the hop county would have given them the Championship.

Interest in the last few weeks of the season was also taken up by the selection of players to tour Australia in 1911–12. S.F. Barnes was among the first to be picked and Spooner one of the first to decline. Spooner was the first batsman in England to reach 2,000 first-class runs, getting to the target on 11 August, ten days before Tom Hayward.

Apart from Spooner, who was for once available all season, the outstanding Lancashire batsman of the year was Makepeace, whose 1,623 Championship runs were gained at an average of 38 per innings. William Tyldesley also had a good year with the bat, but was left out of the side on occasion due to his poor fielding. On that subject the wicket-keeping was not much improved. Garnett took over generally from Worsley, mainly one suspects because the former was a better batsman.

Dean was again the outstanding bowler when Brearley was absent. Cook was the only other bowler who troubled the best batsmen, though Fairclough, a slow left-arm bowler from Bickershaw, promised much on the few occasions when he played.

Season 1912 saw the experimental Triangular Tournament, when both Australia and South Africa sent teams to England and a three-way Test series was arranged. Lancashire, like other counties, cut down their Championship programme and inserted two matches against each of the touring teams, both teams playing at Liverpool and Old Trafford. The first snag which hit the Triangular scheme was the quarrel between the Australian board and many of the principal Australian players. The result meant that Australia sailed to England with a second-rate team.

Ernest Tyldesley greeted the new season with a maiden hundred in the opening game; a hundred as well from Sharp and nine wickets by Dean enabled Lancashire to start the summer with a two-day innings victory over Sussex. The County then travelled to Lord's and inflicted an innings defeat on Middlesex. Another splendid innings from Ernest Tyldesley, helped by Spooner, produced a total of 389, which was much too good for the Metropolitans.

In the Sussex game, F.R.R. Brooke made his Championship debut at the age of 27. Brooke, from Bowdon in Cheshire, was introduced into the side as a wicket-keeper, in the hope that the County might improve in this department, neither of their professionals, Worsley and Blomley, really being of first-class standard, and the amateur Garnett having returned to the Argentine. Unfortunately for Lancashire Brooke was a regular army officer. He had already made his first-class debut in India for the Europeans and whilst he was currently stationed in Aldershot there seemed little likelihood of his being available on more than a stop-gap basis. He celebrated his Lancashire debut with an innings of 61.

The Lancashire committee had had yet another disagreement with Walter Brearley. This time the truculent amateur went so far as to agree to play for Cheshire, thus making himself unavailable for Lancashire even if a change of heart occurred. His move resulted in the curious record that England in 1912 had two minor counties cricketers in their ranks, Brearley and Barnes, both ex-Lancashire bowlers.

Another Lancastrian not seen in the County's team in 1913 was Archie MacLaren. He had been a member of the MCC side to South America in 1911-12 and then on returning taken a job as private secretary to Lionel Robinson at Old Buckenham Hall in East Anglia. Mr Robinson had a private cricket ground at his residence and the first of several first-class matches was staged there in 1912, when the South Africans were the visitors.

The Whitsun game took place at Bradford and was all over in two days. Lancashire could manage only 76 in reply to Yorkshire's 226 and though the County Palatine improved slightly when the follow-on was enforced, Yorkshire won by ten wickets. Whilst the game was being enacted, over at Old Trafford the first Test of the summer was also finished in two days. The weak Australian side slaughtered South Africa, with the Australian leg-break bowler Matthews managing a hat-trick in each innings. His feats however did not win universal approval and of this event unique in the history of Old Trafford Tests, Hamish Stuart commented:

> It was in fact fine fluke. There is also an element of luck in any hat trick, but this double hat trick seemed thrown straight off the wheel of fortune. The last 'c and b' in the second hat-trick was a fine one and that constituted nearly the sole merit in the performance. One might wax very philosophical over the matter, but in the end the only truth reached would be the old truth that the possible is the probable in cricket.

Three weeks later Matthews returned to Old Trafford to bowl against Lancashire and took five for 48 as the County were dismissed for 146, so perhaps his hat-tricks were not quite so much of a fluke. The Australian batting, however, was not up to much and Lancashire recorded their first win over the tourists since 1888, the victory being by 24 runs. Not many spectators turned out to view the success, for the authorities increased the admission price to one shilling and the Mancunians boycotted the game, only 300 coming on the last day.

With the Championship half-way through, Lancashire shared fourth place with Notts, but very little separated the leading sides, Yorkshire, Middlesex and Northants (the Cinderella county) being first, second and third. Dean became the first Englishman to complete 100 wickets for the year, on 12 July, and had displaced Brearley in the England side for the second Test.

Rain ruined the whole of August – on no fewer than 56 occasions during the month a complete day's play was lost in one first-class match or another. The second Test of the year at Old Trafford took place during the last three days of July, but did not escape, just over one innings being completed.

Lancashire were undefeated in their last nine matches of the year, but six of these were drawn and the match against Warwickshire completely washed away. So the positions in the Championship hardly altered and Lancashire had to be content with fourth place.

Seven Lancashire batsmen had Championship averages about 30. Spooner headed the list, though having only 14 innings. The rain meant that Sharp and J.T. Tyldesley alone topped 1,000 Championship runs. Dean was the best bowler, with Huddleston his most useful assistant. Whitehead and Fairclough were the other bowlers to have good seasons.

The financial affairs of the County Club, which had been so buoyant in the 1890s and the early years of the present century, had been apparently growing worse with each passing season. In the four years 1910 to 1913 over £4,500 was lost in total and in the middle of 1913 the committee appeared to believe that the only way out of the downward spiral was to reduce the number of matches. A.H. Hornby, the captain, disagreed, but instead of arguing his point with the committee, he chose to splash his views and criticisms of the committee over the pages of the *Manchester Guardian*.

On the field of play, 1913 was a quite dreadful season for Lancashire cricket, the team finishing eighth with seven wins and eleven losses from 26 games. *Wisden's Almanack* ended its brief survey of the Championship season with: 'Among the great counties, Lancashire were the worst. Not for a long time have they had such a poor season.'

When A.H. Hornby launched his attack, therefore, the public were ready for some fireworks and Lancashire's supporters were keen to discover why the Club was failing both on and off the field. A commission of inquiry was set up to look into the Club's affairs and its findings were the subject of a leading article in the *Manchester Guardian*:

The commission of inquiry into Lancashire county cricket has produced a careful and sane review of the situation. The difficulties, as a result of friendly investigation, already begin to look less serious, and the better understanding between all parties of which there are welcome signs should bring an accession of active interest and co-operative effort into the business of the County Club.

Already a number of minor practical reforms are promised. The entrance fee is to be suspended, season tickets for the ground side are to be issued, second eleven and colts matches are to be more seriously treated as means of recruiting the county team, a more intimate relation is likely to be cultivated with the cricket leagues of Lancashire, the curtailment of the programme of county matches has been arrested, and members are to be allowed occasionally to introduce a friend to the pavilion – under a recognised rule instead of as a capricious favour. The Special Committee are not quite satisfied with the County Committee's reply on three points, the most controversial of which is the rule affecting the election of the President. At present members elect the President annually; they possess an unlimited option to change the President as often as they like, or to re-elect him for as long as they like. The Special Committee wish this option to be restricted by a rule providing for compulsory periodical changes in the Presidency (A.N. Hornby, father of the captain, had been President since 1894). When the point was last raised at a general meeting the feeling was found to be in favour of the continuance of the present unfettered option, under which the members may do exactly what seems best to them at the moment. The Special Committee disapprove, in certain details, of the action both of the Committee and of Mr A.H. Hornby, but they do so with commendable delicacy. The Committee, they think, have made some mistakes, but they recognise, as everyone does, their loyal services to the Club and the difficulties arising from the financial position. As to Mr Hornby, they do not endorse the method he adopted but here again, they admit that the result of his action has been beneficial. So the net result of the statement which Mr Hornby communicated to the *Manchester Guardian* of August 23rd is that Lancashire cricket has benefited. The captain's central object, apart from any minor question of procedure, has thus been served. The committee, the players and the members have got to understand one another better and the fruit of this will be seen, it is hoped in a revival of prosperity next season.

The loss for 1913 was announced at the AGM as £994 10s. Immediately several supporters came forward with financial aid. Lord Derby gave £200 plus a promise of £100 for each of the next three years, Sir William Nelson gave £100 and £50 for the next three years, Sir F.F. Adams £50 for each of three years and Mr Topham £25 for three years.

Turning back to the playing results of 1913, R.H. Spooner, owing to a riding accident, was unable to play all summer, and the batting was thus considerably weakened. J.T. and Ernest Tyldesley, Makepeace and A.H. Hornby all topped 1,000 runs in Championship matches; Sharp however fell right away, his average dropping from 48 to 23.

Brearley was missed in the bowling department, though Heap, Huddleston, Dean and Whitehead all had days of success. MacLeod reappeared in 16 matches, but his merit remained largely in his fielding. With Brooke's matches restricted due to his military duties, the committee brought in R.A. Boddington, who had been in the Rugby school side, but was unable to gain a place in the Oxford eleven. He did however keep wicket quite effectively for Lancashire.

A.H. Hornby, apart from his major outburst, caused a minor storm when he allowed a substitute to bat in the match against Middlesex at Liverpool. P.F. Warner the Middlesex captain was taken ill whilst fielding on the first day and his place was taken by Lee.

A.E. Lawton, the former Derbyshire captain but native of Cheshire, played in four Championship matches, having appeared in two the previous year, but his only day of success was at Trent Bridge when he hit 52 against Notts. The Northants match at Old Trafford was awarded to A.G. Paul, who had acted as coach to the County since retiring as an active cricketer, and had thus been at Manchester for 24 years.

The major news in the spring of 1914 was the announcement that A.C. MacLaren would probably play for the County during July and August. He had founded the magazine *The World of Cricket* in January and in the second issue came the following note from the Editor:

> In reply to numerous enquiries concerning my playing for Lancashire this coming season, I may say that I mean to turn out. Friends who saw my play last year for Mr Lionel Robinson's Elevens at Old Buckenham – where his country-house cricket is certainly of a very high class – suggested that I ought to have been making runs for my county; and after I had met some of my old Lancashire comrades again, I was induced to offer my services for the coming season.

The County made a depressing start to the season. Leicester beat them at Aylestone Road in a low scoring game, which began with the laws being stretched when Heap was taken ill in the field on the first morning and William Tyldesley came on as substitute and was allowed to bat. William Tyldesley actually made the highest Lancashire score in the second innings. Victory was obtained at the expense of Derbyshire, but this was quickly followed by two further defeats at the hands of Northants and Essex. The batting was the weak point – not one of the first eight Lancashire totals realised 250 runs. It is surprising the batting was to blame, since the bowling lacked, for the Essex defeat, Dean,

Heap and Huddleston all injured. Earnest Bowden, the Littleborough amateur came in for Dean and took six for 78, but as stated the batting failed.

So Lancashire came to the Whitsun fixture at Bramall Lane. Some 12,000 spectators watched Yorkshire hit 381. On the Tuesday 10,000 saw Lancashire's batting at last come off. A.H. Hornby and Makepeace put on 130 for the first wicket, and then, when the middle failed, James Tyldesley and Huddleston added 141 in 85 minutes for the ninth wicket. The game meandered to a draw on the third day when Yorkshire declared setting a target of 311 in 190 minutes.

The County brought in J.C.H. Hollins, the Eton and Oxford cricketer, to strengthen the batting against Notts. He made 46, which included a six and five fours, but his lively tactics did not come off again and he disappeared from the side after five matches. The game was a high scoring draw.

In efforts to improve the side a total of eight new players in all were tried, more than in any of the last ten or so years. One only had an immediate effect on the side, but his League engagement meant that he was unable to appear in matches involving Saturday play. *The World of Cricket* contained the following piece of Gossip on July 18:

Parkin, who did such fine work for Lancashire v Leicestershire, though new to the Red Rose ranks, is not a newcomer in county cricket. He played for Yorkshire v Gloucestershire at Leeds in 1906, scoring 0 and taking two for 25. Then the discovery was made that he was born on the wrong side of the Tees. The wrong side, that is, from a Yorkshire point of view: far be it from us to propound the inferiority of Durham even to the biggest county of them all! In consequence of this discovery he was not asked to play again. From 1907 to 1913 he played in a few matches for Durham and generally bowled with success taking in all 56 wickets at a trifle over 13 each.

Parkin, who was the pro at Church CC, took 14 for 99 in this first game for Lancashire, enabling his adopted shire to win by eight wickets. Parkin's feat on debut was a record for the County. He ended the season at the top of the bowling averages. After the First World War he was to win Test recognition with his slow bowling, with 1923 as his best summer in first-class cricket. Known as 'Cricket's Comedian', he was another to win the heart of Neville Cardus, who wrote:

Parkin's cricket was full of the spirit of the age – which of course is an age of jazz. In the artist's sense of the word, he was a grotesque; energy in his work broke the bounds of conventional forms. His slow ball, in the days when he bowled it well, could be called a very gargoyle of a ball, a twisting grin of a ball. An unintelligent criticism of Parkin is that he 'played to the gallery', the implication being that he was not sincere in all his antic humours. But Parkin – and anybody who had studied the man will readily agree with this – was incapable of assuming a pose not genuinely his own; he was, indeed, too much of the egoist to simulate any trait in nature that he did not feel born of his blood. It was his very frankness, his unwavering faith in Parkin, in season and out of season, that occasionally sent him running headlong into the properties.

Parkin was not the only man to make his debut in the Leicester game. F.W. Musson, who earlier in the season had played in the Cambridge freshmen's match, was a second debutant. He was one of three brothers who were notable amateur batsmen, all educated at Tonbridge. A.H. Musson joined the regular army and rose to the rank of Major General, R.G. Musson joined the RAF and died whilst serving with Coastal Command in the Second World War, after having been associated with several record flights. The brothers came from Clitheroe, but only F.W. appeared for their native county.

Cecil Parkin with R. Tyldesley and E.A. McDonald

Yet another of the Tyldesley tribe made his County debut – Harry Tyldesley, brother of James and William; a slow right-arm bowler he made just four appearances for Lancashire between 1914 and 1922.

The match which followed Parkin's debut showed how much Lancashire needed a bowler of his calibre, for Derbyshire hit 524 whilst Parkin was playing in the Leagues. This Derbyshire game ended in farce with the Derby opening bowler, Forester, sending down an over of grubs as Lancashire batted out time.

Cricket in August was overshadowed by the outbreak of the First World War. Spooner, who had intended to play for Lancashire throughout the month was commissioned in the Lincolnshire Regiment and A.H. Hornby left to assist with the job of collecting horses for the cavalry. Of the final five matches of the season, three were drawn and two lost. Lancashire sank to 11th place in the table, having six wins and nine losses.

J.T. Tyldesley topped the batting averages and with Ernest Tyldesley, Sharp and Makepeace formed the backbone of the batting. No one else averaged over 25 or completed 1,000 Championship runs. The bowling averages told a sad tale. Aside from Parkin, Dean had the best record with 59 wickets, 20.49 average. Whitehead took most wickets, but they cost 28 runs each.

During the war the pavilion at Old Trafford was turned into a hospital. County cricket was suspended, though League cricket continued. T.J. Matthews remained in the office in Manchester as Secretary and many members continued their subscriptions. The main changes during the war were first the retirement as President of A.N. Hornby, who had held the post since 1894, and then the resignation of Mr Talbot Fair as honorary treasurer. He died a month after leaving. Apart from being a cricket administrator, he was also keen on golf and did much to promote various tournaments.

THE CHAMPIONSHIP YEARS

LANCASHIRE PROPOSED THAT COUNTY CHAMPIONSHIP matches should be restricted to two days each when the competition was resumed in 1919. According to the reports the County managed to bamboozle the majority of the others into agreeing. The Editor of *Wisden* claimed that Middlesex voted for the plan not realising what it entailed; Lord Harris, on behalf of Kent, decided to let it through purely with the idea that it would prove unworkable and that, in 1920, three-day matches would resume. So the advisory committee sanctioned the scheme by eleven votes to five.

Lancashire began their 1919 Championship season at Old Trafford on 19 May against neighbouring Derbyshire. The team, which won by ten wickets, read: Makepeace, J.C.H. Hollins, J.T. Tyldesley, J. Sharp, V. Norbury, G.S. Rawstorne, M.N. Kenyon (captain), R.A. Boddington (wicket-keeper), H. Dean, Parkin, Bullough. The major changes were the replacement of A.H. Hornby as captain by M.N. Kenyon, the disappearance of Huddleston and Whitehead and that Norbury had been weaned away from Hampshire.

Kenyon, the new leader, was aged 32. He had been educated at Eton, though did not obtain a place in the eleven, but before the war had played for Lancashire Seconds. Like Kenyon, Rawstorne had been at Eton. He captained the 1914 college team, having played for the eleven in the two previous years. His first appearance, however, proved to be also his final one, for he went out to India. Norbury, the Hampshire slow bowler, was engaged by East Lancashire where in 1919 he had an outstanding summer, topping the batting averages for the Lancashire League as well as taking 98 wickets at 10 runs each. He was not therefore available for all County matches. The same was true of Parkin, who was irresistible for Rochdale, taking 115 wickets at 7 runs each, but could play in only a handful of County games. The absence of these two professionals was critical to the success of Lancashire and the fact that L. Cook was not demobilised until the season was well under way caused a further weakening of the attack.

For the second match of the year, Lancashire brought in C.S. Marriott, a leg-break and googly bowler, and he took five for 52 in the first innings in which he bowled. Born at Heaton Moor, he had learnt his cricket at St Columba's in Ireland. He was to obtain his blue at Cambridge in 1920, and after leaving University went to Dulwich College, as master-in-charge of cricket. He qualified by residence for Kent and had a most successful career with that county, gaining a Test cap in 1933.

Another amateur who came into the team was J.R. Barnes, who headed the Ormskirk batting averages in 1919, he being a native of that town. He was to appear for Lancashire on and off until 1930, but as a Liverpool cotton merchant he was yet another player whose opportunities in county cricket were limited. G.O. Shelmerdine, the former Cheltenham schoolboy, who was now at Cambridge, was tried in July. A useful all-rounder, he later joined the Lancashire committee, was chairman of the Forty Club and at the time of his death President of Lancashire.

Yet another of the Tyldesleys made his bow in county cricket – Richard Tyldesley, a right-arm slow bowler and brother of Harry, James and William, was to prove the most important 'discovery' of 1919 and took 33 wickets at an average of 21.

Lancashire finished the season fifth equal with Somerset, having won eight matches and lost four. As instigators of the two-day scheme it was perhaps appropriate that they drew twelve matches – no county drew more.

Ernest Tyldesley took over from his brother, J.T., as the leader of the batting table, but there was little to choose between them with regard to average, even though they were separated by Makepeace. Sharp, now playing as an amateur, came fourth, but made infrequent appearances. Charlie Hallows, a nephew of the former all-rounder, reached 1,000 runs for the first time. An opening left-hand bat from Little Lever, he was to make such rapid progress that in 1921 he was capped by England.

Of the bowlers, Dean played regularly but was much more expensive than before the war; Heap however made the most of any sticky wicket and claimed 62 victims at 16 runs each.

Charles Plairre commented at the end of the year in *Ayres' Cricket Companion*:

> Unwept, unhonoured and unsung, the two-day limitation for county matches – that ill-starred experiment in New World building – passed into its appropriate limbo. It was not so much that it involved an excessive proportion of drawn games – there were drawn games before the war – as that the lengthened day imposed great strain on the players, of whom many came back to the peaceful field of cricket with their physique weakened by wounds and privations. It was not always convenient for spectators, either, to stay till the last ball of the day was bowled. Everyone will welcome the return to three-day matches in 1920.

During the luncheon interval on the first day of the match with Kent at Old Trafford, Archdeacon Aspinall unveiled in the pavilion a tablet erected in memory of Major Garnett, Lieutenant Hartley, Private

Nelson, Lieutenant W. Tyldesley, and Captain E.L. Wright, Lancashire cricketers who gave their lives during the war.

Considering the rather muddled circumstances of the 1919 season and the assortment of players used by Lancashire, as well as the knowledge that no new players of any proven ability were scheduled to join the County in 1920, the results achieved in the second season after the war were quite remarkable.

The County began with three wins, two by an innings. Tantalisingly, Parkin took 13 wickets in the opening game, then went off to his League engagement; Cook and Dean proved they could win matches without Cricket's Comedian at both Northampton and Chesterfield.

The first real test of the side came in the fourth game at Park Avenue, Bradford. Lancashire, having been behind on first innings, came back into the game when Dean took seven for 51 and at the start of the third day, the visitors needed 144 with all second innings wickets intact. Instead of playing their normal game however, he Lancashire batsmen decided to get the runs 'in singles' and Emmott Robinson gained complete domination over them. He returned a career best nine for 36, as Lancashire lost by 22 runs. A drawn game with Middlesex at Old Trafford was followed by six successive victories. This sequence was broken with the return against Middlesex, the Lancashire batting and bowling both failing and Middlesex gaining an innings victory, which was to prove vital to the final destination of the Championship.

The most remarkable game of the year was staged on the Aigburth ground against Hampshire. On the first day, when rain prevented play until 2 o'clock, there was considerable trouble from a crowd of 7,000 and the pavilion was invaded, with a certain amount of damage caused. The two sides were even on first innings, then Lancashire collapsed in their second, being all out for 57, leaving Hampshire wanting only 66. They reached 54 for five, before an inspired spell from Cook and Dean removed the rest of the batsmen for ten runs, producing victory by one run. In the next game, Parkin made one of his appearances and Dean was hardly wanted as Kent were beaten by an innings, Parkin picking up eight for 85.

By the beginning of August, the early runners in the Championship fight – Yorkshire, Surrey and Kent – were beginning to look weary and Lancashire seemed as if they would take the title. The reason why, in the end, they had to settle for second place behind Middlesex, was not so much Lancashire's failure in the closing stages, but the brilliance of Middlesex, who won every one of their last nine matches. Even when it came to the last round of matches, Middlesex were opposed to Surrey, who were to finish third, whereas Lancashire played lowly Worcestershire. It was the most exciting climax to the Championship for years. Lancashire won early on the third morning and a large crowd came in front of the pavilion to congratulate the side on the title, it being assumed that the Middlesex against Surrey game would end in a draw, Middlesex having only just begun the third innings on the second evening. Pelham Warner hit a hundred and he declared the Middlesex innings closed, setting Surrey 244 in about three hours. Surrey had 100 up in 75 minutes for the loss of two wickets. Some good bowling and brilliant fielding took Middlesex to an unexpected victory and robbed Lancashire of the Championship.

The records of the two counties read:

	M	W	L	Won on 1st inns	Lost on	Poss Pts	Pts	NR	%
MX	20	15	2	1	2	100	77	0	77.00
LA	28	19	5	1	1	130	97	2	74.61

Cook was the star of Lancashire. He had developed great accuracy of length combined with some subtle movement off the pitch and these attributes placed him as third best bowler in England, with 156 wickets at an average of 14.88. Dean also took 100 wickets. The third of the regular bowlers was James Tyldesley, who early in the year was looked upon as a possible fast bowler for England. Richard Tyldesley also did his stint.

Good bowling figures are often allied to astute captaincy and a mutual understanding with the wicket-keeper. Lancashire had three wicket-keepers, Musson, Boddington and Blomley and two captains. Kenyon missed over half the season through a variety of indispositions and Sharp acted in his stead. So the bowlers did, in the circumstances, better than anticipated.

With J.T. Tyldesley no longer playing, the batting was not so strong. Makepeace was a marvel of consistency and won a place in the MCC side to Australia; Ernest Tyldesley owed his second place in the averages to a double hundred off Warwickshire and good batting in August. Hallows was reliable, completing 1,000 runs without a century to his name. Spooner played enough to show himself in form and was asked to lead the MCC team in the winter, but business then forced him to stand down.

The finances of the Club were buoyant, and the August Bank Holiday game produced record crowds, with about 68,000 attending over the three days and receipts amounting to £3,321 15s 3d (after deducting tax).

After four seasons without a major Australian tour – 1913, 1914, 1919 and 1920 – the Championship in 1921 had to take second place to Armstrong's all-conquering side. All-conquering save for the famous match engineered by the effervescent MacLaren. The match and the circumstances are described in detail in Michael Down's biography of

MacLaren. England having failed to beat Australia, the visitors were faced with a team gathered by MacLaren at Eastbourne; MacLaren's England XI won an exciting game by 28 runs, due to the batting of the South African Faulkner and the bowling of Faulkner, Falcon and Gibson. Walter Brearley played, but went in at number eleven and was not required to bowl.

The victory contrasted with a win by Australia in two days over Lancashire at Old Trafford, though the country had both Makepeace and Ernest Tyldesley away injured. A fortnight later the Australians were again at Old Trafford for the fourth Test. Continuous drizzle prevented any play on the first day. The game ended in a draw, notable for two breaches of the Laws. First Tennyson, the England captain, illegally declared the innings closed. After the players left the field, the mistake was pointed out and England resumed batting, but in the confusion Armstrong went on to bowl two overs in succession!

Rain marred the Australians' third visit to Lancashire, when they opposed the county at Liverpool. When the third day was washed out, the tourists were heading for a second innings victory, even though Makepeace and Ernest Tyldesley had resumed their places in the home side.

In what was a depressing Test series for England one of the few bright spots was the bowling of Cecil Parkin, who headed the England averages with 16 wickets at 26 runs each. Ernest Tyldesley and Charlie Hallows also represented England.

Middlesex were not beaten in the Championship until mid-July and looked to be comfortable winners until late on when Surrey nearly pipped them. Lancashire began well and towards the end of June were third in the table, but later dropped to fifth, having 15 wins against four losses.

The batting of Ernest Tyldesley and Hallows stood well above the rest. Hallows hit 227 off the Warwickshire attack at Old Trafford, the highest score of his career to date, and with 1,736 runs had the highest Championship aggregate; Ernest Tyldesley had a better average. No one else topped 1,000 in inter-county games, but both Sharp and Makepeace did in all first-class cricket.

The young amateurs, J.R. Barnes and Shelmerdine, both hit Championship hundreds. Shelmerdine, who just missed his blue, hit brilliantly against Kent at Maidstone, his 105 including five sixes and ten fours. Barnes, who often opened the batting in the absence of Makepeace or Hallows, hit a hundred against the rather weak Worcestershire attack; a better innings was his 98 against Surrey.

Two young professionals also forced their way into the team as batsmen. Walker Ellis, from Summerseat, son of Jerry Ellis, the former Lancashire bowler, looked a very useful prospect and scored freely all round the wicket. He scored a hundred in the same match as Shelmerdine. Ellis' career in county cricket was to be a short one, but his colleague in vying for a batting place, Frank Watson, was to become a mainstay of the side. He had played once or twice in 1920, but in 1921 had 22 Championship innings and without any high scores averaged 24.

Cook remained the leading wicket-taker, the only bowler to obtain 100 wickets. His main support came from Richard and James Tyldesley. Parkin was still available only for mid-week matches and Dean sent down less than half his 1920 ration of overs. Blomley and Boddington shared the wicket-keeping duties, but there was a lack of good slip fielders.

Financially the Club was in a good position. Membership reached 4,661 and there was a profit of £2,981 on the year with 251,851 spectators paying through the turnstiles. Ill-health caused the secretary, T.J. Matthews to resign, and he was awarded a Testimonial. His successor was Harry Rylance. Rylance had been on the Old Trafford staff as an all-rounder in 1905, but never played in first-class matches. He was also a useful goalkeeper and then graduated to become a soccer referee, officiating in Football League and FA Cup matches, including the semi-final of 1920. He had also acted as scorer of Lancashire and as assistant secretary to Matthews.

Another appointment at the end of 1921 was that of MacLaren as coach. He was also to captain the Second Eleven.

Parkin was persuaded at last to forsake Rochdale and play a full season with Lancashire in 1922. He easily headed the Lancashire averages and was second to Wilfred Rhodes in all first-class cricket: Parkin proved that he could stand up to a full programme of first-class matches, though towards the end of the season he bowled more loose deliveries. He was unfortunately let down by the wicket-keeper on a number of occasions. R.A. Boddington was rarely available. Parkinson from Barrow was tried in place of Blomley in about half the matches, but did not really come up to county standard. Whewell (pronounced as though the first w is silent) had had the odd game for Lancashire in 1921, and was given a further brief trial behind the stumps in 1922, but he seemed unable to keep still for long and had the habit of taking the ball balanced on one leg. The fielding in general was not as crisp as it might have been.

To support Parkin, Richard Tyldesley and Cook bowled their spinners with intelligence and in all first-class matches both reached a hundred wickets. James Tyldesley was nothing like as effective with his fast bowling as in some previous years and his 31 wickets cost over 30 runs each.

Ernest Tyldesley, Hallows and Makepeace all had excellent batting records, each compiling four Championship hundreds. J.R. Barnes, the

Liverpool amateur, hit 123 not out off the Middlesex attack at Lord's and his style was reminiscent of William Gunn; unfortunately business prevented him playing more often. M.N. Kenyon, the captain, rarely struck form and at the end of the year bowed out of county cricket.

Yorkshire were the outstanding side of the year. They overtook Surrey at the top on 25 July and though Notts and Lancashire competed with Surrey for second place, the Tykes were never really challenged in the closing stages of the campaign, except that due to a quirk in the points system, Notts with the assistance of rain might have robbed them of the title.

The Whitsuntide match took place at Bramall Lane. Ernest Tyldesley made 178 out of Lancashire's first innings total of 307; Yorkshire in reply scored 306. Lancashire then seemed to decide to bat out for a draw, but collapsed – all out 144 – and Sutcliffe hit an unbeaten 73 as Yorkshire won by six wickets. As usual the attendance was very large, but the crowds seemed more partisan than in the past and unfortunately this developed into some ill-feeling between the two sides. The return at Old Trafford provided a very exciting climax. Lancashire were all out for 118 and Yorkshire were 108 for six at the close on Saturday. The Yorkshire captain was then taken ill with appendicitis and the holiday Monday was rained off. Big hitting by James Tyldesley, whilst everyone else failed, meant that Yorkshire required 132 to win in the last innings. The eighth wicket, however, fell with the score on 108, and with Yorkshire having only ten men, Lancashire requested the

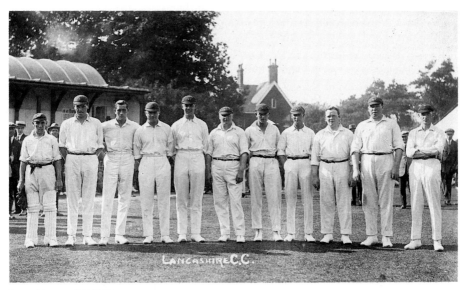

Lancashire 1922 (NCCC)

extra half hour. Rhodes and the last man, Rockley Wilson, gradually built up the total, so that when the final over began four runs were needed. Rhodes batted out the over, but claimed that if the umpire had not been late calling a no-ball, Yorkshire might have won.

The team were involved in another exciting finish at Leicester where the home county needed 153 to win and seemed to be coasting to victory with 100 on the board for the loss of four wickets. Reckless hitting, whilst the bowlers kept their nerve, reduced the target to eight with two wickets left. The tenth man was then dismissed by Richard Tyldesley, and Alec Skelding came in last. He took the score to within three, when he and his partner became hopelessly confused and the latter was run out.

Lancashire won 15 of their 30 matches and lost seven. Financially the season was a good one, though membership dropped slightly, having been boosted by the Australian visit in the previous twelve months. Makepeace obtained £2,110 10s 6d from his benefit – the match v Surrey – and Blomley was awarded £200 in lieu of a benefit.

MacLaren's season as coach had not been completely satisfactory. He won the devotion of many of the young players, but lacked tact when dealing with his brother officials and some of the committee. MacLaren found himself a most pleasant winter occupation for 1922–23, as captain of an experimental MCC side to New Zealand and Australia.

Instead of opting for one of the young amateurs to lead the side in place of Kenyon, the Lancashire committee chose the 45-year-old John Sharp. He had played hardly any Championship games in 1922, but had captained the side quite frequently when Kenyon had been absent in previous years. *The Cricketer* described the appointment as 'an excellent choice which few will be disposed to question'.

Before the 1923 season began Lancashire put forward two proposals with regard to the qualification of county cricketers. In the first place they proposed that players who did not reside in a first- or second-class county could play for the county whose county town was nearest to their place of residence or birth. This with two amendments was carried, but their second proposal that residential qualification be reduced from 24 months to 12 was rejected by the narrow margin of one vote, Notts being the leading county in opposition. Lancashire had an ulterior motive in their proposal – they were waiting for the Australian fast bowler Ted McDonald to qualify and if reduced to 12 months the rule would allow him to play in 1923.

MacLaren officially 'resigned' as Old Trafford coach on his return from New Zealand and the County appointed J.T. Tyldesley to replace him. MacLaren still demonstrated his lack of tact on tour, in one case with amusing results. After one of the minor sides in New Zealand had batted poorly against MCC, MacLaren stated the local players did not know the blade from the handle of the bat. One local man arrived at the crease in the second innings with each part clearly labelled! He ended with the highest score.

The Lancashire season opened with games against Oxford and Cambridge. The County took the opportunity to try out one or two new players, the most notable of whom was the South African left-arm fast bowler, A.E. Hall. Hall was born in Bolton, but had moved to the Transvaal and in the winter had appeared in the Tests against England, taking 27 wickets at 18 runs each. He picked up 15 wickets in his first two games for his native county, but did not play in the Championship matches (Lancashire's application to register him being rejected on the grounds that he could not play for two counties in one year, Transvaal being classified as a county). G.H. Rogerson and Leonard Green were two amateur batsmen who were also played in these games, and both continued to appear during the year.

John Sharp made his first appearance as official captain in the opening Championship match, against Leicestershire, but in the second game,

Jack Sharp greets Cecil Parkin, with Ted McDonald in the background

the Whitsun meeting with Yorkshire, he was unable to play due to a severe cold and J.T. Tyldesley led out the side. Rain washed out the Saturday, but 22,000 spectators appeared on the Monday to see Lancashire dismissed for 108. Most of the third day was also rained off, the report noting: 'The crowd took the hours of waiting in rather bad part.'

Tyldesley decided not to continue as captain and in the third Championship game came another change as Green was given the task. Lancashire suffered a second serious loss when Hallows hurt his hand whilst fielding and this plus influenza kept him out of the team until the end of June. Happily Parkin was bowling well:

> Last season Parkin was singularly unsuccessful against the best sides, and we are glad therefore to note his success against Yorkshire, for he is probably the finest natural bowler we possess at the present time. Moreover he is brimful of life and energy, and if he would discard some of his 'tricks' he used to indulge in last season, and concentrate on a more orthodox method, and a more normal arrangement of his field, he might accomplish great things in the highest class of cricket. For such a fine bowler to bowl with six or seven men on the leg side on a good wicket against batsmen like Hearne and Hendren is a negative form of attack and does not give sufficient scope to his powers.

Having failed to get Hall into the Championship side, Lancashire drafted in the left-arm slow bowler from Kent, W.E. Hickmott. Hickmott had been in splendid form for Ramsbottom, and in 1921 had come second to Cook in the Lancashire League averages with 94 wickets at 8 runs each.

At the end of the first week of June, the Lancashire campaign was going well; they were second in the table to Notts, the two being the only unbeaten sides. Major Green, the temporary leader, celebrated the Gloucestershire match with his maiden Championship hundred. In the same match the County introduced a new wicket-keeper, George Duckworth from Warrington. He was quickly to make the post his own and with his dexterity improve substantially a link in the eleven which had for too many years been weak. Going on to represent England, he became internationally known for his small stature and loud voice.

Sharp returned to the side in the middle of June and his batting was proving a great asset to the side, when, having made a brilliant hundred against Middlesex, his leg gave way and he was unable to play again until the end of July.

Dogged by wet weather, Lancashire slipped down the Championship table, so that on 10 July, though they had been beaten only once, they occupied fifth place. Sussex, who had lost three, had moved into third place behind Yorkshire and Notts. Lancashire, however, did their cause no good by resting Parkin and Richard Tyldesley for the match in mid-July against Essex. They clearly thought Essex of little moment, but it needed a hundred from Makepeace to save the game. Even with Parkin and Richard Tyldesley they couldn't dismiss Surrey in the game which followed, Hobbs hitting a hundred as Surrey declared at 436 for eight. This time Ernest Tyldesley with 236, and some rain, produced another drawn contest. Lancashire dropped to seventh place.

An improvement later in the year meant the County ended third, behind Yorkshire and Notts. Makepeace and Ernest Tyldesley both had excellent batting records and over 1,500 Championship runs. Hallows, despite his long lay-off, also reached 1,000 runs. Frank Watson was the most improved batsman of the side and also sent down some useful deliveries.

Richard Tyldesley earned himself the title of the best leg-spinner in England and so fast did Duckworth develop that in some quarters he was already regarded as the best stumper in the country. Stanley Ellis, the brother of Walker, created a surprise by taking 11 wickets right at the season's end. A right-hand medium-pace bowler he looked very promising. On the other hand, Lawrence Cook, who took his benefit in 1923, was played almost as much as a batsman as a bowler, his accuracy of pitch having been lost. Parkin captured over 200 wickets in all first-class matches and remained the County's best bowler.

The important feature of the preview of the 1924 season was the fact that Hall would now be qualified for the County. The County was also celebrating its Diamond Jubilee with a special dinner at the Midland Hotel, Manchester on 11 June. The guest of honour at the celebration dinner was none other than Lord Harris. Lord Harris was still remembered by Lancastrians as the man who had outlawed Crossland and other bowlers with doubtful actions. The theme of his speech, even on this happy occasion, was not without controversy, for he made it clear that he had forced an inquiry into the residential qualifications of McDonald for Lancashire. Lord Harris went on to say that he might be regarded as a tiresome busybody, but the counties themselves had set up the Laws and he felt that they ought to abide by them.

The first matches of the season belonged to Parkin and so outstanding were his figures that they deserve to be detailed in full (see table on page 124).

Those figures are for Championship matches only, but in all matches to 10 June he had taken 80 wickets at 7.86 runs each. With Richard Tyldesley seventh in the first-class averages on the same date – Parkin of course being top – it is not surprising to find Lancashire still undefeated. At the end of May McDonald qualified and the attack became even

LANCASHIRE *v.* GLAMORGAN

Played on the Aigburth Ground, Liverpool, on 14, 15 and 16 May 1924

LANCASHIRE WON BY 128 RUNS

LANCASHIRE	FIRST INNINGS		SECOND INNINGS	
J.W.H. Makepeace	c Arnott b Mercer	0	c Mercer b Davies	41
C. Hallows	b Mercer	8	st Sullivan b Davies	49
G.E. Tyldesley	b Spencer	6	lbw b Davies	7
F.B. Watson	c Bates b Mercer	0	c Mercer b Spencer	26
Capt R. Howard	b Spencer	7	b Davies	0
*Mr J. Sharp	c Mercer b Ryan	9	c Sullivan b Spencer	7
Mr A. Rhodes	c Clay b Spencer	10	c Clay b Ryan	11
R.K. Tyldesley	c Bates b Ryan	1	not out	5
C.H. Parkin	c Ryan b Spencer	0	not out	4
†G. Duckworth	not out	0	c Clay b Mercer	34
A.E. Hall	c Arnott b Spencer	0		
Extras	b 5, lb 3	8	b 15, lb 6, nb 3	24
Total		49	(8 wkts dec)	208

BOWLING	O	M	R	W	O	M	R	W
Mercer	12	3	27	3	3	0	11	1
Arnott	3	2	5	0	4	1	6	0
Spencer	10.1	5	9	5	21	8	34	2
Ryan	2	2	0	0	30	5	73	1
Davies					25	10	43	4
Clay					7	2	13	0
Bates					1	0	4	0

GLAMORGAN	FIRST INNINGS		SECOND INNINGS	
T.E. Abel	c and b Parkin	0	c sub b Parkin	9
D. Davies	c Howard b Parkin	0	c Makepeace b Parkin	10
W.E. Bates	c R.K. Tyldesley b Parkin	11	b R.K. Tyldesley	0
Mr C.F. Walters	c R.K. Tyldesley b Parkin	0	b Parkin	11
Mr F.W. Matthias	c G.E. Tyldesley b R.K. Tyldesley	2	b R.K. Tyldesley	2
Mr T. Arnott	b Parkin	0	b R.K. Tyldesley	1
*Mr J.C. Clay	c Hallows b Parkin	3	b Watson	8
F.P. Ryan	b R.K. Tyldesley	5	c Duckworth b Parkin	3
J. Mercer	c Watson b R.K. Tyldesley	0	not out	45
H. Spencer	c Rhodes b R.K. Tyldesley	1	b Hall	12
†D. Sullivan	not out	0	b Hall	0
Extras		0	b 3, lb3	6
Total		22		107

BOWLING	O	M	R	W	O	M	R	W
Parkin	8	5	6	6	17	9	30	4
R.K. Tyldesley	7.3	1	16	4	19	6	37	3
Hall					5.2	0	25	2
Watson					3	1	9	1

Umpires: R.D. Burrows and G.P. Harrison

more formidable. Hall, the South African, for whose services Lancashire had fought the authorities, was redundant!

	O	M	R	W
v Derbyshire (Old Trafford)	21.3	13	20	8
v Glamorgan (Liverpool)	8	5	6	6
	17	9	30	4
v Middlesex (Lord's)	48	19	65	8
	9	3	17	1
v Derbyshire (Derby)	34.4	12	57	7
	13	9	6	5
v Warwickshire (Old Trafford)	19	7	44	6
	22	10	34	4

Both Parkin and Ernest Tyldesley were selected for the first Test against the South Africans at Edgbaston. Tyldesley was omitted from the final eleven in favour of A.P.F. Chapman. The South Africans were dismissed by Tate and Gilligan for 30, but following on batted much better and Parkin became increasingly annoyed when he was not asked to bowl. Parkin showed his displeasure by making only feeble attempts to stop the ball in the field and by using his foot to field many of the balls which came close to him, presenting the opposition with several additional runs in the process. After the match he issued a manifesto to the press, saying that as he was more or less ignored as a bowler even though South Africa made nearly 400, he would not be available for selection for the second Test. The press were of the opinion that because of his dreadful exhibition on the field, he wouldn't be chosen anyway and that ended the Test career of Cecil Parkin.

By mid-July Lancashire were still unbeaten and the Championship was very open with Middlesex, Yorkshire, Surrey and Somerset all competing with Lancashire for the premier position. The rain however had a decisive effect on the progress of the County, and by the end of the year only two of the 12 matches arranged at Old Trafford had reached a definite conclusion.

It was not until the middle of August that the County suffered its first reverse. This defeat came at the hands of lowly Glamorgan and was described at the time as the greatest feat yet achieved by Glamorgan in first-class cricket. The men of the match were Maurice Turnbull, a 17-year-old schoolboy from Downside, whose 40 was the highest innings for the Welsh county, and Ryan, whose bowling was unplayable in the fourth innings of the match, when Lancashire required 146 for victory. Glamorgan won by 38 runs.

Yorkshire won the Championship and Lancashire had to be content with fourth place. Lancashire's reaction was to place a proposal before the Advisory Committee, suggesting that first innings points be

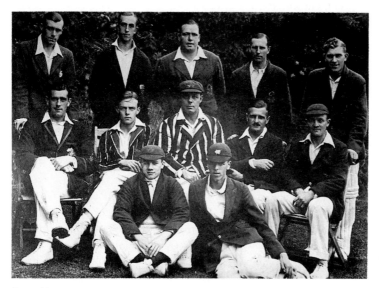

Lancashire 1924.

abolished and only matches with a definite finish taken into account – they were not successful in their proposal.

Parkin took 169 Championship wickets at 13.37 runs each, heading the County's bowling table, but was closely followed by Richard Tyldesley with 135 wickets at 14.00 each. McDonald, being also engaged with Nelson, was not available for all matches and took 62 wickets at 17.35 each. The only other bowler required was Watson – Hickmott, Hall and Stanley Ellis had few opportunities. Ernest Tyldesley and Makespeace continued to dominate the batting. Watson, usually going in at number four built up his reputation for reliability. Hallows declined slightly, though he hit hundreds in both innings against Leicestershire.

Duckworth's qualities achieved official recognition when he appeared in the fourth Test at Old Trafford. Unfortunately rain washed out two of the three days. He was unlucky not to obtain a place in the MCC side to Australia in the winter, but the selectors opted for Strudwick and and the use of the Notts batsman, Whysall, as understudy.

Two young professionals were given fairly long trials in the First Eleven. Jack Iddon came from Mawdesley and was aged 21. His father was for many years professional with Lancaster, and young Jack first achieved note with Leyland Motors. A hard-driving right-hand bat and useful slow left-arm bowler, he gradually developed into a mainstay of the County side and in the mid-1930s gained some Test caps for

England. He was killed in a road accident in 1946. His fellow colt was also a right-hand bat and left-arm bowler and his career ran almost parallel, for he – Len Hopwood – also gained a cap for England in the middle of the next decade and his Championship career also ended in 1939. Hopwood had the edge as a bowler and Iddon as a batsman.

An amateur who played a few games as a batsman in 1924 and 1925 was Don Davies, better known on the soccer field with Bolton Wanderers. He was later to become a sports journalist with the *Manchester Guardian* and was to die tragically in the Munich air disaster of 1958.

Despite the terrible weather, Lancashire made a profit of £1,100 on the year and the membership total was 3,704. T.A. Higson, the former player, was appointed honorary treasurer during the year.

With McDonald no longer under any obligation to Nelson, Lancashire seemed on paper to have the strongest attack in the country for the 1925 season. The County made the early running in the Championship race and at the beginning of June were still on top. Unlike 1924, it was not so much Parkin, but Tyldesley and McDonald, in conjunction with Parkin. On 12 June, Richard Tyldesley was heading the first-class averages with 64 wickets at 10 runs each; McDonald was in sixth place with 68 at 14.10 and Parkin, 11th with 71 at 15.19. Lancashire's first defeat occurred in mid-June, when Middlesex won at Lord's, due to a splendid innings of 142 by Hendren. The report noted: 'McDonald bowled superbly and his six wickets for 145 runs does not represent the splendid work he did for his side. On Saturday his luck was execrable, but he took his misfortune quite calmly, as becomes a great cricketer, and his beautiful action and lovely swing and follow through were a joy to behold.'

It was nearly a month before Lancashire tasted defeat a second time and in the meantime, Hampshire, Leicestershire, Gloucestershire, Sussex and Northants were disposed of by large margins. Yorkshire, however, seemed unstoppable, and when Surrey beat Lancashire on 14 July, Yorkshire were still without defeat with 16 wins from 19 matches. Lancashire in second place had 12 wins from 18, but it was not enough.

What was irritating from the Lancastrian viewpoint was that they gained first innings points in both the Bank Holiday fixtures but in both rain, to some extent, caused draws. At Old Trafford over 35,000 came on the holiday Monday and saw Charlie Hallows fight his way to 111. The Yorkshire press commented on the match:

It does not look as if we in Yorkshire or our fellow-Northerners of Lancashire had any excuse for throwing stones at Australia over slow play in Test Matches. Nothing in last winter's games could possibly have been more funereal than the play in the match that has just ended in a draw at Old Trafford. It is certainly the case that these two counties have an intense respect for each other's abilities, and that their matches are usually conducted in a grimly cautious spirit. But this time they overdid it. They played so dourly that they could not expect to bring the match to a finish; sound defence was carried so far that it lapsed into spiritless plodding ... Strong defensive play has its own very high value in cricket. There are times when it is priceless. But there are other times when it is a nuisance, and we are afraid it must be said that there are two or three batsmen on the Yorkshire side who habitually play as if the Championship depended on their keeping up their wickets at all costs.

In the return fixture at Bramall Lane, when about 30,000 watched the holiday Monday match, Lancashire were accused of playing for a draw from the first morning.

In the middle of August, Surrey overtook Lancashire and from then to the end the positions in the Championship table remained unchanged, with Yorkshire first, followed by Surrey and Lancashire.

Lancashire could claim that their efforts to win the Championship were hampered by the illness to Ernest Tyldesley – struck down by appendicitis – and injury to Hallows. Hallows topped Lancashire's batting, followed by Tyldesley, but the latter missed half the summer. Watson continued to improve, though unlike Hallows he was not regarded as a possibility for England in 1926. J.R. Barnes played in 19 Championship matches and came third in the batting, fractionally above Watson.

Parkin's effectiveness was much reduced as the season wore on. He failed for example to take a wicket when Middlesex hit 410 in the first innings of the match at Old Trafford – the game given to Parkin as a benefit. This match was the cause of the resignation of the Lancashire captain. The crowd gave him such an offensive reception when he dropped a catch, that he announced he would never play at Old Trafford again. The Committee prevailed upon him to continue, but at the end of the season Jack Sharp resigned.

In fact he had not played regularly, and both J.R. Barnes and A.E. Pewtress led the side occasionally.

One departure of 1925 was the decision to stage a Championship game at Nelson, one of the conditions laid down when Nelson released McDonald. The game was well-attended with 10,000 turning up on the Saturday; the visitors, Derbyshire, were beaten by 97 runs.

Of the four young cricketers to make their debuts for the County in 1925, the one who attracted most attention was Frank Sibbles from Oldham. He played in ten matches and with 43 wickets led the bowling table with an average of 13.46. *The Cricketer* commented: 'Sibbles is one of the most promising bowlers we have seen for a long time. He bowls a deceptive swerving ball which dips at the last moment, and he is quite a good bat at No 8.'

Financially the County Club did even better than in 1924 and a new building comprising press box, committee room and scorebox was erected, as well as other improvements at Old Trafford, the total cost being over £4,000. Apart from the good attendance at Nelson, there was a record crowd on the Aigburth Ground for the Sussex match. Further improvements were carried out in the spring, including a new covered stand on the popular side, so the ground wore a refurbished look for the 1926 Australians.

The tourists were first seen on the ground in June, when they outplayed Lancashire. The County were dismissed for 149 of which Hallows, going in first, and last man out, made 85. Macartney then played a magnificent innings. *The Cricketer* commented:

> So surely, so easily did he hit the ball with little apparent effort, that while he lives in the world of cricket Victor Trumper will not be forgotten. There is something of 'Victor the Nonpareil' in Macartney, and no praise can be higher!

Lancashire lost by an innings. The County were again beaten by an innings when the Australians went to Liverpool a month later, Bardsley hitting 155 and Mailey taking nine for 86. The home side did achieve one notable feat, for Makepeace and Hallows put on 114 and 116 for the first wicket, this double never before having been performed against the Australians in England.

The Old Trafford Test began nine days later, but the warning bell on the first morning brought forth not fielders, but rain. Most of the first day was lost, and this being a three-day match a draw was almost certain. Woodfull and Macartney made hundreds in Australia's total of 335. England were 305 for five when stumps were drawn. Despite the weather – rain cut down the playing on the second day as well – 55,000 people paid admission and the takings after tax were £8,700. Ernest Tyldesley was Lancashire's only representative and his 81 was the highest score for England.

For Lancashire at least the presence of the Australians, and even England's famous victory at the Oval, was outshone by the county's progress in the Championship.

At the half-way stage, on 6 July, Yorkshire were leading with eight wins from 14 matches and no defeats, Lancashire were second, also with eight wins, but two defeats and Middlesex, who had played less matches, had six wins and no defeats.

A month later, 10 August, Yorkshire remained undefeated with eleven wins from 24 matches, whilst Lancashire, still in second place, had 12 wins from 26 matches, and still had only two defeats. Middlesex had dropped slightly further behind, but retained third place.

Lancashire then beat Worcestershire, whilst Yorkshire could only gain first-innings points in their parallel fixture, and with Yorkshire having four more games and Lancashire three, the season was building to a thrilling finish.

Lancashire set about the task of winning their final three games – all at home – with determination. In the first, Hampshire, batting first, were bowled out for 109. Lancashire replied with 316 for seven and declared, Watson having made an unbeaten hundred, and although Mead, who had been run out for 0 in the first innings when the ball rebounded from the wicket-keeper's pads, remained for five and a half hours for 132, Lancashire won by eight wickets. Northants were trounced at Blackpool in the three days which followed and then came the final and crucial match against Nottinghamshire.

For once the rain came at the right time for Lancashire. Notts made 292. Tyldesley and Makepeace in a partnership of 279 enabled Lancashire to gain a large lead of 162. In a disastrous 50 minutes on the second evening Notts lost four wickets for 46. Rain overnight then made the pitch very difficult and the visitors' hopes of recovery were dashed. Lancashire won by ten wickets and claimed the title. Yorkshire had one match to play, but even if they won they could not catch Lancashire – as it was the match was not even concluded on first innings.

The veterans, Ernest Tyldesley and Makepeace, formed the backbone of the batting. Tyldesley's record of nine Championship hundreds and 2,365 runs at an average of 69.55 was quite outstanding. He came third behind Hobbs and Sutcliffe in the overall table. Makepeace also completed 2,000 Championship runs and made five Championship hundreds. It was curious that Tyldesley's figures were very similar to those achieved by his brother when Lancashire last won the title in 1904. Makepeace, in contrast to the attractive displays of Tyldesley, was crablike and boring in the extreme to watch, but his dour tactics paid off. Neither Hallows nor Watson really enhanced their reputations. Hallows, a graceful player, fortunately did much better against the stronger sides. Those were the first four batsmen in both batting order and average. Iddon came in at number five and though his highest innings was only 64, he averaged 23 and was dependable. The sixth batting place was shared between M.L. Taylor, a young stylish left-hander from Heywood, whose temperament needed adjusting if he was to win a regular place in the side, and two amateurs. The first was P.T. Eckersley, who failed to make his mark at Cambridge, but played one or two brilliant innings, was exceedingly keen and captained the side occasionally. McDonald, the Australian, was usually at number seven,

LANCASHIRE *v.* NOTTINGHAMSHIRE

Played on the Old Trafford Ground, Manchester, on 28, 30 and 31 August 1926

NOTTINGHAM-SHIRE	FIRST INNINGS		SECOND INNINGS	
G. Gunn	b McDonald	56	b Sibbles	2
W.W. Whysall	b Sibbles	97	b McDonald	6
A. Staples	c Duckworth b McDonald	0	c R.K. Tyldesley b McDonald	10
*Mr A.W. Carr	c Iddon b McDonald	67	lbw b R.K. Tyldesley	10
W.R.D. Payton	lbw b McDonald	2	(7) c Duckworth b McDonald	59
†B. Lilley	b R.K. Tyldesley	13	(8) c Watson b Woolley	45
W.A. Flint	c Sibbles b McDonald	2	(6) lbw b R.K. Tyldesley	17
S.J. Staples	b R.K. Tyldesley	27	(9) not out	9
H. Larwood	lbw b R.K. Tyldesley	10	(10) c Woolley b McDonald	3
F. Barratt	not out	6	(11) b McDonald	4
T.L. Richmond	b Woolley	0	(5) b McDonald	30
Extras	b 5, lb 6, nb 1	12	byes	4
Total		292		199

Fall: 1st inns: 1-120 2-120 3-128 4-227 5-234 6-244 7-246 8-266 9-289
2nd inns: 1-3 2-16 3-23 4-31 5-66 6-82 7-165 8-183 9-187

BOWLING	O	M	R	W	O	M	R	W
McDonald	34	7	· 93	5	21.1	3	80	6
Sibbles	23	5	46	1	12	2	25	1
R.K. Tyldesley	25	7	76	3	11	0	51	2
Woolley	17	3	52	1	4	1	18	1
Iddon	4	1	13	0	5	1	21	0

LANCASHIRE	FIRST INNINGS		SECOND INNINGS	
J.W.H. Makepeace	c A. Staples b S.J. Staples	180	not out	15
C. Hallows	c Carr b Larwood	0		
F.M. Sibbles	c S.J. Staples b A. Staples	34		
G.E. Tyldesley	c Carr b S.J. Staples	140	(2) not out	18
E.A. McDonald	st Lilley b S.J. Staples	24		
J. Iddon	c and b S.J. Staples	18		
R.K. Tyldesley	b Larwood	28		
F.B. Watson	b Barratt	15		
*Mr P.T. Eckersley	b Larwood	8		
A. Woolley	run out	0		
†G. Duckworth	not out	0		
Extras	b 1, lb 4, w2	7	b 4, w 1	5
Total		454	(0 wkt)	38

Fall: 1-0 2-73 3-352 4-358 5-393 6-406 7-439 8-443 9-454

BOWLING	O	M	R	W	O	M	R	W
Barratt	23	5	68	1				
Larwood	18.5	5	42	3				
S.J. Staples	26	2	125	4				
Richmond	23	4	112	0	3	0	24	0
Flint	16	4	50	0				
A. Staples	19	2	50	1				
Carr					3	0	7	0
Gunn					0.4	0	2	0

Umpires: W.A. Buswell and A. Nash

* Captain; † Wicket-keeper

Lancashire won by ten wickets and thus made certain of the County Championship title for the first time since 1904.

but was not really good enough for such a place, though he hit 100 in 100 minutes off the Middlesex attack at Old Trafford.

The new captain, Leonard Green, was perhaps a better batsman than his figures suggest – the highest innings was 61 not out. He certainly understood the character of each of his leading players and with his mastery of tactics, brought the best out of the various situations and individuals.

The bowling was in the hands of McDonald and Richard Tyldesley. The Australian was possibly a little slower in pace than in 1925, but he was still faster than nearly every other bowler in England and was able to make the vital extra effort when needed, notably in the final matches of the season.

Tyldesley, despite being on the bulky side, was capable of long spells and forced mistakes among the legion of firm-footed batsmen in county cricket. Parkin had gone back to League cricket and although he topped the bowling table he bowled in only 14 innings.

Sibbles just topped 50 Championship wickets, but he had made little progress – he needed to develop some variety of pace and more spin. Of the others, Iddon bowled well on slow wickets whilst Watson contained batsmen due to his careful length.

Duckworth's wicket-keeping was excellent and a very good understudy had been found in Farrimond of Bolton.

The traditional Champion County v Rest of England was played at the Oval and provided some astonishing cricket. Lancashire dismissed the rest for 217, with Hendren making 100, but after a good start, Lancashire collapsed and were all out for 177, and that after Hallows and Makepeace had put on 106 for the first wicket. In the second innings the Rest batsmen did what they liked and a declaration was made, the score was 468 for two. Some very reckless batting by Lancashire saw them dismissed in two hours and suffer a very large defeat.

The success of the County Club in the Championship was reflected in the finances: £11,017 17s was received in subscriptions and £14,328 in gate receipts, plus over £2,000 in a fund for ground improvements. Full members numbered 4,151, with 1,327 lady members and 185 juniors. W.E. Howard, the pavilion attendant, received £1,606 for his benefit.

In the winter of 1926–27 one of the cricket controversies which arose and produced some heated argument was the importation of Australian players. Several critics deplored Lancashire's success on the grounds that it was due to McDonald, though it was made clear that McDonald came to England initially purely for League cricket and that he got his place in the County side when Frank O'Keeffe, who came to play for Church CC, died just before he had qualified by residence for the County in 1924. Now the newspapers announced that the record-breaking batsman, W.H. Ponsford, was planning to settle in Blackpool, in order to play in the Ribblesdale League and then qualify for Lancashire.

Lord Hawke was among the first to protest, stating 'I heartily hope that no county will ever again be strengthened by overseas importations, which savour of the long purse and keep home-born cricketers out of the side.'

Memories of MacLaren bringing Kermode over and even earlier of Ferris qualifying for Gloucestershire were revived. In the end the general outcry deterred those who were trying to seduce Ponsford and the matter died a death.

With the same players available for 1927 as in 1926, the Lancashire prospects seemed good. Ernest Tyldesley had been injured in a motor accident whilst touring in the West Indies and missed one or two early games, but the remainder of the team began the summer with an unexpected win. Rain meant that at the end of the first two days of the Warwickshire match at Old Trafford, only the first two innings had been completed and a draw seemed certain, but on the third morning Iddon's spin was unplayable on the damp surface and Warwickshire found themselves dismissed for 64, Lancashire then having the simple task of making 43 to win.

By the time Yorkshire arrived for the Whitsun match, Lancashire were firmly installed at the head of the Championship table with six wins and no losses from nine games. About 15,000 turned out on the Saturday to see the start of what was to be another dour battle. Wilfred Rhodes, leading Yorkshire due to the absence of Major Lupton, came in at number seven to save the side from being routed by McDonald, but even so Yorkshire could muster only 166. Lancashire determined to gain a great advantage but in 150 overs they slowly ground out 234 runs. McDonald again caused all sorts of problems and Lancashire won by eight wickets.

When the halfway stage was reached, Lancashire were still unbeaten and at the head of table, but Nottinghamshire were closing the gap and in the very next week moved into first place with a win over Leicestershire, whilst Lancashire managed a tall-scoring draw at the Oval.

At this time, Lancashire had some bad news, for J.T. Tyldesley, who as coach and Second Eleven captain had kept the supply of young players coming through, suffered a heart attack and was advised to retire from active cricket. T.A. Higson, the genial hon treasurer, was brought out of retirement to lead the Seconds and had the pleasant task of being in the same team as his son, Peter.

The August Bank Holiday fixture, with Notts still in front, was more vital to Lancashire than ever. They gained a lead of more than 200 on the first innings, with Ernest Tyldesley hitting 165, giving no chance, but then Sutcliffe responded with a three-figure innings and the game was another draw. Fortunately the rain and Surrey's batting prevented Notts moving further ahead.

Directly after the Bank Holiday, Notts were beaten in two days by Kent, whereas Lancashire outplayed Middlesex at Old Trafford, Hallows making 134 as Middlesex were beaten by ten wickets; the margin ought to have been larger, but the home side dropped at least six catches.

These two results reversed the position at the top and everything now depended on the last few matches. The next pair of matches, Lancashire v Kent and Notts v Derbyshire, were both rain-ruined draws, but at Trent Bridge not even first innings points could be decided, whereas Lancashire obtained the points at Old Trafford, edging them slightly further into the lead. Both counties won their matches completed on 12 August and then Lancashire went to Trent Bridge, for the game which might decide the Championship. Some 16,000 spectators watched Notts make 300 for seven aided by some dropped catches. By the close of the second day, the home side were on the brink of victory, as Sam Staples took six for 33 and Lancashire's last seven wickets fell for 31. The Lancashire side followed on, 272 in arrears and were 32 without loss at the close. On the final day rain delayed the start until mid-day. Hallows and Watson decided to stonewall and in the 90 minutes play before lunch only 25 runs came. In mid-afternoon, after Voce had taken two wickets, the drizzle turned to heavy rain and the match ended. The positions at the head of the table now read:

	P	W	L	Poss Pts	Actual Pts	%
Lancashire	26	10	0	208	149	71.63
Notts	24	10	2	192	131	68.22

Lancashire had three more matches to play and Notts five. Whilst Lancashire entertained the New Zealand touring team, Notts opposed Northants. Again the rain caused both matches to be drawn. The next set of matches were even more badly affected by the weather. Lancashire's game with Glamorgan failed to start and only three hours play took place over three days in Notts' match with Middlesex. Unfortunately for Notts their match counted in the possible points because some play took place, whereas Lancashire's percentage remained unaltered, because no ball was bowled.

The two sets of matches commencing 24 August, however, saw Notts climb back into the lead, for whilst the midland county won both games, Lancashire not only drew against Leicester, but were trounced by Sussex at Eastbourne – dismissed for 99 and 76 in reply to Sussex's

6

371. Maurice Tate took nine for 49 and the Rev F.B.R. Browne eight for 50. Lancashire had not lost a Championship game since 25 June 1926 and the press, remembering MacLaren's great match at the Saffrons, described Eastbourne as 'the cemetery of cricket hopes'. The Lancashire captain in a desperate effort to save the side batted 50 minutes for 4.

The percentages now read: Notts 70.37, Lancashire 68.75. One match only remained. Lancashire's programme was complete, while Notts went down to Swansea. Glamorgan, whose most famous victory to date had been against Lancashire, now produced another win which eclipsed the previous one, beating Notts by an innings and the final positions read:

	P	W	L	Poss Pts	Actual Pts	%
Lancashire	28	10	1	224	154	68.75
Notts	28	12	3	224	152	67.85

The first point commented upon regarding Lancashire's Championship was that the County won because of their batting, rather than their bowling. *The Cricketer* reported:

A good deal of newspaper and public criticism of none too friendly a nature commented severely on the very slow and uninteresting game played by Lancashire's leading batsmen. There was, possibly, cause for some of these remarks, but there is a great deal to be said in favour of the tactics especially employed by Hallows, Makepeace and Watson, and occasionally by Tyldesley (E), and L. Green. Lancashire's position is prima facie due to the reliable and consistent form of their leading batsmen more than to any other one factor.

Hallows was effectively top of the first-class averages with 2,343 runs, average 75.58, and Ernest Tyldesley averaged 50.17 for his 1,756 runs. Watson completed 1,500 runs, but Makepeace missed half the season through illness. Major Green moved himself further up the order compared to 1926 and averaged nearly 30 in Championship games. Peter Eckersley, who had wintered in India, improved, but nothing was seen of J.R. Barnes.

The bowling relied very much on McDonald, but the wet wickets meant that his average dropped and he again suffered from mistakes in the field, notably by the slips. He bowled more short-pitched deliveries than in the previous summer and some bruised batsmen were unhappy. Richard Tyldesley was McDonald's main ally, but Sibbles, making the new ball swing, had a good year and ended with 97 wickets. Iddon fell away as a bowler and it was felt he should bowl round, rather than over the wicket.

In the opening match of 1928 the Lancashire batsmen demonstrated that they could open their shoulders – on the first day they hit 528 for four. Watson and Hallows put on 200 for the first wicket, Watson and Ernest Tyldesley 179 for the second. Watson went on to make 223 for 255 minutes. The match was won by an innings and 16 runs; the opponents were Northants. The high scoring set the tone for the summer. All over England batting records were broken. In all English first-class cricket 414 hundreds were compiled, compared to 309 in 1927. Five batsmen, including Ernest Tyldesley, reached 3,000 runs. Lancashire's batsmen, who had done well in 1927, now excelled themselves. The County went through the Championship campaign unbeaten and only on three occasions did their opponents even gain a first-innings lead.

Unlike 1927, Lancashire won the Championship with still two matches to play and the success was far more satisfying than it had been the year before. Kent challenged seriously for the title and led the field during most of June and July, but August belonged to Lancashire and three consecutive defeats put Kent in the shade.

The Roses battles were both drawn, neither side giving an inch as the batsmen ground out their runs. The August Bank Holiday game was at Old Trafford and 20,000 came on the Saturday to see Yorkshire make 338 for eight. An even larger crowed, 35,000, saw Lancashire reply with 244 for three on the Monday. Rain prevented any play on the third day. The matches with Notts followed a similar pattern, but it was rather unfortunate that the game at Old Trafford clashed with the Test trial, robbing Lancashire of Hallows, Ernest Tyldesley and Watson, and Notts of Larwood and Sam Staples.

Hallows achieved a quite outstanding feat in the last match of May – against Sussex at Old Trafford. He required 232 to complete 1,000 runs in May. At the end of the first day he was undefeated on 190 and on the second morning reached exactly 232, before being caught next ball. Only W.G. Grace and Walter Hammond had attained the feat before, and with an average of 125.00, Hallows' record was superior to both. He gained a place in the England team for the first Test, when Hobbs withdrew due to a strain, and would have been chosen for the 1928–29 tour to Australia if his fielding had been up to international standard. Later in the summer Hallows was not quite so successful and at the close had to be content with third place in the Lancashire batting table. Ernest Tyldesley was first; he hit eight Championship hundreds, and playing in all three Tests came second to Hobbs in the England averages; one of his very few failures was unhappily in the Test at Old Trafford.

Third of the trio of Lancashire batsmen was Watson. He had more or less taken over Makepeace's role as Hallows' opening partner in 1927. This year the pair put on a century for the first wicket on 12 occasions and in four of those instances the total reached 200 before they were parted. Watson compiled nine Championship hundreds, and against Surrey at Manchester, hit 300 not out, the highest score ever made on the Old Trafford Ground. With Ernest Tyldesley he added 371 for the second wicket, the highest partnership ever recorded for Lancashire.

Makepeace and Iddon batted at numbers four and five. Both completed 1,000 Championship runs. At the end of the year Makepeace was appointed as J.T. Tyldesley's assistant, Of the others, the captain continued his form of 1927 and Hopwood improved, but Taylor had a poor year and Peter Eckersley was prevented from playing due to appendicitis.

The bowling was rather too dependent on McDonald. He finished sixth in the first-class averages and in Championship games took 178 wickets, more than twice Richard Tyldesley's total.

Neville Cardus reported on the bowling of McDonald in the home game against Kent:

> Whence does McDonald draw his terrible strength and velocity? His run to the wicket is so easy, so silent. He does not thunder over the earth like Gregory – like a bull at a gate. No; he runs along a sinister curve, lithe as a panther, his whole body moving like visible, dangerous music. A more beautiful action than McDonald's was never seen on a cricket field, or a more inimical. The man's whole being tells of the sinister destructive forces of nature – he is a satanic bowler, menacing but princely. Yesterday he was at his best; he like a comet burnt, and from his wheeling arm shot pestilence and war. His attack mingled in proportion the strength of the lion and the subtlety of the serpent. He husbanded his forces craftily; for Woolley he slackened his pace reserving the thunderbolts for the frail. He bowled unchanged, never resting once from lunch until the end. When Bryan opposed him with a defence of some science he exploited medium paced off spin, but once, when Bryan would not go for a run – which would have given McDonald a rabbit to shoot at – he sent down, next ball, a streak of lightning that left Bryan standing and missed the off wicket by inches.

In that innings McDonald took eight for 53, giving him 15 wickets in the match. Kent were beaten by an innings and this destroyed in mid-August any vague aspirations Kent still entertained with regard to the Championship.

Of the other bowlers, Tyldesley was losing his nip off the pitch; Sibbles, troubled by injury, was not as effective as in 1927. Iddon was the best of the change bowlers, Watson being in very poor form.

So Major Green, now a Lieutenant-Colonel, retired after three brilliant seasons, in which he took the County to the Championship title. In his first season he had grasped the nettle and made the decision to remove the wayward genius of Parkin from the eleven and from then he managed to control the other characters, and by his example in the field, and his way of distributing praise to others, rather than accepting praise himself, built the successful team.

PETER ECKERSLEY ASSUMES COMMAND

THE REGULATIONS GOVERNING CHAMPIONSHIP cricket were altered for 1929. The percentage system was abolished and every county had to play 28 matches. Eight points were awarded for a win, and in drawn games the side obtaining first innings lead was awarded five points, the other side received three. If no result on first innings could be obtained, each side was awarded four points. Even more revolutionary perhaps, the size of the wickets was increased in order to give bowlers a better chance.

The new rules had no immediate effect on the Whitsun match, which this year fell earlier than usual. On the Saturday, Lancashire spent all day making 196 for seven. Hallows batted throughout and when the innings finally came to an end on Monday, he was still undefeated, having made 152 in 460 minutes. The *Wisden* report opened with: 'Both teams batting in desperately stubborn fashion, there never existed likelihood of any other termination than a draw.'

Immediately following the Whitsun match, Lancashire were completely outplayed by Sussex and in the latter part of June suffered successive defeats at the hands of Gloucestershire and Nottinghamshire. These losses put Lancashire well down the Championship table; they were not again defeated, however, and in fact improved so much that they ended the summer in second place. On 13 August, they were joint equal at the top with Gloucestershire, but had played one more game, and two more than Notts and Yorkshire in third and fourth place. Notts made certain that they did not let their match advantage slip and thus secured the title, breaking Lancashire's sequence.

Whilst Hallows did not enjoy the phenomenal success which had been his in 1928, he still returned good batting figures and remained possibly the best player of slow bowling in England. Ernest Tyldesley and Watson continued to score freely. Iddon made up for any decline in Hallows' figures and had his best season to date. Against Leicestershire he made 222, the highest score of his career, and batted 260 minutes with 25 fours. Makepeace was brought out of retirement in August. He immediately returned to form and hit 163 not out off the Warwickshire attack at Nelson, his strokeplay being as well timed as ever and leading the press to wonder why he had been left out of the team. The stylish M.L. Taylor was not chosen at all all season, but T.M. Halliday, a 24-year-old right-hander from Leyland, reached three figures for the first time and seemed promising, even though he was omitted from the later games. Leslie Warburton of Haslingden, a 19-year-old, hit a mass of runs in local cricket, as well as taking wickets with his fast-medium deliveries. He hit 74 not out against Surrey at the Oval.

The bowling still remained in the hands of McDonald and Richard Tyldesley. Sibbles could play in only nine games due to illness and the famous pair could really only look to Hopwood's left arm for relief.

The new captain seemed rather weighed down by his responsibilities; the fact that he had not played at all in 1928 clearly did not help. He did, however, set an example in the field and it was a pity some of the more established players did not make more effort to follow his example. The

George Duckworth marches to the wicket (NCCC)

outfielding was distinctly sluggish, with returns to the wicket made in a casual manner.

England set rather a poor example in the field during the Old Trafford Test, though they managed to beat the South Africans by an innings. Duckworth was Lancashire's sole representative, indeed the only Lancastrian to appear in any of the Tests.

The Australian team and Don Bradman captured the newspaper headlines in the weeks prior to the 1930 season. 'Donald Bradman is the most discussed cricketer of the time. His run-getting has been phenomenal and he is regarded as a second Trumper. Still only 21, he has already done enough to establish his fame for all time.' So ran just one newspaper comment in April.

The first match which the tourists played in Lancashire was in May at Liverpool. In rather miserable conditions few of the batting stars shone and for Lancashire it was left to Eckersley to score most runs in each innings, Grimmett proving too much of most of the home batsmen. Bad weather cause the game to be drawn. There was one rather delicate point: whether Woodfull was bowled or leg before to Tyldesley. The slow bowler appealed for lbw. The umpire raised his finger and the ball trickled on to the stumps, knocking off a bail. The printed scores show 'bowled', but as according to the Laws the ball is dead immediately the umpire pronounces a batsman out, presumably leg before would be more accurate.

Rain also marred the county match with the tourists at Old Trafford in June. Kippax made a steady hundred. Bradman was brilliantly caught by Duckworth on the leg side for 38. The match petered out on the last day.

After having both these matches interrupted by rain, it was disappointing to have the Old Trafford Test similarly disrupted. The fourth and final day was completely abandoned and very little play took place on the third, so that not even the first innings of each side were completed. About 38,000 attended on the second day, the feature of which was Sutcliffe's innings of 74. Ponsford's 83 was the highest of the match. Lancashire again had Duckworth as their only representative, though Richard Tyldesley had played in the three earlier matches in the series.

Coincidental with the Old Trafford Test, T.A. Higson, the Lancashire hon treasurer, burst into print with his ideas to improve county cricket. He suggested each county play 32 matches of two days each, but each game should depend on one innings per side. This notion did not go down well and came into the category of 'thoroughly interesting but . . .'.

Like the Australians' visits to Lancashire, the 1930 County Championship was thoroughly upset by the weather. Over half of all matches

ended without a definite result, and in the case of Lancashire 18 of their
28 games were drawn. In May they won five of seven Championship
matches and were well in front of the other 16 counties at that stage.
Five successive draws followed which pushed Lancashire down to third
place behind Kent and Notts. Kent then came to Old Trafford, the
match taking place on the same dates as the Lord's Test, so both
Woolley and Chapman, as well as Duckworth, were absent. Outstanding bowling by McDonald, hundreds from Ernest Tyldesley and
Watson, and seven second-innings dismissals by young Farrimond,
standing in for Duckworth, enabled Lancashire to win by an innings
and move up into second place. A week later, McDonald struck again,
this time against Warwickshire, taking four wickets in six balls and
enabling Lancashire to win by seven wickets. Lancashire were now in
the lead, with Notts in second place and Kent third.

Another barren patch – this time eight consecutive draws – was not
so critical, for most other counties were affected likewise and a two-day
win over Leicestershire broke the spell in the middle of August. Richard
Tyldesley, eight for 35 in the final innings, dismissed Leicester for 103.

Gloucestershire had been gradually climbing the table after a very
poor start, and when Lancashire went to Blackpool for their last match,
they needed a definite win to avoid the possibility of the western county
taking the title. They made no mistake and beat Essex by 174 runs early
on the third day. The batsman who played a very skilful second
innings, making 63 out of 176 all out, was Eddie Paynter.

He had made his debut for Lancashire in 1926 at the age of 24, but
developing slowly did not really get into the County side until the
second half of 1930. Once established, he quickly came to the fore,
gaining a Test cap in 1931 and going with Jardine's side to Australia in
1932–33. It was on that tour that Paynter played his historic innings,
emerging from his sickbed to bat for nearly four hours.

Robertson-Glasgow wrote of him:

He found Lancashire cricket plunged in the mastery of delay. Virtue
was to avoid defeat; crime to get out when trying a funny one. All
this Paynter either did not observe or else totally disregarded. There
was nothing wild about his batting. His defence could be as stubborn
as a wall; but in his heart he thought of a ruthless first over as a
personal affront, and of a timid draw as a moral defeat. It is related
that, when he had won a match by some brilliant hitting on a difficult
pitch, he was warned against the repetition of such risky goings-on.
It was like telling Dan Leno not to make faces. His views on the
Lancashire-Yorkshire match were heretical. He wanted it finished,
and said: 'Why should the crowd have all the fun?' He is compact and
nimble, like a gymnast; very quick on the foot against slow bowlers,

EDWARD PAYNTER

Compared with a number of his England contemporaries, Paynter's career in first-class cricket was relatively brief. His name will not be found among those batsmen who scored 20,000 runs for Lancashire, but Paynter remains in the mind after several of those run-goliaths have been forgotten.

He did not gain a regular place in the County side until he was in his 30th year and then the outbreak of war in 1939 finished his serious cricket four or five years earlier than would otherwise have been the case.

His record in Test cricket can be regarded as quite outstanding, for he averaged just under 60, managing four hundreds and seven fifties in 20 Tests.

Essentially he was an attacking batsman and though better against spin, he was particularly savage on fast bowlers who pitched the ball short, being very nimble on his feet. Left-handed, he went in at number four or five and for England at six or seven.

E. Paynter and his colleagues G.E. Tyldesley and G. Duckworth (NCCC)

fearless in hooking the fast. He never looks tired, except when he has nothing to do in the deep field. Then he has a habit of crossing one foot over the other and assuming a comically depressed droop of the shoulders.

Eckersley therefore led Lancashire to his first Championship and the County's fourth in five years. The title had been achieved simply because Lancashire were harder to beat than any other county. The points system in vogue then encouraged counties to fight for a draw, if a win was impossible, and Lancashire did just that. Cardus, writing in the *Manchester Guardian*, noted:

> Seldom, if ever, could anybody feel during a Lancashire innings the absence of a plan. No doubt the plan was at bottom grimly economic, but a plan certainly was there all the time, and the whole team worked accordingly. So, too, with the technique. Nobody last season often saw a Lancashire batsman foozling his work like a country club cricketer of more ambition than accomplishment.

Unlike 1929, Makepeace did not regain his place – he played in just three Championship games. Watson, however, more than adequately filled the role of stonewaller; nobody in England worked harder for their runs. His average was measured as much in time as in runs: about two hours.

Ernest Tyldesley headed the Lancashire batting table followed by Watson and Iddon, but Hallows continued to decline. In August he was dropped from the eleven and various sbustitutes found to replace him as Watson's partner, including Hopwood. Hopwood's tenure at number two was brief, but he was the best all-rounder in the side, and with over 1,000 runs as well as 81 wickets at 19 apiece, had his best summer. Eckersley, after his struggle in 1929, found runs coming much more easily.

The bowling remained largely in the hands of Richard Tyldesley – who had a very good summer – and McDonald, but Hopwood and Sibbles gave much more support. Duckworth was brilliant behind the wicket, but the MCC paid the County a double compliment when for the 1930–31 tour to South Africa they chose Duckworth and his Lancashire assistant, Farrimond, as the two wicket-keepers.

Financially the Club moved back into profit, having made a loss of £1,245 in 1929, but in both years they spent a large sum on maintenance and repairs. The membership for 1930 of 5,741 was a new record.

The fact that Gloucestershire had won 15 matches, yet had to be content with second place to Lancashire, who had won only 10, was not lost on the Advisory Committee and for 1931 the points system was altered yet again. Points for a win were increased from 8 to 15, but those for a draw remained unaltered (5 for lead on first innings, 3 for loss on same, and 4 if no result on first innings). To retain the title Lancashire would need to change their tactics.

Sir Edwin Stockton, Chairman of the Lancashire Committee, stated during a pre-season dinner for the players:

1. The players will not be penalised for getting out in an attempt to force the game.

2. We have been accused sometimes in Lancashire of being rather too cautious and playing too slowly, but I would remind those who criticise in that way that our fellows have played according to the book, according to the game, and the results of their play have been so successful that in five years we have been four times head of the Championship table. That is the best answer to those critics. Under the altered conditions and the change in counting they will have to adopt a different method, and we of the committee have confidence that they will be able to adapt themselves to these conditions and go for the win and the 15 points. It will mean brighter and probably more interesting play, and they may win the Championship on it. It is the Committee's wish that they should adapt themselves, and they will not be penalised for making too big an effort in that direction.

Unfortunately whatever plans were made proved unable to cope with two major catastrophes. Watson, the sheet-anchor, developed pneumonia and was able to play in just six matches. Even more disastrous was the injury and then lack of form of McDonald. The great Australian had lost both his pace and his length and at the end of the year had taken just 26 Championship wickets at 38 runs each. His contract had a year to run, but by mutual agreement it was ended and he signed to play for Bacup in 1932.

The loss of these two stalwarts was too much and the side never appeared to be in the running for the Championship title. They finished in sixth place, having won seven and lost four matches. Yorkshire took the title with 16 wins against one loss – at the hands of Gloucestershire. In contrast, the high point of the Lancashire season was their defeat of Gloucestershire by an innings. Richard Tyldesley bowled the western county out for 101, taking seven for 39; then Hallows and Ernest Tyldesley hit hundreds, allowing Eckersley to declare with a lead of 208. Gloucestershire collapsed a second time to Sibbles and Hopwood, the latter returning an analysis of 4-3-1-4.

Gordon Hodgson was tried fairly regularly in place of McDonald, but despite having played on and off since 1928, the South African was still very inaccurate. The most likely up-and-coming bowlers seemed to be Parkin's son and young Latchford. Butterworth, the Rochdale amateur, who had gained his blue at Cambridge in 1929, was a leg-break bowler of some promise, but he played in only one Championship game.

Turning to the batting, Ernest Tyldesley once more was at the head, while Iddon and Paynter also hit over a thousand runs. Horrocks, who came over to England from Western Australia, qualified immediately for the County, having been born in Warrington, though he left at the age of seven. He made his County debut v New Zealand and later hit a good hundred off the Notts attack. Hallows had another rather indifferent season, as did the captain – Eckersley had stood in the election as National candidate for the Borough of Leigh and polled 21,837 votes, but his Labour opponent had held the seat with a majority of 2,128, so the County did not in the end have a member of Parliament as their leader.

Having decided to release McDonald, the Club then found themselves at odds with Richard Tyldesley. The spinner asked for a guarantee of £400 per year in order to safeguard himself against illness or loss of form. The committee rejected his request and in a final plea Tyldesley stated that he had received many better offers from League clubs, but would prefer to remain in county cricket. If the committee refused his guarantee, then in effect they sacked him. His plea did no good and he went elsewhere.

The team, shorn of its star bowlers, had on paper an outstanding win in the first Championship game of 1932, Sibbles taking 11 for 92, but the opponents were a very weak Worcestershire. They then managed to beat much more robust opponents, Derbyshire, and following a drawn game with Glamorgan went to Bramall Lane for the Whitsun match. On the first day Paynter hit 152 out of Lancashire's total of 263, his final fifty coming in 30 minutes. On the holiday Monday, Sibbles bowled out Yorkshire for 46, taking seven for 10. He captured another five wickets in the second innings and Lancashire won with an innings to spare. The 28-year-old from Oldham had produced the performance of his life and Lancashire, whose chances of winning the Championship seemed nil, were out in front at the beginning of June. It was exceedingly frustrating then to find the next four matches all ruined by the weather. The batting, apart from Paynter, failed against Middlesex when the clouds eventually rolled away. By the beginning of July Lancashire were fourth, behind Kent, Yorkshire and Notts. Yorkshire had their revenge by inflicting an innings defeat on Lancashire in August. Sibbles reached his 100th wicket in this match and Iddon seemed to have rediscovered his bowling, though rather late in the season. Yorkshire won the title and the main challenge in the closing stages came from Sussex. Lancashire had to be content with sixth place, having eight wins and six losses.

The critics still came down heavily on the lethargy of the Lancashire batsmen. Even Paynter came in for comment on some occasions – in one match against moderate bowling he made five in half an hour when some quick runs might have won the game.

Ernest Tyldesley remained out on his own, with nearly 2,000 Championship runs at an average of 51. Watson gradually recovered from his lack of practice in the previous year and Iddon had a good year. Hallows faded altogether and virtually nothing was seen of Horrocks, but Butterworth hit a century and was talked of as the next captain. Eckersley was blamed for being too cautious and more often than not content with a draw.

Sibbles was clearly the outstanding bowler, but apart from Iddon the assistance he received was patchy. Hodgson put a lot of energy into his bowling and reached fifty wickets; Butterworth's slows got wickets at some cost and young Parkin was still in the 'promising' category. On occasions when Eckersley was absent Lt Col Green returned to lead the side and had one or two useful innings.

The weather affected the Club's finances, a loss of £3,329 being made on the year. There had now been three successive wet summers and county treasurers throughout England were wondering how to balance the books. The answer came in the proposal to reduce county matches, but as not all would agree, it was arranged that a minimum of 24 inter-county games be played by each Club in 1933 – the percentage system was thus re-introduced.

The death occurred early in 1932 of the Lancashire secretary Harry Rylance and his position was taken by Captain Rupert Howard. T.A. Higson had taken over as chairman, combining that office with the honorary treasurership.

Lancashire had two representative on the 1932–33 MCC tour to Australia: Paynter, who by dint of his famous 83 topped the Test batting averages, and Duckworth, who was now somewhat on the sidelines, as England preferred Ames for his batting ability. The County were therefore not directly involved in the bodyline contro-versy until later.

The need for new blood in the eleven was to be the feature of the 1933 season. With Hallows, Makepeace, McDonald and Richard Tyldesley all gone and both Ernest Tyldesley and Watson not far off retirement, the County were fortunate to have several likely candidates waiting for the call: Albert Bennett, the all-rounder who had been living in Australia, but was a native of St Helens; the Oxford blue, E.A. Barlow from Ashton-under-Lyne; Len Parkinson, described as a useful batsman with a spice of adventure in his make-up; the amateur soccer inter-national W.H.L. Lister: L.M. Cranfield, the slow bowler and son of the Gloucestershire cricketer; Albert Nutter, Harry Elliott, Norman Oldfield, Eddie Phillipson and Dick Pollard were on the staff at Old

Trafford. The one who made the most immediate impression in the first half of 1933 was none of those mentioned, but a boy from Bridgnorth Grammar School, Cyril Washbrook. In his second Championship game for Lancashire, early in June, he made 152, deputising for Watson. Neville Cardus was one of those who recognised Washbrook's potential:

> Washbrook is potentially one of the best batsmen Lancashire have known since the war. He looks like a cricketer, has a cricketer's face and wears his flannels like a cricketer. All these things count. Washbrook's future is in his own hands now. Let him observe the old axiom – 'a straight bat and a modest mind' – only he need not keep the bat too straight. Some of the best strokes of the game (and Washbrook is rich in strokes for a player of his age) demand a bat that is not at all straight.

Lancashire made a good start to the summer of 1933. Opening their programme, for the first time, at Blackburn, they beat Worcestershire by an innings, as in 1932, Watson making 185 and Iddon being the most successful of the bowlers. Going in at number ten, young Parkinson hit about him and reached fifty in as many minutes.

Frank Booth's medium pace changed the direction of a tame draw at Lord's into an easy Lancashire victory, when, taking six for 24, he removed Middlesex for 69 after lunch on the third day, thus giving his side only 33 to make in the final innings.

After a high-scoring draw at Edgbaston – Iddon chose the occasion to compile an unbeaten 204 – Lancashire met Kent at Old Trafford, for their most important match to date. Watson made 98 in reply to Kent's 276, but it was left to Eckersley and Booth to provide a seasonable first-innings lead. Eckersley, with his rather awkward crouching stance made 69, then Booth at number ten emulated Parkinson's earlier effort in that position and hit a very quick fifty; Parkinson, elevated to number six, was dismissed without scoring. Booth took five wickets in the second innings, which gave Lancashire another win and hoisted them up to second place behind Yorkshire in time for the first battle of the Roses. An audience of 25,000 turned up at Old Trafford on the Monday to see their side completely humiliated, Macaulay bowling them out twice for 93 and 92, in reply to Yorkshire's 341. The wicket had crumbled at both ends, and one of the reasons was the follow-through of the Lancashire fast bowler Hodgson, so the County were to an extent responsible for their own downfall. An innovation for the match was the loudspeaker system, which relayed announcements and popular music. Perhaps the latter was too much for the batsmen! The committee decided that the fault lay with Hodgson and not the loudspeakers and his career came to an abrupt end. One other by-product of the match was the injury to Watson; he was hit on the head by a ball from Bowes and had to miss the next two matches.

The defeat turned out to be the only one suffered all year. The batting remained the County's strength. Iddon, Hopwood, Watson and Ernest Tyldesley all reached 1,000 runs at an average over 40, so even if Paynter seemed somewhat stale after his adventures in Australia, and Washbrook was only finding his feet, the team were so strong overall that of the regular eleven, only Booth averaged below 20.

Dismissing the opposition was the problem. Booth and Sibbles generally opened the bowling, but as the weather turned dry, the successes they enjoyed in May grew less and less. Hopwood's 56 wickets were the only ones to be obtained at less than 20 runs each, and on several occasions, Hopwood turned to leg theory in order to slow down the run rate. Parkinson's leg-breaks broke up partnerships but at great cost. When Phillipson from Flixton was tried, he took only one wicket on his debut, but coming in as last man helped Eckersley to add over a hundred.

Moving to the amateur talent, neither Butterworth or Barlow played, but Lister hit an unbeaten maiden 100 against Middlesex in August and A.D. Baxter, the Scottish cricketer, took six for 50 with his fast bowling in the game against the West Indian tourists – and only seven wickets fell. The Lancashire secretary, Rupert Howard, came out of retirement in this game to captain the County. Watson was supposed to open the innings, but retired on the first day through eye trouble and the West Indies allowed the substitute, Hawkwood, to bat in Watson's place. Hawkwood, the Nelson professional, had one great day, when he made 113 in the August Bank Holiday game at Headingley, but this was to be his sole three-figure innings in first-class cricket.

Lancashire ended the season in fifth place. At about 4,500, membership was down on its peak of a few years back, but the County turned a £3,329 deficit in 1932 to a profit of £2,438 in 1933, some of this being due to an increase in the share of Test match profits.

The first Test at Old Trafford against the West Indians had taken place in 1928, with the visitors beaten by an innings. In that year there had been three three-day matches and the same applied in 1933. This time the West Indies proved as good as England. Headley played one of his greatest Test innings, being not out at the end with 169. The match was marred by fast leg-theory – Jardine was forced to bear the brunt of it as Martindale and Constantine hurled the ball down. *The Cricketer* commented that their reporter was fated to watch in pained silence the full horror of body-line. Jardine seemed unworried by the attack and went on to a maiden Test hundred. Those who were opposed to leg-theory were pleased that the ordinary English spectator could at last see what type of bowling it was and what a menace such tactics were to the true nature of cricket. It remains only to be said that Lancashire did not have a single representative in the English Test side, or indeed in the entire series.

Cecil Parkin returned to Old Trafford in the spring of 1934 as temporary assistant to Harry Makepeace and the County Club had 23 players on their staff: Tyldesley, Watson, Duckworth, Iddon, Farrimond, Hopwood, Sibbles, Oldfield, Paynter, Parkinson, Elliott, Booth, Hawkwood, Greenhalgh, Nutter, Pollard, Phillipson, Bennett, Wilson, Washbrook, Pearson, Wrigley and Nelson. Five players had been released: young Parkin, Hodgson, Cranfield, Latchford and Horrocks. Cranfield had been engaged by Gloucestershire, Parkin and Latchford had gone to Durham. Horrocks had returned to Australia. T.A. Higson, the County chairman, had had further honours thrust upon him as one of the 1934 Test selectors.

The Australian tour clearly grabbed the headlines throughout the summer, but the Championship proved a most unusual campaign.

At the beginning of June Lancashire were nowhere – tenth with a single victory, and that on 10 May v Somerset, out of seven matches – whereas way out in the lead Sussex had already accumulated six successes. In June Lancashire's luck changed and of seven matches, five were won. The turning point came with the match at Bristol. G.A. Brooking noted at the time:

> The Lancashire bowling has been referred to as very weak, but it is not so harmless as some people make it out to be. Sibbles is often adversely criticised, but let me point out to such critics that Sibbles always possesses the virtue of length, which is the keynote of good bowling. Of what use is spin and swerve if your length is faulty?

Sibbles took nine for 45 in the victory at Bristol, whilst Hopwood made the highest score of his career, 220.

The innings win over Gloucestershire was followed by a similar victory against Worcestershire and one by nine wickets over Hampshire. A much sterner test then presented itself in the guise of Notts at Trent Bridge. Before the match began there were several inflammatory statements regarding bodyline bowling and it appeared that the officials of both counties were at odds with each other. The fact that Larwood took six for 51 and Voce four for 49, as Lancashire were dismissed for 119, did little to ameliorate the ill-feeling. Notts replied with 226, but then Lancashire responded quite remarkably, with 394 for seven declared, Tyldesley and Lister being mainly responsible. Hopwood took advantage of a damp wicket and Lancashire won by 101 with the first ball of the final over. Despite this win, feelings between the two clubs did not improve and their fixtures for 1935 were cancelled.

July brought Lancashire five more wins and only one loss – at the hands of Middlesex – so the County entered August second to Sussex in the table, both teams having eleven wins, but Sussex, having played one match fewer, had a better percentage. Victory against Middlesex at Old Trafford on 14 August – very much a team effort – whilst Sussex's match with Kent was drawn due to rain, moved Lancashire to the head of the Championship. Both teams now had four matches to play. Lancashire failed to win any of theirs, but did gain a first innings lead in all four. Sussex not only failed to win any, but were defeated once, so the title returned to Old Trafford.

The veterans, Ernest Tyldesley and Iddon had almost identical figures at the top of the batting, both making over 2,000 runs and averaging over 55. Hopwood, Watson and Paynter all reached 1,000 at an average above 40. Hopwood was decidely the outstanding figure, for he easily topped the bowling with 110 wickets at 17.89 runs each. He reminded spectators of R.G. Barlow, with his stubborn right-handed batting and his slow to medium left-arm bowling. He opened the innings with Watson and usually came on as first change. He was the first player to perform the 'double' for Lancashire since James Hallows in 1904. Length and flight were his chief allies, but he made great use of the damp wickets so often found at Manchester.

The batting of the leading players was so reliable that Washbrook and Hawkwood were superfluous. The bowling, however, required some reinforcement, as Sibbles, crippled with synovitis, and Booth, absent with a strained shoulder, were not always available. Pollard and Phillipson were brought in and filled the gap quite adequately.

The hard-hitting Lister played in 22 matches and stood in as captain when Eckersley was unavailable.

The profit made by the Club over the year owed everything to the share of the Test matches. The final payment was made on the ground, although the fact that the August Bank Holiday was washed out cost the Club dearly. The Second Eleven, captained by Peter Higson, won the Minor Counties' Championship, Farrimond, Washbrook and H.R.W. Butterworth being the leading batsmen, Phillipson and Pollard the principal bowlers.

The Lancashire committee requested that the third, rather than the traditional fourth, Test be staged at Old Trafford. The weather was exceedingly kind, almost too kind, for the sun blazed down on all four days, the heat being at times unpleasant!

The game was a batsman's paradise. Hendren and Leyland scored hundreds and four others made fifties in England's first innings, whilst McCabe hit 137 for Australia. The only unfortunate was Hopwood, who had been brought in for the first time, and scored two and failed to take a wicket.

Ernest Tyldesley threatened to retire at the end of the season, but he

CYRIL WASHBROOK

The angle of his cap and the jauntiness of his walk to the wicket identified Washbrook even at a distance. He was a batsman who took it upon himself to try and dominate the cricket – both the opposing fielders and the rest of the company gathered to watch him. His favourite strokes were the hook and the on-drive, both of which he executed with relish and both of which proved at times his Achilles' heel.

As a fieldsman he was quite brilliant in the covers, regarded in the immediate post-war period as the best in England. It was in 1946 that his Test partnership with Len Hutton became established and, notably on the tours to Australia in 1946–47 and to South Africa in 1948–49 flourished. In county cricket he is linked with Winston Place, the two forming one of the strongest opening partnerships in first-class cricket.

At the end of his career he was appointed a Test selector and as such was picked for England, after an absence of six years – he scored 98.

His benefit match – v Australians in 1948 – created a record £14,000.

C. Washbrook (NCCC)

was persuaded to carry on and there were no major changes on the staff, save that young Arthur Wrigley's name disappeared – he was to return to public notice much later as a scorer and compiler of the records of others.

Lancashire opened their 1935 season on an indifferent wicket at Lord's – in all four innings only Ernest Tyldesley made an individual fifty. The bowlers, Sims, Robins and Pollard, had a field day, and Middlesex won by five wickets. The team moved on to the Parks and young Washbrook took the opportunity to press his case for a permanent place in the eleven, having been ignored in 1934. He hit 228,

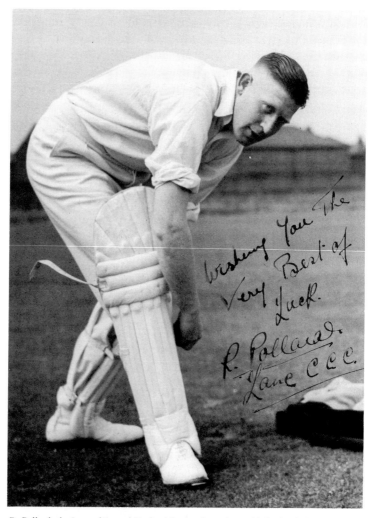

R. Pollard, the Lancashire and England fast bowler, who could also hit the ball very hard (NCCC)

giving only one chance, as Lancashire defeated the undergraduates by an innings. In the next, more serious, contest, he underlined his claims by carrying his bat right through the innings for 49 not out, as his colleagues struggled against Reg Perks, Worcester's fast bowler. Still unsatisfied, Washbrook hit 87 not out in the second innings to bring Lancashire their first win of the summer by nine wickets. In theory Washbrook was only in the side due to the absence of Iddon, but when Iddon did return Washbrook remained, and was in fact awarded his county cap.

The Championship soon turned into a two horse race – Yorkshire and Derbyshire – and the former won the title with ease, having a clear lead with three matches still to play.

Although Lancashire had to be content with fourth place, the development of their younger players was apparent to everyone. Washbrook has been mentioned, but another batsman who seemed to spring from nowhere, Norman Oldfield, reached 1,000 runs and the manner in which he made them provoked the forecast that he would shortly be capped for England. Quick-footed, he got right to the pitch of the ball and his drives were clean and crisp.

As a bowler Dick Pollard made a great advance. His deliveries possessed a bite which most of his rivals missed and he enhanced his chances of an England place by some alert fielding in the slips. Both Washbrook and Oldfield excelled in the outfield, so Lancashire's unwanted tag as a poor fielding eleven was at last thrown off.

Peter Eckersley was returned as an MP for the Exchange Division of Manchester in November and resigned his post as captain; the 24-year-old Lister, who came from Formby, was chosen to replace him.

Another retirement which touched on Lancashire was that of W. Findlay as secretary to MCC. He had left the County in 1907 to join Surrey and then graduated to Lord's.

Season 1936 began, for Lancashire, full of hope. The talented younger players, Washbrook, Oldfield, Phillipson and Pollard, seemed capable of pushing Lancashire back to the top. It was not to be. With the exception of Pollard, the younger generation either stood still or retreated. Washbrook noted:

> The greater the ambitions, the greater the sense of disappointment when they are not fulfilled. Instead of forging ahead and consolidating my position in 1936, I could do little right. In match after match we played on wet wickets and I soon began to realise that I did not possess the experience for them.

In the middle of the summer he came close to being dropped from the eleven, only keeping his place due to others' injuries. Oldfield's average dropped from 35 to 26, and Washbrook's from 40 to 23.

J.L. Hopwood, who performed the Double in 1934 and 1935 (NCCC)

Ernest Tyldesley stated he would play only if needed and then as an amateur – he had two Championship innings all season; Watson also faded from the side. The batting relied very much on Paynter, Iddon and Hopwood.

As for the bowling, *The Cricketer* described it as: 'correctly adequate, of the politely up and down sort of stuff for the most part, keeping the batsmen playing but not over-worrying them'.

Lister did not receive many bouquets for his leadership. On some occasions he made unwise declarations and on the field there were occasions when it was debatable who was in command.

The County could win only seven matches and fell to 11th place in the table. If it had not been for a tremendous boost during August, Lancashire might well have been fighting with Glamorgan and North-ants for the wooden spoon. On 4 August, Lancashire, with just two wins all summer, were in 15th place. Victory over Kent broke the spell, but this win was due only to a sporting declaration by Kent. There were then successes over Northants and Glamorgan which breathed some fight back into the side and with Lister hitting a century in 110 minutes and good bowling by Parkinson, Middlesex were beaten at Lord's by ten wickets.

In the first of the Roses matches, Warburton, who had played for Lancashire very briefly in 1929, impressed with his medium-paced bowling and was catapulted straight into the Test trial a few days later. He had little chance, to shine and disappeared back to the Central Lancashire League, where he played for Littleborough.

India were the 1936 tourists and were allotted three Tests, the second of which took place at Old Trafford. It was a three day game and a high-scoring draw. Duckworth was chosen for all three Tests and this recognition cheered him, for he certainly was back at the top of his form for Lancashire. The County were embarrassingly beaten by the Indians at Liverpool – one of only two counties to suffer that fate.

One domestic point which came up in committee was the fact that certain candidates for the committee had been sending circulars round to members to canvass their vote and 'using even more undesirable methods' to secure election. The committee expressed the hope that members would not in future give their support to such undignified approaches.

With subscriptions and gate receipts dropping, the Club just managed to make a small surplus.

The death occurred in late January of Walter Brearley. He had spent the last few years going to Lord's to give instruction in the nets and his death came as quite a shock to the cricketing community. The Lancashire treasurer, Albert Stockton, stated that only the previous year, Brearley had deplored the lack of first-class bowling in international cricket. Although 59, he claimed that he was the only accurate bowler of pace in England. Mr Stockton went on to recall how Brearley always jumped over the pavilion railings when going in to bat, rather than using the gate, and that once for a bet he had jumped over a billiard table. Brearley took particular delight in not only flattening the stumps but actually breaking them and at home he spent hours on end bowling at a single stump, the extent of his practice only being limited by the supply of old stumps. So passed away one of the greatest and most controversial of all Lancashire's cricketers.

The County made no changes on the ground-staff for 1937. The season opened with three successive draws, in two of which Lancashire were seen at a distinct disadvantage. The Whitsun match came early, on 15 May, and Neville Cardus was not impressed:

A small crowd at Old Trafford on Saturday saw Lancashire play small cricket. The batting was weak in spirit and skill. This match has lost character; the old masters may have been slow making their runs, but they were slow with a difference. The players to-day do not score quickly, because they cannot; the men of the Makepeace–Hallows tradition did not score quickly because they would not ... On

Saturday a ball actually hit a batsman's pad and nobody appealed. What is more the bowler's name was Robinson. The Lancashire and Yorkshire match has obviously gone to the dogs; it has become refined. In the glorious years, if a ball were thrown to the wicket and it accidentally struck a batsman's pad between overs, why, there was, by honoured custom, an involuntary, if half-suppressed 'How's that?' from Emmott. Nobody glares down the wicket nowadays, as George Macaulay always did whenever an umpire said, 'Not out'.

Yorkshire went on to win by ten wickets. The press suggested that H.R.W. Butterworth should be persuaded to turn out for Lancashire. Captain of Littleborough, his only other cricket seemed to be an occasional outing with the Minor Counties or Lancashire Seconds – the latter were now being led by T.A. Higson jun, who had replaced his elder brother Peter.

Butterworth did not appear and by the beginning of June, Lancashire were in 12th place, with a solitary win in seven matches. Phillipson brought some glimmer of a new dawn on a drying wicket at Lord's when he took six for 63 and bowled Lancashire to victory by 22 runs, after they had been 136 behind on first innings. He then took five for 70 to dismiss Essex for 199, Paynter rediscovered his batting with an innings of 266 and Sibbles and Pollard were inspired to remove Essex cheaply in the second innings, so a second win in succession moved Lancashire into the middle of the table.

By the last week in July the side had sunk back to 11th place with a series of draws, one win and two losses. Paynter then exceeded all his previous efforts. He was opening the batting with Washbrook. The pair had put on 268 against Sussex at Hove, when Washbrook went for 108. Oldfield joined Paynter in a stand worth 271 in 135 minutes and by the time Paynter had made 322 in 300 minutes, the total had reached 546. At last the batting had done enough to give the bowlers something to work at and Lancashire gained victory by an innings. Perhaps the all-round improvement was a tribute to Ted McDonald, who had been killed in a motor accident in the early hours of the morning of 22 July, near Bolton; he had been playing for Blackpool this season and was aged 46.

The August Bank Holiday game was staged at Bramall Lane. Sutcliffe scored his 100th century for Yorkshire by tea on the first day, but from then the match belonged to Lancashire. Some good all-round batting, followed by Iddon's bowl of a life-time – nine for 42 – gave Lancashire victory by five wickets. Cardus had forgotten all his wailing in May and suggested that the brass band with mayor and corporation should greet Lancashire on their return to Old Trafford: it was the first Lancashire victory at Sheffield since 1899.

Lancashire celebrated the great event in no uncertain manner. They beat Gloucestershire at Manchester; they beat Notts at Trent Bridge; they beat Kent back at Old Trafford. By the middle of August they found themselves elevated to sixth place. If the two matches which followed had not been ruined by the rain – and in both Lancashire declared soon after obtaining first innings points, they might well have come a respectable fourth, but it was not to be and when the sun broke out again, the County had lost its impetus and fell down badly against Gloucestershire and Essex. The batting failed in both matches and against Essex they could score only 108 and 84. They were fortunate to escape defeat in the final match at Taunton, for when play ended, the last Lancashire pair were at the crease and the deficit 124.

The County had to settle for 11th place. Paynter was out on his own as the best batsman, but both Washbrook and Iddon could feel pleased with their records. Washbrook was ranked as the best young stroke-player in the country, even above Hutton, Compton and Edrich. Oldfield at times played brilliant cricket, but his concentration was apt to waver and a new recruit had been discovered in Winston Place, a 22-year-old from Rawtenstall. He had been carefully tutored by Makepeace and his defensive play was reminiscent of the old coach. Watson did not play regularly and at the season's end retired from county cricket. His perseverance had been equalled by few and annoyed the opposing bowlers more than the spectators.

Of the bowlers, Sibbles had marginally the best record, but Phillipson improved vastly. He was regarded as the best bowler of his type in the country and needed just a little more stamina to push him into Test cricket. Pollard and Phillipson both topped 100 wickets, but the former was not as effective as in 1936 and did not vary his deliveries as much. Two amateurs were tried, A.J. Birtwell, a solicitor from Nelson, who had played for Buckinghamshire, and Cecil Rhodes from Lancaster CC. The former was a leg-break bowler and the latter a slow left-arm. Both were rather expensive. A third spinner was found in Len Wilkinson, who seemed the most promising.

In the close season, Duckworth announced he was retiring to take up journalism, but would be available in emergency. He was only 36 and the Lancashire side would certainly sound different without his appealing, though in Farrimond they had an excellent replacement.

New Zealand, the 1937 tourists, played three Tests, the second being at Old Trafford. England won, but only 15,000 people attended over the three days. Paynter represented Lancashire.

The return of the Australians under Bradman took preference over county news on the sports pages in the spring of 1938. E.E. Burrows, a wicket-keeper from Stockton Heath, E. Price, a slow left-arm bowler from Middleton and J.T. Ikin, an all-rounder from Bignall End, joined the Old Trafford staff, and Tom Jacques, a medium-pace bowler who had appeared in two games in 1937 left to take up a business appointment.

Lancashire began the campaign with wins over Worcestershire and Hampshire, but going to Liverpool for their third match, the County were undone by the weather, in that Derbyshire batted in perfect conditions, whilst Copson, Pope and Mitchell, all bowlers of great resource, revelled in the conditions produced by a drop of rain. Lancashire were dismissed for 171 and 90.

This proved a temporary upset, as the Club beat in succession Essex, Middlesex, Northants and Derbyshire (at Ilkeston). On 31 May, Lancashire were at last back at the head of the counties, with six wins from seven matches.

The Whitsun match at Bradford was watched by 46,000 over the three days, but the Saturday saw Lancashire go back to their tedious style of batting and they spent the whole day, or almost all, making 232. Yorkshire were scarcely any better until Turner and Sellers added 98. The match appeared to be heading for a draw, then directly after lunch on the third day the last six wickets of Lancashire's second innings fell, mainly to Verity, for 18. Yorkshire knocked off the 98 needed with ease. Neville Cardus was aghast – he thought it the worst defeat ever inflicted on Lancashire, because the Yorkshire team was the poorest which had ever taken the field: the fact that it included Hutton, Sutcliffe, Verity, Leyland, Bowes and Mitchell appeared to mean little to the far-famed scribe.

Lancashire then had an exciting win by two wickets over Kent and an easy if protracted win against Glamorgan, which, in combination with several draws meant that on 1 July they were second to Yorkshire, with little to chose between them, though Middlesex in third position were close behind. The County went through July without meeting with defeat, but there were rather too many drawn matches, and so when they entertained Yorkshire at Old Trafford, the teams were actually level on percentages, both having twelve wins from 18 matches.

The match was billed as the tussle of the season. Phillipson was missing from the Lancashire side, but Hutton was unable to play for Yorkshire. Lister won the toss and decided to bat on a rain-affected wicket. Verity, Bowes and Robinson disposed of Lancashire by 4 o'clock. On the holiday Monday nearly 30,000 assembled to see a hundred from Leyland and Yorkshire reach 453. Further rain then made the pitch difficult for Lancashire a second time and by half past twelve it was all over, Verity having taken 5 for 21 and only Paynter lasting long. It was the first time that Yorkshire had done the double against their arch rivals since 1909 and barring accidents it settled the 1938

Championship. Whilst Yorkshire went on to win six more matches, Lancashire, the stuffing knocked out of them, could only chalk up two more successes. They had to be content with 14 wins and fourth place in the table.

No fewer than six Lancashire batsmen reached 1,000 runs in Championship matches. On the hard wickets found during the first half of the season, the leading batsmen usually found runs flowing freely. Paynter, Washbrook, Oldfield, Iddon and Hopwood all enjoyed themselves, as did one unknown, Albert Nutter. *The Cricketer* noted: 'Nutter is that rare thing in modern cricket, a genuine all-rounder, excellent as a bat and a useful medium-pace bowler.' He had appeared on and off before, but this was his first full season and he completely justified his selection. Nutter scored 1,128 runs at 33.77 and took 84 wickets at 24.02.

The difficulty so far as Nutter and Lancashire were concerned was that he bowled in a similar manner to Pollard and Phillipson, so that Wilkinson alone provided the spin. Wilkinson might be regarded as the discovery of the year. He rarely pitched short, and turned the ball from leg, as well as possessing a very craftily disguised googly. His 136 Championship wickets cost 22.66 runs each and there was talk of him being selected for the Test against Australia, but instead he gained a place in the MCC side to South Africa for the coming winter.

There were others who attracted attention. A tall left hander, standing over 6 feet, D.M. Matthews, the amateur from Formby, failed to obtain his blue at Oxford, but he was, according to Cecil Parkin, a brilliant hard-hitting batsman with a great future. Ken Cranston, the Liverpool University student, caused quite a stir with his innings of 289 in about three hours at Eastbourne, for a wandering club side. His days in county cricket were, however, a long way off.

The Test matches proved a great success for Paynter, who scored an unbeaten 216 at Trent Bridge and 99 at Lord's, but failed to score in the famous record-breaking match at the Oval, when England declared at 903 for seven. He was Lancashire's only cricketer to be chosen for England.

For Old Trafford the embarrassment of the season was the third Test. The entire match was washed out with not a single ball bowled, and thus it emulated the 1890 game. Despite this the Club showed a profit on the year of £4,062. Hopwood had been given the Surrey game as a benefit, but he was not so fortunate. Less than £140 came in in the three days, and there was no insurance against rain.

There was an interesting list published at the start of 1939 on the sizes of the various ground in England, and the only ones which could accommodate more than 30,000 spectators were:

Headingley	5 acres playing area	37,000
Old Trafford	170 yds by 160 yds	35,000
The Oval	190 yds by 180 yds	33,000
Trent Bridge	193 yds by 180 yds	32,000
Lord's	180 yds by 145 yds	32,000

The great experiment of 1939 was the eight-ball over. Early impressions were quite favourable; Robertson-Glasgow commented:

> The eight-ball over, I fancy, will pass from a Bill into a Law. It has created widely varying impressions among players and spectators, but in the main the views are favourable. It saves time, and, so far, though it may have taxed the weaker arithmeticians among umpires, it has not been noticed to induce faintness or exhaustion among bowlers.

Lancashire certainly got off to a good start. Lister, afraid of Tom Goddard, put Gloucester in to bat on the Wagon Works ground. Barnett made a hundred, but the rest could do little more between them than double the opener's 120. Lancashire obtained a small first innings lead, then Phillipson, who had been so often absent through injury in the last few seasons, returned figures of 11.6-4-18-7, bowling out Gloucester for 79. Lancashire had an easy win. The rest of May did not prove so fruitful – quite the reverse, for there were two losses and the other games were drawn. The final match of the month was the Yorkshire visit to Old Trafford. On the Saturday Lancashire fiddled about until they were 188 for eight. Pollard then arrived to join Nutter and in 75 minutes the pair added 108. It was a great revival, but Yorkshire were not impressed and ground out their runs until 528 were on the board, at which point Sellers declared, the lead being 228. The last day belonged to Bill Bowes; he took six for 43 and Lancashire lost by an innings.

Lancashire took their revenge on lowly Hampshire, winning by an innings, as Wilkinson's leg-breaks produced the best figures of his career – eight for 53. An innings victory followed as Paynter batted in his best vein, scoring 222 off the Derbyshire attack, and when Hampshire, in the return at Southampton, dared to set Lancashire 385 in the fourth innings, Hopwood and Iddon hit hundreds as a third successive win was added to the ledger. Lancashire moved up into sixth place, but were well behind Yorkshire, Gloucestershire and Middlesex. Those three counties kept adding to their total, whilst Lancashire did little more than tread water. By the time the August Bank Holiday fixture was imminent, Lancashire were in no way going to challenge Yorkshire for the title. The Red Rose county struggled to reach 217 in the first innings, but then caused a surprise by dismissing Yorkshire for

163. Ellis Robinson again caused problems for Lancashire in the later stages of the match and picked up eight for 35, which allowed Yorkshire to knock off the winning runs just before the ground was flooded by a thunderstorm.

Lister was unable to captain the side in this match owing to his Territorial Army duties and T.A. Higson junior came into the side, as did another amateur, J.M. Brocklebank. This in fact was the latter's first-class debut. A native of Cheshire, he had made a name for himself in club cricket on Merseyside as a leg-break bowler. Soon after the match it was announced that Brocklebank was one of three non-regular first-class players to be included in the team to tour India in 1939–40 – Mobey of Surrey and S.C. Griffith being the other two. The team, of course, never left England.

Another young player who hit the headlines in the second half of 1939 was Winston Place. The Rawtenstall opener had been unable to get into the County side in 1938 and his opportunities were very limited in 1939, but he played instead of Paynter against the West Indies at Old Trafford, and opened the innings with Washbrook. Washbrook made 12, but Place hit 164 without making a single mistake, being in 270 minutes.

Lancashire ran into good form in mid-August, beating Notts, Glamorgan, Kent and Northants. The season was then being overtaken by the impending outbreak of war. The Lancashire match with Surrey ended abruptly on the second day due to the political situation, and the final fixture, against Leicestershire, never started. Lancashire finished the season with ten wins and sixth place in the Championship.

Rain badly interfered with the second of the three Tests against West Indies, which was played at Old Trafford, Hardstaff making the highest score in a very unsatisfactory game. For the third Test, England found a place for Norman Oldfield and the debutant played an excellent innings with some beautiful late cuts and leg glances; Oldfield took the place of Paynter, who had failed twice in the previous match.

The main weakness in the 1939 County side was the bowling. Wilkinson suffered a hand injury and he looked a completely different bowler to the one who had gained accolades galore in 1938. Nutter also failed as a bowler, though his batting remained more than useful. Suddenly Lancashire almost returned to the days when they possessed just two effective bowlers, but as pointed out previously Phillipson and Pollard were too much of a muchness. Iddon and Hopwood appeared more as batsmen than bowlers and Brocklebank made little impact. There were two professionals in their mid-twenties who might train on, W.B. Roberts and R.G. Garlick. The former was slow left-arm and hailed from Kirkham, whilst Garlick, medium pace, came from Kirkby Lonsdale.

The war-scarred pavilion at Old Trafford in 1946

The batting, with Iddon, Washbrook, Paynter and Oldfield, was generally very attractive and the fielding vastly superior to what Lancashire supporters had seen in recent years. Washbrook and Oldfield were quite outstanding. Nutter caught some very difficult catches.

On the outbreak of war Old Trafford was requisitioned by the Army and a unit of the Royal Engineers stationed there. In the winter of 1940–41 Manchester suffered from the Luftwaffe and Old Trafford took its share of the blitz. In one raid a sentry on the main gate was killed. Regarding structural damage, the groundsman's house, two of the stands and the top of the pavilion, as well as the great dining room, were the main casualties. The playing area itself was cratered by bombs.

In the latter part of the war, the Army moved out and the Ministry of Supply took charge, filling the site with packing cases of all shapes and sizes. T.A. Higson and Captain Howard, now promoted to Major, continued to do some administrative work for the Cricket Club.

In 1940 the County Club arranged no matches, but appealed to members to continue their subscriptions at half the normal fee; 1,767 members responded. A twelve-a-side match between Lancashire and West Indies was staged at Fazakerley in September 1941 and attracted about 10,000 spectators; the receipts went to the Lord Mayor of Liverpool's Charity Fund. The Lancashire side was C. Hallows, W. Place, C, Washbrook, N. Oldfield, J. Iddon, E. Paynter, F.M. Sibbles, G. Duckworth, W.E. Phillipson, J. Holroyd, L. Warburton and A. Wrigley, thus not far below full strength. The one-day game was drawn.

A series of Lancashire charity matches were played during the 1942 season, organised by A.D. Proctor. The total attendance was about 125,000, which averaged about 5,000 per match and the charities benefited by £3,500.

A similar programme was arranged in 1943, and J.B. Holmes and G.S. Cadman, both of the county committee, assisted by Mr Proctor and Charles Leatherbarrow of Southport, also arranged teams and matches.

In 1944 cricket returned to Old Trafford in the guise of three Services matches and the Club announced that despite the damage to buildings, it would be possible to resume ordinary matches when the war finished. The Lancashire Committee were in the forefront of the proposal for some sort of knock-out competition between the first-class counties. In the first Services match, played on 3 June, the most notable feature was the bowling of Pollard, who took six for 19, dismissing the RAAF XI for 44. The end of the war was in sight.

THE START OF A NEW ERA

THE LANCASHIRE COMMITTEE SAW THE problems which faced them in relation to the rebuilding of Old Trafford as a Test ground and their response was the designing of a magnificent stadium which would accommodate 40,000 people and involve the demolition of all but one of the existing stands. The cost was estimated at £100,000, and in due course an appeal was launched. By December 1945 £11,300 had already been raised.

When the war in Europe ended the County Club inspected its resources. The groundsman, Williams, had returned the actual playing area to its pre-war condition. As to the players, the only leading Lancashire cricketer to be killed on active service was Peter Eckersley, the former captain, who died in 1940 whilst serving in the RNVR. Though Paynter decided he was too old to resume his county career and Farrimond at 42 was nearing his retirement, W.H.L. Lister, Washbrook, Iddon, Oldfield, Pollard, Phillipson, Wilkinson, Nutter and Place formed the nucleus of a good side. In addition there were several of the colts of 1939 keen to build a career in county cricket: Roberts, who had bowled well in wartime matches, E. Price and John Briggs, two left-arm slow bowlers, and J. Bowes the tall fast bowler. Major Howard had two sons, N.D. and B.J. Howard, both keen cricketers. T.L. Brierley, the former Glamorgan player, was now living in Lancashire and it was possible that two amateurs, M.L.Y. Ainsworth and John Dewes might join the County.

A.W. Goodall was appointed in July as the honorary treasurer of the appeal fund and a brochure was issued showing the proposed new pavilion, which itself would provide seating for 5,000 members. This brochure coincided with the first post-war Roses match, staged at Old Trafford on 2 and 3 July 1945. The two-day game, which was played with the same edge as its predecessors, ended in a draw when Yorkshire failed in the final innings to make 100 in 100 minutes. The highest innings of the game was 64 scored by the hard-htting left-hander William Barron from County Durham, who had moved to Lancashire. Pollard was Lancashire's most effective bowler, but for Yorkshire Arthur Booth took eight for 54 in the second innings.

The most important fixture at Old Trafford, however, was the fifth Victory Test, between England and the Australian Services. On the first day the gates were closed with 28,000 spectators in the ground. They saw a brilliant innings by Keith Miller, but also Pollard and Phillipson dismiss the Australians for 173. On the second day, Washbrook, the third Lancashire player in the side, showed that he had possibilities as a

Test cricketer. England won the three-day game by six wickets; 72,463 paid at the gate.

Ideas of two-day cricket and of a knock-out competition did not materialise and by the time April 1946 had arrived, the Advisory County Committee had arranged a Championship fixture list very similar to 1939, though the eight-ball over had vanished.

Lancashire's playing hopes had, however, taken several knocks since the general survey of possible strength which had been undertaken in 1945. Nutter and Oldfield had abandoned the County Club in favour of League cricket; Farrimond had decided he did not have time to devote to county cricket and most tragic of all, Iddon, who had decided to play as an amateur, was killed in a road accident in April 1946. Another serious problem occurred when the proposed captain, T.A. Higson jnr, had to withdraw. The committee chose as replacement J.A. Fallows, son of the honorary treasurer of the County Club. He had captained the Manchester club for ten years up to 1939 and so was familiar with Old Trafford and its players, even if the public at large were unaware of his presence.

To fill the other gaps, the Club engaged B.P. King, formerly of Worcestershire, and two of Bill Edrich's brothers, E.H. and G.A. In reserve were Fred Cooper from Bacup, whose brother played for Worcester, and Alan Wharton from Heywood.

The first-class season for Lancashire began with a warm-up game at Fenner's. The drawn game saw Washbrook, Place, King, Brierley and Phillipson all make runs, as did Ikin, who with Roberts proved the most successful bowler. When the county matches started Lancashire quickly found their feet and by the end of June, with nine wins, including five in succession between 12 and 28 June, they were leading the Championship.

At this stage the Lancashire batsmen were particularly prominent; Washbrook stood third in the averages, whilst King, Phillipson, and G.A. Edrich were also in the top twenty. Price and Roberts were the best of the bowlers.

One of the surprise selections for the first of the Test trials was Jack Ikin. A stylish left-hand batsman and useful leg-break bowler, he took three for 30, as well as scoring 56. Ten days later found Ikin making his Test debut against India. In the second Test trial, Eric Price was given a place, but the slow left-arm bowler from Middleton did not go on to join Ikin on the boat with Hammond's team to Australia. Washbrook's ability was also recognised by the selectors and his partnership with Hutton, which had begun during the Victory Tests in 1945, continued.

The second of the three Tests was staged at Old Trafford towards the end of July. Washbrook and Ikin were joined at the last minute by Pollard in the England side for this Test – Pollard took the place of Peter Smith of Essex who was in the original team, but had to stand down due to injury. Lancashire thus had three players for their home Test. The match ended in great excitement as the last pair of Indian batsmen clung on to avoid defeat.

Returning to the Championship, Lancashire's successes fell away in the second half of the season. Fallows was unlucky with the toss. Two races against the clock failed narrowly and on a few occasions the second string players who were called upon failed to make the necessary adjustments to first-class cricket. Lancashire thus finished in third place, behind Yorkshire and Middlesex, but their tally of fifteen wins from 26 Championship games was very creditable.

The batting, after an initial weakness in the middle order was adjusted, was the County's strong suit. Washbrook, with every shot in the book, including a distinctive square cut, had an outstanding summer – with 2,400 runs in all first-class matches he was second only to Hammond. Place had a deadly cover drive and an ability to hit the ball over the bowler's head; he also played some very good innings on wet wickets. Ikin and Geoffrey Edrich both averaged about 35 and for their first full season of county cricket did more than could be expected. Of King, the *Manchester Guardian* noted:

Winston Place, who opened the innings with Washbrook

King's batting has all the necessary alloys. They have been poured into the mould, but they are not yet cooled off and set. Temperamentally he needs to introduce a rounder philosophy to tone down the spasmodic, often savage, violence of his hitting.

Alan Wharton made two Championship hundreds and his left-handed batting contained a freshness which hopefully he could still retain whilst learning more of his trade. The tail had character and sometimes came off.

Pollard, who missed matches through his army service and also Test calls, was rather overbowled when he did turn out, but still proved very effective. His new ball partner, Phillipson, suffered from ill-health and did not like the soft wickets which sapped his confidence, but he still returned good figures. Roberts, tossing his slow deliveries high, was unfortunate not to be picked for Australia; Price was the more aggressive of the two slow bowlers, and headed the Championship averages with 82 wickets at 18.19 each. Garlick and Ikin were useful supports – Ikin was quite brilliant in the field.

The wicket-keeping was the main weakness. Brierley was tried first, but failed and Eric Edrich took over. Fallows, a genial character, proved a good captain and his leadership produced a side which made the best of all its members. His weakness was that his batting relied too much on a half-hearted defensive prod, when if he had trusted to his attacking strokes he would have made many more runs.   .

Financially the Club did well and £4,500 was added to the building appeal fund. Having enjoyed, considering the unknown factors at the season's opening, a very good summer in 1946, Lancashire's committee, for reasons never fully explained, sacked Fallows. The actual dismissal was bungled as Fallows first learnt of his fate through the press and this ham-fistedness by the committee did not pass unnoticed in the dressing room.

The new captain was Ken Cranston. Cranston was a talented local cricketer, but with no experience of the first-class game, and what was more surprising about his selection was the fact that he made it clear that he did not envisage a long-term future in County cricket.

On the credit side, however, Harry Makepeace, still in 1947 the County's coach, regarded Cranston as the most talented youngster ever to be coached by him. The professional staff of 1947 saw only one absentee compared with 1946: Fred Cooper went to join his brother at Worcester. Three new faces were Roy Tattersall, a tall gangly youth from Bolton, John Kelly, a batsman from Bacup and Alfred Barlow, a wicket-keeper from Little Lever.

The first half of the 1947 fixtures went well up to a point. Not a single defeat was recorded, but there were only five wins. Batting at number six, Cranston rarely failed to score some useful runs, and his medium-pace bowling picked up several wickets in most matches. His all-round figures were such that he caught the eye of the selectors, and when the Old Trafford Test arrived, found himself joining Cyril Washbrook in the England side. It was a rapid and remarkable race up cricket's ladder and to take Cranston's story a stage further, he went to the West Indies with the 1947–48 MCC side, and in Allen's absence led his country in a Test, scarcely nine months after he had first set foot in first-class cricket.

The main criticism of Cranston in his first year of captaincy was his failure to take advice from the senior professionals, preferring instead the mandarins in the committttee room. Certainly on one or two occasions Lancashire might have won matches which through the captain's inexperience were drawn. The difference this made in the Championship race was crucial, for it meant that Lancashire trailed behind in third, fourth or fifth place, whilst the battle for the title was fought between Gloucestershire and Middlesex. In August Lancashire came nearer their true potential, winning six out of seven matches following a drawn Roses battle, and the seventh game ended as a tie.

The tie was at Dean Park, Bournemouth, where Hampshire set the visitors 221 in 135 minutes. Washbrook and Place appeared to have the game well in hand with an opening stand of 142 in 90 minutes, but Bailey then took six for 29 in six overs. The scores were level when the ninth man was run out, but Roberts had earlier broken a finger and was unable to come to the wicket, so the match was tied.

The two Roses games lived up to the traditional image and attracted huge crowds, though at Bramall Lane in August Lancashire were very much on the defensive when stumps were drawn.

The successes in August placed Lancashire clearly in third place with 13 wins from 26 matches – and only one loss, at Frome when Washbrook, Cranston and Place (the last as twelfth man) were representing England. In this low-scoring match some hurricane hitting from Wellard at number ten proved decisive.

The chief reason for Lancashire's run of August victories was the return to form of Pollard. He ended the summer with 131 Championship victims at 18.52 each. His partner, Phillipson, though given ample opportunity, failed to find his form and was dropped from the side in favour of Bowes, but the latter tried to bowl too fast. Of the spinners, Price was unable to command a place in the side, Roberts being preferred, and though Roberts finished second to Pollard in the table, he was not at all effective on the dry wickets of August. Garlick lost his place in the side, perhaps because he was torn between off-breaks and swing bowling. Both Price and Garlick left Lancashire for other counties at the end of the year.

The batting maintained the standard of the end of 1946. Washbrook

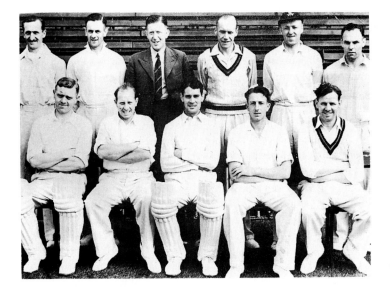

Lancashire 1947. Standing: R.G. Garlick, W.E. Phillipson, R. Pollard, Williamson, E. Price, T.L. Brierley. Seated: W. Place, E.H. Edrich, J.T. Ikin, G.A. Edrich, W.B. Roberts (Lancashire CCC)

and his partner, Place, both had very productive seasons, Place actually reaching 2,000 runs in the 26 Championship games, whilst Washbrook was third behind Compton and Edrich in the first-class averages. With his jaunty walk and his air of mastery, Washbrook was the Cock O' the North.

Ikin, though no longer in the England side and handicapped by illness and injury, did not find his feet until late on, but Geoffrey Edrich made a significant advance.

Brierley scored a hundred against Glamorgan, but Eric Edrich did little and Barlow took over as wicket-keeper. B.J. Howard, the younger son of the secretary, scored two Championship hundreds, after doing little in his first few matches. The elder brother also played, captaining the side when Cranston was absent.

The appeal fund reached £37,149 by the year's end, still a long way short of the £100,000 requested.

After an absence of ten years, the Australians came to England in 1948. Once more Don Bradman stole the headlines and county cricket was overshadowed. At Old Trafford, Brierley was appointed as Makepeace's assistant, and four youngsters were brought on to the staff: Greenwood, the Burnley centre forward; Berry, from Longsight, a slow left-arm bowler; E.F.W. Highton from Formby, who bowled medium pace; and F.D. Parr from Wallasey Grammar School, a wicket-keeper. Of those who no longer remained, King went to Bingley in the

Bradford League; Wilkinson, who scarcely played in 1946, went to Barrow.

For Lancashire 1948 was a season of high scores. Only on three occasions did Lancashire fail to obtain a first-innings lead over their opponents and more often than not the lead was a substantial one. Cranston came in for criticism on account of his delayed declarations and there was no doubt that some of the 15 drawn Championship matches could have been turned into victories, if a more adventurous spirit had lurked at Old Trafford. In the great run glut, Washbrook turned in an average of 92.73 for Championship games and in all first-class matches was far ahead of the rest of English batsmen. Washbrook was appropriately rewarded, for he was given the match against the Australians for his benefit and endded with a record £14,000. Place, after his winter in the West Indies, had a poor summer and his average depended very largely on four big innings, including a double hundred against Somerset at Taunton.

Ikin came second to Washbrook in terms of average and was particularly good in August. Geoffrey Edrich and Wharton both missed games through illness and Nigel Howard among the younger players

(second from left in front row) Ken Cranston, who captained Lancashire and England during his brief first-class career, pictured with some England colleagues, including T.G. Evans, J.A. Young, R.E.S. Wyatt and R. Pollard (NCCC)

made the biggest advance, reaching nearly 1,000 runs; little was seen of his brother.

Cranston remained the principal all-rounder, but appeared in only one Test. Roberts was the top of the bowling and some of his admirers were disappointed that he failed to interest the Test selectors. A younger bowler who became a nine-day wonder was Malcolm Hilton, who in his third County match dismissed the Don twice. The 19-year-old left-arm spinner from Oldham caught the headlines. He went on to appear in about half the Lancashire matches and came second to Roberts in the bowling table.

The County's main concern was not spin, however, but the lack of an opening partner for Pollard. Two bowlers who were more naturally of a slower variety were persuaded to bowl quickies as Pollard's assistant, but Tattersall and Greenwood were neither happy nor effective.

The wicket-keeping problem resurfaced. Barlow suffered from injured hands and both Eric Edrich and Brierley were reinstated. Both scored a fair amount of runs, but it did not solve the keeper's post.

Ken Cranston, having made it clear that he could afford only two full seasons of county cricket, resigned as captain when the 1948 summer ended and the committee chose Nigel Howard to be the 1949 leader. His father had left the secretary's post at Old Trafford, and rather confusingly, another Howard, Cecil Geoffrey, took over. C.G. Howard, no relation to Rupert, had been assistant secretary at the Oval and had played three games for Middlesex as a middle order batsman in 1930. Geoffrey Howard was a southerner coming into a job which was one of the most complex in England, if for no other reason than the juxtaposition of the County Club and the powerful Leagues. The County Club was still ruled by T.A. Higson, whose spell as chairman of the committee now outran the memories of all the current playing staff and most of the other officials. This Manchester City Councillor ruled the County Club almost as a dictator. He had developed over the years a knack of controlling both Annual General Meetings and committee meetings and his refusal to tolerate opposition produced many enemies, but his firm hand, hard work and dedication to Lancashire cricket did a vast deal of good for cricket in the County.

The full professional staff for 1949 was: R. Alderson, A. Barlow, R. Berry, G.A. Edrich, T. Greenough, P. Greenwood, K.J. Grieves, E. Highton, J. Hilton, M. Hilton, J.T. Ikin, J. Ingham, J. Kelly, J.G. Lomax, F.D. Parr, W. Place, R. Pollard, W.B. Roberts, S. Smith, R. Tattersall, C. Washbrook, A. Wharton, A. Wilson.

The most noteworthy recruit was Ken Grieves, the 23-year-old all-rounder from Sydney, who had played for New South Wales. He had been engaged in the Leagues and thus qualified by residence for Lancashire.

Before the season opened it was announced that the re-building fund had reached £40,793 and would close at the end of the summer. The idea of demolishing and rebuilding the Pavilion had been abandoned, since it had been discovered that it was not so seriously damaged by the wartime bombing as had been originally assumed.

By the time the first month of the season had gone it was clear that on the dry wickets the County did not have the fast bowlers to dismiss the opposition cheaply. Runs were needed but unfortunately Washbrook damaged a hand and was forced to miss several matches, whilst Place took some time to find his form. So when the Whitsun game against Yorkshire came round, the County found themselves 12th in the Championship table with only one win from six matches.

Len Hutton became only the third player to score 200 in a Roses match and his batting – he made an unbeaten 91 in the second innings – enabled Yorkshire to declare twice. Grieves and Wharton, the former dropped four times, managed to force a draw after Lancashire had lost four cheap wickets in their second innings when requiring 318 to win.

The first Test of 1949 – at Headingly against New Zealand – came a week after the drawn match with Yorkshire. To the surprise of many, there were two Lancashire cricketers in the England side: Washbrook, who scored an unbeaten 100, and Alan Wharton, who was batting in quite brilliant form and at the time of selection was fifth in the first-class averages. He was in fact rapidly approaching his total run aggregate for the previous year. The one depressing event in the Test was that Washbrook pulled a leg muscle and scored much of his hundred with a runner. This injury was to irritate him for the remainder of the season.

Whilst the Test was being played, Lancashire produced their most emphatic victory so far, beating Kent by an innings and 23 runs. Grieves took eight for 90 and was awarded his county cap, whilst Alderson, on his Championship debut, made 55. This win had to be measured against defeats at the hands of Warwickshire, Middlesex, Derbyshire and Gloucestershire, and Lancashire fell to 14th in the table, claiming just two victories. The Derbyshire defeat was the first time that that county had beaten Lancashire since 1938. The single crumb of comfort was the bowling of the 23-year-old fair-haired Bob Berry. A slow left-hander, he was not afraid to give the ball air. Further misfortune occurred when Wharton was injured and had to withdraw from the team for the second Test – it was a personal tragedy for Wharton never again played for England.

The Bacup batsman, Kelly, who had been scoring heavily in the Second Eleven, was brought into the First Eleven, but could hardly be expected to replace the talents of Washbrook or Wharton.

The third Test was staged at Old Trafford. It saw Freddie Brown as

England's captain for the first time; the debut of England's youngest-ever cricketer, 18-year-old Brian Close; a brilliant hundred by Reg Simpson on his Test debut in England, his second fifty coming in 27 minutes. The match, like all the others that year was drawn, but on the Saturday 38,000 watched the game and the gates were closed on a full house.

Three victories in August cheered up Lancashire supporters and the County ended the campaign in 11th place. Surrey were overwhelmed at Old Trafford, when Greenwood and Tattersall bowled well and Greenwood took ten wickets in the victory over Northants. Green-wood was bowling with the new ball and making pace off the pitch, rather than as an off-spinner.

The most pleasant memory of 1949 in Lancashire terms was the dinner to celebrate 100 years of Roses matches, held in the Grand Hotel at Sheffield on 7 October, at which such famous players of the past as E.B. Rowley, R.H. Spooner, C.S. Marriott, Ernest Tyldesley, Harry Makepeace and many more reminisced on times past.

The 1949 season did not contain so many happy memories on the field. The review in *The Cricketer* called the team, like W.S. Gilbert's Navy, an eleven in which all were admirals. The young captain tried to please everyone and ended up by pleasing no one. The Committee came in for much criticism for the way the sides were selected. It was felt that both Kelly and Lomax deserved extended trials, but both were shuffled in and out of the eleven without having a chance to establish themselves. There was an embarrassment of riches in the slow spin department, with the result that Hilton, Berry and Roberts were chosen in rotation. Grieves' leg-breaks did well at the start of the season, but after one or two bad spells he scarcely bowled at all.

The wicket-keeping problem remained unsolved. Alan Wilson from Newton-le-Willows was tried, looked competent, but was then drop-ped in favour of a return to Barlow. The fielding on the whole was variable, despite the presence of such acknowledged experts as Wash-brook, Ikin and Grieves. To an extent this chopping and changing might be attributable to lack of leadership at the top, for T.A. Higson had been severely ill for some time and died at his home, Grange-over-Sands, on 2 August. The committee were in need of a new guiding light.

There were very few changes on the playing staff for 1950. Kelly asked to be released and was specially registered for Derbyshire; Smith and Greenhough were called up for National Service and the Mac-clesfield left-hand bat, P. Hough, was engaged. Stan Worthington, the old Derbyshire and England Test player, replaced Duckworth as Makepeace's assistant. The new chairman of the county committee was Dr J.B. Holmes. A keen club cricketer before the First World War, he was also a director of Manchester United. He announced at the beginning of the year that a new sub-committee whose job was to unearth fresh talent had been formed and that he was anxious to cement firmer ties between the leagues and the County Club.

The most urgent need was for some new faces to open the attack, though it was to be hoped that Pollard would regain his lost form. In the event Pollard was dropped from the side in late May, just after the first victory of the year, against Warwickshire, and the spin of Berry and Tattersall beat Yorkshire at Bramall Lane by 14 runs in the next game. The sudden emergence of Tattersall as a match-winning bowler added to Lancashire's abundance of spinners. Tattersall had a casual, slightly flat-footed run up to the wicket and used his height to great advantage when flighting the ball, and could also make deliveries turn sharply.

Having enabled Lancashire to beat Yorkshire, Tattersall then took eight for 60 in the following drawn match with Surrey, before bringing the County another victory, this time over Gloucestershire, when his match figures were 12 for 68 – Malcolm Hilton took the other eight wickets. By the halfway point, Lancashire were top of the Championship table with eight wins from 16 games and Tattersall top of the first-class bowling averages with 78 wickets at 13.96 each. It was a remarkable change of fortune for both County and bowler – Tattersall had taken 36 wickets at 26 runs each during the whole of 1949.

Inevitably there were some who wondered at the change and the Old Trafford wicket was suspected as being the principal cause. Rex Pogson on 24 June noted

> The Old Trafford wicket is setting the county committee some problems. In order to take advantage of it, Berry and Hilton (as well as Tattersall) were both played against Gloucestershire and Kent, and only one opening bowler was included. This move can be defended for Hilton is good enough for a regular place . . . but in away games on hard wickets the side will find itself in trouble.

However on 17 June, after just three weeks on the staff at Old Trafford, a young fast bowler who had completed his National Service at the beginning of May, made his Championship debut – 'he is tall and has a very good action' was the brief comment. The bowler was Brian Statham.

Statham, from the Manchester suburbs, hit the headlines in the August Bank Holiday match at Old Trafford. The match was crucial to the destiny of the Championship. Lancashire, with 13 wins from 21 games, were 20 points ahead of Yorkshire, at the top of the table, with Surrey third, another 12 points behind. Yorkshire batted first, and Statham, opening the bowling, actually skidded and fell down twice in

JOHN BRIAN STATHAM

At the time of the last of his 70 Test appearances, in 1965, Statham had taken 252 wickets for England. In the history of the game to that year, it was a total exceeded by only one player. In partnership with Trueman or Tyson, Statham was an integral part of the English attack for nearly 15 years. Whilst Trueman and Tyson in their different ways probably frightened out as many batsman before actually delivering the ball as by the skill of their bowling, Statham was content to rely on his two faithful friends, line and length.

Thirteen times he took one hundred wickets in an English season. His domination of the Lancashire bowling was such that he topped the County's Championship averages every year, from 1951 to 1966. In the history of the Club, no other bowler can claim such a record and, looking at the other first-class counties, few can equal such a long run of success, especially fast bowlers.

Statham was a cricketer to be relied upon, and in the time of crisis the County Club turned to him, their senior professional, to captain the side, which he did for three seasons.

J.B. Statham (NCCC)

the first over before knocking over Lowson's off stump with his sixth ball. Within six overs Yorkshire were 13 for four, three of the wickets being Statham's, and only five of the total had come from the bat. Yardley then played a determined captain's innings, rescuing his side with 119 and in the later stages the match fizzled out.

The final match of Lancashire's season was against Surrey at the Oval. Lancashire required four points from a first-innings lead, provided Surrey did not win, to gain the Championship title outright. Lancashire had a disastrous start, however, losing both Washbrook and Place in the second over, both clean bowled by Stuart Surridge; Ikin was lucky to be dropped when he had made nine – he went on to the innings' highest score of 52. Nigel Howard made 51, but was also dropped early in his innings. Lancashire were all out for 221. The County took a gamble with their attack, dropping Berry and bringing in Tom Dickinson, an amateur fast bowler for Blackburn Grammar School. Statham removed Fishlock for two, but the young Cambridge University student, Peter May, remained undisturbed for five hours, compiling 92 and achieving first innings points for Surrey – he was awarded his county cap. Surrey's lead was 66 and Lancashire batted out time, there being no hope of victory.

R. Tattersall, the Lancashire and England spin bowler (NCCC)

This result meant that Lancashire, having completed their Championship programme, could only look on as Surrey met Leicestershire in their last match. Alec Bedser took twelve wickets, Fishlock hit a century and Surrey won, despite interruptions by the weather, by ten wickets. They drew level with Lancashire and tied for the Championship – in fact Lancashire were fortunate that the rule stating that if two teams tied on points, then the side with the most wins gained the title was not then in force. Surrey had 17 wins to Lancashire's 16.

It was Lancashire's best season since 1934. Tattersall was the bowler of the year, with 163 wickets at 12.19 runs each, an outstanding return for his first full Championship summer. Malcolm Hilton also made a great advance, with 125 wickets at 15.04 each in the Championship. Hilton's ability to spin the ball gave him more opportunities than Berry's method of beating batsmen through the air, and the latter took 45 wickets at 21.84 each. Third in the bowling came the 20-year-old Statham, who by the end of the year was the most talked about young fast bowler in England. The close-to-the-wicket fielding was vastly improved – Grieves, Ikin and Edrich all being brilliant, whilst Barlow returned as the regular wicket-keeper and missed few chances.

The batting, though managing to make enough runs, was not so successful. Washbrook and Ikin both missed matches through injury and Place had a moderate year. Wharton lost his place in the side, but Grieves held the middle order together and was very consistent. In the second half of the season, Howard found runs coming more easily and topped 1,000 for the season; he also led the side with much more authority than in 1949. A surplus of £3,993 on the year's workings came from a small rise in membership and a large increase in gate receipts.

The West Indians toured England, bringing with them the unknown 'spin twins' Ramadhin and Valentine. There were four Tests, the first of which was staged at Old Trafford and signalled the Test debut of Bob Berry, who took nine wickets in the match, bowling in harness with Eric Hollies of Warwickshire, who took eight. England won by 202 runs – the day of the West Indians had not yet quite dawned. Berry failed to take a wicket in the second Test, when West Indies won with ease, and in the fourth Test Malcolm Hilton made his bow, but returned figures of none for 91. West Indies won the match and the rubber.

Berry was selected to go to Australia with the 1950–51 MCC side under F.R. Brown, but he never struck form, and when injury depleted the side, both Tattersall and Statham were flown out. Both made their Test debuts and Tattersall took six for 44 in the final innings of the second Test against New Zealand.

Washbrook was the other Lancashire player in the side. He found the lower bounce unsuitable for his favourite strokes and that, combined with great trouble combating the mysterious Iverson, meant he did very little in the Tests, though succeeding in the state games. Ikin and Grieves went to India with the Commonwealth side and both had splendid records – Ikin topped the unofficial Test batting averages.

April of 1951 saw Old Trafford buzzing with anticipation. In the winter the members' dining room had been converted into an indoor school and Place and Edrich had spent their time coaching youngsters. Pollard and Roberts had left county cricket, but with four young Test bowlers in Statham, Tattersall, Hilton and Berry, the county had a potential attack only Surrey could rival.

By coincidence the Championship season began where the previous one had ended – at the Oval. The first day was washed out, but on the Monday Ikin carried his bat for 125 not out to produce a total of 197 and then Statham took five for 25, giving Lancashire first innings lead of 60. Tattersall's off-breaks in the final innings had Surrey battling to save themselves from defeat. A war of attrition was played with Yorkshire, then Surrey came to Old Trafford for the return. Statham took nine wickets, as Lancashire won by nine wickets. Kent and Middlesex were beaten in the next two fixtures. The prospects looked bright – Statham on 1 June was top of the bowling averages, Hilton fourth and Tattersall seventh, whilst Ikin was second to Denis Compton in the batting.

The success of these cricketers proved a double-edged sword, for Ikin, Tattersall and Statham were all in the England side for the second Test at Lord's – Tattersall with twelve wickets almost beat the South Africans on his own. In the meantime, however, Lancashire had gone off to Portsmouth without their stars and suffered their first defeat of the year, Shackleton, bred in the north, being the most successful player for Hampshire. When Hampshire came to Liverpool a month later, Lancashire were even further depleted, as this second game clashed with the Gentlemen v Players fixture. Ikin, Tattersall, Statham and Hilton were representing the Players, whilst Howard had been invited to captain the Gentlemen. Geoffrey Edrich made 155, his highest score in first-class cricket to give Lancashire a first innings lead of 118 and then the reserve bowler, Greenwood, returned figures of 19-12-10-5 with his off-breaks to bring an innings victory.

The next match drew record crowds to Edgbaston to watch Lancashire play Warwickshire – the midland county, under Tom Dollery, were having a brilliant season and were leading the Championship table at this stage, whilst Lancashire were in third place. An audience of 25,000 on the first day saw Tattersall take six for 53, dismissing the home side for 184; then Washbrook continued to press Lancashire's claims, with one of the best innings of his long career – 209 not out from a total of 333 for nine declared. Warwickshire had to bat out the final day to avoid defeat and were saved by Dollery, who made an undefeated 108.

N.D. Howard, Lancashire Captain 1949–1953 (NCCC)

Just prior to the match Lancashire received a double recognition from the selectors – N.D. Howard was appointed captain of the MCC side to tour India in 1951–52 and the secretary, C.G. Howard, was appointed as manager.

This draw against Warwickshire was the beginning of a sad decline. Lancashire failed to win any of the last twelve matches of 1951, eleven being unfinished and one, against Glamorgan at Old Trafford, being lost. So as the County stood still in the table, Warwickshire's points rose steadily. Although ending third in the table, Lancashire were 80 points behind the leaders and 48 behind Yorkshire in second place.

Rain was the cause of many of the drawn games, but on more than one occasion it saved Lancashire from defeat. On too many occasions Lancashire failed to press home an early advantage. Tattersall had a good year, but was unable to reproduce the astonishing figures of 1950, having seemed to have lost his ability to spin the ball sharply. Hilton took 112 Championship wickets, the only Lancashire player to reach 100, but he was second in the averages to Statham. In his first complete season, Statham faded somewhat towards the end, but he was a man with a great future. Wharton was introduced as Statham's new ball partner and produced some lively spells. Berry's opportunities were limited and Greenwood, between injuries, bowled well. C.S. Smith, an 18-year-old amateur from William Hulme's Grammar School, opened the bowling in some matches when Statham was away, and though not much above medium pace as yet, had a nice action and also batted with the look of someone who knew what he was about.

Place, Washbrook, Geoffrey Edrich and Grieves all completed 1,000 Championship runs; Ikin, missing half the matches, hit 927 at 54.52, but Howard was disappointing. The death occurred just before the season ended of W.B. Roberts. He had left the staff only the previous year. Ill health had prevented him playing in 1951, and he had had an operation from which he seemed to recover, only to die a few weeks later, aged 37.

Harry Makepeace finally severed his connection with the County Club and the committee granted him an annual pension of £150: Worthington became the new chief coach. The number of members increased, but this was offset by a drop in receipts through the turnstiles, so the overall surplus for the year remained virtually unchanged.

There were no major changes on the playing staff for 1952. R. Alderson, D. Stone and P. Hough were released, but they had had a total of only eight first team matches between them over three seasons. Peter Barcroft, an all-rounder from Bacup, was the only newcomer.

In the absence of Howard, recovering from his winter in India, Washbrook captained the County in the opening Championship game and 13 wickets by Tattersall beat Kent with ease. Howard returned and victories were recorded against Notts, Derbyshire, Worcestershire and most surprisingly against Warwickshire at Edgbaston, Washbrook again leading the team in this last win as Howard, due to lack of form, dropped himself. Warwickshire were completely outplayed and lost by an innings with Ikin not only making 118, but taking six wickets.

Five wins from ten matches and no losses was a good start to the season, but Surrey were in even more impressive form with eight wins from eleven, whilst Middlesex and Yorkshire, having each played an extra game, were marginally above Lancashire on points.

The match with Essex at Brentwood towards the end of June finished in a tie. Because of rain a decision on first innings was not reached until 11.05 on the third morning, but after that the match really came alive with 457 runs hit in the day. Howard declared to set Essex 242 in 140 minutes. Trevor Bailey faced Hilton for the last over with one wicket to fall, and nine runs needed. Bailey hit the first ball for six, was dropped in the deep off the second, acquiring two runs in the process, and was caught at mid-off from the fourth ball to create a tie. From this excitement the team went to Trent Bridge and were easily beaten by the weakest county, Notts. They were further humiliated four days later by losing to the Indian tourists by ten wickets, being dismissed for 68, with Ramchand taking seven for 27. It was the tourists' first county win of their visit.

The season continued with the County charting an erratic course – good wins interspersed with unexpected defeats. The final position of third, the same as in 1951, was somewhat more satisfactory since the wins increased from eight to twelve, but at no time did the County challenge Surrey.

Tattersall returned to his form of two years previously and Hilton and Berry shared the second spinner's spot. Statham completed 100 Championship wickets at the same average as Tattersall and the attack was further strengthened by the form of J.G. Lomax, the professional from Rochdale, now aged 27. He had made his first-class debut for Lancashire in 1949, but had remained on the 'promising' list without being able to gain a regular first-team place. Now, both as a fast-medium bowler and middle order batsman, he was making a useful contribution and was awarded his county cap.

The five principal batsmen, Ikin, Grieves, Place, Edrich and Washbrook, all hit over 1,000 runs at an average above 35, though a damaged thumb marred Washbrook's summer.

Three young players made their debuts: Peter Marner, a 16-year-old from Oldham who sprang to the limelight by taking six for 9 in a local league match; James Hilton, brother of Malcolm, another off-break bowler; and Sidney Smith from Heywood – not related to C.S. Smith. The wicket-keeping position changed hands. Barlow disappeared, Wilson lost his place and F.D. Parr took over. He was quite brilliant taking the fast bowlers, but not so good with the slows. He also could hold down an end successfully, as he demonstrated against Yorkshire, when he survived over an hour for nine.

The financial affairs of the Club remained bouyant – with nearly 10,000 members, the Committee decided to restrict the number of new members and a waiting list was in operation. The problem was that the capacity on the ground for members had been reached.

Rain was blamed for Lancashire's failure to challenge Surrey for the 1953 Championship. Eight complete days were washed out at Old Trafford and several away games were ruined through the weather. The visit of the Australians under Hassett, with the hope that the reviving fortunes of England might bring the Ashes home, naturally took interest away from the Championship. Surrey fought harder for the title than in 1952, but it was Middlesex and Sussex who were the main challengers, rather than Lancashire.

Ikin was forced to retire hurt with back trouble during the first Championship match, and for the second game young Marner was brought into the side: he hit 72 well made runs and looked as if he might

ESSEX *v.* LANCASHIRE

Played on the Old County Ground, Brentwood, on 21, 23 and 24 July 1953

MATCH TIED

LANCASHIRE	FIRST INNINGS		SECOND INNINGS	
A. Wharton	lbw b Smith	85	c Avery b Smith	16
J.G. Lomax	c Gibb b Smith	10	c Bailey b Greensmith	47
G.A. Edrich	c Insole b Smith	35	st Insole b Smith	69
W. Place	c Avery b Preston	63		
K.J. Grieves	b Preston	34	c and b Smith	0
*Mr N.D. Howard	c Avery b Preston	0	b Smith	5
P. Greenwood	b Smith	14	b Smith	8
M.J. Hilton	b Preston	8	not out	48
R. Tattersall	b Smith	1	not out	7
J.B. Statham	b Preston	1	c Greensmith b Smith	15
†A. Wilson	not out	0		
Extras	b 10, lb 3, nb 2	15	b 9, w 1, nb 1	11
Total		266	(7 wkts dec)	226

Fall: 1st inns: 1-20 2-111 3-153 4-237 5-237 6-240 7-255 8-265 9-266
2nd inns: 1-32 2-103 3-104 4-114 5-138 6-175 7-208

BOWLING	O	M	R	W	O	M	R	W
Bailey	21	6	44	0	14	3	34	0
Preston	20.3	2	49	5	11	2	26	0
Smith	39	5	105	5	33	4	122	6
Greensmith	24	12	30	0	12	5	33	1
Insole	4	0	23	0				

ESSEX	FIRST INNINGS		SECOND INNINGS	
T.C. Dodds	c Howard b Lomax	46	c Tattersall b Lomax	26
A.V. Avery	c Wilson b Lomax	41	st Wilson b Hilton	4
†P.A. Gibb	c Edrich b Hilton	13	c Grieves b Tattersall	33
R. Horsfall	c Edrich b Hilton	3	lbw b Statham	10
*Mr D.J. Insole	b Lomax	2	b Statham	18
Mr T.E. Bailey	c Wharton b Hilton	34	c Howard b Hilton	52
R. Smith	run out	27	c Wharton b Tattersall	48
F.H. Vigar	not out	25	not out	1
Mr C. Griffiths	c Edrich b Tattersall	6	c Wilson b Tattersall	19
W.T. Greensmith	b Statham	56	b Statham	5
K.C. Preston	b Statham	1	c Grieves b Tattersall	10
Extras	b 4, lb 2, nb 1	7	b 3, lb 2	5
Total		261		231

Fall: 1st inns: 1-86 2-89 3-92 4-104 5-111 6-164 7-181 8-187 9-259
2nd inns: 1-33 2-50 3-61 4-89 5-150 6-156 7-167 8-183 9-206

BOWLING	O	M	R	W	O	M	R	W
Statham	24.4	3	50	2	12	1	59	3
Lomax	21	4	37	3	3	0	14	1
Tattersall	25	5	46	1	18	3	61	4
Hilton	37	15	47	3	10.4	0	69	2
Grieves	22	7	44	0				
Wharton	3	0	11	0				
Greenwood	12	4	19	0	3	0	23	0

Umpires: T.W. Spencer and C.H. Welch

* Captain: † Wicket-keeper

Nine runs were required by Essex to win with Hilton bowling the last possible over. Bailey scored six off the first delivery, ran a two off the second, but was caught at mid-off from the fourth.

force himself into the side permanently. This innings, however, proved to be his season's best.

Ikin recovered just in time for his benefit match, against Surrey at the very end of May. Surrey had little difficulty in winning by eight wickets, but a week later came the sensation of the season at Bath, when the Somerset v Lancashire match was all over in a single day. Tattersall took seven for 25 as Somerset were dismissed for 55. Lancashire then made 158, the highest scorer being Marner who hit four gigantic sixes in his 44. Somerset collapsed to Statham and Tattersall for 79 and the whole game ended by six o'clock.

For the third successive year the County finished the season in third place. Statham and Tattersall remained the principal bowlers, but Hilton conceded his regular place to Berry, who ended with 92 Championship wickets, and against Worcestershire at Blackpool took all ten wickets in an innings, the first time this feat had been achieved for Lancashire since 1900. C.S. Smith, when available (he was doing his National Service), was the best of Statham's new ball partners. The batting saw five players reach 1,000 Championship runs: Grieves, Edrich, Washbrook, Ikin and Place, but in general the scoring was lower than in recent years and in the first-class averages, Washbrook, in 15th position, was the highest.

The extent of Lancashire's contribution to England's Test series against Australia was a single appearance each by Tattersall and Statham – no one from the County played in the fifth and decisive Test at the Oval. Australia had the best of the Test at Old Trafford. The attendance for the game was 151,000 and receipts £48,313. The 'H' stand was rebuilt for the start of the summer.

Harry Williams, who had been groundsman at Old Trafford since 1935, announced that he intended to retire at the end of the 1953 season. He had originally learnt his profession under Fred Hunt at Worcester and for 20 years had been a familiar sight around the ground, more often than not accompanied by his dog.

The County broke with tradition in 1954 by appointing Cyril Washbrook as their first professional captain, when Howard announced that he could no longer afford the time for county cricket on a regular basis. Washbrook had wanted the captaincy in 1949 when it was thrust on Nigel Howard; now the office had been awarded to him almost too late. Brought up in the dressing room of the 1930s, he was not in tune with the more easy-going atmosphere of the mid-1950s and expected a code of discipline which the young players on the staff found difficult to swallow.

If the rain had had an effect on Lancashire in 1953, it was nothing compared to its effect in 1954. In three Lancashire games not a single ball was bowled and in a total of seven – one quarter – of the Championship matches rain prevented even first innings points being decided. Even allowing for this tale of depression, the final position in the Championship of tenth was poor. The batting seemed in complete disarray. Only Washbrook and Wharton managed 1,000 Championship runs, and only those two averaged over 30 – Washbrook, the leading batsman, was 29th in the first-class averages. Of the rest, Edrich hit two hundreds, one of which was against the Pakistani tourists, but failed on wet wickets, which used to suit his style. Ikin had a serious operation in the spring and was unable to play in the early part of the season. Place, apart from 148 v Glamorgan, never found his form and Grieves proved little better. In the absence of runs from the more senior men, S. Smith was given an extensive trial, but his 21 Championship innings produced only 303 runs.

Two young amateurs who were registered and drafted into the eleven were R.W. Barber, captain of Ruthin School and later in 1954 captain of the Schools at Lord's. He was a left-hand bat and leg-break bowler. G. Pullar of Werneth CC was a second left-hander – both Barber and Pullar were 18 years old. The groundstaff contained one new batsman in G.H. Blight of Longsight. Barber appeared in seven Championship matches and Pullar in six, and neither managed an individual fifty, but both looked like cricketers of the future.

Lancashire 1954

The bowling was the County's strong point, except for the lack of a partner for Statham. Wharton usually fulfilled this role, but C.S. Smith, after a successful summer at Cambridge, came in to the team for nine matches and F.W. Moore, a fast-medium right-arm bowler from Rochdale, was tried once or twice. Statham was now the leading bowler in England, topping both the first-class and Lancashire averages – he missed a number of games through Test calls. There were some unkind comments about the fact that the committee had allowed Frank Tyson, from Middleton, to be signed by Northants. Tyson was now regarded as the fastest bowler in England and won his first Test cap during the summer.

The spin department was in the capable hands of Roy Tattersall, the only Lancashire player to take a hundred wickets in 1954, and Malcolm Hilton – brother James and J.G. Lomax had both left the Old Trafford staff in the winter and emigrated to Somerset. Bob Berry, who early in the season played for MCC v Pakistan, was given so few opportunities with Lancashire that he requested his release and signed for Worcestershire for 1955. A young leg-spinner who did receive more encouragement was Tommy Greenhough from Rochdale, and in nine matches he took 23 wickets at 19 runs each. Parr lost his wicket-keeping place and like Berry requested his release but later changed his mind. Wilson resumed behind the stumps.

The poor weather – three days of the Old Trafford Test were also washed out – meant that 84,000 less people came through the turnstiles, but accommodation for members was increased and improved and membership figures showed an upward trend, so that the loss on the year was £6,613, most of it attributable to the loss on catering. It is interesting in passing to note that the membership subscription rates for 1954 were: Life £50; Full £3 3s; Country £1 11s 6d.

Bert Flack was appointed head groundsman for 1955, and another non-playing change was the election of T.E. Burrows to succeed Dr J.B. Holmes as chairman. Dr Holmes was elected president.

Tommy Burrows had made a name for himself in local cricket administration and had been for ten years a member of the MCC Youth Council; later he became chairman of the NCA Junior and Youth Committee. He had come to the attention of Lancashire cricket at county level when he helped to organise the record benefit for Cyril Washbrook in 1948. Burrows saw that it was his job to persuade the leagues in Lancashire that they formed part of the overall pattern for county cricket. He was a very hard-working chairman and did all he could to encourage cricket at all levels, but, unlike T.A. Higson, he did not have the personality to dominate the County committee and accepted the conservative views expressed, a policy which was to slowly drag the County Club downward.

After a hesitant start, Lancashire won three successive Championship matches in June, against Middlesex, Leicester and Worcester and this moved the County into third place in the Championship table, but Surrey and Yorkshire were well in front, whilst Lancashire were marginally ahead of a bunch of five or six counties. By the end of July they had drifted to tenth place and ended the summer ninth equal with Warwickshire. The now familiar cry for a second pace bowler of quality was the main feature of critical comment. When Statham was absent, playing for England or injured, the seam attack looked threadbare. Fred Goodwin from Heywood bowled at a lively pace in seven matches and his ability to move the ball enabled him to take 22 Championship wickets at 17 runs each, but he was still very raw. K.B. Standring, a local grammar school boy playing for Clitheroe in the Ribblesdale League managed to dismiss Len Hutton. Very tall, he had an easy action, but at little more than a medium pace – he played in six Championship games. Moore was given a longer trial, but proved expensive. Statham was again the leading Lancashire bowler, his 79 wickets costing 12 runs each – of the regulars Tattersall came second with 105 wickets, but they cost 20 runs apiece. Hilton remained Tattersall's partner, Greenhough's leg-spin accounting for only 10 wickets.

With Ikin restored to health – and briefly back in the England team – the batting looked stronger. Grieves, Washbrook, Ikin and Wharton all topped 1,000 runs. Place dropped out of the eleven and Edrich had a moderate year. Barber, at Cambridge, failed to get his blue, but appeared for the County in the vacation and was looked upon as the white hope, but Pullar could appear in only three matches. Marner had completed his National Service and played once or twice.

The fielding, brilliant on some days, was too variable and the wicket-keeping position again changed hands, Wilson giving way to John Jordan.

The drier weather improved gate receipts and a small surplus was made on the year's workings.

The announcement that Cyril Washbrook had been chosen as a Test selector for 1956 – the Australians were the visitors – was greeted with satisfaction, but it meant that Lancashire would be deprived of his services for quite a number of matches. This absence would put a strain on the batting, more especially because Ikin was again ill and would miss much of the summer. The signs at the start of 1956 were not too promising, but when the County won their first four Championship games the gloom lifted. Somerset were beaten by ten wickets, due to a century from Wharton and some accurate bowling by Statham. More pleasure was gleaned from the second win – by 153 runs over Yorkshire. Tattersall took 14 for 90 and Grieves hit the highest score in each innings. Over 66,000 turned up at Headingley for the match, which was Lancashire's second win in the Roses series since the war.

Glamorgan were beaten just after tea on the second day, Tattersall and Statham proving too much for the Welshmen and Tattersall picked up another ten wickets at the expense of Warwickshire in a 162-run win.

Lancashire were now second to Sussex to the Championship table, but had played three matches fewer. Wharton was at the head of the first-class batting averages and Tattersall second in the bowling.

Of the eight matches the County played in June, only three came to a definite result. There were two wins and the first loss, against Warwickshire at Edgbaston, when Statham was away playing for England.

By coincidence at the time of this defeat the Lancashire committee sacked five young players: Barcroft, Bowling, Johnson, Goodwin and Wood, all being axed from the groundstaff. The most surprising dismissal was that of Goodwin. His rival as an opening partner for Statham took 11 wickets, including the hat-trick, against Essex at Chelmsford, but as it turned out this was to be the only time he ever obtained ten wickets in a match and the green wicket was tailor-made for his medium deliveries.

Sussex came to Old Trafford on 7 July and a hundred from Wharton combined with Statham's first hat-trick for Lancashire gave the team an impressive victory which moved them to the top of the Championship.

Immediately following this success came the news that Washbrook had been brought into the England side for the third Test, at Headingley, and though the choice of one of the Test selectors came in for much adverse comment, Washbrook scored 98 and England won the game by an innings. Ten days later came the fourth Test at Old Trafford, when Jim Laker broke all existing Test records with his 19 wickets, giving England another innings victory and the Ashes.

In between times Lancashire were creating a curious record. They beat Leicestershire without losing a single wicket, the first such instance in first-class cricket.

Two more victories by the end of July kept Lancashire in top place, but tied on points with Surrey; Surrey however had a game in hand.

By the time Lancashire went to the Oval for their penultimate match, the Surrey team had gained such a lead in the table that Lancashire had to win both this and their last match, whilst Surrey failed in all three of theirs. As it turned out Surrey picked up just four points from the three games, but unfortunately Lancashire could only gain the same number from their two, so had to be content with second place; this, however, was a great improvement on the last two seasons and, apart from 1950, the County's best result since the war.

LANCASHIRE *v*. LEICESTERSHIRE

Played on the Old Trafford Ground, Manchester on 14, 16 and 17 July 1956

LEICESTERSHIRE	FIRST INNINGS		SECOND INNINGS	
G. Lester	c Statham b Wharton	2	c Jordan b Greenhough	52
M.R. Hallam	c Pullar b Statham	13	c Collins b Hilton	42
J. van Geloven	b Greenhough	14	c Jordan b Statham	3
M. Tompkin	lbw b Statham	0	c Dyson b Hilton	8
*Mr C.H. Palmer	c Edrich b Hilton	24	b Statham	1
V.E. Jackson	c Collins b Statham	7	c Wharton b Hilton	2
Mr R.A. Diment	c Pullar b Hilton	12	lbw b Greenhough	0
V.S. Munden	c Grieves b Greenhough	0	b Hilton	6
†J. Firth	b Statham	14	c Jordan b Hilton	1
R.L. Pratt	b Hilton	9	b Statham	0
T.J. Goodwin	not out	5	not out	0
Extras	b 2, lb 3, nb 3	8	b 5, nb, 2	7
Total		108		122

Fall: 1st inns: 1-7 2-17 3-22 4-34 5-49 6-75 7-75 8-75 9-85
2nd inns: 1-59 2-78 3-94 4-95 5-102 6-115 7-116 8-117 9-122

BOWLING	O	M	R	W	O	M	R	W
Statham	17.3	7	32	4	15.1	3	36	3
Wharton	6	2	10	1	3	0	8	0
Hilton	16	9	19	3	26	17	23	5
Greenhough	27	16	29	2	16	6	41	2
Tattersall	5	2	7	0	8	5	7	0
Collins	4	2	3	0				

LANCASHIRE	FIRST INNINGS		SECOND INNINGS	
A. Wharton	not out	87	not out	33
J. Dyson	not out	75	not out	31
*G.A. Edrich				
K.J. Grieves				
G. Pullar				
R. Collins				
M.J. Hilton				
†J. Jordan				
J.B. Statham				
T. Greenhough				
R. Tattersall				
Extras	b 1, lb 1, nb 2	4	b 1, nb 1	2
Total	(0 wkt dec)	166	(0 wkt)	66

BOWLING	O	M	R	W	O	M	R	W
Goodwin	10	0	41	0	7	1	36	0
Pratt	7	0	37	0	6	1	19	0
Palmer	11	5	22	0	5	0	9	0
Jackson	16	7	37	0				
Munden	6	0	25	0				

Umpires: C.S. Elliott and F.W. Shipston

* Captain; † Wicket-keeper

Lancashire won by ten wickets and became the first team in the history of first-class cricket to win a match without losing a single wicket.

A glance at the first-class bowling averages goes a long way to explain the County's success. Hilton, Tattersall and Statham were all in the first seven. Hilton had one of the best seasons of his career and in Championship games took 128 wickets. Greenhough with his leg-breaks was the best of the other bowlers, picking up 62 Championship wickets at 16 runs each.

Wharton was the outstanding batsman, though his form declined in the latter part of the season. Grieves and Washbrook also did well, but the great advance was the batting of Pullar, who had decided to become a professional and averaged 30 in Championship games. A second young player who gained a regular place and latterly opened the batting was Jack Dyson, the Manchester City inside left, who, in all first-class matches, completed 1,000 runs. Almost nothing was seen of Barber, but Roy Collins, who had made his debut in 1954, played in 18 Championship matches. A big, lusty youth he could hit the ball very hard and also bowled off-breaks, which took some useful wickets. Marner hit a hundred against Oxford, but was then absent through illness. Jordan was the regular wicket-keeper.

When the season ended, an extensive scheme of development began, scheduled to be completed in April 1958 and costing £70,000, with dressing rooms, players' dining room and many other facilities improved and refurbished. This was despite a loss of £5,439 on the year.

The Centenary of cricket at Old Trafford was marked in 1957 with a special match to be played against MCC, as well as a dinner in Manchester Town Hall. The County began the season in astonishing form, winning every one of their first five matches, and at the end of May were clear leaders in the Championship. Then, deprived of Washbrook and Statham for the first Test, the County lost two matches in succession, and after the last pair staved off defeat against Yorkshire, the County then lost three more Championship matches and suffered an innings defeat at the hands of Cambridge University.

The downward tumble ended with an innings victory over Somerset at the end of June, when Statham took nine for 31 and Somerset were dismissed for 90 and 74. Middlesex were beaten in the next game at Lord's, but the see-saw continued when not a win came in the ten Championship matches which followed. Not until August 20 could Lancashire claim another victory.

The Lancashire correspondent in *The Cricketer* was nearing despair, but he found one ray of hope on August 17:

The Blackpool match (a defeat at the hands of Northants) enjoyed glorious weather and should have replenished the County coffers; otherwise there was little satisfaction in it for Lancashire supporters. One could not blame the bowlers, and indeed Greenhough did very well up to a point. A veil might decently be drawn over most of the batting, but there was one bright spot in the innings of young Bond, who confirmed high opinions formed in recent games. Coming in on top of the failure of some older batsmen, he showed judgment and a well-organised defence, coupled with a healthy notion of what to do with a bad ball. Since finding a place in the side, Bond has progressed so rapidly that his prospects must be bright. His fielding is an added asset; quite a crop of excellent catches close to the wicket have recently come his way, suggesting that he could well carry on the Ikin and Grieves tradition.

Two wins right at the end of the programme meant that Lancashire ended the year in sixth place, but it had been a season on a switchback railway. Statham remained the outstanding figure in the side and came second to Tony Lock in the first-class averages; he and Tattersall completed 100 Championship wickets, but Hilton was less accurate with his left-arm spinners and the soft wickets were not to Greenhough's liking.

Wharton and Ikin were the only two to reach 1,000 Championship runs. Ikin announced his retirement from first-class cricket. His career had not reached the heights promised in 1946, due mainly to illness which forced him to miss so many matches. Ikin had been a great servant of his adopted County and an unselfish player who regarded cricket as a team game. Few players have excelled him as a close fielder and his all-round figures tend to understate his value. He returned to Staffordshire cricket and until he died in 1984 was an excellent coach. In 1965–66 he was assistant manager of the MCC side to Australia.

Washbrook and Grieves both had modest seasons, whilst Edrich confined his efforts mainly to captaining the Second Eleven. Of the younger batsmen, Pullar scored a couple of Championship hundreds and his graceful style was noted by the discerning public. Injury prevented Barber joining the side directly after the University season, but in his few later innings he looked very much a Test batsman in the making. Jordan missed many matches through injury and Wilson and young Heys from Oswaldtwistle deputised. At the end of the year Jordan decided to leave cricket for an alternative career. One very promising player who missed the entire year was Peter Marner, seriously injured on the rugby field, but it was hoped he would gain a First Eleven place in 1958 – he had appeared using a surgical aid to his right leg in the Second Eleven in 1957.

The County Club were making an all-out effort to find the right bowler to partner Statham. For the 1958 season they engaged Ken Higgs the 21-year-old Port Vale footballer from Kidsgrove, to add to Colin Hilton from Atherton, who had appeared once or twice in 1957,

Jack Roberts from Bolton and A. Collier. There were also two amateurs, R.D. Bailey of Repton School and Richard Bowman, the Oxford blue.

July 1958 was a good month for Lancashire. They won five matches, including two victories by an innings, both with a day to spare. In the first against Leicester, the report notes: 'Statham badly upset Leicestershire on the first day.' In fact his analysis was 16.5-6-20-6 and he took a further seven wickets in the second innings as Leicestershire were dismissed for 99 and 87. Against Gloucestershire in the second great win, Statham had seven for 29 in the first innings but it was Tattersall who destroyed the western county when they batted again, taking six for 41.

Each side of July Lancashire continued their zig-zag course, almost winning and losing by turn, with the usual helping of washed-out matches thrown in.

By the end of their successful spell in July, the County had risen well up the table, but eventually they had to settle for seventh place. The attack at last had a balanced took as young Higgs gained a regular place, and in his debut season took 62 Championship wickets at 21 runs each. Hilton and Tattersall both played throughout the year and could point to good returns, but Statham was out on his own. Though in the full first-class averages he came third behind Les Jackson of Derbyshire and Tony Lock of Surrey, he still captured his wickets at six runs less per victim than any of his Lancashire colleagues.

It was the batting which let the County down, the bottom being reached when they were dismissed for 27 by Surrey at Old Trafford in Wharton's Benefit Match – Higgs at number ten was the highest scorer with six. A week previously they had been bowled out by Kent for 80 and 117, and against Somerset at Weston the Lancashire totals were 89 and 59 – in the latter innings again not a single double-figure score.

The reason for the failures was the lack of form of Wharton and Grieves, and though Washbrook had his moments, he failed to hit a century. The retirement of Ikin and virtual disappearance of Edrich added to the distress, so the youngsters were floundering on their own. In fact Marner and Pullar both reached 1,000 runs, the only Lancashire players to do so in Championship matches. Marner had overcome his football injury and hit about him in gay abandon as his elders muddled along. He became noted for his hits which cleared the boundary and he hit no less than eight sixes in one innings against the New Zealanders. Pullar, using his reach to advantage and playing mainly off the front foot, had a variety of strokes at his command, and though he went off the boil in mid-season he hit a splendid 128 against Glamorgan late in August and came second to Marner in the batting table.

Barber, with his upright stance and style which made batting look so easy, was happiest on hard wickets. He still had a flaw on the leg side and this caused his dismissal too often.

None of the other young batsmen averaged above 20. Bond, light on his feet, proved a neat batsman and played in eight Championship games. Noel Cooke, an amateur from Liverpool College, made his first-class debut, but his best batting was confined to the Second Team, in which D.M. Green of Manchester Grammar School gave promise of runs to come. He appeared for the Public Schools at Lord's.

Of concern off the field was the financial situation. In 1957 the club, despite having 11,000 members, lost £12,641. This was attributed to the lack of a Test at Old Trafford. In 1958 the loss, despite the presence of the New Zealand Test, was still £9,033. The catering side had steadily lost money and for the 1958 season this hole was plugged by bringing in a firm of outside caterers, Messrs Pattison-Hughes of Birmingham. Another move was the idea of letting the pavilion out for functions during the winter months, and in 1958 certain alterations were made to the building to cope with this experiment. The Lancashire CCC Auxiliary Association and the Supporters' Association both grew up and one of their sources of income was the football pool, and various sweepstakes and draws.

Cyril Washbrook announced that 1959 would be his last season. In acknowledgement of this final campaign, the weather cheered up. The 1959 summer was one of the sunniest on record and for day after dry day there were blue skies and dry wickets. Pullar was particularly appreciative – in both innings of the first and second matches he hit the highest scores and provided two easy wins, the second of which was against Yorkshire at Old Trafford. By July he was opening for England in the Test side, and hit 75 off the Indian attack in his only innings at Leeds. Coming to Old Trafford for his second Test, Pullar treated his supporters to a century, the first Lancastrian ever to make a Test hundred at home. By the summer's close he was bloated with runs, 2,647 at an average of 55.14, only Mike Smith of Warwickshire making more. *Wisden* made him one of the 'Cricketers of The Year'. At 23, he was being compared with Charlie Hallows and Eddie Paynter.

Unlike 1958, Lancashire began the season well, failed badly in the middle and then recovered. The worst patch was in July when they lost successively to Hampshire, Notts and Middlesex.

To support the prolific Pullar, Grieves, so long in the shadows, loved the dry conditions and became the hard-hitting batsman of distant memory. Wharton reached 2,000 Championship runs and matched Pullar's four Championship hundreds. Barber, available for half the matches, did well without approaching Pullar's standard and Bond scored his first Championship hundred. He was promoted to number three and made his runs quickly.

Marner played a brilliant innings of 137 against Derbyshire, when no one else could reach fifty, but his form was variable and he briefly lost his place in the eleven.

The bowling was once more spearheaded by Statham – who performed a 'hat-trick' by topping the Test, first-class and Lancashire bowling averages. His action was so smooth and apparently effortless that batsmen were too often surprised by his unexpected pace, in contrast to the thundering and bellowing of Trueman.

Higgs continued to improve and took 100 wickets in all matches, and though not as fast as Statham he kept a good length and could use the old ball as well as the new. The biggest fundamental change in the attack was the almost overnight disappearance of both Hilton and Tattersall. Dyson and Collins were looked upon as possible successors, but the bowler who hit the headlines was Greenhough. To the embarrassment of *The Cricketer*'s Lancashire correspondent, Greenhough found himself selected for the first Test of 1959. On 9 May, *The Cricketer* had noted:

> Much as one would welcome a chance for Greenhough, it would be idle to pretend that he is of Test class. There have been moments during his many years at Old Trafford when a real development seemed possible, but he is much the same bowler as in the early years, and he had never managed to make his position in the county side secure.

Greenhough took five for 35 in the first innings of the second Test, but then had trouble with his run-up and in the middle of the season changed his style, bowling a fuller length and flighting the ball more, also bowling too many googlies. Even with these alterations he ended with 122 first-class wickets. Dyson bowled his off-breaks intelligently on the usually unhelpful hard wickets, and the committee persevered with him rather than bringing Tattersall back – Dyson was certainly a better batsman than the ex-England spinner.

Washbrook was unfortunate to find his last season marred by injury, but he played some innings reminiscent of former days. Lancashire discovered a new wicket-keeper in Geoff Clayton, a 21-year-old, who had rejoined the staff on completion of his National Service. He ousted poor Wilson from the First Eleven place – Clayton also scored runs, so with Tattersall and Wilson gone the long tail had been eliminated.

ONE STEP FORWARD, TWO STEPS BACK

WASHBROOK HAD MADE IT CLEAR AT THE START of 1959 that he was going to retire when the season finished. The Lancashire committee were now forced to look for a successor to this great player. They turned round only to discover that they had sacked his natural replacement a few months before. Edrich had captained the Second Eleven in 1958, he had received a glowing tribute at the end of that year and there is no doubt that the younger players thought a great deal of him and he brought the best out in them. He had a difference of opinion over the disciplining of some of the young players at the beginning of 1959 and left the Club abruptly.

The committee therefore dumped the captaincy for 1960 on their up-and-coming all-rounder, Bob Barber. To help ease him into the job the Club reverted to the pre-war system of segregating him (an amateur) from the professional herd. There was a return to the days of the captain and committee on one side and the players on the other.

Statham, Higgs and Greenhough had outstanding seasons. Statham topped the first-class averages and the other two were both in the top 15 bowlers of the year. With an attack of this calibre, the County beat Yorkshire at Whitsun and then achieved the double over the August Bank Holiday, Statham and Higgs dismissing the old enemy twice for 154 and 149. It was the first time since 1893 that Lancashire had won both games. The County were top of the Championship table and it appeared as if no one would catch them. They proceeded to beat Gloucestershire at Bristol in the next game and after a draw against Kent – when Barber made some controversial comments about his opposite number (Colin Cowdrey) – Lancashire, even without Statham, beat Leicestershire by seven wickets.

Six Championship matches remained when the team, within sight of goal, fell apart. Not one of these matches were won and four ended in defeat. In the meantime Yorkshire, in second place, grabbed three wins and seized the title. Lancashire with a total of 13 victories came second: Yorkshire won 17. Lancashire could not even claim that the weather robbed them, for Yorkshire were involved in three 'no decision' matches, as opposed to Lancashire's one.

On paper Barber had given Lancashire a great season, but the fact that they failed to take the title after being so close seemed to upset the members more than ending lower down the table would have done. Four capped players were missing when the cricketers reported for duty at Old Trafford in April 1961. Wharton had resigned on the grounds

Lancashire 1960. Standing: J.D. Bond, K. Higgs, G. Pullar, R. Collins, P.T. Marner, B.J. Booth, K. Goodwin. Seated: K.J. Grieves, A. Wharton, R.W. Barber, J.B. Statham, T. Greenhough (Lancashire CCC)

that at 37 he would get few opportunities in the First Eleven – he was snapped up by Leicestershire. Tattersall had been released. Dyson had been sacked for indiscipline the previous August and the wicket-keeper, Wilson, having lost his place to Clayton, was the fourth to go. These moves caused quite a rumpus at the Annual General Meeting, when several members severely criticised the committee's decisions. The Club, however, had a surplus of £397 on the year, despite giving the receipts of the Yorkshire match as a joint benefit for Hilton and Tattersall.

The change to 85 overs before the new ball could be taken was regarded as a bonus to Lancashire with its surfeit of spinners, and in particular the leg-spin of Greenhough, Barber and Brian Booth, the Blackburn all-rounder. The last named however made news in May by his batting, scoring 150 out of a total of 194 for the Second Eleven against Yorkshire.

In the first-class Roses match however, all Lancashire's batsmen, except for sixties from Bond and Collins, failed – Illingworth took eight for 50 in the second innings and Yorkshire won by ten wickets. This was Lancashire's fifth Championship match of 1961 and they had yet to achieve a win. *Playfair Cricket Monthly* contained this cryptic comment:

> For any one not intimately concerned with the team, Lancashire's fall from grace, since their Championship bid last August and extending up to the present time, is one of the major mysteries of the day.

Ken Higgs, fast bowler for Lancashire and England, in action, 1958 (Allsport)

In the end the County did win nine matches, including beating the eventual Champions, Hampshire, by eight wickets, when Statham took eight for 47. The strain of Test cricket was beginning to show on the county's star bowler. He played in 20 of the 32 Championship games and his wickets cost considerably more than in 1960. Colin Hilton was the third seamer, and his final figures of 65 wickets at 25 runs each were better than Higgs'. Higgs seemed to have lost his nip. Peter Lever, a 20-year-old from Todmorden, was specially registered in 1960 and his fast bowling used in five matches, but he was very green. The expected success of the spinners failed to materialise. Greenhough injured a finger and was unable to regain a permanent place in the side when he recovered. Collins was overbowled but had some bright moments, whereas the captain seemed reluctant to bowl himself – he played in ten more matches than Collins, but sent down 74 fewer overs. Booth's leg-breaks were very expensive.

Pullar and Bond, the former opening for England in all five Tests, were the most reliable batsmen. Grieves, Barber and Booth also completed 1,000 runs, but Marner, after a brilliant innings against the Australians in May, lost form, heart and confidence. Gerald Houlton, an amateur from St Helens, played frequently in the latter part of the season and despite an ungainly style made some good scores.

Lancashire sank to 13th place in the table and the committee placed the blame squarely on the shoulders of Barber. The following statement was issued on 12 October:

> The cricket committee of the Lancashire County Cricket Club are unanimously of the opinion that the responsibilities of captaincy with a natural disinclination to give himself the bowling his talents demand, are holding up R.W. Barber's development as an England cricketer, and have decided in the circumstances not to invite him to captain the side in 1962.

The committee then drew up a short list of possible replacements: C.S. Smith, who was now an architect in London, R.W. Bowman, D.M. Green who had been playing for Oxford in 1961 and had hit 138 v Northants on his return to Lancashire, and J.R. Blackledge a 33-year-old amateur with Chorley CC in the Northern League. Blackledge drew the short straw. This followed Yorkshire's example of selecting J.R. Burnet a few years ago. Either by design or coincidence, Grieves, the senior professional, and Malcolm Hilton decided to leave Old Trafford. Grieves signed for Stockport and joined his former colleague, wicket-keeper Wilson, who had agreed to play for that club as an amateur. There was no definite reaction from Bob Barber, who was with the MCC in India. Would he remain with Lancashire? He decided to stay.

Lancashire experienced the worst season in the Club's history. By the end of the summer they had avoided the wooden spoon by a fraction and no one could blame the weather – Lancashire lost 16 matches, four more than any other county and won two, a number equalled only by the bottom club, Leicestershire.

On paper the batting was strong. Pullar, Bond, Marner, Barber and Booth all reached 1,000 runs, but the bowling lacked the spinners which a few years back had been too numerous. Barber's leg-breaks proved expensive, and Greenhough was for some unexplained reason left out of ten matches. Marner was used but only to keep down the run rate. Of the fast bowlers, Statham was beset with domestic worries, but still proved easily the best bowler. Colin Hilton and Higgs came next to

Statham in the bowling table, but too often, after the opening bowlers had taken a vital wicket of two, there was no one to follow up. The Club chairman, Tommy Burrows, issued a 'news letter' to members apologising for the disaster.

As in 1961, the committee decided that the head to roll was the captain's. Out went Joe Blackledge. The list of possible amateurs was confined to the waste paper basket and Ken Grieves was asked to come and clear up the mess. He obtained permission from his employer and accepted.

Unrelated to the catastrophe was the resignation of Stan Worthington as coach – this had been announced twelve months earlier and the Club

Peter Lever, who created a good impression in 1962 (Patrick Eagar)

engaged Tom Reddick, the old Notts player, who had emigrated to South Africa, to replace Worthington.

Barber, however, decided to leave Lancashire and on 26 February 1963 Warwickshire announced that they were applying for his special registration.

Grieves began the season with a victory in the new knock-out competition sponsored by Gillette, but Lancashire were without their best batsman, Pullar, who had been sent home early from the MCC tour of Australia with a knee injury which required an operation. A fortnight after the start of the season, Bond had his hand broken by Wes Hall in the match against the West Indian tourists and so both the leading Lancashire batsmen were absent until the middle of July.

In order to strengthen the side Dyson was forgiven and returned to Old Trafford. Lancashire won their second-round match in the knock-out competition and also gained their first Championship victory of 21 May at Rushden. The County reached the semi-finals of the Gillette Cup, and then suffered total collapse against Worcester. They were dismissed for 59 and Worcester won by nine wickets.

By the end of the summer Lancashire had only marginally improved on 1962. Statham returned to his best form, but Higgs had a modest year, whilst Colin Hilton disappeared back to the Second Eleven, his place being taken by Peter Lever. Greenhough was the best of the spinners, but could take only 55 wickets in 25 matches and Dyson's opportunities were reduced by injury, though when he did bowl he was very expensive.

Marner came out with the best batting record, followed by Grieves. The diminutive Harry Pilling, from Ashton-under-Lyne, scored a maiden hundred against Hampshire and appeared in 16 Championship games. Bob Entwistle for Burnley had one good innings against Notts, but nothing was seen of D.M. Green or the Cambridge blue, E.J. Craig.

The Club made two further moves to improve the team's performance for 1964. Sonny Ramadhin, the old West Indian Test spinner, who had been playing in the Lancashire League for Radcliffe, was specially registered and Cyril Washbrook, now on the committee, was appointed team manager. Lesser changes were that Colin Hilton, Brian Booth and G. Houlton had left the staff, but D.M. Green had signed as a contracted player and K. Shuttleworth, a right-arm fast bowler from St Helens, and K. Snellgrove, a batsman from Bootle, had been engaged.

The County Club celebrated its Centenary Year in 1964, but there was little success on the field to enthuse over. It was unfortunate that Washbrook and Grieves, whose combined efforts might have brought about some improvement, were at odds with each other.

The whole bag of tricks exploded in error during the Centenary

Match v MCC at the end of August, when it was leaked to the press that Grieves, Marner, Clayton and Dyson had all been released. The committee then issued a statement:

> The committee have reviewed the performance of the team both on and off the field during the current season in conjunction with a special report which had been called for. A firm decision was taken not to re-engage P. Marner and G Clayton on the grounds that their continued retention was not in the best interests of the playing staff or the Club. In the case of J. Dyson he will not be offered re-engagement terms because it is felt he is not now up to the playing standards required. The committee regret the publicity given to the question of the captaincy before they had an opportunity to interview Grieves; this was deliberately deferred to the end of the season when his appointment as captain normally terminated. The committee now have the problem of captaincy to solve and intend, in accordance with established custom, to make an appointment in the New Year.

The detailed reasons for the sacking of the four players was never published. Statham, in his book 'A Spell At The Top', was of the opinion that Clayton's dismissal stemmed from the Gillette Cup semi-final match against Warwickshire. Clayton arrived at the wicket with the score 161 for five and 134 required off 20 overs. He proceeded to defend stubbornly for the rest of the match, being 19 not out when the game ended. He even refused easy singles offered by his partner, Pilling. The Committee omitted Clayton from the side 'until the responsibility for his attitude had been determined'. Dyson's dismissal was attributed to his poor form, but his sharp temper did not help his cause. Marner never reached his full potential. He was a batsman of moods and needed the right type of captain to guide his way. It was unfortunate that in his formative years, Lancashire should be switching from one leader to another with such alacrity.

The County received complaints from several opposing counties regarding the behaviour of the Lancashire players – specifically bad language and rude gestures – and thus Grieves as captain was blamed and dismissed.

Members were discontented and an extraordinary General Meeting was held in September. The committee suffered an overwhelming vote of no confidence and decided to resign en bloc, though nearly all of them stood for re-election. The result was that six of the old committee retained their seats, including the chairman, T.E. Burrows, but six fresh faces appeared. What was almost as important was the abolition, at the Annual General Meeting, of the old rule that vice-presidents had the right to attend committee meetings and the power to vote at those meetings. Burrows retired as chairman and the new chairman for 1965

Cedric Rhoades, whose energetic Chairmanship revived the County Club in the 1970s

was T.A. Higson. Higson, while he lacked the commanding personality of his father, was a bridge between the old order and the new – the
new being led by Cedric Rhoades.

One point that had angered members was the old committee's
decision to advertise in *The Times* for a captain to replace Grieves. Who
applied is irrelevant, for the new committee decided that Statham was
the only real choice the Club had. Leaving aside other considerations,
the fast bowler was the senior player and by his deeds for England
commanded the respect of the up-and-coming cricketers on the staff.
The committee also released Reddick as coach and brought back Charlie
Hallows. There was also a change in the office. Geoffrey Howard had
accepted the post of secretary of Surrey and returned to his old haunts.
Lancashire appointed the secretary of the Wigan Rugby League Club,
Jack Wood, to replace Howard.

The results achieved in 1965 were on the face of it not dissimilar to
those of 1964. Fortunately Statham's new appointment made no
difference to his bowling, and as well as topping the Lancashire
averages, he came third in the overall first-class table. He was recalled
by the Test selectors for the final Test at the Oval v South Africa and
joining him was Ken Higgs, who made his Test debut and took eight
wickets, four in each innings, whilst Statham had five for 40 in the first.
The two Lancastrians came close to providing England with victory, 91
runs being needed in 70 minutes when rain ended the game.

So Lancashire had a strong opening attack, with Lever proving a useful third man. The spin attack however was weak. Ramadhin, who had enjoyed some success in 1964, his first year, proved ineffective and was dropped – at the end of the season he left the County. This meant that Greenhough was the only slow bowler of any established value. David Lloyd, a young all-rounder from Accrington, sent down some left-arm spin, which looked as if it might develop. Ken Howard's off-breaks took 19 Championship wickets at 28 runs each, but there was little else.

The batting depended far too much on the opening pair of D.M. Green – now vice-captain – and Pullar. Green had a quite remarkable season, scoring in all matches over 2,000 runs, yet failing to reach a century. Harry Pilling was awarded his county cap and averaged above 30, but the others had a very moderate summer. Gerry Knox, the former Tynemouth schoolmaster, hit two centuries, but managed less than 500 runs in his other 34 innings. The other main batsmen, Bond and Beddows, had very modest records. Goodwin took over from Clayton as the wicket-keeper.

Apart from the absence of Ramadhin, there was very little change at Old Trafford for Statham's second season as captain. Unfortunately none of the young players made much progress. The fast bowling of Statham, Higgs and Lever comprised virtually all the attack, as Greenhough became more expensive and was released at the end of the year, and the hopeful Howard failed to inspire much confidence in his off-breaks – he also left Old Trafford.

The batting was as disappointing as the spin bowling. Green, after his good summer in 1965, just managed 1,000 runs, but could average only 22 and Pullar, the only other 1,000-run batsman also found his average dropping. Bond recovered ground lost in 1965 and D.R. Worsley, the Oxford University blue from Bolton, after being moved down the order, established himself in the eleven with some sound innings. He was awarded his cap at the end of the year. Knox, Pilling and David Lloyd all had occasional days of success. Barry Wood, the Ossett batsman, who had joined the County having already played for Yorkshire, played in ten matches, but his highest innings was only 39.

In order to provide some immediate improvement in the side, two players discarded by other counties were engaged for 1967. The 29-year-old Graham Atkinson, a right-hand bat with 13 seasons of Somerset cricket behind him, was brought in as an opening partner for David Green. John Savage, nine years older, had spent his career as an off-spinner with Leicestershire, and as he was born in Ramsbottom, he was returning to his native county.

It was irritating that Lancashire, with the best new ball attack in the country, were unable to win more than four Championship matches.

Higgs actually took over from Statham at the top of the Lancashire bowling table, but only by a fraction of one run. Both bowlers missed matches through injury and Higgs also had to heed the claims of England for four Tests. Ken Shuttleworth, who had been operating in the shadow of Higgs, Statham and Lever for three years, had more opportunities and came third in the bowling table, with figures much better than Lever. Savage was played in nearly every match, but Statham seemed to doubt his ability and he did not bowl as many overs as might have been expected.

As for the batting, Green and Pullar were handicapped by illness and injury. Pilling returned the best record, which included three centuries, and, with Atkinson, was one of only two players to reach 1,000 runs.

Season 1968 was that in which the authorities decided that instant registration of overseas players would be allowed. Lancashire wanted Sobers, but had to settle for Farokh Engineer, the Indian wicket-keeper-batsman, and agreed terms with Haslingden, the Lancashire League club, regarding the signing of the West Indian, Clive Lloyd, for the 1969 season.

Statham announced that he would not be able to play for the full season, due to a business commitment, and declined the captaincy. Jack Bond was appointed in his place.

The season opened badly. Lancashire were tipped as favourites for the Gillette cup, but Notts, under Sobers, knocked them out in the first round by a convincing win with 10 overs to spare. This was followed by defeat at the hands of Kent in the first Championship match and by 14 June, the County had played eight Championship games, recording three losses and five draws. The second half of the season saw the side coming together, and from the bottom of the table they rose to a final sixth place, with eight wins. Bond appropriately topped the batting average, although Pilling was the only player to reach 1,000 runs. Engineer had a moderate season with the bat, but kept wicket with efficiency. Of the younger players, Barry Wood made progress as both a batsman and medium-pacer bowler. He, as well as David Lloyd, Engineer and Shuttleworth, gained his county cap. Another all-rounder who impressed was David Hughes from Newton-le-Willows, a 22-year-old slow left-arm bowler who twice captured five wickets in an innings. The bonus point system was now in vogue in Championship matches and the fact that Lancashire gained 105 bowling points, the second highest, and 24 batting points, the second lowest, gives a clear indication of the side's strengths and weaknesses.

Pullar was released from his contract and decided to join Gloucestershire.

Season 1969 saw the introduction of the Sunday League sponsored by John Player; a change of chairmanship, with Cedric Rhoades taking

JACK SIMMONS

Although he ws 27 before he made his debut for the County, Simmons established himself as the leading all-rounder in the eleven – he seemed to be playing better, and certainly obtaining better figures, in his mid-40s, than ever he did in his 30s.

As a teenager he had had trials with Lancashire, but initially refused to join the Old Trafford staff in order to complete his apprenticeship, and then was 'forgotten' by the County Club.

Although he has never featured in Test cricket, he went to Tasmania as captain-coach and led that state to its first Sheffield Shield success and also to one-day success. This ability to raise the standard of the Tasmanian side made many people wonder why Simmons was not chosen to captain Lancashire in the ten years after Bond retired.

His accurate off-breaks are equally useful in both three-day and one-day cricket and he is a more than effective batsman in the lower middle order. His popularity was made plain when he received a record £128,000 benefit in 1980.

Jack Simmons (Patrick Eagar)

over from T.A. Higson; and the debut, in the second half of the season, of Clive Lloyd.

Rhoades had led the 'rebels' against the old committee in 1964. He had gained most votes when the election for the new committee had taken place. In his first years on the committee he had taken up the financial problems of the Club and steered through the Annual General Meeting the controversial scheme to build office blocks at Old Trafford. This development had placed the Club back on a sound footing. Now his reward was the chairmanship of the committee and he was regarded generally as one of the up-and-coming younger generation of cricket administrators.

On the field Lancashire found the new John Player League suited their style – of the first ten matches the Club played in the competition, nine were victories. They won the League with their 15th match, beating Warwickshire by 51 runs, Clive Lloyd and John Sullivan having a splendid partnership of 105 for the fourth wicket.

Bad weather seriously interfered with the Championship matches – every game at Old Trafford was drawn. With Statham now retired, the County found Lever, Higgs and Shuttleworth not quite so effective. The only contrast to the seam bowling was provided by the left-arm of David Hughes and to a lesser extent Jack Simmons. The one point that shone out on the field was the performance of Bailey, Hughes and David Lloyd close to the wicket.

Pilling and David Lloyd were the most successful batsmen and Engineer improved a great deal on his first season's efforts. He suffered two serious finger injuries which kept him out of several matches and thus prevented him reaching 1,000 runs – the Championship had been cut down to 24 matches per side, making the target of 1,000 runs more difficult.

The Sunday League proved so popular in Lancashire that the gate receipts from the eight matches exceeded all the money taken from the 12 three-day Championship games and the tourist fixtures. The Club however still lost £12,675 on the year, compared with £6,825 in 1968, mainly due to a large increase in the wages bill. Membership had steadily declined and from the total of 11,000 ten years before was now at 8,000. The Lancashire chairman, Cedric Rhoades, was against any increase in one-day cricket, considering that the development of all the year facilities at Old Trafford was the answer to the financial problems.

The surprise of the 1969–70 winter was the announcement that Ken Higgs had decided at the age of 32 to retire and go into League cricket. The staff for 1970 was bolstered by the signing of three youngsters, Frank Hayes, the young Marple batsman, Derek Parker, a leg-spinner and former Lancaster pro, and Michael Staziker, the fast-medium bowler from Preston. The other 17 members of the staff were: J.D.

Bond (Captain), G. Atkinson, D. Bailey, F.M. Engineer, P. Gooch, K. Goodwin, D. Hughes, P. Lever, C.H. Lloyd, D. Lloyd, H. Pilling, J.S. Savage, K. Shuttleworth, J. Simmons, K. Snellgrove, J. Sullivan and B. Wood. Brian Statham was elected to the committee.

The season began with all the problems of the South African tour and the campaign to stop it. That saga having run its course and a Rest of The World v England series substituted, interest in domestic cricket increased.

The young Lancashire side had the Player League title to defend, but clearly their horizon stretched beyond that. Apart from losing two 'joke' matches, when rain reduced the allotted overs, the County had a brilliant season in the Sunday League. The climax was reached at Old Trafford in the last match – by chance against Yorkshire – when 33,000 packed the ground. It was the first time since 1948 that the gates were closed and 'ground full' notices posted. Yorkshire, batting first, scored much too slowly and then lost wickets trying to rectify the problem. Lancashire found the target of 166 easy to achieve and won by seven wickets with 4.1 overs remaining. The crowd swarmed over the ground and there were scenes of great jubilation as Jack Bond accepted the Sunday League trophy. The averages show clearly the advantage Lancashire had over their rivals. In the top dozen batsmen, Clive Lloyd came second with an average of 57.88, Pilling was fourth and Sullivan twelfth. The bowling was even more impressive with Shuttleworth at the top, his 24 wickets costing 11.04 runs each; Simmons was third and David Hughes fourth and Peter Lever not too far behind him.

A week after the great match at Old Trafford the side travelled to Lord's for the final of the Gillette Cup. On the way to the final Lancashire had beaten Gloucestershire by 27 runs in their first match, David and Clive Lloyd both hitting fifties in a total of 278 for eight, which the Western County found too much for them. In the second match Peter Lever took five for 30 as Hampshire were dismissed cheaply. In the semi-final, Lancashire went to Taunton, where a capacity crowd of 10,000 saw the home side dismissed for 207, with Roy Virgin making a splendid 65, but then useful innings from all the Lancashire batsmen, save young Hayes, brought victory with 3.4 overs in hand.

Sussex, Lancashire's opponents in the final, batted first, but found runs hard to make. It was not so much the bowling as the fielding:

Lloyd was magnificent; lithe and swift, the ball either thudding into Engineer's gloves, or shattering the stumps. Pilling, this little dynamo of a man, was throwing in from the boundary with commendable speed and accuracy. In fact, the whole bearing of Lancashire in the field left one with the feeling that the batsmen were on a hiding to nothing.

CLIVE HUBERT LLOYD

Under his captaincy the West Indies cricket team dominated world cricket. By the time he decided to retire he had led West Indies in 74 Tests – no other player for any of the Test playing countries can approach this figure.

A very tall man with something of a stoop, Lloyd had the reach to make bowlers worry about their length. He hit the ball very hard and possessed a splendid array of strokes, thus being able to dominate all but the very best attacks.

In the field he was a real live wire, no batsman chancing a run if the ball was hit in Lloyd's vicinity in the covers.

On several occasions it looked as if a knee injury might end his career early, but each time he bounced back and though not as agile in his later years, he still scored runs with ease.

With 110 Tests to his name, it is not surprising that he has hit well over 7,000 Test runs and is second to Sobers in the West Indian run aggregate total.

Clive Lloyd (Patrick Eagar)

Thus ran the report in the *Playfair Cricket Monthly*. Three run-outs were achieved and what is as surprising in the game which was made for seamers, Hughes took three for 31 in twelve overs with his slows. Lancashire lost both openers cheaply, but Pilling, building an innings which had a good quantity of quick singles, was never in trouble and his unbeaten 70 won the match and the Man of the Match award. It was a great match for Lancashire, but not a great match in itself, because Bond and his merry band were better in every respect. Bond's field placings could scarcely be faulted, the Lancashire bowlers knew all about line and length and the batsmen used their feet – it was all completed in the 56th over.

In the Championship, Lancashire also found success. By the beginning of July they had won four out of eleven matches, were the only unbeaten side in the competition and were in fourth place seven points behind the leaders with matches in hand over all their rivals. There was spaculation on 5 August, when Lancashire moved up to third, still a game in hand over the two teams above them and only five points separating the three, that Lancashire might win a triple crown. M.H. Stevenson in *The Cricketer* noted:

> It is always difficult to apportion credit, as it is embarrassing to attach blame but, perhaps, the three individuals who have had the major share in Lancashire's meteoric rise, are Cedric Rhoades (I heard the other day from a senior player: 'Oh, yes, they can criticise him, but he's a good man for the players') and the two Jacks – messrs Wood and Bond. Both have acquired that priceless commodity, the respect of members and players alike, without which any club must at best be rather insecure.

Until the last match, Lancashire had outside hopes of taking the title, but they lost their realistic chances when they failed to beat Glamorgan in the penultimate match. Lancashire made 303 for five declared, then bowled out the Welsh side for 138, enforced the follow on and took two cheap wickets, but made no further progress as Tony Lewis and Peter Walker added 195 for the third wicket. In the final match, a win plus a record number of bonus points might have still won the title. As it was rain killed off that very remote hope.

There is clearly a connection between Lancashire's playing success in 1970 and the efforts of the chairman and the secretary of the Club, but quite rightly the press placed on Bond's shoulders the credit for winning matches and titles. Clive Lloyd's batting played a vital role, but he did miss a third of the Championship matches, and it was the fact that all the team were chivvied and cajoled into producing their best –by Bond – which made the difference. David Lloyd and Barry Wood became the regular opening pair – Atkinson was confined to the Second

Eleven and announced his retirement at the end of the year. Pilling came in at number three and Clive Lloyd at number four. They were followed by Engineer, Bond and Sullivan. With Simmons and Hughes as all-rounders lower in the order, the tail was negligible.

The leading wicket-takers were Lever and Shuttleworth, followed by Hughes, but both Sullivan and Wood managed to pick up more than 20 wickets each at a lower cost than any of the mainstream bowlers, and with Clive Lloyd also taking 20 wickets, it was a team of all-rounders.

Despite the success on the field, the financial corner had yet to be turned and Lancashire lost £13,692 on the year – the worst figures ever recorded. On the other hand the public recognised the debt they owed to Jack Bond, who received £7,230 from his Testimonial Fund.

Lancashire made a determined effort to retain their two titles in 1971 and add the Championship crown. The playing staff remained almost unchanged. By the first week of August, the County found itself in a similar position to that of the same time in 1970. They were second in the Championship, twelve points behind Warwickshire, both clubs having six wins from 19 matches. On 28 July they had played and won the famous semi-final Gillette Cup match at Old Trafford against Gloucestershire. In this match, attended by 23,520 spectators, rain had interrupted play and it was thus in very dark conditions at half past eight that Jack Bond and David Hughes attempted to score the final 27 runs off six overs. Hughes hit spinner Mortimore for 24 off the 56th over and made the winning run from the fifth ball of the 57th.

Turning back to the Championship, Lancashire ended their pro-gramme on 31 August with an innings victory over Worcestershire at Old Trafford and moved to the top of the table, but both Warwickshire and Surrey had matches in hand and all Lancashire could do for once was to pray for rain! It did not materialise and both their rivals overhauled them. With nine wins and four losses, Lancashire could look back at a satisfactory Championship year. Before the destiny of the Championship could be decided, there was a lull in three-day cricket, as the final of the Gillette Cup was played at Lord's, Lancashire meeting Kent.

Unlike the previous year's match, this was a much closer affair. Clive Lloyd's innings of 66 was the backbone of Lancashire's 224 for seven, but Simmons and Hughes hit a priceless 39 off the last four overs. Kent entrusted their all to Asif Iqbal. He took Kent to 197 for six – only 28 runs required at about six per over. Then an astonishing right-handed catch at extra cover by Bond removed Asif and the other three wickets simply faded away, Lancashire winning by 24 runs. Asif took the Man of the Match Award.

The race for the Sunday League continued after the other two trophies had been decided. On 12 September Glamorgan (and 30,000

LANCASHIRE *v.* GLOUCESTERSHIRE
Gillette Cup Semi-Final

Played on the Old Trafford Ground, Manchester on 28 July 1971

LANCASHIRE WON BY THREE WICKETS AT 8.50pm

GLOUCESTERSHIRE

R.B. Nicholls	b Simmons	53
D.M. Green	run out	21
R.D.V. Knight	c Simmons b Hughes	31
M.J. Procter	c Engineer b Lever	65
D.R. Shepherd	lbw b Simmons	6
M. Bissex	not out	29
*A.S. Brown	c Engineer b Sullivan	6
H.J. Jarman	not out	0
J.B. Mortimore		
†B.J. Meyer		
J. Davey		
Extras	b 2, lb 14, w 1, nb 1	18
Total	(6 wkts, 60 overs)	229

Fall: 1-57 2-87 3-113 4-150 5-201 6-210

BOWLING	O	M	R	W
Lever	12	3	40	1
Shuttleworth	12	3	33	0
Wood	12	3	39	0
Hughes	11	0	68	1
Simmons	12	3	25	2
Sullivan	1	0	6	1

LANCASHIRE

D. Lloyd	lbw b Brown	31
B. Wood	run out	50
H. Pilling	b Brown	21
C.H. Lloyd	b Mortimore	34
J. Sullivan	b Davey	10
†F.M. Engineer	hit wkt b Mortimore	2
*J.D. Bond	not out	16
J. Simmons	b Mortimore	25
D.P. Hughes	not out	26
P. Lever		
K. Shuttleworth		
Extras	b 1, lb 13, nb 1	15
Total	(7 wkts, 56.5 overs)	230

Fall: 1-61 2-105 3-136 4-156 5-160 6-163 7-203

BOWLING	O	M	R	W
Procter	10.5	3	38	0
Davey	11	1	22	1
Knight	12	2	42	0
Motrimore	11	0	81	3
Brown	12	0	32	2

Umpires: H.D. Bird and A. Jepson

* Captain: † Wicket-keeper

spectators) arrived at Old Trafford for the final match. Lancashire had to win in order to keep the title – the position at the top was that Worcestershire and Essex could both finish level on points with Lancashire, but the Lancastrians' run rate was superior to both the rivals and according to the rules, run rate decided the title if teams were equal on points and wins.

Glamorgan batted first but failed against some accurate bowling by Lever and Simmons, being dismissed in 37.4 overs for 143. Unfortunately Engineer was dismissed for a single when Lancashire began their replay. Snellgrove and David Lloyd added 39 for the second wicket, but that proved the best partnership of the innings and Lancashire, all out for 109, lost the title, Worcestershire taking the trophy.

Although Lancashire had to be content with only one title in 1971, they had earned a reputation as the most attractive and entertaining side in county cricket. They were able to field a side which changed very little – Barry Wood, Harry Pilling, David Lloyd, Jack Simmons and David Hughes played in every Championship match, Jack Bond missed one and Clive Lloyd two. Simmons was the most improved player, being an ideal all-round cricketer. Clive Lloyd topped the batting, with Wood second. Lever was the top bowler, but missed matches through Test calls; Hughes took most wickets, followed by Simmons.

The tide finally turned on the financial front, the popularity of the team combined with the income from the redevelopment of Old Trafford having their effect. The surplus for 1971 was £21,937, the largest in the Club's history and the first time since 1964 that the Club had not recorded a deficit. The membership rose to 10,500.

The successful side showed little change for 1972, though three new names appeared as 'apprentice professionals': John Abrahams, son of a professional in the Central Lancashire League, a left-hand bat and off-break bowler, aged 19; John Lyon, a 21-year-old wicket-keeper from St Helens; and Bob Ratcliffe, an all-rounder from Accrington. The County had also signed Tony Good, voted the outstanding schoolboy cricketer of 1971, who was a fast bowler from Worksop College and now at Durham University. Lancashire also jumped in and signed Peter Lee, the Northants fast bowler, who had been released by his native county. The reason was that Lever and Shuttleworth might be needed for England.

The unexpected happened and both Lever and Shuttleworth failed to live up to their reputations. Lever took 20 Championship wickets at 29.25 runs each, Shuttleworth 30 at 34.06. The poor weather did not help, but Lancashire could only win two Championship matches. The County finished in 15th place. Things were little better in the Sunday League, where they slipped to eighth place and though they qualified for the knock-out section of the new Benson & Hedges Cup, Lancashire lost in the quarter finals to Leicestershire, being completely outplayed.

The one Trophy in which they held their own was the Gillette. In the first match at Old Trafford, Somerset were narrowly defeated by nine runs, failing to reach a target of 243 set by the home Club. Lancashire had an easier time beating Hampshire, though the game was dominated by Barry Richards. The South African opener hit a brilliant 129 – the next best score in the all-out total of 223 was 28. Lancashire's innings was a team effort, the first seven batsmen all contributing something in the four-wicket win.

Jack Bond leaves the ground after this final match for Lancashire in 1972 (Patrick Eagar)

About 20,000 turned out for the semi-final at Old Trafford. It was a great game, with Kent, in the shape of Colin Cowdrey and Mike Denness, opting to bat on in very bad light on the first evening, but the match continued on to the second day, when Kent needed 125 with seven wickets in hand and the contest moved from the advantage of one side to the other until Lancashire dismissed the last Kent batsman with the last ball and Lancashire won by seven runs. Harry Pilling gained the Man of the Match Award through his well constructed innings of 70.

The final was against Warwickshire. M.J.K. Smith, the Warwickshire captain, decided to bat – Lever and Shuttleworth were not in the Lancashire side and Clive Lloyd opened the bowling with Peter Lee. Lloyd bowled his 12 overs for 31 runs and then later in the day hit 126, striking the ball with such force that it often passed the fielder before he could move; his innings included three sixes and 14 fours. Clive Lloyd won the match – by four wickets – and the Man of the Match Award. Lancashire under Bond had gained three successive Gillette Cup titles.

Jack Bond had already announced his retirement from county cricket. He wrote at the end of the season:

My view, when I was appointed Lancashire's captain, was fairly simple: there was a great deal of hard work to be done, but I wanted the players to go out and enjoy themselves. It's a formula which has worked in other sports, and I felt it was the right approach for us. My view was that it wasn't sufficient for us to be grimly concerned with not losing; we had to try to be positive – because the spectators of cricket were entitled to entertainment and enjoyment. I have never, ever had reason to change this point of view and Lancashire's success in the one-day competitions has given tremendous pleasure to thousands of people. They may not appreciate all the finer points of the three-day game but, by gum, they know what they want to see in the Gillette Cup and on a Sunday!

If there is one disappointment, it is the fact that Lancashire did not win the County Championship, under my leadership. We tried, how we tried ... and, after twice finishing third, we really thought we could do it last season. Instead things just didn't go right. But I'm not grumbling, for we have all had so much out of the past five years.

THE PARTY'S OVER

IN FIVE YEARS, JACK BOND, CEDRIC RHOADES and Jack Wood had converted a no-hope side to the most exciting eleven in the country. Could this bubbling enthusiasm survive the retirement of Bond?. He was not to disappear completely, for the committee appointed him joint-coach with Savage. 'Whoever succeeds', wrote M.H. Stevenson, 'he will not find it easy to follow Bond of Lancashire, humble, humorous, dedicated yet unselfish; but he could not base his approach to captaincy upon a better model.'

What was not known in the autumn of 1972 was that 12 months later Bond would be offered and accept the captaincy of Nottinghamshire, and by November 1974 Jack Wood, the pivot of Lancashire's all-round success, was to retire, at the age of 47, through ill-health. So the pyramid which Cedric Rhoades had so carefully constructed had fallen apart, when it appeared on the surface that there were several years remaining to it.

To return to 1973. David Lloyd, the 26-year-old left-hand opening batsman was appointed captain, a not unexpected choice, since he had led the side on several occasions in 1972 in the absence of Bond. The major obstacle to Lancashire's bid for trophies in 1973 was the fact that Clive Lloyd would be unavailable for most matches, being a member of the West Indies touring team. Much depended on the recovery of form and fitness of Peter Lever and Ken Shuttleworth.

The first indications of 1973 were promising, both David Lloyd and Frank Hayes hit hundreds in the preliminary Benson & Hedges matches. Hayes, the middle order batsman who had been given his county cap in 1972, looked as if he was going to fulfil the promise which he had shown over the last three years. Peter Lee was the other Lancashire player to make the news. He took six for 53 against Derbyshire at Old Trafford, his career best, then beat this with eight for 53 against Sussex at Hove a fortnight later, and not long afterwards took eight for 80 against Notts at Old Trafford. On 10 July, he was second in the first-class averages with 58 wickets at 16.55 runs each.

Frank Hayes made his one-day international debut in the two-match series against New Zealand and then his Test debut in the first Test v West Indies at the Oval in July. Hayes became only the fourth Englishman to score a century on his debut since the war, making an undefeated 106, as England fell to 255 all out and lost by 158 runs.

Lancashire progressed to the semi-finals of the Benson & Hedges Cup, before being beaten by the narrowest of margins. Batting first Lancashire reached 159 all out in 55 overs, Pilling making the highest score. Worcestershire in reply made 159 for 9, making a single off the last ball to tie the scores, but win the match. The County's hopes in the Gillette Cup ended in the third round, when despite 90 from Pilling they lost to Middlesex by four wickets with an over to spare.

In the Sunday League, Lancashire finished fourth, but Kent had an outstanding year and neither Lancashire nor any other county looked likely to overtake the southerners. In the Championship there was a marginal improvement on the poor showing of 1972. Critics were quick to point out that David Lloyd lacked the flair of Bond, so that, despite the good figures returned by Lever and Lee (fourth and seventh in the first-class bowling averages), the new captain was unable to make the most of half-chances and inspire the side to the extra effort required to win.

On the other hand the loss of Clive Lloyd's brilliant batting was impossible to overcome, more especially so when Hayes was taken away for Test duty. The middle order batting tended to be very fragile. Wood and David Lloyd as the openers had good seasons and Lloyd actually gained a one-day cap against West Indies. Four youngsters who looked very promising were John Abrahams, a whiz-kid in the field, Bernard Reidy, who was the pro at Blackpool, Andrew Kennedy of Blackburn, and in the Colts side, Paul Tipton of Sale, an off-spinner.

Secretary Jack Wood wrote in his pre-season notes for 1974 that much depended on the fitness of the three fast bowlers, Lee, Lever and Shuttleworth and so it turned out. Lee, the main success of 1973, was troubled with illness and injury all summer and could play in only nine Championship matches and even in those was rarely effective. Shuttleworth made a partial return to the form he had shown two years before. Lever began modestly, but after not appearing in any of the six Tests, was chosen for the two one-day internationals at the end of the year and booked himself a place on the MCC tour to Australia for the winter. Also on that tour was David Lloyd. He hit a century against the Indian tourists when they played Lancashire early in the season, then a double century in the third Test against them – his form being regarded as so good that he kept Boycott out of the England side for the rest of the summer.

David Lloyd's selection for England meant that he played in only seven Championship matches and that Clive Lloyd took over the leadership in his absence. The West Indian had an oustanding summer with 1,403 runs at an average of 63.77, and ended the year as the leading batsman in England. Hayes, the only other player to reach 1,000 runs in Championship matches, was proving very unpredictable. He seemed to possess all the strokes and when he had played himself in there were few more attractive batsmen in England. He had, however, a weakness for the hook, which led to his demise too often and he was clearly over-nervous at the start of an innings.

In the frequent absence of David Lloyd, the 24-year-old left-hander from Colne, Andrew Kennedy, was drafted in as Barry Wood's opening partner, and averaged over 30, without the aid of any hundreds. Pilling, despite two hundreds, had an uneven summer, possibly due to work on his benefit year which realised £11,500. Barry Wood was the team's all-rounder, heading the bowling table, whilst still opening the batting. Simmons also proved valuable on both counts and was as usual one of the best limited-overs bowlers.

Lancashire were the only County to go through the year undefeated in the Championship, but they were in the lower reaches of the table until three consecutive wins in August pushed them to eighth place.

Farokh Engineer appeals for a catch during the 1974 Gillette Cup Final (Patrick Eagar)

They made little impact in the Sunday League – the other Counties had watched and learnt from Jack Bond. In the Gillette Cup the County once more reached the final, meeting their old adversaries, Kent. The Saturday was rained off, but a prompt start made on Monday. The rain in the previous week had made the outfield slow and the pitch devoid of bounce. Lancashire batted first, lost two quick wickets, and then the running out of Clive Lloyd took the stuffing out of them – all out for 118. Shuttleworth wrenched a knee whilst batting and broke down in his opening over, and Kent won in the 47th over with four wickets to spare.

The Lancashire batting had also failed in the semi-final of the Benson & Hedges Cup. Set to make 194 off the 55 overs, by Surrey, they were all out for 130, of which Clive Lloyd made 50. Hayes had the misfortune to be dismissed without scoring in both this and the Gillette semi-final.

A.K. 'Jimmy' James, the Secretary of Somerset, took over Jack Wood's post at Old Trafford in the spring of 1975. There were, however, few other changes. Keith Goodwin, who had lost his first team place to Engineer and in 1974 saw young Lyon move into the second wicket-keeping slot, retired and Frank Beirne, whose bowling efforts had been confined to Second Eleven matches, also left. It was hoped that Tony Good and Paul Tipton would be available after the college term ended.

The first World Cup competition was the centrepiece of 1975, combined with a four-match Test series against Australia. Old Trafford not only failed to be allotted a Test match, but also obtained the least interesting of the World Cup ties – Sri Lanka v West Indies and India v New Zealand. Wood, Hayes and Lever appeared in the semi-final, when England were beaten by Australia at Leeds, then Wood appeared in three Tests and Lever in one.

The County recovered their appetite for the Championship and by beating Warwickshire, Northants, Derby, Middlesex and Derby a second time they were at the top of the table. Lever and Lee were near the top of the bowling averages, Clive Lloyd and Wood high in the batting. The elation at the Club's run of success, however, was marred by some unpleasant headlines on the players' salaries. The argument revolved around 'cost of living' increases and also the large difference between the money paid to English professionals and to the overseas players in county cricket. For reasons relating officially to indiscipline, Wood was suspended for six matches, Lever and Hayes for two each. All three were absent on 1 July, when Lancashire suffered their first Championship defeat of the season.

After going through a very sticky patch, the County revived latterly. With three matches to play, they beat Notts by ten wickets and then

Barry Wood, the Lancashire and England batsman, in full flow at Lord's in 1974 (Patrick Eagar)

Gloucester by the same margin, so going to Hove for the final match they were still in a position to challenge for the title. The points tally of the four principal counties prior to the last round of matches was:

Leicestershire	224
Lancashire	213
Yorkshire	207
Hampshire	205

Leicestershire were favourites, for led by Illingworth, they had won each of their last five matches and shot up the table during August. Lancashire in their last match managed to obtain four bowling bonus points, dismissing Sussex for 160, and two batting points, then the weather prevented a definite decision being reached. All the rivals won and Lancashire had to be content with fourth place – good compared with recent years, but poor when viewed from the hopes raised in mid-season.

Lancashire were among the also-rans in the Sunday League, but flourished in the Gillette Cup. Northants were cast aside in the first match – Lancashire won by nine wickets, Peter Lever taking four for 18;

the second game followed a similar pattern, but Wood (4-17) and Ratcliffe (4-25) were the bowlers who dismissed Hampshire for 98, Lancashire winning by six wickets. Gloucestershire were not so easily disposed of in the semi-final. Sadiq hit 122 and the total reached 236. Lancashire won with three deliveries remaining, Simmons and Ratcliffe delivering the *coup de grâce*.

The final was against Middlesex. Receipts were a record £66,921 and the crowd numbered 24,195. David Lloyd won the toss and decided to break with tradition and put the opposition in. Middlesex lost four for 64, both openers being removed by Lever, and the home county never recovered its poise, though the later batsmen took the total to 180 for eight. A brilliant innings by Clive Lloyd was the feature of the match as Lancashire won by seven wickets.

Clive Lloyd, though he had to be content with third spot in the first-class averages, was easily Lancashire's most prolific scorer. David Lloyd played during May in some discomfort from an injury received in Australia and then suffered a further setback in the form of a broken hand. Hayes, Kennedy and Wood all had good seasons, though Wood missed many matches. Pilling fell right away and was dropped from the side, but young Abrahams looked impressive.

With four Lancashire bowlers, Lever, Lee, Wood and Shuttleworth, in the top ten of the first-class averages at the summer's end, there could be few complaints about the bowling, especially as Ratcliffe, Simmons and Hughes could also claim to take their wickets at less than 27 runs each.

There was an embarrassment of wicket-keepers. Engineer performed quite up to international standard, so Lyon had very few opportunities: several other counties were casting sidelong glances at him.

Financially the Club had a good year, gate receipts increasing by about £30,000 and a profit of £7,577 being made. Shuttleworth and Sullivan, the latter now confined to the Second Team, shared a benefit worth £14,000.

The absence of Clive Lloyd in 1976 – playing for West Indies – caused Lancashire to lose all the ground they had made in the Championship in the previous season. They plummeted to 16th place in the table with only three victories and seven losses. Harry Pilling had an Indian summer, scoring nearly twice as many runs as the next on the list, averaging 53.34, and coming seventh in the overall first-class averages. Barry Wood, troubled by injuries, missed half the matches, but with the aid of 198 against Glamorgan, came second to Pilling. His bowling deserted him: two years earlier he had been described as a deceptive bowler, his casual run-up concealing a well disguised late swing. The batsmen now appeared to have rumbled him. The other bowlers either stood still or declined, Lever, in particular, being very disappointing.

David Lloyd batting in the Cup Final of 1975 (Patrick Eagar)

Injury prevented Shuttleworth from playing more than a few Second Eleven games and at the end of the season he left Old Trafford. There was some glimmer of hope for the future when the left-hand spinner, Arrowsmith, was given a chance late on and with 18 wickets at 22.16 each, topped the bowling. Kennedy and Reidy, the young batting hopes of the previous year, contributed little, save an unbeaten 176 by the former against Leicestershire.

Results in the Sunday League were slightly more agreeable, but ninth place with eight wins was not good by Lancashire's one-day standards. They did make more effort in the Gillette Cup and reached the final for the sixth time in seven years. This time their opponents were Northants. Lancashire batted first, but the cheap dismissal of Engineer and Pilling allied to the retirement of Wood with a broken finger was too much of a handicap and Northants won by four wickets.

F.M. Engineer retired at the end of the season and signed for Woodhouses in 1977 – his benefit realised a record £26,159. The Club achieved a profit of £11,289, despite an increase in wages and match expenses of £13,000. Apart from Engineer, Shuttleworth (going to Leicestershire) and Sullivan were also absent when the staff reported for the 1977 season. The three most important newcomers were Colin

Croft, the gangling West Indian fast bowler recommended by Clive Lloyd, William Hogg, the 21-year-old fast bowler from Ulverston and Chris Scott, a 17-year-old wicket-keeper. After hesitation, Peter Lever declined a one-year contract and also departed.

The Packer Affair burst on the scene as the 1977 Australians under Greg Chappell prepared for their tour of England. The first one-day international was staged at Old Trafford and 15,000 turned up to see Australia beaten. No Lancastrians featured in either the one-day internationals or the Test series.

The County itself had a dreadful year. Clive Lloyd played in May, then withdrew for a cartilage operation. The batting was unreliable, with only Hayes and Barry Wood reaching 1,000 runs, and it might have been wise to recall Engineer, for his replacement, Lyon, though a competent wicket-keeper, increased the tail.

The bowling relied on Lee and Simmons; Croft was erratic and his wickets cost 29 runs each. Ratcliffe, who had seemed so promising, was dropped due to a back complaint. Rumours circulated concerning the reason for the sudden retirement of Lever, but these did not help the attack to mend itself. Hogg remained on the 'promising' list and was a no-ball specialist. Hughes, whose 18 wickets at 19.05 each placed him at the head of the bowling table was dropped in favour of Arrowsmith, which did nothing for the batting, the latter managing 32 runs in 12 innings.

Only two Championship wins were recorded all summer and the County ended in 16th place for the second successive season. They held the same lowly position in the Sunday League and even in their speciality, the Gillette Cup, they were removed in the second round.

The Old Trafford wicket came in for much criticism. Bert Flack had retired in the spring and Gordon Prosser, the Worcester groundsman, was appointed, but within five weeks and on the eve of the one-day international, he walked out and returned to Worcester. Bernard Flack, the Edgbaston groundsman and TCCB Inspector of Pitches, was released temporarily by Warwickshire to sort out the problems at Old Trafford.

On 5 October, David Lloyd resigned as captain, and Frank Hayes was appointed as the leader for 1978. A.K. James, the secretary, moved at the end of the year to take a similar post with Hampshire, and was succeeded by Chris Hassell, a 35-year-old assistant secretary at Arsenal, who had also been secretary at Crystal Palace, Everton and Preston North End. Brian Fitch of Canterbury was approached regarding the groundsman's job, but declined and Chris Hawkins, the former Warwickshire cricketer and groundsman at Aigburth, took over instead.

On the playing staff for 1978 came a new batsman from Rawtenstall,

Graeme Fowler, but in his first year his only outing with the First Eleven was a Sunday League match. The County improved slightly on 1977, but had a terrible time with injuries to their fast bowlers. Peter Lee played in the first match, then broke down with a shoulder injury and was seen no more; Willie Hogg lasted until mid-summer before his back gave way and Ratcliffe also retired hurt later in the season. Croft survived, but his deliveries seemed to hit the batsman more often than the wicket and at the close of the year his contract was not renewed.

The spin attack of Arrowsmith and Simmons was expensive and Hughes, the most economical of the bowlers, was not bowled a great deal.

The batting also had its share of misfortune. Barry Wood could play in only seven Championship matches and in eleven innings his highest was 22. His fall was quite dramatic, for at the beginning of the summer he played as England's opening bat in the first two one-day internationals and the first Test, but apparently later on, though fit, he was not chosen for the County side.

Clive Lloyd, though a shadow of his brilliant best, topped the batting averages and both David Lloyd and Frank Hayes were consistent. Andrew Kennedy had a good year, but John Abrahams improved only in fits and starts.

While David Lloyd created a new Lancashire record with a benefit worth £40,171, the Club suffered a record loss of £33,816. the results in 1979 showed little sign of improving – though Lancashire got through the first-round Gillette tie against Essex, the latter reporting the Old Trafford pitch to Lord's. About 150 members rebelled and forced a Special General Meeting, proposing a vote of no confidence in the committee. Before the meeting could take place, the committee took the sting out of the attack by announcing the appointment of Jack Bond as cricket manager for 1980 and signing Mick Malone, the Australian fast bowler. Malone appeared in the last two Championship matches, taking 18 wickets at 10 runs each. The no-confidence vote failed.

The county's positions in the Championship and Sunday League were 13th and 10th. After their first-round victory in the Gillette Cup, they were knocked out in the second and they failed to qualify for the Benson & Hedges knock-out section. Clive Lloyd, Hayes, Wood and David Lloyd had fair seasons with the bat, but only Simmons took 50 Championship wickets. Injuries were still very frequent but there were one or two promising youngsters who might be brought forward by Bond – Fowler, Ian Cockbain and fast bowler Paul Allott were mentioned in that context. The financial situation improved, with a profit of £6,315 being registered for 1979.

The most controversial news of the winter of 1979–80 was that Barry Wood, who had received a new record benefit of £62,429, had refused to sign for 1980 for the £7,000 offered. He later signed for Derbyshire and by the end of 1980 was that county's captain. John Lyon was another player to decline terms and he left Old Trafford.

In the spring of 1980, Bond assessed the possibilities – he had been coaching in the Isle of Man for the two previous years:

> The potential is there, otherwise I wouldn't have taken the job. But there has been something of a decline. One of my first priorities is to get pride of County back. It might take between three and five years to realise my ideals, as I want to give everyone a thorough chance. I have no intention of taking on new overseas players, and I want to give the youth of the County every opportunity.

The fact that Clive Lloyd would be unable to play due to the West Indies touring team being in England combined with Wood's defection seriously to reduce the batting strength. Bernard Reidy, a hard-hitting batsman for Whalley, hit a brilliant hundred against Worcestershire at Old Trafford to bring a welcome victory in the third Championship match. Illness and injury marred the rest of the season for him and Lancashire managed only three more victories, to end the season in 15th place.

The fast bowling continued to pose problems. Malone, after his great debut in 1979, had a modest year and Hogg, still a no-ball expert, was the only bowler to reach 50 wickets. Ratcliffe missed virtually the whole year and Lee, who played in six Championship games was wildly expensive, his wickets costing 40 runs each. Only Kennedy and Hayes managed 1,000 runs and Pilling was brought back in a forlorn attempt to bolster the batting.

Jack Bond still had a lot to do when the season closed.

CLIVE LLOYD TO THE RESCUE

CLIVE LLOYD WAS APPOINTED COUNTY CAPTAIN for 1981. Michael Holding, the West Indian fast bowler, was signed on a part-time basis, appearing also for Rishton in the Lancashire League. Neal Radford, the Transvaal fast bowler, was also secured. Willie Hogg, however, had moved over to Warwickshire and Mick Malone was no longer at Old Trafford. It was to be hoped therefore that Peter Lee would manage to avoid injury and that Allott would grow in stature.

The Championship season began poorly. There was a one-innings a-side match at Worcester (rain only allowing five hours play) which was won, but that apart, Lancashire did not record victory in what was now the Schweppes County Championship until August. Three late victories prevented them taking the wooden spoon and they settled for 16th place. In the Sunday League six wins gained the County 10th place. They failed to survive the preliminary section of the Benson & Hedges Cup, but in the main knock-out competition (now sponsored by NatWest Bank, rather than Gillette) Lancashire had picked up a few crumbs of comfort.

Durham were beaten in the first round, Kennedy making an unbeaten 102. David Lloyd was the leading scorer and Man of The Match in the second round win against Middlesex, whilst Clive Lloyd, dropped twice, made 82 not out to bring a three-wicket win in the quarter finals against Hampshire. The semi-final match against Northants at Northampton built up to an exciting climax. When the last batsman for Northants, Griffith, who had one of the worst batting records in county cricket, arrived at the crease, 13 runs were needed off eight overs. Eventually Northants won with one delivery remaining – of the 13, 11 were scored in singles. Play was actually held up for five minutes before the final over was bowled, in order that the scoring rates could be checked – the scores at that point were level.

The two West Indians, Lloyd and Holding, both made great contributions to the side. Lloyd topped the batting by a margin of eight runs and Holding topped the bowling, taking his wickets at nearly six runs less per victim than the next in the list, who proved to be Paul Allott.

Allott was the great bowling discovery of 1981. He took 85 wickets and made his Test debut at Old Trafford in the fifth Test, taking the place of Old. The bespectacled 24-year-old caused a surprise by hitting 52, though he also did enough with the ball to earn himself a place in the England touring side to India in the winter.

The fast bowling of Allott was not the only sign of youthful success, for Graeme Fowler took over as an opening batsman from David Lloyd and scored 1,384 Championship runs and was an England cricketer in the making. He was also given the job of wicket-keeper for some matches, but this was not so satisfactory and Chris Scott resumed the position in the later part of the season.

Hughes completed 1,000 first-class runs for the first time, but Frank Hayes was beset with injuries. His namesake, Kevin Hayes, who played for England Under 19s and gained a blue at Oxford, played in one Championship game and looked a good prospect, as did Steve O'Shaughnessy. There was also Tim Taylor, the young left-arm spinner, so Bond could point to several hopeful signs, even if the 1981 results did not bring much cheer.

Lancashire took part in the experimental seven-a-side floodlit county tournament at the end of the season, and they won the final, after beating Yorkshire and Notts, playing against Somerset at Chelsea Football Ground.

Off the field, the 100-bedroom hotel scheme for Old Trafford, which had received much publicity, was officially abandoned when it was discovered that the scheme would cost £6 million. The 1981 financial

David Lloyd batting in the Benson & Hedges Semi Final v Notts at Trent Bridge in 1982 (Patrick Eagar)

year brought a new record surplus of £118,641. The subscriptions brought in £128,829 and gate receipts were £44,319. The County's share from the TCCB amounted to £142,636.

Because of the tightening of the rules regarding overseas players, Lancashire were forced to abandon any attempt to take Holding on the staff full time and reverted to Croft. Since both Clive Lloyd and Croft had been engaged by the County before 1978, they could both be played in Championship matches, whereas if Holding had been played Clive Lloyd would have had to drop out of the eleven. The difference in the side of 1982 compared with 1981 was broadly the difference between Holding (40 wkts at 17.87) and Croft (33 wkts at 30.39 in 1982).

The batting in 1982 was strong – Kennedy lost his place in the side and David Lloyd reverted to opening with Fowler. Both had excellent seasons with 1,000 runs each at an average above 40. Hughes, Clive Lloyd and Abrahams all scored lots of runs and the last named in his tenth season at old Trafford finally won a county cap.

The bowling was weak – Simmons with 49 wickets at 26.20 each was top of the averages. Allott could not repeat his 1981 performance and after playing in two Tests and two one-day internationals against India, lost his England place for the second half of the season against Pakistan. He was plagued with injuries, which did nothing to help his career.

The policy of engaging young cricketers continued. Ian Folley from Burnley and Stephen Crawley were signed in the winter, followed by Les McFarlane, a Jamaican, but with English registration. Chris Maynard, a wicket-keeper on the Edgbaston staff, was signed after the season began and soon took Scott's place – Scott left Old Trafford at the end of the summer.

In the results themselves the County showed very little improvement on the last few years – 12th in the Championship with four wins; tenth equal in the Sunday League; and they made no noticeable impact in the other two competitions. The jam tomorrow promises of Bond and the Committee were beginning to have a rather fly-blown look.

The financial affairs of the club showed a terrible nosedive – from their record profit of £118,641 in 1981, the Club swung to a loss of £150,852. This was partially due to the collapse of the firm dealing in ground advertising – the firm owed the Club £80,000.

Colin Croft, due to injury, was released by the County, but Neal Radford and Steve Jefferies were registered. Jefferies had played one match for Derbyshire in 1982 and was the Western Province fast bowler. Radford would qualify as an English player in 1983 and in the meantime could play when Clive Lloyd was absent.

The only memorable point in 1983 for Lancashire was O'Shaughnessy's infamous 35-minute century in the last match of the season,

LANCASHIRE *v.* WARWICKSHIRE

Played at Southport on 28, 29 and 30 July 1982

LANCASHIRE WON BY TEN WICKETS

WARWICKSHIRE	FIRST INNINGS		SECOND INNINGS	
*D.L. Amiss	c Abrahams b McFarlane	6	c Scott b McFarlane	24
R.I.H.B. Dyer	c Simmons b McFarlane	0	c Abrahams b McFarlane	0
T.A. Lloyd	c Scott b Folley	23	b McFarlane	0
A.I. Kallicharran	not out	230	(5)c D. Lloyd b O'Shaughnessy	0
†G.W. Humpage	b D. Lloyd	254	(6)c Abrahams b O'Shaughnessy	21
Asif Din			(4)c Hughes b O'Shaughnessy	21
S.H. Wootton			b McFarlane	0
C. Lethbridge			c Hughes b Folley	18
G.C. Small			lbw b McFarlane	0
P.J. Hartley			c Scott b McFarlane	16
S.P. Sutcliffe			not out	7
Extras	b 1, lb 6, w 1, nb 2	10	b 1, lb 2, w 1	4
Total	(4 wkts dec)	523		111

Fall: 1st inns: 1-5 2-6 3-53 4-523
2nd inns: 1-1 2-1 3-47 4-47 5-47 6-47 7-76 8-81 9-99

BOWLING	O	M	R	W	O	M	R	W
McFarlane	11	2	90	2	20	3	59	6
Folley	15	3	64	1	11	5	19	1
O'Shaughnessy	15	2	62	0	7.1	0	29	3
Simmons	20	2	97	0	1	1	0	0
Hughes	20	2	79	0				
Abrahams	15	3	76	0				
D. Lloyd	10.1	1	45	1				

LANCASHIRE	FIRST INNINGS		SECOND INNINGS	
G. Fowler	b Asif Din	126	not out	128
D. Lloyd	c Humpage b Small	10	not out	88
†C.J. Scott	lbw b Brown (sub for Small)	9		
I. Cockbain	c Amiss b Kallicharran	98		
*C.H. Lloyd	c Humpage b Kallicharran	45		
D.P. Hughes	c Small b Kallicharran	14		
J. Abrahams	not out	51		
S.J. O'Shaughnessy	not out	26		
J. Simmons				
I. Folley				
L.L. McFarlane				
Extras	lb 13, w 3, nb 19	35	lb 2, nb 8	10
Total	(6 wkts dec)	414	(no wkt)	226

Fall: 1-34 2-109 3-194 4-305 5-327 6-333

BOWLING	O	M	R	W	O	M	R	W
Small	15	4	38	1	11	2	30	0
Hartley	14	0	66	0	9	1	38	0
Sutcliffe	38	9	103	0	19	5	60	0
Lethbridge	14	5	58	0	9	2	27	0
D.J. Brown (sub)	13	3	47	1				
Asif Din	6	1	35	1				
Kallicharran	13	3	32	3	6	0	35	0
Lloyd					1	0	1	0

Umpires: H.D. Bird and J. van Geloven

Jack Simmons batting at Lord's in the Benson & Hedges Semi-Final in 1983 (Patrick Eagar)

when opponents Leicestershire put on their joke bowlers in the hope of enticing a declaration. Fowler and O'Shaughnessy hit 201 for the first wicket in 43 minutes, but Clive Lloyd did not bother to declare and the game was a total farce in the last session.

Only three Championship wins were recorded, which gave the Club 12th place. They again failed in the one-day competitions. The bowling lacked bite. Taking a qualification of 20 wickets, Lancashire's best bowler came 30th in the first-class averages – Jefferies with 32 wickets at nearly 25 runs each. Only Simmons took over 50 wickets. Allott, after being dropped by England, regained a place in the World Cup squad of

1983, but his Championship record was modest indeed, with 38 wickets at 30 runs each. Mike Watkinson, a 21-year-old medium-pace bowler from Westhoughton, joined the 'promising brigade. The club added Nasir Zaidi, a Pakinstani from the Lord's groundstaff, to their books. He appeared in 12 Championship games, but took only 15 wickets, though he looked a useful batsman and an asset in the field.

Aside from a sad decline in Clive Lloyd's average, the batsmen had good returns. Fowler and Abrahams reached 1,000 runs, young Neil Fairbrother scored 94 on his first-class debut against Warwickshire and then hit seven more fifties. A 19-year-old left-hand batsman from Lymm Grammar School, he was chosen for the three matches against Young Australia and was the most impressive of the Young England batsmen, making 90 in the final mini-Test.

David Lloyd missed half the season through a neck injury. He returned to the side and scored a century against Northants, only to break a finger in the same game. Disillusioned, David Lloyd decided to retire from county cricket. There was a change of head groundsman, Peter Marron taking over from Chris Hawkins.

With Clive Lloyd deciding to captain West Indies, Lancashire were forced to find a new leader for 1984. The choice fell on John Abrahams, who had captained the team when Lloyd was absent in 1983 and won praise for his work as deputy. With both Lloyds being away from Old Trafford for the new season, Alan Ormrod, the 41-year-old Lancastrian who had spent over 20 years with Worcester, was recruited. There were also several much younger rookies – David Varey from Birkenhead School and Cambridge, David Makinson, an all-rounder from Leyland and Mark Chadwick, a right-hand batsman from Rochdale were the most notable. In the last few years the Lancashire groundstaff had been almost doubled in size – for 1984 there were 30 players. The most for any other county was 23 and the average spread over the 17 first-class counties was 21.

The youthful enthusiasm engendered by Jack Bond and his two coaches – Peter Lever had been brought in as assistant to Savage – translated itself to much better results in the one-day competitions of 1984.

Lancashire got through to the knock-out rounds of the Benson & Hedges Cup, beat Essex in the quarter-finals, when Abrahams and Hughes put on 107 for the fourth wicket (by the time the partnership ended only 16 runs were needed with overs in hand) and beat Notts in the semi-finals, when Mark Chadwick made 87 as Lancashire scored 224 for four, winning by six wickets.

The final was against much-fancied Warwickshire. Allott and Jefferies took advantage of a damp pitch to dismiss Warwickshire for 139. With the wicket easier in the afternoon Lancashire had no difficulty in hitting off the runs. The match adjudicator, Peter May, gave the Man of the Match Award to John Abrahams for the way he had captained the side throughout the competition. It was the first time that the County had won the Benson & Hedges title.

In the Sunday League, Lancashire were sixth at the beginning of July and a month later were third. In the end they had to settle for fourth place, but this was a great improvement on 1983, and ten of their 16 matches were won.

The team's batting fell apart in the quarter-final of the NatWest Trophy at Lord's, Lancashire making 105 in reply to Middlesex's 276 for eight. The real disappointment of the season though was the County Championship. Only one victory was recorded, the worst season's work ever; the wooden spoon was avoided by four points.

Although the loss of the two Lloyds, then just after season began the retirement on medical advice of Frank Hayes, plus Graeme Fowler's absence on England duty (he missed 14 Championship games) clearly caused a major rethink in the batting department, the combination of O'Shaughnessy, Abrahams, Ormrod and Fairbrother, with Simmons and Watkinson, meant that runs were not lacking.

The bowling averages, as so frequently in the past, told their own sad tale. Allott, with 58 wickets at 17 runs each, was almost on his own as an attacking bowler who expected to dismiss the opposition. England noticed him again and he missed ten Championship games.

For the rest, Simmons remained the venerable trundler – his 63 wickets cost 26 runs each. No one else averaged under 29. McFarlane, Jefferies and Radford all had disappointing summers; McFarlane and Radford were released at the end of the season. In what appeared to be a moment of panic at the end of July, Pat Patterson, the West Indian fast bowler, was registered and within 24 hours pushed from the Saddleworth League into the Lancashire team. He took one for 69 on his debut in the NatWest Trophy and failed to take a wicket in his one Championship game.

Off the field of play, the Club had built 20 executive boxes at the Stretford End of the ground and these were rented out to various companies, providing a good income – profits rose from £15,013 to £134,704 in 1984. There was no beneficiary in 1984, an appeal being made instead for the Centenary of the first Old Trafford Test.

There was quite a change in the playing staff for 1985. Pat Patterson was taken on full time, as were Andrew Hayhurst, a batsman from Davyhulme; the fast bowler from Denmark, Soren Henriksen; and Tony Murphy, a bowler from Manchester; but no fewer than seven players were released: Crawley, McFarlane, Neal Radford, who moved to Worcestershire (with embarrassingly good results), Taylor, Wallwork and Nasir Zaidi.

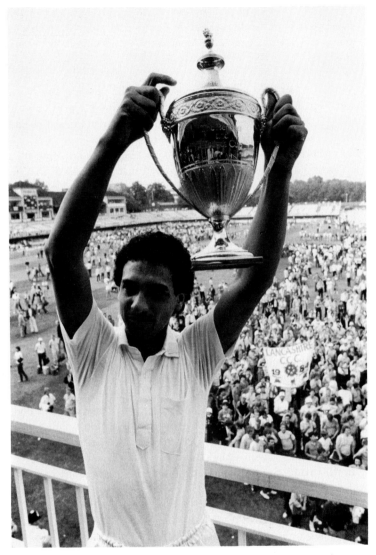

John Abrahams with the Benson & Hedges Trophy after the 1984 victory at Lord's
(Patrick Eagar)

Bond was confident that he had now groomed the right youngsters and he commented before the season began:

We have been prepared to be patient with our young players because everybody deserves a chance to learn how to play the game. Now the learning process and the transitional period is over and we expect everybody to take full responsibility for an improvement in results. We have quite a few players who can no longer use inexperience to excuse any underachievement this summer. We will expect the batsmen to score quickly enough to earn us a lot more batting bonus points and to give our bowlers longer to bowl sides out in the second innings.

When the season's results were analysed, the bowling had failed (apart from Allott) completely. In the 24 Championship matches only once was the opposition bowled out twice – at Bristol in the second match against Gloucestershire. Only Allott had an average under 30. Allott had returned early from England's touring team to India with a bad back injury, but he recovered so well that he regained his Test place, in the process missing ten Championship games. Patterson was usually preferred to Jefferies or Clive Lloyd as the overseas player in Championship matches, but captured only 34 wickets, at 31 runs each. Makinson, the local left-arm fast bowler, played regularly, but his 31 wickets cost 33 runs each. Watkinson, another seam bowler, was even more expensive and the spin attack of left-arm Folley and veteran Simmons rarely did more than contain the batsmen.

In contrast to the revival of Allott, Fowler's career collapsed in pieces around him. Opening in the Tests in India and scoring his famous double century at Madras, he seemed certain of a good future, but he lost confidence after a string of low scores, was omitted from the England side, injured his neck and finally found himself in the Lancashire Second Eleven. His opening County partner suffered a similar fate – Ormrod also failed in the first few matches, went into the Second Team and at the end of the season was released. With both openers failing, it was quite catastrophic to find that the number three batsman also lost the ability to make runs. In 13 matches O'Shaughnessy averaged 13, with a highest score of 63.

In the circumstances the Club had the very difficult choice of trying to bolster the batting by including Clive Lloyd, or hoping that the tide would turn and staying with Patterson or Jefferies. They stayed with the overseas bowlers – Clive Lloyd, appearing in only four Championship games, topped the batting averages.

Fairbrother was the most successful batsman, the only one to complete 1,000 runs, and with three centuries to his name he was awarded his county cap. Later on, Kevin Hayes, Mark Chadwick and David Varey, the last two opening the innings, looked the best of the other youngsters. Abrahams, the captain, found the problems quite depressing and his batting reflected his mood. He was relieved of the post at the end of the year.

The doom and gloom of the Championship results – three wins and 14th place – were not brightened in any way by the one-day results, which are best passed by.

The 1985 season saw the retirement after 26 years of Harry Pilling – Ormrod was re-engaged as Second Eleven coach. The Club also decided to release Jefferies on the grounds that with Clive Lloyd and Patterson on the books, the South African would be given few opportunities to prove himself in the First Eleven. Ian Austin from Rossendale, a 19-year-old batsman with Haslingden, joined the staff as did two youngsters on the Young Opportunity Scheme, Warren Hegg, a wicket-keeper from Bury and Nick Speak of Didsbury.

It was decided to appoint Clive Lloyd as 1986 captain, with Jack Simmons as vice-captain. This decision was on the face of it not a very happy one, for Lloyd could not play if Patterson was chosen.

Two early Championship victories at the expense of Sussex and Worcestershire seemed to give promise of some improvement in the County's first-class record. The signing of Mendis, the Sri Lankan opening batsman, who had played for Sussex since 1974, added some authority at the top of the order. He opened the innings with Fowler and both completed 1,000 runs. Varey and Chadwick were tried first wicket down, but the job eventually went to Abrahams, who was much more consistent. At number four, the left-handed Fairbrother had an excellent season and all in all the batting looked much stronger than in 1985, but there was little to enthuse about when the bowling figures were inspected. As in 1985 no one managed 50 Championship wickets. Simmons won the last match of the year with five for 53 against Somerset, after Botham had astonished everyone with 100 off 60 balls in the first innings. The veteran bowler also returned one or two other good analyses and topped the bowling averages, but he missed 11 Championship games. Allott came second to Simmons and Patterson had one or two good days, his 40 wickets costing 30 runs each.

The early Championship wins soon disappeared from view and the County sank back to 15th place in the table. Their position in the Sunday League was little better – 12th with six wins. Only one victory was recorded in the Benson & Hedges Cup, the County even being defeated by Scotland – the first ever win by that country in the competition.

The one Trophy which afforded some consolation was the NatWest. An easy win over Cumberland led to a great match at Taunton, which Lancashire won by three runs, after batting first – Mendis hit 72 and Abrahams 52. An undefeated 93 by Fairbrother beat Leicestershire and took the side into the semi-finals. The match took place at the Oval, where Sylvester Clarke exploited a pitch with plenty of bounce. Clive Lloyd, however, mastered him and Lancashire made 229. Surrey's batsmen hit out in a vainglorious manner and only Jesty reached 20 – he went on to 112 and fortunately for Lancashire was caught in the penultimate over on the long-on boundary – Lancashire won by four runs.

The final, against Sussex, proved a run feast. Lancashire made 242 for eight, Fairbrother scoring 63 and young Hayhurst 49. Sussex had to score a record 243 in the second innings. They managed the task with ease, losing only three wickets and having 1.4 overs to spare.

Having failed in all the other competitions, the Lancashire Club had set their hearts on winning the Trophy, which over the last two decades had been so often at Old Trafford. When the news of the humiliating defeat sank in, heads rolled and the following day it was announced that both Bond and his coach, Lever, were sacked.

The most vociferous reaction to the demise of Bond and Lever came a week or so later from Birtles Bowl, the home in Cheshire of Tim Hudson, who had stood for the Lancashire committee two years before, but failed to be elected. Hudson stated that he could sign up Botham and Richards (just sacked by Somerset) for Lancashire and would accept the chairmanship of the Lancashire committee.

The committee did not take too kindly to this suggestion. Hudson then requested the addresses of all the members of the Club so that he could write to them. The Club refused and Hudson then launched his campaign to oust Cedric Rhoades from the chairmanship. A proposal was put forward for consideration at the AGM that a chairman should resign after five years.

Before this AGM could take place the committee chose David Hughes as captain for 1987.

At the AGM in December, Hudson attacked Rhoades, but was told by members at the meeting to shut up and sit down. The proposal to force a change of chairman after five years in office failed to obtain a two-thirds majority. The rule that committee members should retire at 75 was, however, carried.

During the meeting Rhoades stated that Bond and Lever had agreed that Clive Lloyd should captain Lancashire in 1986. After the meeting Bond denied this and provoked the following comment from Clive Lloyd:

> As a manager he had his good and bad points, but it was the team's lack of success over a number of years which cost him his job – not me.

On 2 February, Cedric Rhoades issued the following statement:

> Since September there have been continuous, and in some cases, vicious attacks upon me personally and on the committee as a whole. I find this situation quite intolerable and am submitting by resignation to the committee. I trust that they will accept it, but I must make it clear that there has been no pressure of any kind from any direction.

Murray Birnie, the Bury businessman, seemed favourite to succeed

Rhoades, but the committee took the unusual step of appointing someone not at present on the committee – Bob Bennett. Bennett, who had played for the County as an opening batsman in the 1960s, had previously been on the committee for a dozen years, but did not stand for re-election in December 1985.

The committee took a look at the structure of the Club and in Februrary decided to create a new public relations sub-committee under the chairmanship of John Brewer and a marketing committee under Murray Birnie.

The development of the ground had continued through the in-fighting and for the 1987 season the new press box and allied facilities were opened. With the decision not to appoint a new cricket manager, Alan Ormrod took on the coaching department, working in conjunction with the new captain, Hughes.

The team itself went off to Jamaica in March for a two week pre-season tour, and when they returned the public waited to see if all the changes of the winter months could bring some revival on the field. Most important of the new players signed for 1987 was the Manchester Grammar school batsman, Michael Atherton, now at Cambridge.

The team won three of their first five Championship matches, but then as in the previous year seemed to fade, though not to the same degree. In mid-August they beat Sussex at Lytham and there followed five more successive victories. If they had gained maximum points in the last match (v Essex) they stood the possibility of taking the title. As it was Lancashire had to be content with second place. This position and the ten victories were so far in advance of any achievement in the three-day game in recent years that the new captain and the rest of the officials of the Club won the congratulations of all and sundry.

Fowler and Mendis formed a strong opening pair, both reaching 1,000 runs at an average above 40. Fairbrother had an excellent season, even if he disappointed when selected for England. The 19-year-old Atherton joined the side in the vacation and established himself as number three in the order, Abrahams being unable to hold a regular place. Watkinson was given a chance in June and did so well that he became the best all-rounder in the eleven, usually going in at number five. Chris Maynard, the senior wicket-keeper, was absent through injury all season; Stanworth took over, but when he was injured, young Warren Hegg had his chance and surprised his admirers with a century against Northants.

The change in the bowling compared with the last few seasons was quite remarkable. In most of the recent years it had been unusual for Lancashire to have more than one bowler in the top 30 in the averages – in 1987 all five of the major Lancashire bowlers were featured. Simmons, at the age of 46, had one of the best years of his long career, with 63 Championship wickets at 22 runs each. Allott topped the bowling and Watkinson, Folley and Patterson all took wickets at a reasonable cost.

On the other hand several of the young hopefuls fell by the wayside and at the end of the season left Old Trafford: Kevin Hayes, Soren Henriksen, Ian Davidson, Mark Chadwick and David Varey. Of the older players, O'Shaughnessy lost his place in the side and was released.

The success in the Championship did not carry itself forward to the one-day competitions, though in the Sunday League the Club moved up three places. The League was badly affected by the weather and Lancashire suffered five no-result games, but two other counties were even more cruelly affected, so for once Lancashire could not really complain too bitterly on this front.

Off the field, Jim Cumbes, the former county cricketer, was appointed as marketing manager to cope with the growing sponsorship activities. The library was brought to life by the appointment of the Rev Malcolm Lorimer as hon librarian and he also took over from Charles Oliver the task of keeping the Club's cricketing records – Mr Oliver had supplied the record section in the *Year Book* for more than 30 years. Keith Hayhurst was acting as the archivist for the Club and the museum was benefiting greatly from his enthusiasm and expertise in this area.

For 1988 Lancashire determined to recruit some seasoned players to reinforce the up-and-coming youngsters. With Patterson a member of the West Indian touring team, Wasim Akram, who had been a leading all-rounder with the 1987 Pakistan touring side to England, was signed. Wasim, however, would not be available for some early matches so Chris Matthews, the Australian left-arm seamer, who was engaged with Little Lever, was also put on the books. A third experienced player to sign was Trevor Jesty, the 39-year-old former Hampshire cricketer, who had more recently played for Surrey.

Lancashire were certainly going in for a belt and braces policy. The team got off to a traumatic start, by meeting Hick in the first Championship match. The Rhodesian-Worcestershire batsman struck 212 and Worcestershire never looked back. Chris Matthews dismissed Warwickshire for 155 in the second game, and Lancashire were deprived of victory by rain, but in the third match good bowling by Folley, who took nine wickets, brought the first Championship win of the summer.

Wasim Akram made his impact felt with an unbeaten hundred at the end of May against Somerset, though the batting failed in the second innings and Somerset won an exciting match by two wickets.

By the halfway stage, Lancashire were doing well with five victories and were joint third in the table. The match at Southport in late July, the 14th of the season, was full of incident. Wasim achieved a hat-trick

Lancashire 1988: Back row: W. Davies (scorer), I. Folley, M.A. Atherton, A.J. Murphy, A.N. Hayhurst, M. Watkinson, I. Austin, T.E. Jesty, J.A. Ormrod (coach). Front row: G.D. Mendis, N.H. Fairbrother, P.J.W. Allott, D.P. Hughes (Capt.), J. Simmons, G. Fowler, W. Hegg (Bill Smith)

and then hit 98 off 78 balls, with four sixes and nine fours – two more runs would have provided him with the fastest century of the season at that date. Lancashire required 272 to win, but when the final ball was bowled were 271 for 9, so the game was officially a draw with the scores level. Lancashire were awarded 12 points.

The next five matches proved crucial to any hopes the county entertained of winning the Championship. Unfortunately four of the five were lost – Hughes publicly read the riot act, but this failed to produce any further Championship victories and the County had to settle for ninth place. In the single victory during the later stages, against Sussex at Hove, Atherton hit 152 which enabled him to top the Lancashire batting averages.

Both Fowler and Fairbrother hit two hundreds each, but both only just reached the 1,000 run mark at an average of 30 and 29 respectively, which for players on the fringes of the England team is not outstanding. Wasim Akram had a good year with both bat and ball and Lancashire were unfortunate that he missed matches due to injury.

Although no success attended the team in the NatWest or B & H Cups, they had a good year in the Sunday League and finished third, qualifying for the new knock-out Refuge Assurance Cup. In the semi-

LANCASHIRE v. WORCESTERSHIRE REFUGE ASSURANCE CUP FINAL

Played at Edgbaston on 18 September 1988

LANCASHIRE WON BY 52 RUNS

LANCASHIRE

G.D. Mendis	b Weston	0
G. Fowler	c Neale b Pridgeon	26
A.N. Hayhurst	st Rhodes b Weston	1
N.H. Fairbrother	c Radford b Newport	38
T.E. Jesty	b Radford	59
M. Watkinson	not out	42
I.D. Austin	not out	6
*D.P. Hughes		
P.J.W. Allott		
J. Simmons		
†W.K. Hegg		
Extras	b 4, lb 12, w 13	29
Total	(5 wkts, 40 overs)	201

Fall: 1-1 2-4 3-69 4-113 5-194

BOWLING	O	M	R	W
Weston	8	0	19	2
Newport	8	0	40	1
Radford	8	0	44	1
Pridgeon	8	1	48	1
Illingworth	8	0	34	0

WORCESTERSHIRE

T.S. Curtis	c Hegg b Hayhurst	32
S.J. O'Shaughnessy	c Mendis b Allott	4
G.A. Hick	b Watkinson	2
D.A. Leatherdale	b Simmons	30
*P.A. Neale	c Watkinson b Austin	42
M.J. Weston	c Hegg b Hayhurst	1
†S.J. Rhodes	c Hughes b Hayhurst	20
P.J. Newport	c Hegg b Austin	2
N.V. Radford	c Hegg b Hayhurst	0
R.K. Illingworth	c Hegg b Austin	0
A.P. Pridgeon	not out	2
Extras	lb 10, w 4	14
Total	(35.5 overs)	149

Fall: 1-9 2-24 3-75 4-79 5-90 6-134 7-145 8-145 9-146

BOWLING	O	M	R	W
Watkinson	6	2	10	1
Allott	6	2	10	1
Austin	7.5	0	51	3
Simmons	8	0	22	1
Hayhurst	8	0	46	4

Umpires: J. Birkenshaw and J.W. Holder

* Captain: † Wicket-keeper

final Lancashire beat Gloucestershire by three wickets, then proceeded to the final at Edgbaston, where they beat Worcestershire with relative ease, Jesty making the most of some poor fielding by hitting 59.

So 1988 finished with a substantial consolation prize, which hopefully will inspire the County to greater heights in 1989.

STATISTICAL SECTION

LANCASHIRE RECORDS

The records in this section, unless otherwise stated, refer to all Lancashire first-class matches since the county's first match in 1865. As far as possible the records follow the definition of first-class matches as compiled by The Association of Cricket Statisticians.   M.G.L.

BIOGRAPHICAL DETAILS
OF LANCASHIRE PLAYERS

NAME AND EXTENT OF CAREER	BIRTHPLACE	DATE OF BIRTH	DATE OF DEATH
John Abrahams 1973–	Cape Town, South Africa	21. 7.1952	
Thomas Ainscough 1894–1906	Parbold	23. 2.1865	20.11.1927
Jerry Lionel Ainsworth 1899	Formby	11. 9.1877	30.12.1923
Ralph Alderson 1948–1949	Newton-Le-Willows	7. 6.1919	2. 4.1988
Paul John Walter Allott 1978–	Altrincham	14. 9.1956	
Arthur Appleby 1866–1887	Clayton-Le-Moors	22. 7.1843	24.10.1902
James Frederick Arnold 1896	Withington, Manchester	2. 3.1869	26. 3.1944
Robert Arrowsmith 1976–1979	Denton, Manchester	21. 5.1952	
John Thomas Ashworth 1871–1873	Haslingden	27. 2.1850	20.10.1901
Michael Andrew Atherton 1987–	Manchester	23. 3.1968	
Graham Atkinson 1967–1969	Wakefield	29. 3.1938	
Ian David Austin 1987–	Haslingden	30. 5.1966	
David Bailey 1968–1969	West Hartlepool	9. 9.1944	
George Robert Baker 1887–1899	Malton	18. 4.1862	6. 2.1938
Stanley Tattersall Banham 1939	Bacup	21. 9.1913	29.12.1984
Horatio William Barber 1866–1867	Salford	27. 2.1843	27. 4.1869
John Benjamin Barber 1874–1876	Stretford, Manchester	6. 2.1849	21. 2.1908
Robert William Barber 1954–1962	Withington, Manchester	26. 9.1935	
Harry George Barchard 1888	Cheetham, Manchester	25. 6.1860	28. 7.1935
Peter Barcroft 1956	Bacup	14. 8.1929	26. 8.1977
Robert Vickers Bardsley 1910–1920	Prestwich	28. 6.1890	26. 7.1952
Gerald Roscoe Bardswell 1894–1902	Woolton, Liverpool	7.12.1873	29.12.1906
Alfred Barlow 1947–1951	Little Lever	31. 8.1915	9. 5.1983
Edwin Alan Barlow 1932	Ashton-Under-Lyne	24. 2.1912	27. 6.1980
Richard Gorton Barlow 1871–1891	Bolton	28. 5.1851	31. 7.1919
John Reginald Barnes 1919–1930	Ormskirk	18. 5.1897	22. 7.1945
Sydney Francis Barnes 1899–1903	Smethwick	19. 4.1873	26.12.1967
Ben Barrell 1911–1923	Orford	14. 5.1885	14. 7.1969
William Barron 1945	Herrington	26.10.1917	
Frederick William Baucher 1903	Wigan	6.11.1878	7. 6.1947
Arthur Douglas Baxter 1933–1934	Edinburgh	20. 1.1910	28. 1.1986
Fred Demetrius Beattie 1932	Manchester	18. 8.1909	
Alan Michael Beddow 1962–1966	St Helens	12.10.1941	
Albert Bennett 1932–1933	St Helens	21. 5.1910	
Henry Simpson Bennett 1894	Bakewell	3. 9.1869	18. 2.1965
Robert Bennett 1962–1966	Bacup	16. 6.1940	
Charles Henry Benton 1892–1901	Glossop	8. 1.1868	19. 5.1918
Robert Berry 1948–1954	Manchester	29. 1.1926	
George Henry Biddolph 1885	Manchester	28. 3.1858	21. 4.1937
George Ashburner Bigg 1887	Barrow	24. 7.1861	27.10.1931
George Bird 1880	Middlesex	30. 7.1849	28.10.1930
Morice Carlos Bird 1907	Liverpool	25. 3.1888	9.12.1933

Francis Hornby Birley 1870–1872	Chorlton, Manchester	14. 3.1850	1. 8.1910
Alexander Joseph Birtwell 1937–1939	Burnley	17.12.1908	20.11.1974
Joseph Frederick Blackledge 1962	Chorley	15. 4.1928	
Richard Blackstock 1865	Oxton, Cheshire	13. 7.1838	3. 2.1893
Wilfred Blake 1877	Skipton	29.11.1854	—
Edward Overall Bleackley 1919	Salford	10. 3.1898	17. 2.1976
Benjamin Blomley 1903–1922	Chadderton	10. 6.1879	12. 3.1949
Robert Alan Boddington 1913–1924	Manchester	30. 6.1892	5. 8.1977
Reginald George Boden 1907	Ashby-de-la-Zouch	13. 9.1884	11. 2.1966
Alan Bolton 1957–1961	Darwen	1. 7.1939	
John David Bond 1955–1972	Kearsley	6. 5.1932	
Arthur Booth 1950–1951	Droylsden	8. 1.1926	
Brian Joseph Booth 1956–1963	Blackburn	3.12.1935	
Frank Stanley Booth 1927–1937	Cheetham Hill	12. 2.1907	21. 1.1980
Edwin James Bousfield 1865–1878	Chorlton	21. 5.1838	8. 1.1895
Ernest Bowden 1914	Lancaster	13. 6.1892	14.10.1972
William Henry Bower 1885–1886	Bradford	17.10.1857	31. 1.1943
John Barton Bowes 1938–1948	Stretford	2. 1.1918	22. 5.1969
Kenneth Bowling 1954	Preston	10.11.1931	
Richard Bowman 1957–1959	Cleveleys	26. 1.1934	
Richard Boys 1877	Burnley	17. 6.1849	4. 1.1896
Thomas Farrell Bradbury 1881	—	1856	26. 4.1934
J. Braddock 1873	—	—	—
Walter Brearley 1902–1911	Bolton	11. 3.1876	13. 1.1937
Thomas Leslie Brierley 1946–1948	Southampton	15. 6.1910	
John Briggs 1879–1900	Sutton-in-Ashfield	3.10.1862	11. 1.1902
Jack Briggs 1939	Haslingden	8. 4.1916	1. 6.1984
Sir John Montague Bart Brocklebank 1939	Hoylake	3. 9.1915	13. 9.1974
Francis Ralph Russell Brooke 1912–1913	Bowdon	2.10.1884	20. 6.1960
Abraham Worthington Brooks 1877	Swannington, Leicestershire	7.10.1853	7. 5.1925
John Jarvis Broughton 1901–1902	Grantham	8. 9.1873	3. 4.1952
William Brown 1894	—	1892	—
William Brown 1919–1922	Brierley Hill	13. 6.1866	—
Leslie Bulcock 1946	Colne	5. 1.1913	—
John Bullough 1914–1919	Bolton	1893	3. 6.1967
William Burrows 1867–1873	Preston	31.12.1844	—
Clifford Burton 1956	Moston	15. 6.1931	20. 5.1978
Henry Rhodes Whittle Butterworth 1931–1936	Rochdale	4. 2.1909	9.10.1958
Wilfred Selkirk Butterworth 1876–1882	Rochdale	11.10.1855	9. 4.1908
George Augustus Campbell 1866	Tunbridge Wells	7. 7.1847	12. 9.1930
Frederick Carlisle 1869	Liverpool	4.11.1849	22.10.1920
Edmund Leach Chadwick 1875–1881	Rochdale	31. 8.1847	6. 8.1918
Mark Robert Chadwick 1983–1987	Milnrow	9. 2.1963	
Albert Champion 1886	Handforth, Yorks.	27.12.1851	30. 6.1909
Ian Michael Chappell 1963	Unley, S. Australia	26. 9.1943	
J. Clarke 1905	—	—	—
Geoffrey Clayton 1959–1964	Mossley	3. 2.1938	
Ian Cockbain 1979–1983	Bootle	19. 4.1958	
Terence George Owen Cole 1904	Llanrhaiadr	14.11.1877	15.12.1944
Roy Collins 1954–1962	Clayton	10. 3.1934	
Lawrence Whalley Cook 1907–1923	Preston	28. 3.1885	2.12.1933
William Cook 1905–1907	Preston	16. 1.1882	18.12.1947
Noel Henry Cooke 1958–1959	West Derby, Liverpool	5. 1.1935	

Fred Cooper *1946*	Bacup	18. 4.1921	22.12.1986
William Copeland *1885*	Trimdon,	10. 6.1856	28. 1.1917
	Co. Durham		
Samuel Corlett *1871–1875*	Withington	8. 5.1852	2. 1.1921
Josiah Coulthurst *1919*	Blackburn	24.12.1893	6. 1.1970
Cornelius Coward *1865–1876*	Preston	27. 1.1838	15. 7.1903
Frederick Coward *1867–1868*	Preston	11. 2.1842	15.12.1905
John Michael Cownley *1962*	Sheffield	24. 2.1929	
Frederick Crabtree *1890*	Baildon,	10. 3.1867	28.11.1893
	Yorkshire		
Herbert Crabtree *1902–1908*	Colne	25. 5.1880	2. 3.1951
James Stanley Cragg *1908*	Stockport	18.10.1866	27. 7.1979
Edward John Craig *1961–1962*	Formby	26. 3.1942	
Walter Reid Craig *1874*	Bury	29.12.1846	6. 7.1923
Kenneth Cranston *1947–1948*	Aigburth	20.10.1917	
Colin Everton Hunte Croft *1977–1982*	Demerara, British	15. 3.1953	
	Guiana		
Frederick James Crooke *1865*	Liverpool	21. 4.1844	6. 8.1923
Sydney Morland Crosfield *1883–1899*	Warrington	12.11.1861	30. 1.1908
John Crossland *1878–1885*	Sutton-in-Ashfield	2. 4.1852	26. 9.1903
Henry Cudworth *1900*	Burnley	6.12.1873	5. 4.1914
James Cumbes *1963–1971*	East Didsbury	4. 5.1944	
Willis Robert Cuttell *1896–1906*	Sheffield	13. 9.1864	9.12.1929
Ian Charles Davidson *1985–1987*	Worsley	21.12.1964	
Harry Donald Davies *1924–1925*	Pendleton	13. 3.1892	6. 2.1958
Harry Dean *1906–1921*	Burnley	13. 8.1884	12. 3.1957
John Harold Greenway Deighton *1948–1950*	Prestwich	5. 4.1920	
Charles Edmund de Trafford *1884*	Trafford Park	21. 5.1864	11.11.1951
Robert Dewhurst *1872–1875*	Clitheroe	11. 5.1851	15. 3.1929
Thomas Eastwood Dickinson *1950–1951*	Parramatta,	11. 1.1931	
	Australia		
J. Dixon *1878*	—	—	—
Percy Dobell *1886–1887*	Huyton	29. 4.1864	5. 1.1903
Harold Douthwaite *1920–1921*	Lancaster	12. 8.1900	9. 7.1972
George Duckworth *1923–1938*	Warrington	9. 5.1901	5. 1.1966
George Colquhoun Hamilton Dunlop *1868*	Edinburgh	28. 7.1846	7. 6.1929
Arthur Durandu *1887*	Liverpool	25.12.1860	4. 2.1903
Jack Dyson *1954–1964*	Oldham	8. 7.1934	
Alexander Eccles *1898–1907*	Ashton-on-Ribble	16. 3.1876	17. 3.1919
Henry Eccles *1885–1886*	Huyton	4. 3.1863	10. 2.1931
Joseph Eccles *1886–1889*	Accrington	13. 4.1863	2. 9.1933
Peter Thorp Eckersley *1923–1935*	Newton-Le-	2. 7.1904	13. 8.1940
	Willows		
Cyril Arthur Edge *1936–1938*	Ashton-Under-	14.12.1916	4.10.1985
	Lyne		
Harold Emerton Edge *1913*	Market Drayton	18. 6.1892	24. 1.1944
James William Edmonds *1975*	Smethwick	4. 6.1951	
Eric Harry Edrich *1946–1948*	Lingwood,	27. 3.1914	
	Norfolk		
Geoffrey Arthur Edrich *1946–1958*	Lingwood,	13. 7.1918	
	Norfolk		
Harold Elliott *1930*	Wigan	15. 6.1904	15. 4.1969
Jeremy Ellis *1892–1898*	Summerseat	15. 2.1866	14. 8.1943
Stanley Ellis *1923–1924*	Ramsbottom	12. 2.1896	14. 2.1987
Walker Ellis *1920–1923*	Summerseat	27. 1.1895	25.11.1974
Farokh Maneksha Engineer *1968–1976*	Bombay, India	25. 2.1938	
Robert Entwistle *1962–1966*	Burnley	20.10.1941	
Neil Harvey Fairbrother *1982–*	Warrington	9. 9.1963	

STATISTICAL SECTION

Name	Place	Born	Died
Peter Moss Fairclough *1911–1923*	Bickershaw	25. 9.1887	16.11.1952
John Armstong Fallows *1946*	Woodley	25. 7.1907	20. 1.1974
Andrew William Farnsworth *1919*	Sydney, Australia	1887	30.10.1966
Harry Farrar *1955*	Radcliffe	14. 3.1930	
Hubert Lister Farrar *1904*	Broughton Park	2. 4.1881	4. 7.1939
William Farrimond *1924–1945*	Daisy Hill	23. 5.1903	15.11.1979
William Findlay *1902–1906*	Liverpool	22. 6.1880	19. 6.1953
John Dexter Fitton *1987–*	Littleborough	24. 8.1965	
Ian Folley *1982–*	Burnley	9. 1.1963	
Graeme Fowler *1979–*	Accrington	20. 4.1957	
Frederick Ducange Gaddum *1884*	Didsbury	28. 6.1860	14.10.1900
Richard Gordon Garlick *1938–1947*	Kirkby Lonsdale	11. 4.1917	16. 5.1988
Harold Gwyer Garnett *1899–1914*	Aigburth	19.11.1879	3.12.1917
Arthur Buchwald Edgar Gibson *1887*	Salford	15. 6.1863	11. 3.1932
Peter Anthony Gooch *1970*	Timperley	2. 5.1949	
Antony John Good *1973–1976*	Kumasi, Gold Coast	10.11.1952	
Fred Goodwin *1955–1956*	Heywood	28. 6.1933	20. 1.1931
Francis Herbert Goodwin *1894*	Rainhill	4. 1.1866	
Keith Goodwin *1960–1974*	Oldham	25. 6.1938	
David Michael Green *1959–1967*	Llanengan	10.11.1939	
Leonard Green *1922–1935*	Whalley	1. 2.1890	2. 3.1963
Eric Washington Greenhalgh *1935–1938*	Sale	18. 5.1910	
Thomas Greenhough *1951–1966*	Rochdale	9.11.1931	
Peter Greenwood *1948–1952*	Todmorden	11. 9.1924	
William Russell Gregson *1906*	Lancaster	5. 8.1878	18. 6.1963
Kenneth James Grieves *1949–1964*	Sydney, Australia	27. 8.1925	
George Henry Grimshaw *1868*	Ashton	1838	21. 1.1898
Stell Haggas *1884–1885*	Keighley	18. 4.1856	14. 3.1926
Walter Haggas *1903*	Oldham	1. 4.1881	14.11.1959
Charles Henry Haigh *1879–1887*	Rochdale	26. 9.1854	15. 3.1915
Alfred Ewart Hall *1923–1924*	Bolton	23. 1.1896	1. 1.1964
Albert William Hallam *1895–1900*	East Leake, Notts.	12.11.1869	24. 7.1940
Thomas Maxwell Halliday *1925–1929*	Leyland	1. 7.1904	28. 2.1977
Charles Hallows *1914–1932*	Little Lever	4. 4.1895	10.11.1972
James Hallows *1898–1907*	Little Lever	14.11.1873	20. 5.1910
Frank Hardcastle *1869*	Bolton	12. 5.1844	5.11.1908
Walter Mitchell Hardcastle *1869–1874*	Bolton	10. 2.1843	27. 4.1901
Frederick William Hargreaves *1881*	Blackburn	16. 8.1858	5. 4.1897
George (Minto) Harper *1883*	London	30. 8.1865	—
Frank Harrison *1936*	—	1909	9. 6.1955
J. Harrop *1874*	—	—	—
Frank Harry *1903–1908*	Torquay	22.12.1876	27.10.1925
Alfred Hartley *1907–1914*	New Orleans, U.S.A.	11. 4.1879	9.10.1918
Charles Robert Hartley *1897–1909*	New Orleans, U.S.A.	13. 2.1873	14.11.1927
Fred Hartley *1924–1945*	Bacup	24. 4.1906	24.12.1976
George Hartley *1871–1872*	Heywood	17. 3.1849	9. 9.1909
Baron Harwood *1877*	Darwen	14. 8.1852	16.12.1915
Clifford Hawkwood *1931–1935*	Nelson	16.11.1909	15. 5.1960
Frank Charles Hayes *1970–1984*	Preston	6.12.1946	
Kevin Anthony Hayes *1980–1986*	Thurnscoe	26. 9.1962	
Andrew Neil Hayhurst *1985–*	Davyhulme	23.11.1962	
Francis Somerville Head *1868–1869*	London	30. 6.1846	2. 4.1941
John Garsden Heap *1884*	Accrington	5. 1.1857	20. 4.1931
James Sutcliffe Heap *1903–1921*	Burnley	12. 8.1882	30. 1.1951
Warren Kevin Hegg *1987–*	Radcliffe	23. 2.1968	

Name	Years	Place	Born	Died
Soren Henrikson	1985–1986	Copenhagen	1.12.1964	
Joseph Hewitson	1890	Bolton	27.10.1865	4.12.1925
William Heys	1957	Oswaldtwistle	19. 2.1931	
Henry Hibbard	1884	—	1854	12. 2.1902
George Hibbard	1867	Sheffield	8. 2.1845	24. 8.1911
William John Hibberd	1900–1901	Nottingham	11. 7.1873	6. 6.1934
William Edward Hickmott	1923–1924	Boxley, Kent	10. 4.1893	16. 1.1968
William Hickton	1867–1871	Hardstoft, Derbyshire	14.12.1842	25. 2.1900
Kenneth Higgs	1958–1969	Kidsgrove, Staffs.	14. 1.1937	
Edward Frederick William Highton	1951	Formby	29. 8.1924	9.10.1985
Peter Higson	1929–1931	Bramhall	1.12.1904	19. 4.1986
Thomas Atkinson Higson	1905–1923	Stockport	18.11.1873	3. 8.1949
Thomas Atkinson Higson (Jun.)	1936–1946	Whaley Bridge	25. 3.1911	
Rev. Lyonel D'Arcy Hildyard	1884–1885	Bury	5. 2.1861	22. 4.1931
Rowland Wright Davenport Hill	1871	Hajepoor, India	5. 9.1851	29. 8.1912
John Ritson Hilkirk	1871–1877	Manchester	25. 6.1845	18.10.1921
Colin Hilton	1957–1963	Atherton	26. 9.1937	
Jim Hilton	1952–1953	Oldham	29.12.1930	
Malcolm Jameson Hilton	1946–1961	Oldham	2. 8.1928	
Sydney Francis Hird	1939	Balmain, New South Wales	7. 1.1910	20.12.1980
Geoffrey Hodgson	1928–1933	Huddersfield	24. 7.1938	
Gordon Hodgson	1965	Johannesburg, South Africa	16. 4.1904	14. 6.1951
William Hogg	1976–1980	Ulverston	12. 7.1955	
Cecil Holden	1890	Liverpool	1. 6.1865	22. 8.1928
Michael Anthony Holding	1981	Kingston, Jamaica	16. 2.1954	
Gideon Holgate	1866–1867	Barnoldswick	23. 6.1839	11. 7.1895
John Holland	1900–1902	Nantwich	7. 4.1869	22. 8.1914
Sir Frank Hubert Hollins	1902–1904	Bowness	31.10.1877	31. 1.1963
John Chard Humphrey Lancelot Hollins 1914–1919		Preston	3. 6.1890	13.11.1938
Edwin Holroyd	1878	Halifax	27.10.1855	9. 4.1914
John Holroyd	1927–1933	Oldham	15. 4.1907	15. 9.1975
John Leonard Hopwood	1923–1939	Newton Hyde	30.10.1903	15. 6.1985
Albert Henry Hornby	1899–1914	Nantwich	29. 7.1877	6. 9.1952
Albert Neilson Hornby	1867–1899	Blackburn	10. 2.1847	17.12.1925
Cecil Lumsden Hornby	1877	Blackburn	25. 7.1843	27. 2.1896
Edgar Christian Hornby	1885–1887	Liverpool	14. 9.1863	2. 4.1922
Leonard Horridge	1927–1929	Adlington	18. 8.1907	1. 9.1976
Richard Horrocks	1880–1882	Church	29. 8.1857	19. 6.1926
William John Horrocks	1931–1933	Warrington	18. 6.1905	15.11.1985
William Harry Houldsworth	1893–1894	Levenshulme	6. 4.1873	19. 4.1909
Gerrard Houlton	1961–1963	St Helens	25. 4.1939	
Barry John Howard	1947–1951	Hyde	21. 5.1926	
Kenneth Howard	1960–1966	Manchester	2. 6.1941	
Nigel David Howard	1946–1953	Hyde	18. 5.1925	31. 5.1979
Rupert Howard	1922–1933	Ashton-Under-Lyne	17. 4.1890	10. 9.1967
Richard Howe	1876–1877	Denton	17. 2.1853	21. 1.1914
Theodore Rathbone Hubback	1892	Liverpool	17.12.1872	1942
William Huddleston	1899–1914	Earlestown	27. 2.1873	21. 5.1962
Bennett Hudson	1886–1888	Sheffield	29. 6.1852	11.11.1901
George Neville Hudson	1936	Clitheroe	12. 7.1905	24.11.1981
David Paul Hughes	1967–	Newton-Le-Willows	13. 5.1947	
Campbell Arthur Grey Hulton	1869–1882	Manchester	16. 3.1846	23. 6.1919

Name	Years	Place	Born	Died
Harrington Arthur Harrop Hulton	1868	Ashton-Under-Lyne	9.11.1846	28. 1.1923
John I'Anson	1896–1908	Scorton	26.10.1868	14. 9.1936
Roger Iddison	1865–1870	Bedale	15. 9.1834	19. 3.1890
William Holdsworth Iddison	1867–1868	Bedale	5. 2.1840	6. 3.1898
John Iddon	1924–1945	Mawdesley	8. 1.1902	17. 4.1946
John Thomas Ikin	1939–1957	Bignall End, Staffs.	7. 3.1918	15. 9.1984
Charles Willis Ingleby	1899	Leeds	19.12.1870	15.11.1939
Frederic Isherwood	1881	Over Darwen	30. 8.1858	20. 2.1927
Edward Jackson	1871–1885	Lancaster	17. 3.1849	—
J. Jackson	1867	—	—	—
Tom Jaques	1937	Middleton	9.11.1911	13. 8.1976
Stephen Thomas Jefferies	1983–1985	Cape Town, South Africa	8.12.1959	
William Swynfen Jervis	1874	Stafford	18.11.1840	3. 4.1920
Trevor Edward Jesty	1988	Gosport, Hants.	2. 6.1948	
Henry Celestine Robert John	1881	Agra, India	26. 5.1862	24. 6.1941
William Turner Jolley	1947	Smallthorne, Staffs.	3. 8.1923	
Charles Langton Jones	1876–1888	Liverpool	27.11.1853	2. 4.1904
James Lindley Jones	1910	Liverpool	1876	—
John Jordan	1955–1957	Rossendale	7. 2.1932	
George Edwin Jowett	1855–1889	Roby, Prescot	20. 8.1863	19. 5.1928
Joseph Lowther Kaye	1867	Huddersfield	21. 6.1846	12.10.1882
Edward Arthur Kelly	1957	Bootle	26.11.1932	
John Martin Kelly	1947–1949	Bacup	19. 3.1922	13.11.1979
Arthur Twiss Kemble	1885–1894	Carlisle	3. 2.1862	13. 3.1925
Sir George Kemp	1885–1892	Rochdale	9. 6.1866	24. 3.1945
Andrew Kennedy	1970–1982	Blackburn	4.11.1949	
Richard William Kentfield	1888	Bognor	25. 5.1863	16.10.1904
Myles Noel Kenyon	1919–1925	Bury	25.12.1886	21.11.1960
Alexander Kermode	1902–1908	Sydney, New South Wales	15. 5.1876	17. 7.1934
John Edward Kershaw	1877–1885	Heywood	12. 1.1854	29.11.1903
Joseph Henry Kevan	1875	Bolton	13. 9.1855	9.12.1891
Edward Kewley	1875	Eton	20. 6.1852	17. 4.1940
Philip Benjamin King	1946–1947	Leeds	22. 4.1915	31. 3.1970
Arthur Knowles	1888	Pendlebury	10. 4.1858	10. 7.1929
Gerald Keith Knox	1964–1967	North Shields	22. 4.1937	
Brian Egbert Krikken	1966–1967	Horwich	26. 8.1946	
Oswald Philip Lancashire	1878–1888	Newton Heath	10. 2.1857	23. 7.1934
Thomas Lancaster	1894–1899	Huddersfield	11. 2.1863	12.12.1935
Charles Whittington Landon	1874–1875	Bromley	30. 5.1850	5. 3.1903
John Richard Latchford	1930–1932	Delph	16. 6.1909	30. 4.1980
Geoffrey Francis Lawson	1979	Wagga Wagga, New South Wales	7.12.1957	
Albert Edward Lawton	1912–1914	Dukinfield	31. 3.1879	25.12.1955
William Lawton	1948	Ashton-Under-Lyne	4. 6.1920	
Edward Leach Cecil Leach	1923–1924	Featherstall	28.11.1896	4. 1.1973
Harold Leach	1881	Rochdale	13. 3.1862	15. 2.1928
John Leach	1866–1877	Rochdale	17.10.1846	1. 2.1893
Rev Robert Leach	1868–1876	Rochdale	18.12.1849	10. 9.1939
Roger Chadwick Leach	1885	Rochdale	21. 9.1853	21. 4.1889
William Edmund Leach	1885	Rochdale	7.11.1851	30.11.1932
Peter Granville Lee	1972–1982	Arthington	27. 8.1945	

Name	Place	Born	Died
Charles Philip Leese *1911*	Manchester	22. 5.1889	19. 1.1947
Ernest Leese *1880–1884*	Bowdon	30.11.1854	15.11.1913
Sir Joseph Francis Leese *1865–1881*	Manchester	28. 2.1845	29. 7.1914
James Leigh *1887*	West Leigh	1862	25. 9.1925
Edwin Charles Leventon *1867*	Nottingham	1845	21. 8.1909
Peter Lever *1960–1976*	Todmorden	17. 9.1940	
William Hubert Lionel Lister *1933–1939*	Formby	11.10.1911	
George William Littlewood *1885*	Holmfirth	10. 5.1857	5. 3.1928
George Hubert Littlewood *1902–1904*	Friarmere, Yorks.	12. 5.1882	20.12.1917
Clive Hubert Lloyd *1968–1986*	Georgetown, British Guiana	31. 8.1944	
David Lloyd *1965–1983*	Accrington	18. 3.1947	
Graham David Lloyd *1988*	Accrington	1. 7.1969	
Richard Averill Lloyd *1921–1922*	Dungannon, N. Ireland	4. 8.1891	23.12.1950
James Geoffrey Lomax *1949–1953*	Rochdale	20. 5.1925	
John Lyon *1973–1982*	St Helens	17. 5.1951	
Edgar Arthur McDonald *1924–1931*	Launceston, Tasmania	6. 1.1891	22. 7.1937
Leslie Leopold McFarlane *1982–1984*	Portland, Jamaica	19. 8.1952	
Hugh McIntyre *1884*	Glasgow	16. 1.1857	25. 6.1905
William McIntyre *1872–1880*	Eastwood, Notts.	24. 5.1844	13. 9.1892
Donald William MacKinnon *1870–1871*	Bangalore, India	3. 3.1842	19.11.1931
Archibald Campbell MacLaren *1890–1914*	Whalley Range	1.12.1871	17.11.1944
Frederic Grahame MacLaren *1903*	Worsley	5.11.1875	10. 5.1952
Geoffrey MacLaren *1902*	Whalley Range	28. 2.1883	14. 9.1966
Dr James Alexander MacLaren *1891–1894*	Whalley Range	4. 1.1870	8. 7.1952
Kenneth Grant MacLeod *1908–1913*	Liverpool	2. 2.1888	7. 3.1967
Kenneth Walcott McLeod *1987*	St Elizabeth, Jamaica	18. 3.1964	
Roy MacNairy *1925*	Barrow-in-Furness	11. 2.1904	5. 9.1962
Joseph William Henry Makepeace *1906–1930*	Middlesbrough	22. 8.1881	19.12.1952
David John Makinson *1984–1988*	Eccleston	12. 1.1961	
Joseph Makinson *1865–1873*	Higher Broughton	25. 8.1836	14. 3.1914
Michael Francis Malone *1979–1980*	Perth, Australia	9.10.1950	
Walter James Marchbank *1869–1870*	Preston	2.11.1838	9. 8.1893
Peter Thomas Marner *1952–1964*	Oldham	31. 3.1936	
Charles Stowell Marriott *1919–1921*	Heaton Moor	14. 9.1895	13.10.1966
William Morton Massey *1883*	Scotland	11. 4.1846	19. 4.1899
Christopher Darrell Matthews *1988*	Cunderin, Western Australia	22. 9.1962	
Dudley Muir Matthews *1936–1938*	Rainhill	11. 9.1916	3.12.1968
James Mayall *1885*	Oldham	8. 1.1856	13. 9.1916
Christopher Maynard *1982–*	Haslemere	8. 4.1958	
Francis Melhuish *1877*	Birkenhead	17. 5.1857	—
John Melling *1874–1876*	Clayton-Le-Moors	6. 4.1848	31. 1.1881
Horace Mellor *1874–1875*	Paddington	21. 2.1851	27. 2.1942
Gehan Dixon Mendis *1986–*	Colombo, Ceylon	24. 4.1955	
Frank N. Miller *1904*	South Africa	8. 4.1880	—
Henry Miller *1880–1881*	Liverpool	18. 9.1859	11. 4.1927
Josiah Mills *1889*	Oldham	25.10.1862	23.11.1929
Walter George Mills *1871–1877*	London	2. 6.1852	6. 1.1902
Robert Oswald Milne *1882*	Manchester	10. 9.1852	6. 9.1927
Arthur (Webb) Mold *1889–1901*	Middleton Cheney	27. 5.1863	29. 4.1921
Frederick Moore *1954–1958*	Rochdale	17. 1.1931	
Edward Moorhouse *1873–1875*	Haslingden	11. 4.1851	10. 3.1927
Lewis Henry Moorsom *1865*	—	1835	10. 3.1914
Sir Ralph George Elphinstone Mortimore *1891*	Newcastle-Upon-Tyne	7. 7.1869	3. 5.1955

Name	Years	Place	Date 1	Date 2
Francis Hugh Mugliston	1906–1908	Singapore	7. 6.1886	3.10.1932
Anthony John Murphy	1985–	Manchester	6. 8.1962	
Francis William Musson	1914–1921	Clitheroe	31. 5.1894	2. 1.1962
Rev John Russell Napier	1888	Preston	5. 1.1859	12. 3.1939
George Nash	1879–1885	Aylesbury	1. 4.1850	13.11.1903
Syed Mohammad Nasir Zaidi	1983–1984	Karachi, Pakistan	25. 3.1961	
John Nelson	1913	Blackpool	28.10.1891	12. 8.1917
Duncan Victor Norbury	1919–1922	Bartley, Hants.	3. 8.1887	23.10.1972
Albert Edward Nutter	1935–1945	Burnley	28. 6.1913	
Ezra Nutter	1885	Colne	21.11.1858	17.11.1903
William Oakley	1893–1894	Shrewsbury	6. 5.1868	—
Norman Oldfield	1935–1939	Dukinfield	5. 5.1911	
Alfred Ollivant	1873–1874	Stretford	14. 1.1839	26. 5.1906
William Edward Openshaw	1879–1882	—	5. 2.1852	7. 2.1915
Joseph Alan Ormrod	1984–1985	Ramsbottom	22.12.1942	
Steven Joseph O'Shaughnessy	1980–1987	Bury	9. 9.1961	
Septimus Palmer	1879–1880	Australia	23. 8.1858	14.12.1935
Wilfred Parker	1904	—	—	
Cecil Harry Parkin	1914–1926	Eaglescliffe	18. 2.1886	15. 6.1943
Reginald Henry Parkin	1931–1939	Tunstall, Staffs.	25. 7.1909	
Herbert Black Parkinson	1922–1923	Barrow-in-Furness	11. 9.1892	27. 4.1947
Leonard Wright Parkinson	1932–1936	Salford	15. 9.1908	16. 3.1969
Francis David Parr	1951–1954	Wallasey	1. 6.1928	
Henry Bingham Parr	1872–1876	Grappenhall	6. 6.1845	24. 3.1930
Balfour Patrick Patterson	1984–	Williamsfield, Jamaica	15. 9.1961	
William Seeds Patterson	1874–1882	Liverpool	19. 3.1854	20.10.1939
Arthur George Paul	1889–1900	Belfast	24. 7.1864	14. 1.1947
James Payne	1898	—	—	
John Henry Payne	1883	Broughton	19. 3.1858	24. 1.1942
Edward Paynter	1926–1945	Oswaldtwistle	5.11.1901	5. 2.1979
Harry Pennington	1900	Salford	21. 4.1880	17. 3.1961
William Perry	1865	Oxford	12. 8.1830	15. 3.1913
Alfred William Pewtress	1919–1925	Rawtenstall	27. 8.1891	21. 9.1960
William Phillips	1904–1908	—	—	
William Edward Phillipson	1933–1948	North Reddish	3.12.1910	
Charles Carlisle Pilkington	1895	Liverpool	13.12.1876	8. 1.1950
Harry Pilling	1962–1980	Ashton-Under-Lyne	23. 2.1943	
Richard Pilling	1877–1889	Bedford	5. 7.1855	28. 3.1891
William Pilling	1891	—	1858	27. 3.1924
Winston Place	1937–1955	Rawtenstall	7.12.1914	
Dr. Leslie Oswald Sheridan Poidevin	1904–1908	Merrila, New South Wales	5.11.1876	18.11.1931
Richard Pollard	1933–1950	Westhoughton	19. 6.1912	16.12.1985
Edward Horatio Porter	1874–1882	Liverpool	13.10.1846	31.10.1918
George Potter	1902	Oldham	3.10.1878	—
Thomas Owen Potter	1866	Calcutta, India	10. 9.1844	27. 4.1909
William Henry Potter	1870	Gufsey, India	20. 8.1847	10. 4.1920
Stephen Preston	1928–1930	Heywood	11. 8.1905	
Alfred Price	1885	Ruddington, Notts.	5. 1.1862	21. 3.1942
Eric James Price	1946–1947	Middleton	27.10.1918	
Geoffrey Pullar	1954–1968	Swinton	1. 8.1935	
George Radcliffe	1903–1906	Ormskirk	25. 9.1877	27.10.1951
Lees Radcliffe	1897–1905	Rochdale	23.11.1865	22. 1.1928
Neal Victor Radford	1980–1984	Luanshya, N. Rhodesia	7. 6.1957	

Name	Years	Place		
Robert Burns Rae	*1945*	Littleborough	23. 7.1912	
Sonny Ramadhin	*1964–1965*	Esperance, Trinidad	1. 5.1929	
Henry John Ramsbottom	*1868*	Enfield	21.10.1846	9. 4.1905
Edgar Ratcliffe	*1884*	Liverpool	19. 1.1863	29. 7.1915
Robert Malcolm Ratcliffe	*1972–1980*	Accrington	29.11.1951	
Elisha Barker Rawlinson	*1867*	Yeadon	10. 4.1837	17. 2.1892
William Rawlinson	*1870–1871*	Burnley	5. 9.1850	—
George (Streynsham) Rawstorne	*1919*	Croston	22. 1.1895	15. 7.1962
Bernard Wilfrid Reidy	*1973–1982*	Whalley	18. 9.1953	
Frederick Reginald Reynolds	*1865–1874*	Bottisham, Cambridgeshire	7. 8.1834	18. 4.1915
Albert Rhodes	*1922–1924*	Saddleworth	9. 4.1889	10. 3.1970
Cecil A. Rhodes	*1937–1938*	—	1906	
William Richmond	*1868*	Burnley	1.12.1843	11.11.1912
James Ricketts	*1867–1877*	Manchester	9. 2.1842	3. 6.1894
William Rickman	*1876*	South Yarra, Victoria	1849	6. 6.1911
David Mawdsley Ritchie	*1924*	Liverpool	12. 8.1892	10. 9.1974
John Francis Esdale Roberts	*1957*	Bolton	4. 3.1933	
R. Roberts	*1872–1874*	—	—	—
William Braithwaite Roberts	*1939–1949*	Kirkham	27. 9.1914	24. 8.1951
Paul Andrew Robinson	*1979*	Boksburg, South Africa	16. 7.1956	
Walter Robinson	*1880–1888*	Greetland	29.11.1851	14. 8.1919
George Henry Rogerson	*1923*	Nantwich	13. 3.1896	29. 5.1961
Edward Roper	*1876–1886*	Richmond	8. 4.1851	27. 4.1921
Daniel Rowland	*1868*	—	1826	1.10.1891
Leslie Samuel Rowlands	*1903–1910*	Aston	29. 8.1880	1.10.1947
Alexander Butler Rowley	*1865–1871*	Manchester	3.10.1837	9. 1.1911
Edmund Butler Rowley	*1865–1880*	Manchester	4. 5.1842	8. 2.1905
Ernest Butler Rowley	*1893–1898*	Manchester	15. 1.1870	4.10.1962
Rev Vernon Peter Fanshawe Archer Royle	*1873–1891*	Brooklands	29. 1.1854	21. 5.1929
Frank Rushton	*1928–1929*	Bolton	21. 4.1906	15.10.1975
Thomas Henry Rushton	*1870*	Horwich	14. 5.1845	1. 7.1903
Frederick John Rutter	*1868*	Hillingden	12. 9.1840	19. 1.1907
Sir Lancelot Sanderson	*1884*	Lancaster	24.10.1863	9. 3.1944
Richard Withington Bromiley Sanderson	*1870*	Cheetham Hill	15. 1.1847	—
John Scholes Savage	*1967–1969*	Ramsbottom	3. 3.1929	
Charles Montague Sawyer	*1884*	Broughton	1856	30. 3.1921
J. Schofield	*1876*	—	—	—
Frank Beaumont Scholfield	*1911*	Bury	16.11.1886	1. 3.1950
Sandford Sandford Schultz (later known as S.S. Storey)	*1877–1882*	Birkenhead	29. 8.1857	18.12.1937
Christopher John Scott	*1977–1982*	Swinton	16. 9.1959	
William Ainslie Scott	*1874*	—	1845	17. 6.1899
Alfred Seymour	*1869*	—	16. 2.1843	31. 1.1897
John Sharp	*1899–1925*	Hereford	15. 2.1878	28. 1.1938
George Owen Shelmerdine	*1919–1925*	Manchester	7. 9.1899	31. 7.1967
Charles Shore	*1886*	Sutton-in-Ashfield	21.11.1858	5. 6.1912
Kenneth Shuttleworth	*1964–1975*	St Helens	13.11.1944	
Frank Marshall Sibbles	*1925–1937*	Oldham	15. 3.1904	20. 7.1973
William Silcock	*1899–1902*	Croston	22. 2.1868	30. 7.1933
Jack Simmonds	*1968–*	Clayton-Le-Moors	28. 3.1941	
Arthur Redman Sladen	*1903–1904*	Bradford	22. 7.1877	25. 7.1934
R. Slater	*1865*	—	—	—

Name	Place		
J. Smalley *1869*	—	—	—
Alfort Smith *1867–1871*	Bury	7. 7.1846	21.12.1908
Arthur Price Smith *1886–1894*	Ruddington	3.12.1857	3. 6.1937
Charles Smith *1893–1902*	Calverley	24. 8.1861	2. 5.1925
Colin Stansfield Smith *1951–1957*	Didsbury	1.10.1932	
Donald James Smith *1951–1952*	Accrington	1. 5.1929	
John Smith *1865–1869*	Yeadon	23. 3.1833	12. 2.1909
Dr Reginald Smith (also known as Starkey-Smith) *1893*	Warrington	1. 5.1868	5.10.1943
Stanley Smith *1952–1956*	Heywood	14. 1.1929	
Thomas Smith *1867*	Glossop	26. 8.1848	—
Kenneth Leslie Snellgrove *1965–1974*	Shepton Mallet	12.11.1941	
Gary John Speak *1981–1982*	Chorley	26. 4.1962	
Nicholas Jason Speak *1987–*	Manchester	21.11.1966	
Helm Spencer *1914*	Padiham	31.12.1891	7.12.1974
Archibald Franklin Spooner *1906–1909*	Litherland	21. 5.1886	11. 1.1965
Reginald Herbert Spooner *1899–1921*	Litherland	21.10.1880	2.10.1961
Kenneth Brooks Standring *1955–1959*	Clitheroe	17. 2.1935	
Henry Duncan Stanning *1906–1908*	Leyland	14.11.1881	5. 3.1946
John Stanning *1900–1903*	Leyland	10.10.1877	19. 5.1929
John Stanworth *1983–*	Oldham	30. 9.1960	
John Brian Statham *1950–1968*	Gorton	17. 6.1930	
Michael William Staziker *1970*	Croston	7.11.1947	
Allan Gibson Steel *1877–1893*	Liverpool	24. 9.1858	15. 6.1914
Douglas Quintin Steel *1876–1887*	Liverpool	19. 6.1856	2.12.1933
Ernest Eden Steel *1884–1903*	Liverpool	25. 6.1864	14. 7.1941
Harold Banner Steel *1883–1896*	Liverpool	9. 4.1862	29. 6.1911
Frederick Stephenson *1875–1877*	Todmorden	24. 4.1853	1927
Wilfred Bowring Stoddart *1898–1899*	Liverpool	27. 4.1871	8. 1.1935
Donald Harry Stone *1949–1950*	Clayton	9. 1.1927	
Enoch Storer *1865–1878*	Clay Cross	18. 5.1838	1. 7.1880
Frank Howe Sugg *1887–1889*	Ilkeston	11. 1.1862	29. 5.1933
John Sullivan *1963–1976*	Stalybridge	5. 2.1945	
Richard John Sutcliffe *1978*	Rochdale	18. 9.1954	
Samuel Henry Swire *1865–1868*	Ashton-Under-Lyne	3. 1.1839	29.12.1905
Roy Tattersall *1948–1960*	Bolton	17. 8.1922	
Roger Hartley Tattersall *1971*	Nelson	12. 3.1952	
Frank Taylor *1874–1888*	Rochdale	4. 5.1855	14. 8.1936
Fred Taylor *1920–1922*	Oldham	1891	4. 7.1968
James Taylor *1871–1873*	Littleborough	25. 5.1846	16. 8.1915
Malcolm Lees Taylor *1924–1931*	Heywood	16. 7.1904	14. 3.1978
Robert Joseph Taylor *1898*	Liverpool	1.11.1873	—
Timothy John Taylor *1981–1982*	Romiley	28. 3.1961	
Kevan Tebay *1961–1963*	Bolton	2. 2.1936	
Alfred Teggin *1886*	Broughton	22.10.1860	23. 7.1941
Hector Norman Tennent *1865–1870*	Hobart, Tasmania	6. 4.1842	19. 4.1904
William Middleton Tennent *1867*	Hobart, Tasmania	6.10.1845	5. 7.1883
Alan Thomas *1966*	Bolton	7. 1.1947	
Richard Thomas *1894–1902*	Wales	15. 7.1867	18.12.1918
Harry Thornber *1874*	Manchester	9.11.1851	28. 7.1913
Sydney Maguire Tindall *1894–1898*	Margate	18. 2.1867	19. 9.1922
Alfred Tinsley *1890–1895*	Malton	12. 3.1867	25. 9.1933
Henry James Tinsley *1894–1896*	Malton	20. 2.1865	10.12.1938
Enoch Tranter *1875–1876*	Old Park, Shropshire	27. 4.1842	23. 9.1910
Geoffrey Edward Trim *1976–1980*	Openshaw	6. 4.1956	
(George) Ernest Tyldesley *1909–1936*	Worsley	5. 2.1889	5. 5.1962

Harry Tyldesley *1914–1922*	Bolton	4. 7.1892	30. 8.1935
James Darbyshire Tyldesley *1910–1922*	Ashton-in-Makerfield	10. 8.1889	31. 1.1923
John Thomas Tyldesley *1895–1923*	Worsley	22.11.1873	27.11.1930
Richard Knowles Tyldesley *1919–1931*	Westhoughton	11. 3.1897	17. 9.1943
William Knowles Tyldesley *1908–1914*	Wigan	10. 8.1887	26. 4.1918
James Unsworth *1871*	Everton	4. 3.1844	1. 1.1893
David Saunders Van Der Knapp *1967*	Johannesburg, South Africa	7. 9.1948	
David William Varey *1984–1987*	Darlington	15.10.1961	
Ernest Wadsworth *1871–1879*	Manchester	30. 9.1850	7. 1.1918
Roger Walker *1874–1875*	Bury	18. 9.1846	11.11.1919
Henry Wall *1877*	Wigan	21. 4.1852	13.10.1914
Thomas Wall *1868*	Wigan	27.11.1841	18. 4.1875
William Wall *1877*	Wigan	8. 1.1854	18. 4.1922
Mark Andrew Wallwork *1982*	Urmston	14.12.1960	
George Walsh *1874–1877*	Blackburn	16. 2.1852	22. 5.1904
Mathew Walton *1867*	Glossop	10.12.1837	7. 1.1888
Leslie Warburton *1929–1938*	Haslingden	30. 4.1910	11. 2.1984
Albert Ward *1889–1904*	Leeds	21.11.1865	6. 1.1939
Frank Ward *1884–1896*	Carlisle	9. 1.1865	
Charles Wardle *1867–1872*	Arnold	20. 2.1837	10. 8.1907
Cyril Washbrook *1933–1959*	Barrow	6.12.1914	
Wasim Akram *1988–*	Lahore, Pakistan	3. 6.1966	
Michael Watkinson *1982–*	Westhoughton	1. 8.1961	
Alexander Watson *1871–1893*	Coatbridge	4.11.1844	26.10.1920
Frank (Bramley) Watson *1920–1937*	Nottingham	17. 9.1898	1. 2.1976
Roger Graeme Watson *1982–1985*	Rawtenstall	14. 1.1964	
Sidney Webb *1899–1903*	Brompton	1. 2.1875	4. 4.1923
Fred Webster *1925–1927*	Accrington	7. 5.1897	28. 7.1931
George Edward Wharmby *1894*	Sutton-in-Ashfield	7.12.1870	15.11.1951
Alan Wharton *1946–1960*	Heywood	30. 4.1923	
Thomas Whatmough *1871*	Manchester	26. 3.1844	19. 3.1911
John William Whewell *1921–1927*	Rishton	8. 5.1887	2. 7.1948
Ralph Whitehead *1908–1914*	Ashton-Under-Lyne	16.10.1883	23. 8.1956
Thomas Whitehead *1884*	—	1852	2.11.1937
Peter Whiteley *1957–1958*	Rochdale	12. 8.1935	
John Parkinson Whiteside *1888–1890*	Fleetwood	11. 6.1861	8. 3.1946
David Whittaker *1884–1888*	Church	25.10.1857	17.12.1901
Edwin Whittaker *1865–1868*	Ashton-Under-Lyne	4.12.1834	25. 6.1880
Leonard Litton Wilkinson *1937–1947*	Northwich	5.11.1916	
Alan Wilson *1948–1962*	Newton-Le-Willows	24. 4.1920	
George Alexander Winder *1869*	Bolton	16. 7.1850	1. 2.1913
Barry Wood *1966–1979*	Ossett	26.12.1942	
James Wood *1956*	Royton	26. 6.1933	30. 6.1977
Reginald Wood *1880–1884*	Woodchurch	7. 3.1860	6. 1.1915
Albert Woolley *1926*	Salford	26. 9.1902	5. 1.1978
Duncan Robert Worsley *1960–1967*	Bolton	18. 7.1941	
William Worsley *1903–1913*	Wandsworth	11. 9.1869	13.11.1918
Egerton Lowndes Wright *1905–1910*	Chorley	15.11.1885	11. 5.1918
Rev Frank Wynyard Wright *1869–1875*	Woodstock	6. 4.1844	15. 2.1924
Calvart Yates *1882*	Oswaldtwistle	28.11.1851	10. 6.1904
George Yates *1885–1894*	Haslingden	6. 6.1856	21. 8.1925

CAREER AVERAGES IN ALL FIRST-CLASS LANCASHIRE MATCHES, 1865–1988

	Mt	Inns	NO	Runs	H.S.	Aver.	100s	Runs	Wkts	Aver.	Best	5wI
J. Abrahams	251	388	52	9980	*201	29.70	14	2811	56	50.19	3/27	—
T. Ainscough	2	3	0	40	24	13.33	—					
J.L. Ainsworth	4	6	1	17	11	3.40	—	289	18	16.05	6/84	1
R. Alderson	2	2	0	55	55	27.50	—					
P.J.W. Allott	166	183	42	2480	88	17.58	—	11079	475	23.32	8/48	23
A. Appleby	58	93	14	1052	99	13.31	—	3474	245	14.17	9/25	18
J.F. Arnold	3	5	0	94	37	18.80	—					
R. Arrowsmith	43	40	12	286	39	10.21	—	2796	99	28.24	6/29	4
J.T. Ashworth	2	3	0	28	19	9.33	—					
M.A. Atherton	19	33	4	1058	*152	36.48	2	429	8	53.62	3/32	—
G. Atkinson	62	99	9	2468	124	27.42	5	24	1	24.00	1/19	—
I.D. Austin	8	10	2	253	64	31.62	—	431	18	23.94	5/79	2
D. Bailey	27	36	1	845	136	24.14	2					
G.R. Baker	228	350	29	7170	186	22.33	4	3475	138	25.18	6/18	6
S.T. Banham	1	—	—	—	—	—	—					
H.W. Barber	3	6	0	41	15	6.83	—					
J.B. Barber	3	6	3	39	*12	13.00	—					
R.W. Barber	155	264	25	6760	175	28.28	7	4768	152	31.36	7/35	3
H.G. Barchard	1	2	0	45	40	22.50	—					
P. Barcroft	3	3	0	40	29	13.33	—					
R.V. Bardsley	7	8	0	46	15	5.75	—	23	0	—	—	—
G.R. Bardswell	21	28	1	429	56	15.88	—	342	8	42.75	4/37	—
A. Barlow	74	87	20	707	44	10.55	—	0	0	—	—	—
E.A. Barlow	7	8	1	84	40	12.00	—	389	12	32.41	4/33	—
R.G. Barlow	249	426	45	7765	117	20.38	2	10010	736	13.60	9/39	55
J.R. Barnes	89	136	22	3271	*123	28.69	3	53	0	—	—	—
S.F. Barnes	46	58	20	452	35	11.89	—	4459	225	19.81	8/37	19
B. Barrell	3	3	1	45	25	22.50	—	135	9	15.00	3/10	—
W. Barron	1	2	0	3	2	1.50	—					
F.W. Baucher	1	2	0	12	8	6.00	—					
A.D. Baxter	3	1	0	0	0	0.00	—	208	16	13.00	6/50	2
F.D. Beattie	5	9	1	120	36	15.00	—					
A.M. Beddow	33	54	3	775	*112	15.19	1	473	15	31.53	3/10	—
A. Bennett	16	14	1	238	51	18.30	—	865	24	36.04	4/49	—
H.S. Bennett	1	2	0	16	11	8.00	—					
R. Bennett	49	82	3	1814	112	22.96	2	49	0	—	—	—
C.H. Benton	29	50	6	663	68	15.06	—					
R. Berry	93	85	34	427	*27	8.37	—	5900	259	22.77	10/102	13
G.H. Biddulph	1	2	0	19	18	9.50	—	13	0	—	—	—
G.A. Bigg	1	1	0	16	16	16.00	—	13	1	13.00	1/13	—
G. Bird	1	2	0	0	0	0.00	—					
M.C. Bird	5	10	0	36	10	3.60	—	84	4	21.00	2/9	—
F.H. Birley	4	6	1	58	18	11.60	—	120	4	30.00	3/76	—
A.J. Birtwell	14	16	6	103	31	10.30	—	999	25	39.96	4/78	—
J.F. Blackledge	26	41	4	569	68	15.37	—	10	0	—	—	—
R. Blackstock	1	2	0	23	18	11.50	—					
W. Blake	1	1	0	26	26	26.00	—					
E.O. Bleackley	2	3	0	31	21	10.33	—					
R. Blomley	70	87	32	316	41	5.74	—					
R.A. Boddington	52	75	19	663	*58	11.83	—					
R. Boden	1	2	0	8	5	4.00	—					

Name	M	I	NO	Runs	HS	Avge	100	Balls	Wkts	Avge	Best	5wi
A. Bolton	40	71	6	1223	96	18.81	—	80	2	40.00	1/17	—
J.D. Bond	344	522	76	11867	157	26.60	14	69	0	—	—	—
A. Booth	4	5	0	81	49	16.20	—					
B.J. Booth	117	210	17	5075	*183	26.29	5	3183	106	30.02	7/143	1
F.S. Booth	140	157	25	1330	54	10.07	—	11180	457	24.46	7/59	24
E.J. Bousfield	12	21	2	279	32	14.68	—					
E. Bowden	4	6	0	27	10	4.50	—	453	12	37.75	6/78	1
W.H. Bower	4	6	0	45	23	7.50	—					
J.B. Bowes	10	13	1	106	39	8.83	—	602	21	28.66	4/103	—
K. Bowling	1	2	1	7	*4	7.00	—					
R. Bowman	9	12	1	189	58	17.18	—	459	11	41.72	2/28	—
R. Boys	1	2	1	13	10	13.00	—					
T.F. Bradbury	1	2	1	6	*6	6.00	—					
J. Braddock	1	2	0	13	11	6.50	—					
W. Brearley	106	145	23	749	38	6.13	—	12907	690	18.70	9/47	79
T.L. Brierley	46	62	8	1286	*116	23.81	1	12	0	—	—	—
J. Briggs	391	602	39	10707	186	19.01	9	26464	1696	15.60	10/55	161
J. Briggs	4	2	2	0	*0	—	—	391	10	39.10	4/48	—
J.M. Brocklebank	4	4	1	5	4	1.66	—	279	5	55.80	3/61	—
F.R.R. Brooke	29	35	0	566	61	16.17	—	9	1	9.00	1/9	—
A.W. Brooks	1	1	0	6	6	6.00	—					
J.J. Broughton	6	7	0	153	99	21.85	—	69	2	34.50	2/28	—
W. Brown	2	3	0	17	7	5.66	—	12	0	—	—	—
W. Brown	10	17	2	239	39	15.93	—	474	22	21.54	4/22	—
L. Bulcock	1	1	0	1	1	1.00	—	90	2	45.00	2/41	—
J. Bullough	8	8	3	24	17	4.80	—	573	13	44.07	5/123	1
W. Burrows	14	26	1	255	39	10.20	—	6	0	—	—	—
C. Burton	2	1	0	0	0	0.00	—	80	0	—	—	—
H.R.W. Butterworth	25	34	5	584	107	20.13	1	1392	36	38.66	6/85	1
W.S. Butterworth	9	14	1	73	22	5.61	—					
G.A. Campbell	1	2	0	18	10	9.00	—					
F. Carlisle	2	4	0	37	18	9.25	—					
E.L. Chadwick	13	24	3	254	42	12.09	—					
M.R. Chadwick	33	56	1	1197	132	21.76	1	71	0	—	—	—
A. Champion	1	2	0	4	4	2.00	—					
I.M. Chappell	1	1	0	3	3	3.00	—					
J. Clarke	1	1	0	0	0	0.00	—	35	0	—	—	—
G. Clayton	183	277	49	4382	84	19.21	—					
I. Cockbain	46	78	9	1456	98	21.10	—	14	0	—	—	—
T.G.O. Cole	1	1	0	0	0	0.00	—					
R. Collins	119	181	18	3332	*107	20.44	2	4782	159	30.07	6/63	4
L.W. Cook	203	258	91	2051	*54	12.28	—	17537	821	21.36	8/39	45
W. Cook	11	17	3	307	46	21.92	—	946	51	18.54	7/64	3
N.H. Cooke	12	16	0	242	33	15.12	—	93	3	31.00	2/10	—
F. Cooper	4	8	2	96	*33	16.00	—					
W. Copeland	1	2	1	21	*21	21.00	—	23	1	23.00	1/23	—
S. Corlett	2	3	0	6	4	2.00	—					
J. Coulthurst	1	—	—	—	—	—	—					
C. Coward	36	65	2	912	85	14.47	—	44	0	—	—	—
F. Coward	7	13	1	35	9	2.91	—					
J.M. Cownley	2	4	0	45	25	11.25	—	36	2	18.00	2/36	—
F. Crabtree	1	1	0	1	1	1.00	—					
H. Crabtree	5	8	0	116	49	14.50	—	34	0	—	—	—
J.S. Cragg	1	2	0	10	9	5.00	—					
E.J. Craig	6	11	1	214	89	21.40	—					
W.R. Craig	1	2	0	8	7	4.00	—					
K. Cranston	50	57	9	1928	*155	40.16	2	3267	142	23.00	7/43	10
C.E.H. Croft	49	50	10	433	*46	10.82	—	3604	136	26.50	7/54	3

Name													
F.J. Crooke	1	2	0	55	35	27.50	—						
S.M. Crosfield	90	140	13	1909	★82	15.03	—	111	2	55.50	1/1	—
J. Crossland	71	109	21	1002	★48	11.38	—	3125	245	12.75	7/14	17
H. Cudworth	1	1	0	4	4	4.00	—						
J. Cumbes	9	5	4	5	5	5.00	—	563	19	29.63	4/42	—
W.R. Cuttell	213	294	30	5389	137	20.41	5	14890	760	19.59	8/105	50
I.C. Davidson	2	4	0	14	13	3.50	—	85	4	21.25	2/24	—
H.D. Davies	11	15	0	260	46	17.33	—						
H. Dean	256	354	118	2448	★49	10.37	—	22828	1267	18.01	9/31	96
J.H.G Deighton	7	9	1	206	79	25.75	—	509	20	25.45	5/52	2
C.E. de Trafford	1	1	0	0	0	0.00	—						
R. Dewhurst	13	22	1	267	59	12.71	—						
T.E. Dickinson	4	5	3	10	9	5.00	—	98	3	32.66	1/20	—
J. Dixon	1	2	0	2	2	1.00	—						
P. Dobell	7	12	1	96	28	8.72	—						
H. Douthwaite	3	5	0	85	29	17.00	—						
G. Duckworth	424	455	170	4174	75	14.64	—	66	0	—	—	—
G.C.H. Dunlop	1	2	0	17	16	8.50	—						
A Durandu	1	1	0	5	5	5.00	—						
J. Dyson	150	242	35	4433	★118	21.41	1	4447	161	27.62	7/83	8
A. Eccles	123	196	20	4179	139	23.74	4	30	0	—	—	—
H. Eccles	5	7	0	37	14	5.28	—						
J. Eccles	47	75	5	1787	184	25.52	2	38	0	—	—	—
P.T. Eckersley	256	293	45	4588	★102	18.50	1	145	1	145.00	1/7	—
C.A. Edge	8	5	2	2	1	0.66	—	759	25	30.36	4/71	—
H.E. Edge	1	1	0	3	3	3.00	—	101	0	—	—	—
J.W. Edmonds	1	—	—	—	—	—	—	82	3	27.33	3/52	—
E.H. Edrich	33	40	4	854	121	23.72	2						
G.A. Edrich	322	479	55	14730	★167	34.74	24	199	2	99.50	1/19	—
H. Elliott	1	1	0	4	4	4.00	—						
J. Ellis	6	9	1	56	★26	7.00	—	240	21	11.42	8/21	1
S. Ellis	8	7	1	57	25	9.50	—	525	14	18.00	5/21	1
W. Ellis	36	55	4	846	★138	16.58	1						
F.M. Engineer	175	262	39	5942	141	26.64	4	10	0	—	—	—
R. Entwistle	48	79	4	1554	85	20.72	—						
N.H. Fairbrother	131	208	28	6826	★164	37.92	13	314	4	78.50	2/91	—
P.M. Fairclough	20	27	14	140	19	10.76	—	1158	52	22.26	7/27	2
J.A. Fallows	25	22	1	171	35	8.14	—						
A.W. Farnsworth	1	2	0	3	3	1.50	—						
H. Farrar	1	—	—	—	—	—	—	25	0	—	—	—
H.L. Farrar	1	2	0	28	25	14.00	—						
W. Farrimond	134	142	38	2202	63	21.17	—	16	0	—	—	—
W. Findlay	58	82	20	1223	81	19.72	—	15	0	—	—	—
D.J. Fitton	3	3	1	50	36	25.00	—	143	8	17.87	6/59	1
I. Folley	129	151	48	1353	69	13.13	—	8186	272	30.09	7/15	10
G. Fowler	161	268	17	9483	226	37.78	21	117	5	23.40	2/34	—
F.D. Gaddum	1	2	0	15	10	7.50	—	14	0	—	—	—
R.G. Garlick	44	56	7	753	50	15.36	—	2797	120	23.30	6/27	4
H.E. Garnett	144	231	17	5599	139	26.16	5	224	8	28.00	2/18	—
A.B.E. Gibson	2	4	0	25	16	6.25	—						
P.A. Gooch	4	3	1	0	★0	0.00	—	252	6	42.00	4/52	—
A.J. Good	8	8	2	10	6	1.66	—	482	17	28.35	5/62	1
F. Goodwin	11	10	4	47	★21	7.83	—	715	27	26.48	5/35	1
F.H. Goodwin	3	6	1	14	10	2.80	—	47	0	—	—	—
K. Goodwin	122	149	42	618	23	5.77	—						
D.M. Green	135	242	10	6086	138	26.23	4	1849	41	45.09	3/6	—
L. Green	152	173	28	3575	★110	24.65	1	299	9	33.22	2/2	—
E.W. Greenhalgh	14	18	5	366	★53	28.15	—	282	3	94.00	2/75	—

T. Greenhough	241	298	79	1868	*76	8.52	—	15540	707	21.98	7/56	32
P. Greenwood	75	92	15	1270	113	16.49	1	5090	208	24.47	6/35	9
W.R. Gregson	5	7	1	62	26	10.33	—	428	24	17.83	5/8	1
K.J. Grieves	452	696	73	20802	224	33.39	26	6769	235	28.80	6/60	8
G.H. Grimshaw	1	2	0	11	11	5.50	—					
S. Haggas	3	5	0	59	18	11.80	—					
W. Haggas	2	2	0	6	4	3.00	—					
C.H. Haigh	24	33	3	435	80	14.50	—					
A.E. Hall	9	10	4	11	*5	1.83	—	630	24	26.25	6/23	2
A.W. Hallam	71	93	25	570	*31	8.38	—	4063	211	19.25	6/28	9
T.M. Halliday	41	55	11	996	*109	22.63	1	16	0	—	—	—
C. Hallows	370	569	62	20142	*233	39.72	52	784	19	41.26	3/28	—
J. Hallows	138	202	27	4997	*137	28.55	8	6610	279	23.69	9/37	13
F. Hardcastle	2	4	1	17	9	5.66	—					
W.M. Hardcastle	4	7	0	33	11	4.71	—					
F.W. Hargreaves	1	1	0	0	0	0.00	—					
G.M. Harper	1	1	0	1	1	1.00	—					
F. Harrison	3	3	1	4	*2	2.00	—	118	4	29.50	2/30	—
J. Harrop	1	2	0	5	5	2.50	—	14	0	—	—	—
F. Harry	69	106	9	1528	88	15.75	—	3795	207	18.33	9/44	14
A. Hartley	112	185	9	4963	234	28.20	6	61	1	61.00	1/39	—
C.R. Hartley	160	168	11	3729	139	23.75	4	53	0	—	—	—
F. Hartley	2	1	0	2	2	2.00	—	44	1	44.00	1/44	—
G. Hartley	3	3	0	37	24	12.33	—					
B. Harwood	1	2	2	0	*0	—	—	16	1	16.00	1/16	—
C. Hawkwood	24	26	5	596	113	28.38	1	92	1	92.00	1/63	—
F.C. Hayes	228	339	48	10899	187	37.45	22	11	0	—	—	—
K.A. Hayes	18	24	1	586	117	25.47	1	25	0	—	—	—
A.N. Hayhurst	32	46	3	892	107	20.74	1	1436	43	33.39	4/27	—
F.S. Head	6	10	0	75	24	7.50	—					
J.G. Heap	2	2	0	0	0	0.00	—	4	0	—	—	—
J.S. Heap	210	312	41	5146	*132	18.98	1	9513	412	23.08	9/43	25
W.K. Hegg	41	59	9	858	130	17.16	1					
S. Henrikson	3	4	3	17	*10	17.00	—	105	2	52.50	1/26	—
J. Hewitson	4	5	0	99	56	19.80	—	235	14	16.78	6/57	1
W. Heys	5	7	0	74	46	10.57	—					
H. Hibbard	1	2	0	7	4	3.50	—	54	2	27.00	2/35	—
G. Hibberd	1	2	1	4	*2	4.00	—	37	0	—	—	—
W.J. Hibbert	14	22	4	445	79	24.72	—	116	3	38.66	2/41	—
W.E. Hickmott	34	35	9	272	*31	10.46	—	2042	82	24.90	5/20	2
W. Hickton	24	42	9	373	55	11.30	—	2024	144	14.05	10/46	14
K. Higgs	306	374	131	2655	60	10.92	—	23661	1033	22.90	7/19	37
E.F.W. Highton	1	1	0	6	6	6.00	—	49	1	49.00	1/49	—
P. Higson	3	3	2	22	*13	22.00	—					
T.A. Higson	5	7	1	123	42	20.50	—	58	1	58.00	1/18	—
T.A. Higson Jnr.	20	20	1	153	*32	8.05	—	302	6	50.33	1/14	—
L.D. Hildyard	8	13	1	174	39	14.50	—					
R.W.D. Hill	1	2	0	8	5	4.00	—					
J.R. Hillkirk	30	46	4	596	*56	14.19	—					
C. Hilton	91	110	35	537	36	7.16	—	7039	263	26.76	6/38	7
J. Hilton	8	7	0	99	33	14.14	—	152	2	76.00	2/27	—
M.J. Hilton	241	294	35	3140	*100	12.12	1	17419	926	18.81	8/19	48
S.F. Hird	1	—	—	—	—	—	—					
G. Hodgson	56	52	17	244	20	6.97	—	4107	148	27.75	6/77	4
G. Hodgson	1	1	0	1	1	1.00	—					
W. Hogg	44	40	12	120	19	4.28	—	2960	122	24.26	7/84	5
C. Holden	3	5	1	43	*27	10.75	—	11	0	—	—	—
M.A. Holding	7	8	2	66	32	11.00	—	715	40	17.87	6/74	4

G. Holgate	8	15	1	281	65	20.07	—					
J. Holland	12	21	4	324	63	19.05	—					
F.H. Hollins	12	18	0	290	114	16.11	1					
J.C.H.L. Hollins	20	30	0	454	65	15.13	—	99	1	99.00	1/45	—
E. Holroyd	1	2	0	6	4	3.00	—					
J. Holroyd	11	9	5	33	*18	8.25	—	652	23	28.34	5/47	2
J.L. Hopwood	397	571	54	15519	220	30.01	27	14905	672	22.18	9/33	35
A.H. Hornby	283	426	40	9441	129	24.45	8	168	1	168.00	1/21	—
A.N. Hornby	292	467	28	10649	188	24.25	10	94	3	31.33	1/2	—
C.L. Hornby	1	2	0	4	4	2.00	—	3	1	3.00	1/3	—
E.C. Hornby	9	13	1	229	82	19.08	—	98	3	32.66	1/15	—
L. Horridge	3	3	1	33	*11	16.50	—	79	3	26.33	2/46	—
R. Horrocks	6	10	0	116	61	11.60	—					
W.J. Horrocks	15	19	3	371	*100	23.18	1	44	0	—	—	—
W.H. Houldsworth	10	16	1	156	21	10.40	—					
G. Houlton	20	33	2	688	86	22.19	—	6	0	—	—	—
B.J. Howard	32	45	3	996	109	23.71	2					
K. Howard	61	82	35	395	23	8.40	—	3175	104	30.52	7/53	3
N.D. Howard	170	234	29	5526	145	26.95	3	23	0	—	—	—
R. Howard	8	9	2	166	*88	23.71	—	18	0	—	—	—
R. Howe	3	6	0	24	13	4.00	—					
T.R. Hubback	4	6	1	63	33	12.60	—					
W. Huddleston	183	258	32	2765	88	12.23	—	12007	684	17.55	9/36	42
B. Hudson	5	6	0	207	98	34.50	—	59	3	19.66	2/14	—
G.N. Hudson	2	2	1	1	1	1.00	—	82	0	—	—	—
D.P. Hughes	392	515	92	9350	153	22.10	8	17505	596	29.37	7/24	20
C.A.G. Hulton	8	12	3	80	19	8.88	—					
H.A.H. Hulton	2	4	1	13	6	4.33	—					
J. I'Anson	57	76	9	986	*110	14.71	1	3072	148	20.75	7/31	7
R. Iddison	16	31	5	621	106	23.88	1	875	56	15.62	6/29	4
W.H. Iddison	4	8	0	46	19	5.75	—	95	1	95.00	1/33	—
J. Iddon	483	683	90	21975	222	37.05	46	14214	533	26.66	9/42	14
J.T. Ikin	288	431	51	14327	192	37.70	23	8005	278	28.79	6/21	10
C.W. Ingleby	1	2	1	40	29	40.00	—	17	0	—	—	—
F. Isherwood	1	1	0	0	0	0.00	—					
E. Jackson	15	23	4	105	11	5.52	—					
J. Jackson	1	2	0	6	3	3.00	—					
T. Jacques	2	2	0	4	2	2.00	—	70	1	70.00	1/45	–
S.T. Jefferies	32	47	7	1167	93	29.17	—	2568	87	29.51	8/46	4
W.S. Jervis	1	2	0	6	6	3.00	—	4	0	—	—	—
T.E. Jesty	16	28	3	704	73	28.16	—	56	0	—	—	—
H.C.R. John	1	1	1	15	*15	—	—	13	0	—	—	—
W.T. Jolley	2	2	1	21	13	21.00	—	132	5	26.40	4/31	—
C.L. Jones	5	10	1	52	*20	5.77	—	6	1	6.00	1/6	—
J.L. Jones	4	5	4	10	*7	10.00	—					
J. Jordan	62	75	7	754	39	11.08	—					
G.E. Jowett	19	32	2	507	58	16.90	—	55	0	—	—	—
J.L. Kaye	1	2	0	21	20	10.50	—	16	0	—	—	—
E.A. Kelly	4	6	2	38	*16	9.50	—	284	4	62.00	3/77	—
J.M. Kelly	6	11	3	150	58	18.75	—	14	0	—	—	—
A.T. Kemble	76	112	13	1050	50	10.60	—					
G. Kemp	18	33	2	355	109	11.45	1					
A. Kennedy	149	241	20	6232	180	28.19	6	398	10	39.80	3/58	—
R.W. Kentfield	2	4	0	39	18	9.75	—	94	2	47.00	2/52	—
M.N. Kenyon	91	127	30	1435	*61	14.79	—					
A. Kermode	76	102	22	631	*64	7.88	—	7260	321	22.61	7/44	21
J.E. Kershaw	33	54	3	575	66	11.27	—					
J.H. Kevan	2	4	0	12	12	3.00	—					

Name	M	I	NO	Runs	HS	Avge	100	Runs	Wkts	Avge	Best	5wi
E. Kewley	1	2	0	3	3	1.50	—					
B.P. King	37	56	3	1505	145	28.39	2					
A. Knowles	1	2	0	6	6	3.00	—					
G.K. Knox	52	92	3	1698	108	19.07	3	161	2	80.50	1/10	—
B.E. Krikken	2	2	0	4	4	2.00	—					
O.P. Lancashire	97	158	10	1911	★76	12.91	—					
T. Lancaster	27	40	11	554	66	19.10	—	1456	66	22.06	7/25	5
C.W. Landon	6	10	0	121	47	12.10	—	69	2	34.50	1/10	—
J.R. Latchford	7	10	1	154	63	15.40	—	181	4	45.25	1/6	—
G.F. Lawson	1	2	0	19	17	9.50	—	88	5	17.60	4/81	—
A.E. Lawton	12	20	1	269	52	14.15	—	259	14	18.50	4/33	—
W. Lawton	2	2	0	3	3	1.50	—	64	1	64.00	1/0	—
E.L.C. Leach	12	15	0	161	79	10.73	—					
H. Leach	1	1	0	33	33	33.00	—					
J. Leach	5	9	0	103	34	11.44	—					
R. Leach	3	5	0	35	14	7.00	—					
R.C. Leach	1	2	0	49	39	24.50	—					
W.E. Leach	5	9	1	208	56	26.00	—	11	0	—	—	—
P.G. Lee	152	119	54	500	25	7.69	—	11817	496	23.82	8/34	24
C.P. Leese	1	2	0	16	10	8.00	—					
E. Leese	8	11	1	146	62	14.60	—					
J.F. Leese	24	42	1	556	44	13.56	—	94	5	18.80	3/49	—
J. Leigh	1	2	0	2	1	1.00	—					
E.C. Leventon	1	2	0	6	6	3.00	—	24	2	12.00	2/24	—
P. Lever	268	285	59	3073	83	13.59	—	17647	716	24.64	7/70	25
W.H.L. Lister	158	210	17	3561	★104	18.45	2	74	1	74.00	1/10	—
G.H. Littlewood	14	19	5	129	42	9.21	—	1123	58	19.36	7/49	5
G.W. Littlewood	3	6	1	28	★8	5.60	—					
C.H. Lloyd	219	326	42	12764	★217	44.94	30	1809	55	32.89	4/48	—
D. Lloyd	378	605	70	17877	195	33.41	37	7007	234	29.94	7/38	5
G.D. Lloyd	1	2	0	22	22	11.00	—					
R.A. Lloyd	3	5	0	100	51	20.00	—					
J.G. Lomax	57	78	2	1137	78	14.96	—	2519	81	31.09	5/18	1
J. Lyon	84	89	18	1010	123	14.22	1					
E.A. McDonald	217	215	31	1868	★100	10.15	1	22079	1053	20.96	8/53	94
L.L. McFarlane	35	34	18	115	★15	7.18	—	2563	73	35.10	6/59	1
H. McIntyre	1	1	1	1	★1	—	—					
W. McIntyre	72	112	20	758	66	8.23	—	5141	441	11.65	8/31	49
D.W. MacKinnon	3	5	0	65	24	13.00	—	72	5	14.40	3/13	—
A.C. MacLaren	307	510	37	15772	424	33.34	30	247	1	247.00	1/44	—
F.G. MacLaren	1	2	0	19	19	9.50	—	7	0	—	—	—
G. MacLaren	2	4	0	7	3	1.75	—	13	2	6.50	1/5	—
J.A. MacLaren	4	4	0	9	6	2.25	—					
K.G. MacLeod	75	124	9	2619	131	22.77	4	2019	81	24.92	6/29	2
K.W. MacLeod	6	6	0	92	31	15.33	—	409	17	24.05	5/8	2
R. McNairy	1	1	1	4	★4	—	—	73	1	73.00	1/23	—
J.W.H. Makepeace	487	757	64	25207	203	36.37	42	1971	42	46.92	4/33	—
D.J. Makinson	35	39	17	486	★58	22.09	—	2486	70	35.51	5/60	2
J. Makison	5	9	0	131	45	14.55	—	73	4	18.25	4/49	—
M.F. Malone	19	16	3	181	38	13.92	—	1421	64	22.20	7/88	5
W.J. Marchbank	4	7	1	20	15	3.33	—					
P.T. Marner	236	391	38	10312	★142	29.21	10	4116	109	37.76	5/46	1
C.S. Marriott	12	16	2	78	16	5.57	—	967	34	28.44	8/98	2
W.M. Massey	1	2	0	6	5	3.00	—					
C.D. Mathews	3	3	0	38	31	12.66	—	225	7	32.14	4/47	—
D.M. Mathews	7	8	0	130	46	16.25	—					
J. Mayall	1	1	0	0	0	0.00	—					
C. Maynard	91	120	21	1934	★132	19.53	1	8	0	—	—	—

F. Melhuish	3	6	0	32	13	5.33	—					
J. Melling	3	5	0	39	20	7.80	—	16	0	—	—	—
H. Mellor	2	4	0	28	17	7.00	—					
G.D. Mendis	73	124	13	4214	*203	37.96	7	77	0	—	—	—
F.N. Miller	1	2	0	37	37	18.50	—					
H. Miller	5	8	0	84	27	10.50	—	202	10	20.20	5/46	2
J. Mills	1	1	0	1	1	1.00	—					
W.G. Mills	6	11	1	57	26	5.70	—	97	6	16.16	3/52	—
R.O. Milne	1	1	1	7	*7	—	—					
A.W. Mold	260	347	114	1675	57	7.15	—	23384	1543	15.15	9/29	143
F.W. Moore	24	26	7	151	18	7.94	—	1516	54	28.07	6/45	2
E. Moorhouse	5	9	3	75	34	12.50	—					
L.H. Moorsom	1	2	0	12	7	6.00	—					
R.G. Mortimer	1	1	1	22	*22	—	—					
F.H. Mugliston	7	11	0	117	35	10.63	—					
A.J. Murphy	13	13	6	18	5	2.57	—	993	24	41.37	4/115	—
F.W. Musson	16	27	1	510	75	19.61	—					
Rev J.R. Napier	2	3	1	48	37	24.00	—	102	11	9.27	4/0	
G. Nash	54	80	24	295	30	5.26	—	2503	202	12.39	8/14	14
S.M. Nasir Zaidi	19	22	9	313	51	24.07	—	827	19	43.52	3/27	—
J. Nelson	1	2	0	7	5	3.50	—					
D.V. Norbury	14	23	0	594	100	25.82	1	448	23	19.47	4/28	—
A.E. Nutter	70	90	16	2200	*109	29.72	1	4453	152	29.29	6/66	7
E. Nutter	1	1	0	18	18	18.00	—					
W. Oakley	20	31	8	131	24	5.69	—	638	37	17.24	6/50	2
N. Oldfield	151	220	24	7002	*147	35.72	12	85	2	42.50	1/0	—
A. Ollivant	2	3	1	36	*24	18.00	—					
W.E. Openshaw	4	5	0	29	16	5.80	—					
J.A. Ormrod	27	47	3	1253	*139	28.47	1					
S.J. O'Shaughnessy	100	161	27	3567	*159	26.61	5	3947	110	35.88	4/66	—
S. Palmer	6	9	0	28	8	3.11	—	11	0	—	—	—
W. Parker	2	3	0	66	40	22.00	—	175	4	43.75	2/47	—
C.H. Parkin	157	189	27	1959	57	12.09	—	14526	901	16.12	9/32	85
R.H. Parkin	20	18	4	231	60	16.50	—	845	23	36.73	3/52	—
H.B. Parkinson	15	18	5	34	8	2.61	—					
L.W. Parkinson	88	112	13	2132	93	21.53	—	5654	192	29.44	6/112	7
F.D. Parr	48	51	10	493	42	12.02	—					
H.B. Parr	10	14	0	167	61	11.92	—					
B.P. Patterson	52	48	18	167	29	5.56	—	3863	141	27.39	7/49	9
W.S. Patterson	7	11	1	132	50	13.20	—	241	24	10.04	7/30	4
A.G. Paul	95	150	15	2958	177	21.91	4	146	2	73.00	1/7	—
J. Payne	1	2	0	0	0	0.00	—	48	0	—	—	—
J.H. Payne	9	15	3	158	33	13.16	—					
E. Paynter	293	445	47	16555	322	41.59	36	1250	24	52.08	3/13	—
H. Pennington	4	5	1	41	*29	10.25	—					
W. Perry	1	2	0	16	16	8.00	—	29	0	—	—	—
A.W. Pewtress	50	73	5	1483	89	21.80	—	10	1	10.00	1/10	—
W. Phillips	10	18	3	109	18	7.26	—					
W.E. Phillipson	158	202	46	4050	113	25.96	2	13508	545	24.78	8/100	28
C.C. Pilkington	2	4	0	38	18	9.50	—	100	3	33.33	3/70	—
H. Pilling	323	525	65	14841	*149	32.26	25	195	1	195.00	1/42	—
R. Pilling	177	258	86	1854	78	10.77	—					
W. Pilling	1	1	1	9	*9	—	—					
W. Place	298	441	43	14605	*266	36.69	34	42	1	42.00	1/2	—
L.O.S. Poidevin	105	163	14	4460	*168	29.93	8	1786	46	38.82	8/66	2
R. Pollard	266	298	52	3273	63	13.30	—	22492	1015	22.15	8/33	55
E.H. Porter	17	29	1	301	61	10.75	—	9	0	—	—	—
G. Potter	10	17	1	449	86	28.06	—					

T.O. Potter	1	2	0	39	39	19.50	—					
W.H. Potter	1	2	0	23	12	11.50	—					
S. Preston	5	4	2	46	33	23.00	—	212	6	35.33	2/42	—
A. Price	1	2	0	8	8	4.00	—					
E. Price	35	36	14	305	54	13.86	—	2373	115	20.63	6/34	6
G. Pullar	312	524	45	16853	*167	35.18	32	305	8	38.12	3/91	—
G. Radcliffe	7	11	0	171	60	15.54	—					
L. Radcliffe	50	67	22	275	25	6.11	—					
N.V. Radford	24	33	8	549	*76	21.96	—	1805	33	54.69	5/95	2
R.B. Rae	1	1	0	74	74	74.00	—	29	0	—	—	—
S. Ramadhin	33	40	19	151	13	7.19	—	2267	97	23.37	8/121	7
H.J. Ramsbottom	1	2	0	1	1	0.50	—	11	0	—	—	—
E. Ratcliffe	1	2	0	9	7	4.50	—	8	0	—	—	—
R.M. Ratcliffe	82	84	22	1022	*101	16.48	1	5411	205	26.39	7/58	15
E.B. Rawlinson	1	2	1	15	14	15.00	—					
W. Rawlinson	3	6	0	24	10	4.00	—					
G.S. Rawstorne	1	1	0	2	2	2.00	—					
B.W. Reidy	107	162	26	3641	*131	26.77	2	2508	60	41.80	5/61	1
F.R. Reynolds	38	65	20	293	*34	6.51	—	1823	94	19.39	6/92	6
A. Rhodes	17	25	3	382	70	17.36	—	475	15	31.66	2/24	—
C.A. Rhodes	8	10	4	11	6	1.83	—	619	22	28.13	4/37	—
W. Richmond	1	2	0	1	1	0.50	—					
J. Ricketts	34	66	4	1120	*195	18.06	1	250	12	20.83	4/40	—
W. Rickman	1	1	0	5	5	5.00	—					
D.M. Ritchie	1	1	0	3	3	3.00	—					
J. Roberts	2	4	2	5	5	2.50	—	90	0	—	—	—
R. Roberts	10	16	0	100	20	6.25	—					
W.B. Roberts	114	113	39	810	51	10.94	—	7971	382	20.86	8/50	25
P.A. Robinson	1	1	0	15	15	15.00	—	58	2	29.00	2/57	—
W. Robinson	115	186	10	3597	154	20.43	4	61	0	—	—	—
G.H. Rogerson	12	20	1	340	*47	17.89	—					
E. Roper	28	47	2	586	65	13.02	—					
D. Rowland	1	2	0	0	0	0.00	—	23	0	—	—	—
L.S. Rowlands	6	10	4	27	9	4.50	—	322	16	20.12	4/29	—
A.B. Rowley	12	21	3	282	*63	15.66	—	603	24	25.12	5/71	1
E.B. Rowley	81	131	8	1626	78	13.21	—	17	0	—	—	—
E.B. Rowley Jnr	16	25	4	553	65	26.33	—					
Rev V.P.F.A. Royle	74	120	8	1754	81	15.66	—	114	2	57.00	1/22	—
F. Rushton	6	5	0	59	28	11.80	—	362	10	36.20	4/30	—
T.H. Rushton	1	1	0	7	7	7.00	—					
F.J. Rutter	2	4	1	15	*8	5.00	—	11	0	—	—	—
L. Sanderson	1	1	0	0	0	0.00	—					
R.W.B. Sanderson	1	2	0	7	6	3.50	—					
J.S. Savage	58	64	33	197	19	6.35	—	3051	114	26.76	5/1	2
C.M. Sawyer	2	2	1	21	*11	21.00	—	65	0	—	—	—
J. Schofield	4	6	2	27	11	6.75	—					
F.B. Scholfield	1	2	1	17	17	17.00	—	2	0	—	—	—
S.S. Schultz	9	17	3	215	*42	15.35	—	23	0	—	—	—
C.J. Scott	46	51	13	262	*27	6.89	—					
W.A. Scott	1	2	1	14	9	14.00	—					
A. Seymour	1	2	0	45	25	22.50	—					
J. Sharp	518	776	70	22015	211	31.18	36	11821	434	27.23	9/77	18
G.O. Shelmerdine	31	45	4	980	105	23.90	1	97	0	—	—	—
C. Shore	1	2	0	3	3	1.50	—	11	0	—	—	—
K. Shuttleworth	177	179	62	1929	71	16.48	—	11097	484	22.92	7/41	17
F.M. Sibbles	308	311	79	3436	*71	14.81	—	20538	932	22.03	8/24	41
W. Silcock	6	7	1	82	43	13.66	—	367	5	73.40	2/62	—
J. Simmons	422	519	137	8716	112	22.81	5	26140	982	26.61	7/64	40

A.R. Sladen	2	3	0	8	5	2.66	—	175	6	29.16	3/77	—
R. Slater	1	2	0	0	0	0.00	—	3	0	—	—	—
J. Smalley	2	4	0	24	17	6.00	—					
A. Smith	4	8	3	56	30	11.20	—					
A.P. Smith	48	76	5	1440	124	20.28	2	517	29	17.82	5/49	1
C. Smith	167	234	50	2248	81	12.21	—	18	1	18.00	1/18	—
C.S. Smith	45	55	4	768	67	15.05	—	2815	101	21.63	5/39	2
D.J. Smith	3	4	0	26	14	6.50	—	205	4	51.25	1/19	—
J. Smith	6	12	1	153	*40	13.90	—	290	12	24.16	4/46	—
R. Smith	1	1	0	6	6	6.00	—	11	0	—	—	—
S. Smith	38	54	4	865	*72	17.30	—					
T. Smith	2	3	0	18	12	6.00	—	36	1	36.00	1/8	—
K.L. Snellgrove	105	170	16	3906	138	25.36	2	27	3	9.00	2/23	—
G.J. Speak	5	6	4	27	*15	13.50	—	230	1	230.00	1/78	—
N.J. Speak	2	4	0	49	35	12.25	—					
H. Spencer	2	3	1	5	4	2.50	—	139	3	46.33	1/0	—
A.F. Spooner	18	33	1	500	83	15.62	—					
R.H. Spooner	170	280	14	9889	247	37.17	25	554	5	110.80	1/5	—
K.B. Standring	8	14	2	110	41	9.16	—	375	11	34.09	3/44	—
H.D. Stanning	33	54	1	898	86	16.94	—	3	0	—	—	—
J. Stanning	4	7	0	97	33	13.85	—					
J. Stanworth	34	38	11	236	*50	8.74	—					
J.B. Statham	430	501	98	4237	62	10.51	—	27470	1816	15.12	8/34	109
M.W. Staziker	2	2	2	1	*1	—	—	269	1	269.00	1/114	—
A.G. Steel	47	72	5	1960	105	29.25	1	3134	238	13.16	9/63	26
D.Q. Steel	22	35	1	560	82	16.47	—					
E.E. Steel	40	58	4	861	*69	15.94	—	2598	122	21.29	6/69	11
H.B. Steel	22	37	3	765	100	22.50	1					
F. Stephenson	2	4	1	0	*0	0.00	—	17	1	17.00	1/17	—
W.B. Stoddart	15	25	4	294	*43	14.00	—	899	37	24.29	6/121	3
D.H. Stone	6	8	2	86	46	14.33	—	472	9	52.44	4/30	—
E. Storer	6	11	5	46	23	7.66	—	245	15	16.33	5/12	1
F.H. Sugg	235	387	24	9620	220	26.50	15	259	10	25.90	2/12	—
J. Sullivan	154	241	32	4286	*81	20.50	—	2216	76	29.15	4/19	—
R.J. Sutcliffe	1	2	2	10	*10	—	—	37	1	37.00	1/37	—
S.H. Swire	5	9	1	93	*18	11.62	—	37	0	—	—	—
R. Tattersall	277	312	128	1786	58	9.70	—	20316	1168	17.39	9/40	83
R.H. Tattersall	2	—	—	—	—	—	—	219	1	219.00	1/44	—
F. Taylor	52	85	4	1451	96	17.91	—	73	3	24.33	1/4	—
F. Taylor	15	18	6	188	*29	15.66	—	1026	40	25.65	6/65	3
J. Taylor	3	6	0	52	33	8.66	—	13	0	—	—	—
M.L. Taylor	95	112	15	2216	*107	22.84	1	26	0	—	—	—
R.J. Taylor	2	3	0	6	6	2.00	—	96	2	48.00	1/25	—
T.J. Taylor	4	4	1	2	2	0.66	—	238	5	47.60	2/63	—
K. Tebay	15	27	2	509	106	20.36	1					
A. Teggin	6	8	0	31	9	3.87	—	176	16	11.00	6/53	2
H.N. Tennent	2	3	0	45	21	15.00	—					
W.M. Tennent	1	2	0	3	3	1.50	—					
A. Thomas	1	2	0	4	4	2.00	—	7	0	—	—	—
R. Thomas	20	22	5	60	17	3.52	—					
H. Thornber	1	2	0	0	0	0.00	—					
S.M. Tindall	42	62	1	1039	86	17.03	—	28	1	28.00	1/11	—
A. Tinsley	58	91	10	1348	65	16.64	—	7	0	—	—	—
H.J. Tinsley	4	6	0	57	18	9.50	—					
E. Tranter	3	5	0	9	5	1.80	—	94	3	31.33	2/11	—
G.E. Trim	15	25	0	399	91	15.96	—	13	0	—	—	—
G.E. Tyldesley	573	850	93	34222	*256	45.20	90	332	6	55.33	3/33	—
H. Tyldesley	4	7	3	63	*33	15.75	—	101	3	33.66	2/37	—

J.D. Tyldesley	116	169	16	2885	*112	18.85	3	8092	309	26.18	7/34	15
J.T. Tyldesley	507	824	52	31949	*295	41.38	73	170	2	85.00	1/4	—
R.K. Tyldesley	374	435	47	6126	105	15.78	1	24139	1449	16.65	8/15	100
W.K. Tyldesley	87	137	7	2979	152	22.91	3	383	8	47.87	2/0	—
J. Unsworth	2	3	0	25	23	8.33	—	75	3	25.00	3/52	—
D.S. Van der Knapp	1	—	—	—	—	—	—	69	2	34.50	2/24	—
D.W. Varey	44	70	7	1752	112	27.80	1	6	0	—	—	—
E. Wadsworth	7	13	0	69	30	5.30	—	13	0	—	—	—
R. Walker	2	4	1	27	19	9.00	—					
H. Wall	3	4	0	24	15	6.00	—					
T. Wall	2	4	0	48	37	12.00	—	17	0	—	—	—
W. Wall	1	2	1	17	*17	17.00	—					
M.A. Wallwork	1	—	—	—	—	—						
G. Walsh	2	3	0	16	15	5.33	—					
M. Walton	1	2	0	6	6	3.00	—					
L. Warburton	6	5	1	159	*74	39.75	—	217	5	43.40	3/47	—
A. Ward	330	544	47	15392	185	30.96	24	2380	65	36.61	6/29	4
F. Ward	47	74	6	986	145	14.50	1	538	27	19.92	4/14	—
C. Wardle	3	5	2	25	*7	8.33	—	17	0	—	—	—
C. Washbrook	500	756	95	27863	*251	42.15	58	268	4	67.00	1/4	—
Wasim Akram	10	18	2	496	*116	31.00	1	666	31	21.48	7/53	2
M. Watkinson	116	170	23	3465	106	23.57	1	7990	239	33.43	7/25	11
A. Watson	283	423	88	4187	74	12.49	—	17516	1308	13.39	9/118	98
F.B. Watson	456	664	48	22833	*300	37.06	49	12811	402	31.86	5/31	5
R.G. Watson	2	3	0	33	18	11.00	—					
S. Webb	73	94	27	513	*38	7.65	—	5226	265	19.72	8/36	15
F. Webster	2	3	1	12	10	6.00	—	122	7	17.42	3/34	—
G.E. Wharmby	6	8	2	29	11	4.83	—	209	8	26.12	3/35	—
A. Wharton	392	589	55	17921	199	33.55	25	7094	225	31.52	7/33	2
T. Whatmough	2	4	2	42	*28	21.00	—	79	3	26.33	2/52	—
J.W. Whewell	12	13	5	19	12	2.37	—					
R. Whitehead	107	158	36	2571	*131	21.07	4	7260	300	24.20	8/77	17
T. Whitehead	1	1	0	8	8	8.00	—	20	0	—	—	—
P. Whiteley	5	8	2	86	32	14.33	—	266	9	29.55	3/70	—
J.P. Whiteside	6	8	0	25	12	3.12	—					
D. Whittaker	9	14	1	128	26	9.84	—	46	1	46.00	1/26	—
E. Whittaker	11	21	2	232	39	12.21	—	125	1	125.00	1/26	—
L.L. Wilkinson	63	61	24	296	48	8.00	—	6091	232	26.25	8/53	15
A. Wilson	171	186	59	760	*37	5.98	—					
G.A. Winder	2	4	0	23	9	5.75	—					
B. Wood	260	424	56	12969	198	35.24	23	6910	251	27.52	7/52	8
J. Wood	1	—	—	—	—	—	—	103	4	25.75	3/56	—
R. Wood	6	9	2	167	52	23.85	—	72	4	18.00	1/23	—
A. Woolley	7	9	0	61	24	6.77	—	351	11	31.90	4/56	—
D.R. Worsley	62	108	9	2508	120	25.33	2	904	27	33.48	4/21	—
W. Worsley	136	167	63	628	*37	6.03	—					
E.L. Wright	4	8	0	53	17	6.62	—					
Rev. F.W. Wright	15	22	2	416	*120	20.80	1	156	3	51.66	2/44	—
C. Yates	1	2	0	28	24	14.00	—					
G. Yates	92	135	15	1632	74	13.60	—	934	30	31.13	4/112	—

RESULTS OF ALL INTER-COUNTY FIRST-CLASS MATCHES 1865–1988

	DY	EX	GM	GS	HA	KT	LE	MX	NR	NT	SM	SY	SX	WA	WO	YO
1865								WL								
1866						LL						DL				
1867												DD				LLL
1868										LL		WL				-L
1869												WL	WL			
1870				WW								WL				
1871	LW			LW												LW
1872	WW															WW
1873	WW			L–								WW				LL
1874	LD			DL												LW
1875	DW			WW												WL
1876	WW			WL						WL			LW			LL
1877	LW			LL						LW			WW			WW
1878	WL		DL	WW						LW						WD
1879	WW		WD	WD						DD						WL
1880	WW		DL	WW						LL		WW				DD
1881	WW		WD	WW		D–				WD		WW				WW
1882	WW		WW	WW				WW		LD	WW	DW				DW
1883	WW		WL	WL						WD		WL				LL
1884	WW		DL	WL							WW	LW				LW
1885	LW		WW	W–								LD	WW			DL
1886	DW		DL	WL						LD		LW	WL			WD
1887	WW		WW	WW						LW		LW	WW			DL
1888			DW	LL				WW		DD		LW	DL			DL
1889			WL	WW	LW			LW		DL		WW	WW			WW
1890			DD	WW	LW			LW		DW		LL	WW			DW
1891			WW	AW	LL			LL		LD	WW	LD	DW			WW
1892			WD	WD	DL			LW		LW	LW	DL	WW			WL
1893			WW	LL	WL			WL		WL	WD	LW	DW			WW
1894	LW		WW	LL	DW	WL				WL	WD	LT	WW			LLD
1895	DL		WD	WW	WW	LW				WW	AW	LW	WW	LW		WD
1896	WD		WW	WD	WD	LL				WD	WD	WW	WD	WD		LL
1897	WW	WL		WW	WW	DW	WW	WD		DW	WW	LL	DW	DD		DW
1898	WD	LL		DW	DD	DD	DW	WL		WD	WW	DD	WL	LW		DL
1899	WW	DW		WW	DW	AD	LW	LD		DW	LW	LL	WL	WD		WD
1900	WW	DD		DL	WW	DD	DW	WD		WW	WW	WL	DW	WD	WW	DD
1901	WD	DD		WD	WD	WL	WD	DD		DW	LW	WD	LD	WL	WW	LD
1902		DW		WD	WW	DD	AD			DL	DL	WL	DW	LD	WD	LD
1903	WW	LW		DD	LW	WW	DD			DW	DL	WD	LD	WD	WD	DL
1904	WW	WD		WW	WW	WD		WD		DD	WW	WW	DD	WD	WD	DD
1905	WD	WD		WL	WW	WD	DD			DW	WW	AL	DD	WD	WD	WL
1906	WW	WW		WW		WL	WW	LL		WD	WW	DW	WD	WD	DL	LL
1907	DW	LL				WW	WW	DL	DW	DL	WW	WL	WD	DW	LD	DL
1908	DD	LW			LD	WW	LD	WL	WW	WW	AL	DL	WW	LD		LL
1909	WD	WD			DW	WD	DW	LW		WW	WW	WW	WW	WD	WL	LL
1910	WD	DW		DW	WW	AL	LW	DD	WD	WL	WW	LD	WL	WD	DW	DW
1911	LW	DW		WD	WW	LW	WD	LW	WW	DL	WW	DD	WD	LL	WW	LD
1912	DW	AD			WL	WW	WD			DD	DW	WD	AD	DW		LD
1913	WD	DD		DW		LL	WW	DW	LD	LD	DL	LL	LW	LL		WLW
1914	WD	LD		WW	WD	WD	LW	DL	LD	DD	LL	DL	DL			DLD
1919	WW	LD		WW		LD	DD	DL	DD	DW	DD	WL	DW			WD
1920	WW	DW		DW	WW	WW	WW	DL	WW	WW		LL	WL	WW	WW	LD

263

Year																
1921		WD	WW	WW	WD	WL	DL	WW	LD		DD	WW	WL	WW	DD	
1922	WW	WD	WW	WW	DL	DD	WW	WL	WW	WL		LL	DL	DW	WD	LD
1923	DW	DW	WW	WD	DD	DW	WW	WW	WW	LW		DD	DD	WD	DW	DL
1924	DW	WW	WL	WD	DD	DL	WW	DD	WW	DD		DD	WD	DD	DD	WD
1925	WW	DD	WW	WD	WW	WL	WW	LL	WW	DD	WW	WL	WW	DD	WW	DD
1926	WW	DW	DW	DW	WW	DW	WL	DD	WW	WW	DW	WD	DD	DW	DW	LD
1927	DD	DD	AW	DW	WW	DD	DD	DW	DW	DD	WD	DD	DL	WD	WD	WD
1928	DW	WW	WD	WD	WW	WW	DD	DW	WD	DD		DW	WW	DW	DD	DD
1929	WD		WW	LD	WW	DW	DD	DD	DW	LD		WD	LD	WW	WW	DD
1930		DW	WD	WD	DD	WW	WW	DD	WW	DD		DD	DD	WD	DD	DD
1931	DW	WL	WD	WL	AD	DD		WD		DD	WW	DD	AL	DD	LD	DD
1932	WW		DD	LD	DD	DL	DW	LW		LD	LW	AD	DD	DD	WW	WL
1933	WD	DW	DD	DD	WD	WD	WW	WW		DD		DD	DD	DD	WD	LD
1934	DW	DD	DW	WW	WD	LD	DW	LW	WW	WD	WD	DD	DD		WW	LD
1935	LD	LW	DW	WW	DD	DW	LW	LL	WD		DD	DW	WW		WW	DL
1936	DD		DW	LD	DL	WW	DW	DW	WW	LD	DD	DL	LD	DL	DD	DD
1937	DD	WL	DD	WL	DD	DW	DD	WL	WD	DW	DD	DL	DW	WD	DD	LW
1938	LW	WD	WD	DL	WW	WL	DW	WD	WW	DD	DL	DW	DW	WD	WD	LL
1939	WD	DD	DW	WD	WW	WL	D–	LD	DW	DW	DD	LD	AD	LD	WW	LL
																D–
1946	WW	WL	LD	W–	LW	L–	WW	W–	D–	WD	W–	DW	WD	WW	W–	DD
1947	WW	DW	DD	W–	WT	W–	WW	W–	W–	DW	L–	DD	WW	DD	D–	DD
1948	DD	D–	DD	DD	D–	LW	W–	DW	DD	WD	WW	L–	W–	DW	D–	DD
1949	LD	W–	DD	LL	D–	WL	D–	DL	DW	DD	WW	W–	L–	DL	D–	DD
1950	DL	W–	WW	WD	DW	WW	DW	LW	D–	WW	W–	DD	DW	WD	W–	WD
1951	WD	D–	DL	DD	LW	WW	DD	WD	D–	DD	D–	DW	WD	WD	D–	DD
1952	WD	TD	DW	D–	W–	WW	L–	DW	DW	WL	DD	W–	DL	DW	WW	DD
1953	LD	DD	WD	W–	W–	WD	D–	DD	DL	WW	WW	L–	WL	DD	WD	DD
1954	DL	W–	WW	AD	DD	DD	DA	AD	D–	DD	–W	DL	DW	WD	–D	LD
1955	WW	–D	DD	WL	DL	WD	WW	LW	–D	LL	W–	LL	DL	WD	W–	LD
1956	DD	DW	WD	W–	–W	DL	W–	WD	DW	DD	WW	–D	WD	WL	DD	DW
1957	LD	DL	LW	–D	W–	WD	–L	DW	LL	DD	WW	L–	DL	WW	WW	DD
1958	WW	L–	DD	WL	WL	AL	WW	DD	D–	DD	–L	LL	AD	WW	–D	DW–W
1959	DL	–W	DL	DW	WL	WD	LW	DL	–W	WL	W–	WW	LD	DW	D–	WD–L
1960	LW	DL	LD	DW	WW	DL	WW	DL	DL	LW	DL	DW	DW	WD	DW	WW
1961	WL	LD	DD	WW	WL	DD	DD	DD	DD	WW	DD	DW	WL	LD	LW	LD
1962	DD	LL	LL	DL	DL	DL	DD	DL	DD	LL	LL	WL	DL	WD	DL	DL
1963	DD	DD	WL	L–	–D	WD	D–	WL	DW	LL	LL	–D	LD	LD	DD	DL
1964	LD	WD	DD	–D	D–	DD	–W	LL	DD	DL	DW	D–	WL	LL	LL	DL
1965	WD	W–	LL	LL	LD	DD	DL	LL	L–	WD	–L	DD	WL	DW	–L	DL
1966	LW	–D	DL	DW	WD	LW	LL	DD	–L	WD	L–	DL	WD	DD	L–	LL
1967	DD	DW	DD	–D	W–	DL	–D	DL	DW	WD	DD	D–	DD	AD	DL	AD
1968	WD	WD	LL	W–	–D	DL	D–	WD	DW	LD	DW	–D	DW	DW	LD	DL
1969	LD	D–	DD	–D	D–	DD	–D	DW	–D	DD	–W	D–	DD	DD	D–	DD
1970	DL	–D	DD	D–	–D	DD	W–	WW	W–	DD	D–	–D	WD	DL	–D	DW
1971	WD	D–	–W	–W	DW	L–	–L	D–	WW	WD	DD	L–	–L	DW	WD	DD
1972	DA	D–	D–	–D	D–	W–	–D	–L	D–	DD	–D	D–	D–	LL	–D	WD
1973	DD	–W	–W	D–	L	–W	D–	–L	WL	D–	–L	D	LL	D–		DD
1974	DD	D–	D–	–D	–D	D–	–W	–W	D–	WD	–D	D–	W–	WD	–D	DD
1975	WW	–D	–L	W–	L–	–L	D–	W–	–W	WD	W–	–D	–D	WW	D–	DD
1976	DL	D–	W–	–D	–D	D–	–D	–D	L–	WD	–W	D–	L–	LL	–L	LD
1977	DD	–D	–D	D–	D–	–D	D–	L–	–D	DW	W–	AD	–D	DL	DL	DL
1978	LD	L–	D–	–W	–W	D–	–L	–L	A–	WD	–L	DD	D–	LD	WD	LL
1979	DD	–L	–D	D–	D–	–D	W–	W–	–W	DD	D–	DD	–L	DD	WL	DL
1980	DA	D–	D–	–D	–W	D–	–D	–D	D–	WD	–A	DL	L–	DD	WL	WD
1981	DD	–D	–W	D–	L–	–D	L–	L–	–D	DL	L–	DL	–L	DD	WW	DW
1982	DD	D–	W–	–D	–L	D–	–D	–D	D–	DL	–W	WD	D–	WD	DL	DD
1983	DD	D–	DD	W–	DD	–D	D–	DD	–D	DL	W–	–D	–W	LL	DL	DD

1984 DL	LL	–D	DD	–L	DD	–W	D–	LD	LL	–D	–D	L–	LD	D–	DD
1985 WD	–D	–D	–W	L–	L–	DD	–D	D–	DD	WL	DL	DL	DL	–L	DD
1986 DD	W–	DD	D–	DA	–L	D–	DL	–L	DL	W–	–L	–W	DD	DW	DD
1987 LD	LW	–L	WD	–D	DW	–W	D–	DL	DD	–W	W–	W–	WW	W–	DD
1988 DD	–W	–W	D–	W–	–L	D–	L–	–D	LW	L–	DL	–W	DW	LD	DL

LANCASHIRE IN THE GILLETTE/NATWEST CUP

ELIMINATED IN				FINAL	
1st Round	2nd Round	¼ Final	Semi-Final	Runners Up	Winners
			1963		
			1964		
	1965				
		1966			
			1967		
1968					
	1969				
					1970
					1971
					1972
		1973			
				1974	
					1975
				1976	
	1977				
			1978		
	1979				
	1980				
			1981		
1982					
	1983				
		1984			
	1985				
				1986	
1987					
	1988				

LANCASHIRE IN THE BENSON & HEDGES CUP

ELIMINATED IN:			FINAL	
Zonal Group	¼ Final	Semi-Final	Runners Up	Winners
	1972			
		1973		
		1974		
	1975			
	1976			
1977				
1978				
1979				
	1980			
1981				
		1982		
		1983		
				1984
1985				
1986				
1987				
1988				

LANCASHIRE'S SUNDAY LEAGUE RECORD

Year	Position	Won	Lost	Tied	No result
1969	1st	12	3	–	1
1970	1st	13	2	–	1
1971	3rd	10	6	–	–
1972	7th★	8	7	–	1
1973	4th	8	4	–	4
1974	12th★	5	9	1	1
1975	8th	8	7	1	–
1976	9th	8	8	–	–
1977	16th	5	10	–	1
1978	5th	9	6	–	1
1979	10th	6	7	–	3
1980	13th	6	9	–	1
1981	11th	6	8	1	1
1982	10th	6	7	1	2
1983	8th	5	5	1	5
1984	4th	10	6	–	–
1985	15th	3	6	2	5
1986	12th	6	9	–	1
1987	9th	5	6	–	5
1988	3rd	10	4	–	2

1988: Winners of Refuge Cup.

GROUNDS USED BY LANCASHIRE 1865–1988

Alexandra Meadow, Blackburn	1932–1935
Stanley Park, Blackpool	1905–1988
Lune Road, Lancaster	1914
Church Road, Lytham	1985–1988
Aigburth, Liverpool	1881–1988
Old Trafford, Manchester	1865–1988
Nelson	1925–1938
West Cliff, Preston	1936–1952
Sparthbottoms Road, Rochdale	1876
Dover Road, Birkdale, Southport	1959–1988
Station Road, Whalley	1867

HIGHEST AND LOWEST SCORE AGAINST LANCASHIRE BY EACH COUNTY

Opponents	Highest	Venue	Year	Lowest	Venue	Year
				37 ⎱	Old Trafford	1923
Derbyshire	577	Old Trafford	1896	37 ⎰	Chesterfield	1922
Essex	559-9	Leyton	1904	59	Liverpool	1931
Glamorgan	425	Old Trafford	1938	22	Liverpool	1924
Gloucestershire	561	Bristol	1938	33	Liverpool	1888
Hampshire	487	Liverpool	1901	37	Old Trafford	1900
Kent	479	Canterbury	1906	38	Maidstone	1881
Leicestershire	493	Leicester	1910	33	Leicester	1925
Middlesex	501-3	Lord's	1914	69	Lord's	1933
Northants	517-9	Northampton	1955	48	Northampton	1922
Nottinghamshire	504-5	Old Trafford	1949	35	Trent Bridge	1895
Somerset	561	Bath	1901	29	Old Trafford	1882
Surrey	634	Oval	1898	33	Oval	1873
Sussex	485	Old Trafford	1903	24	Old Trafford	1890
Warwickshire	532-4	Edgbaston	1901	49	Edgbaston	1896
Worcestershire	492	Old Trafford	1906	48	Worcester	1910
Yorkshire	590	Bradford	1887	33	Headingley	1924
Australia	548-6	Old Trafford	1961	66	Old Trafford	1888
South Africa	429	Old Trafford	1907	44	Liverpool	1912
West Indies	454-7	Old Trafford	1950	108	Old Trafford	1928
New Zealand	410-9	Liverpool	1931	104	Old Trafford	1965
India	493	Liverpool	1932	85	Old Trafford	1911
Pakistan	303	Old Trafford	1962	219	Old Trafford	1954
Oxford Univ.	419-8	Oxford	1960	47	Oxford	1985
Cambridge Univ.	416	Liverpool	1957	31	Old Trafford	1882
MCC	404	Lord's	1897	30	Lord's	1886

HIGHEST AND LOWEST SCORE FOR LANCASHIRE AGAINST EACH COUNTY

Derbyshire	546	Old Trafford	1898	25	Old Trafford	1871
Essex	510	Clacton	1947	70	Southport	1978
Glamorgan	564-9	Old Trafford	1938	49	Liverpool	1924
Gloucestershire	474-3	Liverpool	1903	45	Preston	1936
Hampshire	676-7	Old Trafford	1911	54	Portsmouth	1937
Kent	531	Old Trafford	1906	61	Canterbury	1884
Leicestershire	590	Leicester	1899	73	Leicester	1935
Middlesex	484-8	Old Trafford	1920	63	Lord's	1891
Northants	528-4	Old Trafford	1928	33	Northampton	1977
Nottinghamshire	627	Trent Bridge	1905	37	Liverpool	1907
Somerset	801	Taunton	1895	48	Taunton	1892
Surrey	588-4	Old Trafford	1928	27	Old Trafford	1958
Sussex	640-8	Hove	1937	55	Old Trafford	1892
Warwickshire	526	Edgbaston	1920	70	Old Trafford	1955
Worcestershire	592-4	Worcester	1929	55	Worcester	1965
Yorkshire	509-9	Old Trafford	1926	30	Holbeck	1868
Australia	346	Old Trafford	1961	28	Liverpool	1896
South Africa	445-6	Old Trafford	1924	90	Blackpool	1960

West Indies	405	Old Trafford	1923	79	Old Trafford	1957
New Zealand	487	Liverpool	1931	116	Old Trafford	1973
India	511	Old Trafford	1974	68	Old Trafford	1952
Pakistan	324	Old Trafford	1954	98	Old Trafford	1954
Oxford Univ.	512–8	Oxford	1947	47	Oxford	1985
Cambridge Univ.	470–4	Old Trafford	1960	65	Cambridge	1907
MCC	365–6	Old Trafford	1957	49	Lord's	1880

HIGHEST AND LOWEST SCORES IN LIMITED OVERS MATCHES

HIGHEST

Competition	Score	Opponents and Venue	Year
John Player/Refuge Assurance	255–5 (40 overs)	Somerset at Old Trafford	1970
Benson & Hedges Cup	290–5 (55 overs)	Northants at Old Trafford	1983
Nat. West/Gillette Cup	349–6 (60 overs)	Gloucestershire at Bristol	1984

LOWEST

John Player/Refuge Assurance	71 (20.4 overs)	Essex at Chelmsford	1987
Benson & Hedges Cup	82 (47.2 overs)	Yorkshire at Bradford	1972
Nat. West/Gillette Cup	59 (31.1 overs)	Worcestershire at Worcester	1963

DOUBLE CENTURIES IN FIRST CLASS MATCHES

Score	Batsman	Opponents	Venue	Year
424	A.C. MacLaren	Somerset	Taunton	1895
322	E. Paynter	Sussex	Hove	1937
300*	F. Watson	Surrey	Old Trafford	1928
295*	J.T. Tyldesley	Kent	Old Trafford	1906
291	E. Paynter	Hampshire	Southampton	1938
272	J.T. Tyldesley	Derbyshire	Chesterfield	1919
266*	W. Place	Oxford Univ.	Oxford	1947
266	E. Paynter	Essex	Old Trafford	1937
256*	E. Tyldesley	Warwickshire	Old Trafford	1930
253	J.T. Tyldesley	Kent	Canterbury	1914
251*	C. Washbrook	Surrey	Old Trafford	1947
250	J.T. Tyldesley	Nottinghamshire	Nottingham	1905
249	J.T. Tyldesley	Leicestershire	Leicester	1899
248	J.T. Tyldesley	Worcestershire	Liverpool	1903
247	R.H. Spooner	Nottinghamshire	Nottingham	1903
244	A.C. MacLaren	Kent	Canterbury	1897
244	G.E. Tyldesley	Warwickshire	Birmingham	1920
243	J.T. Tyldesley	Leicestershire	Leicester	1908
242	G.E. Tyldesley	Leicestershire	Leicester	1928
240	R.H. Spooner	Somerset	Bath	1906
239	G.E. Tyldesley	Glamorgan	Cardiff	1934
236	G.E. Tyldesley	Surrey	The Oval	1923
236	F. Watson	Sussex	Brighton	1928
234	A. Hartley	Somerset	Old Trafford	1910
233*	C. Hallows	Hampshire	Liverpool	1927
232	C. Hallows	Sussex	Old Trafford	1928
228	C. Washbrook	Oxford Univ.	Oxford	1935
227	C. Hallows	Warwickshire	Old Trafford	1921
226*	A.C. MacLaren	Kent	Canterbury	1896
226*	W. Place	Nottinghamshire	Nottingham	1949
226	E. Tyldesley	Sussex	Old Trafford	1926
226	G. Fowler	Kent	Maidstone	1984

225	J.T. Tyldesley	Nottinghamshire	Nottingham	1904
225	G.E. Tyldesley	Worcestershire	Worcester	1932
224	R.H. Spooner	Surrey	The Oval	1911
224	K.J. Grieves	Cambridge Univ.	Cambridge	1957
223	F. Watson	Northamptonshire	Old Trafford	1928
222	J. Iddon	Leicestershire	Liverpool	1929
222	E. Paynter	Derbyshire	Old Trafford	1939
221	J.T. Tyldesley	Nottinghamshire	Nottingham	1901
220	F.H. Sugg	Gloucestershire	Bristol	1896
220	J.L. Hopwood	Gloucestershire	Bristol	1934
219★	C. Washbrook	Gloucestershire	Bristol	1938
217★	J. Iddon	Worcestershire	Old Trafford	1939
217★	C.H. Lloyd	Warwickshire	Old Trafford	1971
216	K.J. Grieves	Cambridge Univ.	Old Trafford	1960
215	R.H. Spooner	Essex	Leyton	1904
211★	C. Washbrook	Somerset	Old Trafford	1952
211	J. Sharp	Leicestershire	Old Trafford	1912
210	J.T. Tyldesley	Somerset	Bath	1904
210	J.T. Tyldesley	Surrey	The Oval	1913
209★	C. Washbrook	Warwickshire	Birmingham	1951
209	J.T. Tyldesley	Warwickshire	Birmingham	1907
208★	E. Paynter	Nothamptonshire	Northampton	1935
207	F. Watson	Worcestershire	Worcester	1929
204★	J. Iddon	Warwickshire	Birmingham	1933
204★	C. Washbrook	Sussex	Old Trafford	1947
204	A.C. MacLaren	Gloucestershire	Liverpool	1903
203★	G.D. Mendis	Middlesex	Old Trafford	1987
203	J.W.H. Makepeace	Worcestershire	Worcester	1923
202★	K.J. Grieves	Indians	Blackpool	1959
201★	J. Abrahams	Warwickshire	Nuneaton	1984
201	J. Iddon	Sussex	Old Trafford	1932
200★	R.H. Spooner	Yorkshire	Old Trafford	1910
200★	H. Makepeace	Northamptonshire	Liverpool	1923
200★	J. Iddon	Nottinghamshire	Old Trafford	1934
200	J.T. Tyldesley	Derbyshire	Old Trafford	1898
200	W. Place	Somerset	Taunton	1948
200	C. Washbrook	Hampshire	Old Trafford	1948

CENTURIES IN LIMITED-OVER MATCHES

(a) SUNDAY LEAGUE (JOHN PLAYER/REFUGE ASSURANCE)

Score	Batsman	Opponents	Venue	Year
134*	C.H. Lloyd	Somerset	Old Trafford	1970
116*	N.H. Fairbrother	Nottinghamshire	Trent Bridge	1988
112	G. Fowler	Kent	Canterbury	1986
108	C.H. Lloyd	Glamorgan	Old Trafford	1985
107	G. Fowler	Worcestershire	Old Trafford	1986
105*	C.H. Lloyd	Leicestershire	Old Trafford	1975
105*	C.H. Lloyd	Middlesex	Old Trafford	1981
103*	D. Lloyd	Northants	Bedford	1971
103*	J. Abrahams	Somerset	Taunton	1986
102*	N.H. Fairbrother	Glamorgan	Old Trafford	1987
102	N.H. Fairbrother	Somerset	Old Trafford	1987
101*	C.H. Lloyd	Yorkshire	Headingley	1975
101	D. Lloyd	Essex	Southport	1974
101*	S.J. O'Shaughnessy	Leicestershire	Leicester	1984
100*	C.H. Lloyd	Nottinghamshire	Trent Bridge	1974
100*	G. Fowler	Somerset	Old Trafford	1987

(b) BENSON AND HEDGES CUP

Score	Batsman	Opponents	Venue	Year
124	C.H. Lloyd	Warwickshire	Old Trafford	1981
116*	N.H. Fairbrother	Scotland	Old Trafford	1988
113	D. Lloyd	Minor Counties North	Old Trafford	1973
113	D. Lloyd	Scotland	Old Trafford	1980
109*	B.W. Reidy	Derbyshire	Chesterfield	1980
109*	H. Pilling	Glamorgan	Old Trafford	1973
102	F.C. Hayes	Minor Counties North	Old Trafford	1973
101	C.H. Lloyd	Yorkshire	Old Trafford	1986
100*	D. Lloyd	Derbyshire	Chesterfield	1980

(c) NAT WEST TROPHY/GILLETTE CUP

Score	Batsman	Opponents	Venue	Year
131	A. Kennedy	Middlesex	Old Trafford	1978
126	C.H. Lloyd	Warwickshire	Lord's	1972
122	G. Fowler	Gloucestershire	Bristol	1984
121*	D. Lloyd	Gloucestershire	Old Trafford	1978
121	P Marner	Leicestershire	Old Trafford	1963
119*	C.H. Lloyd	Gloucestershire	Old Trafford	1978
116	B. Wood	Kent	Canterbury	1978
109	C.H. Lloyd	Essex	Chelmsford	1971
105	B. Wood	Warwickshire	Edgbaston	1976
102*	A. Kennedy	Durham	Old Trafford	1981
101	G. Fowler	Buckinghamshire	Old Trafford	1984

CARRYING BAT THROUGH A COMPLETED FIRST-CLASS INNINGS

Year	Batsman	Opponents and venue	Score	Total
1867	J. Ricketts	Surrey, at the Oval	195	429
1874	R.G. Barlow	Kent, at Maidstone	26	116
1876	R.G. Barlow	Nottinghamshire, at Trent Bridge	34	187
1878	R.G. Barlow	MCC, at Lord's	34	99
1880	R.G. Barlow	Yorkshire, at Old Trafford	10	47
1882	R.G. Barlow	Australians, at Old Trafford	66	269
1882	R.G. Barlow	Nottinghamshire, at Trent Bridge	5	69
1882	R.G. Barlow	Nottinghamshire, at Aigburth	44	93
1882	R.G. Barlow	Gloucestershire, at Clifton	58	240
1885	R.G. Barlow	Gloucestershire, at Clifton	62	183
1889	R.G. Barlow	Kent, at Maidstone	51	215
1890	R.G. Barlow	Surrey, at the Oval	29	131
1876	A.N. Hornby	Yorkshire, at Old Trafford	23	56
1893	A. Ward	Australians, at Old Trafford	45	97
1893	A. Ward	Gloucestershire, at Bristol	140	281
1895	A. Ward	Leicestershire, at Old Trafford	75	168
1899	A. Ward	Hampshire, at Southampton	109	337
1899	A. Ward	Middlesex, at Lord's	83	262
1913	J.W.H. Makepeace	Kent, at Maidstone	39	88
1921	J.W.H. Makepeace	Cambridge University, at Cambridge	71	185
1923	J.W.H. Makepeace	Nottinghamshire, at Trent Bridge	106	208
1926	J.W.H. Makepeace	Nottinghamshire, at Trent Bridge	92	159
1921	C. Hallows	Sussex, at Old Trafford	109	230
1921	C. Hallows	Leicestershire, at Old Trafford	110	183
1923	C. Hallows	Essex, at Southend	179	393
1925	C. Hallows	Leicestershire, at Leicester	158	297
1925	C. Hallows	Derbyshire, at Nelson	65	103
1929	C. Hallows	Yorkshire, at Old Trafford	152	305
1931	J.L. Hopwood	Somerset, at Nelson	60	153
1935	J.L. Hopwood	South Africans, at Old Trafford	73	128
1935	C. Washbrook	Worcestershire, at Old Trafford	49	124
1949	J.T. Ikin	Middlesex, at Old Trafford	119	261
1951	J.T. Ikin	Surrey, at the Oval	125	197
1950	W. Place	Warwickshire, at Edgbaston	101	244
1963	B.J. Booth	Derbyshire, at Liverpool	62	140
1988	G.D. Mendis	Glamorgan at Swansea	65	163

CENTURY IN EACH INNINGS OF A FIRST-CLASS MATCH

Year	Batsman	Opponents and venue	Score	
1897	J.T. Tyldesley	Warwickshire at Birmingham	106	and 100★
1910	J.T. Tyldesley	Hampshire at Old Trafford	136	and 101
	(First time ever performed at Manchester)			
1921	G.E. Tyldesley	Essex at Leyton	165	and 123★
1924	C. Hallows	Leics. at Ashby-de-la-Zouch	112★	and 103★
1928	C. Hallows	Warwickshire at Birmingham	123	and 101★
1933	G.E. Tyldesley	Glamorgan at Cardiff	109	and 108★
1938	E. Paynter	Warwickshire at Birmingham	125	and 113★
1947	W. Place	Notts. at Old Trafford	105	and 132★
1947	C. Washbrook	Sussex at Eastboune	176	and 121★
1970	H. Pilling	Warwickshire at Old Trafford	119★	and 104★
1979	D. Lloyd	Worcestershire at Southport	116	and 104★
1982	G. Fowler	Warwickshire at Southport	126	and 128★

CENTURY ON FIRST-CLASS DEBUT FOR LANCASHIRE

Year	Batsman	Opponents and venue	Score
1867	J. Ricketts	Surrey, at The Oval	*195
1890	A.C. MacLaren	Sussex, at Brighton	108
1908	R. Whitehead	Nottinghamshire, at Old Trafford	*131

2,000 FIRST-CLASS RUNS IN A SEASON FOR LANCASHIRE

Batsman	Runs	Average	Year
J.T. Tyldesley	2633	56.02	1901
E. Paynter	2626	58.35	1937
C. Hallows	2564	65,74	1928
F. Watson	2541	63.52	1928
G.E. Tyldesley	2487	57.83	1934
G.E. Tyldesley	2467	77.09	1928
G.E. Tyldesley	2432	62.35	1926
G.E. Tyldesley	2420	59.02	1932
W. Place	2408	68.80	1947
J. Iddon	2381	52.91	1934
J.W.H. Makepeace	2340	48.75	1926
J.T. Tyldesley	2335	66.71	1904
J.W.H. Makepeace	2286	50.80	1923
K. Grieves	2253	41.72	1959
G. Pullar	2197	54.92	1959
C. Hallows	2185	52.02	1925
A. Wharton	2157	40.69	1959
F. Watson	2137	46.45	1929
C. Hallows	2119	73.06	1927
J.D. Bond	2112	37.05	1962
G.E. Tyldesley	2070	46.00	1922
G. Pullar	2047	47.60	1961
F. Watson	2031	45.13	1930
E. Paynter	2020	57.71	1938
E. Paynter	2016	45.81	1936

INDIVIDUAL BOWLING RECORDS

HAT-TRICKS IN FIRST-CLASS MATCHES

1876	A. Watson, *v* Kent (Castleton)
1879	R.G. Barlow, *v* Derbyshire (Old Trafford)
1881	J. Crossland, *v* Surrey (The Oval)
1881	R.G. Barlow, *v* Derbyshire (Derby)
1882	G. Nash, *v* Somerset (Old Trafford) (four in four balls)
1886	R.G. Barlow, *v* Nottinghamshire (Old Trafford)
1894	A.W. Mold, *v* Somerset (Old Trafford)
1895	A.W. Mold, *v* Nottinghamshire (Nottingham) (four in four balls)
1905	W. Brearley, *v* Somerset (Old Trafford) (four in four balls)
1906	A. Kermode, *v* Leicestershire (Leicester)
1906	W.R. Gregson, *v* Leicestershire (Blackpool)
1912	R. Whitehead, *v* Surrey (Old Trafford)
1914	J. Bullough, *v* Derbyshire (Derby)
1920	J.D. Tyldesley, *v* Derbyshire (Old Trafford)
1922	J.D. Tyldesley, *v* Worcestershire (Old Trafford)
1925	E.A. McDonald, *v* Sussex (Hove)
1926	E.A. McDonald, *v* Kent (Dover)
1929	R. Tyldesley, *v* Derbyshire (Derby) (four in four balls)
1930	E.A. McDonald, *v* Warwickshire (Birmingham)
1938	L.L. Wilkinson, *v* Sussex (Hove)
1939	R. Pollard, *v* Glamorgan (Preston)
1947	R. Pollard, *v* Warwickshire (Blackpool)
1949	J.T. Ikin, *v* Somerset (Taunton)
1953	R. Tattersall, *v* Nottinghamshire (Old Trafford)
1956	F.W. Moore, *v* Essex (Chelmsford)
1956	J.B. Statham, *v* Sussex (Old Trafford)
1958	J.B. Statham, *v* Leicestershire (Old Trafford)
1960	K. Higgs, *v* Essex (Blackpool)
1968	K. Higgs, *v* Yorkshire (Leeds)
1969	P. Lever, *v* Nottinghamshire (Old Trafford)
1977	J. Simmons, *v* Nottinghamshire (Liverpool)
1988	Wasim Akram *v* Surrey (Southport)

NINE OR MORE WICKETS IN AN INNINGS FOR LANCASHIRE

Analysis	Bowler	Opponents	Venue	Year
10–46	W. Hickton	Hampshire	Old Trafford	1870
10–55	J. Briggs	Worcestershire	Old Trafford	1900
10–102	R. Berry	Worcestershire	Blackpool	1953
9–25	A. Appleby	Sussex	Brighton	1877
9–29	J. Briggs	Derbyshire	Derby	1885
9–29	A. Mold	Kent	Tonbridge	1893
9–31	H. Dean	Somerset	Old Trafford	1909
9–32	C.H. Parkin	Leicestershire	Ashby	1924
9–33	J.L. Hopwood	Leicestershire	Old Trafford	1933
9–35	H. Dean	Warwickshire	Liverpool	1909
9–36	W. Huddleston	Nottinghamshire	Liverpool	1906
9–37	J. Hallows	Gloucestershire	Gloucester	1904
9–39	R.G. Barlow	Sussex	Old Trafford	1886
9–40	R. Tattersall	Nottinghamshire	Old Trafford	1953
9–41	A.W. Mold	Yorkshire	Huddersfield	1890
9–42	J. Iddon	Yorkshire	Sheffield	1937
9–43	J.S. Heap	Northamptonshire	Northampton	1910
9–44	F. Harry	Warwickshire	Old Trafford	1906

9–46	H. Dean	Derbyshire	Chesterfield	1907
9–47	W. Brearley	Somerset	Old Trafford	1905
9–62	A.W. Mold	Kent	Old Trafford	1895
9–62	H. Dean	Yorkshire	Liverpool	1913
9–63	A.G. Steel	Yorkshire	Old Trafford	1878
9–69	J.L. Hopwood	Worcestershire	Blackpool	1934
9–77	J. Sharp	Worcestershire	Worcester	1901
9–77	H. Dean	Somerset	Bath	1910
9–80	W. Brearley	Yorkshire	Old Trafford	1909
9–88	J. Briggs	Sussex	Old Trafford	1888
9–109	H. Dean	Leicestershire	Leicester	1912
9–118	A. Watson	Derbyshire	Old Trafford	1874

FIFTEEN OR MORE WICKETS IN A MATCH FOR LANCASHIRE

Analysis	Bowler	Opponents	Venue	Year
17–91	H. Dean	Yorkshire	Liverpool	1913
17–137	W. Brearley	Somerset	Old Trafford	1905
16–103	H. Dean	Somerset	Bath	1910
16–111	A. Mold	Kent	Old Trafford	1895
15–47	W. McIntyre	Derbyshire	Derby	1877
15–70	F. Harry	Warwickshire	Old Trafford	1906
15–85	A.W. Mold	Nottinghamshire	Nottingham	1895
15–87	A.W. Mold	Sussex	Brighton	1894
15–89	J.B. Statham	Warwickshire	Coventry	1957
15–95	C.H. Parkin	Glamorgan	Blackpool	1923
15–108	H. Dean	Kent	Old Trafford	1912
15–108	J.B. Statham	Leicestershire	Leicester	1964
15–112	J.L. Hopwood	Worcestershire	Blackpool	1934
15–131	A. Mold	Somerset	Taunton	1891
15–154	E.A. McDonald	Kent	Old Trafford	1928

SIX WICKETS IN A LIMITED-OVERS MATCH

(a) SUNDAY LEAGUE (JOHN PLAYER/REFUGE ASSURANCE)

Analysis	Bowler	Opponents	Venue	Year
6–29	D.P. Hughes	Somerset	Old Trafford	1977

(b) BENSON & HEDGES CUP

6–10	C.E.H. Croft	Scotland	Old Trafford	1982

(c) NAT WEST/GILLETTE CUP
None

125 WICKETS IN A SEASON FOR LANCASHIRE (100 SINCE 1964)

Total	Bowler	Year	Total	Bowler	Year
198	E.A. McDonald	1925	140	R. Pollard	1938
194	C.H. Parkin	1924	137	J. Briggs	1894
192	A.W. Mold	1895	137	A. Mold	1896
190	E.A. McDonald	1928	137	R. Tyldesley	1925
189	A.W. Mold	1894	137	R. Pollard	1947
186	C.H. Parkin	1923	136	H. Dean	1912
181	C.H. Parkin	1922	135	R. Tattersall	1953
179	H. Dean	1911	135	R. Tattersall	1957
175	E.A. McDonald	1926	133	R. Tyldesley	1923
171	R. Tattersall	1950	133	R. Tyldesley	1930
167	R. Tyldesley	1924	133	W.E. Phillipson	1939

155	J. Briggs	1897	
154	R. Tyldesley	1929	
154	W. Brearley	1908	
150	L. Cook	1920	
150	C.H. Parkin	1925	
150	E.A. McDonald	1927	
150	M.J. Hilton	1956	
148	L. Cook	1921	
146	R. Tattersall	1952	
145	J. Briggs	1896	
145	L.L. Wilkinson	1938	
142	A. Mold	1893	
142	L. Cook	1922	
142	E.A. McDonald	1929	

133	H. Dean	1910
133	W. Brearley	1905
131	S.F. Barnes	1903
131	F.M. Sibbles	1932
131	W.E. Phillipson	1937
130	J.B. Statham	1965
129	A. Mold	1891
129	H. Dean	1908
128	R. Tyldesley	1926
128	J. Briggs	1893
127	M.J. Hilton	1950
125	J.B. Statham	1958
112	P. Lee	1975
101	P. Lee	1973

RECORD WICKET PARTNERSHIPS

Score		Batsmen	Opponents	Venue	Year
1st WICKET					
1	368	A.C. MacLaren & R.H. Spooner	Gloucestershire	Liverpool	1903
2	350★	C. Washbrook & W. Place	Sussex	Old Trafford	1947
3	299	D. Lloyd & B. Wood	Leicestershire	Leicester	1972
2nd WICKET					
1	371	F. Watson & G.E. Tyldesley	Surrey	Old Trafford	1928
2	363	A.C. MacLaren & A. Paul	Somerset	Taunton	1895
3	336	F. Watson & G.E. Tyldesley	Worcestershire	Worcester	1929
3rd WICKET					
1	306	E. Paynter & N. Oldfield	Hampshire	Southampton	1938
2	296	R.H. Spooner & J. Hallows	Essex	Leyton	1904
3	279★	E. Tyldesley & J. Iddon	Worcestershire	Worcester	1932
4th WICKET					
1	324	A.C. MacLaren & J.T. Tyldesley	Nottinghamshire	Nottingham	1904
2	300	E. Tyldesley & J. Iddon	Leicestershire	Leicester	1928
3	268★	E. Tyldesley & J. Iddon	Glamorgan	Swansea	1933
5th WICKET					
1	249	B. Wood & A. Kennedy	Warwickshire	Birmingham	1975
2	235★	N. Oldfield & A.E. Nutter	Nottinghamshire	Old Trafford	1939
3	230	T.M. Halliday & J. Iddon	Surrey	The Oval	1928
6th WICKET					
1	278	J. Iddon & H.R.W. Butterworth	Sussex	Old Trafford	1932
2	260	A.C. MacLaren & R. Whitehead	Worcestershire	Worcester	1910
3	260	K. Cranston & A. Wharton	Warwickshire	Birmingham	1948
7th WICKET					
1	245	A.H. Hornby & J. Sharp	Leicestershire	Old Trafford	1912
2	206	A.H. Hornby & W.R. Cuttell	Somerset	Old Trafford	1904
3	200	F. Watson & M.L. Taylor	Oxford University	Oxford	1930
8th WICKET					
1	158	J. Lyon & R.M. Ratcliffe	Warwickshire	Old Trafford	1979
2	150	A. Ward & C.R. Hartley	Leicestershire	Leicester	1900
3	149	K.J. Grieves & J.B. Statham	Middlesex	Old Trafford	1952
9th WICKET					
1	142	L.O.S. Poidevin & A. Kermode	Sussex	Eastbourne	1907
2	141	J.D. Tyldesley & W. Huddleston	Yorkshire	Sheffield	1914
3	138	C. Washbrook & E. Price	Middlesex	Old Trafford	1946
10th WICKET					
1	173	J. Briggs & R. Pilling	Surrey	Liverpool	1885
2	141	J.T. Tyldesley & W. Worsley	Nottinghamshire	Nottingham	1905
3	131	E. Tyldesley & R. Whitehead	Warwickshire	Birmingham	1914

RECORD WICKET PARTNERSHIPS IN LIMITED-OVER MATCHES

RECORD PARTNERSHIPS FOR LANCASHIRE FOR EACH WICKET IN THE REFUGE ASSURANCE/JOHN PLAYER LEAGUE 1969–1988

1st	177 G. Fowler and G.D. Mendis v Kent, Canterbury	1986
2nd	149 S.J. O'Shaughnessy and J. Abrahams v Leicestershire at Leicester	1984
3rd	182 H. Pilling and C.H. Lloyd v Somerset at Old Trafford	1970
4th	157* C.H. Lloyd and J. Abrahams v Gloucestershire at Bristol	1983
5th	107 J. Sullivan and A. Kennedy v Glamorgan at Old Trafford	1974
6th	109 D.P. Hughes and N.H. Fairbrother v Surrey at the Oval	1983
7th	130 D.P. Hughes and A.N. Hayhurst v Kent at Old Trafford	1987
8th	65 J. Simmons and R.M. Ratcliffe v Warwickshire at Birmingham	1977
9th	87 D.P. Hughes and P. Lever v Essex at Leyton	1973
10th	30* M. Watkinson and I. Folley v Hampshire at Old Trafford	1983

RECORD PARTNERSHIPS FOR LANCASHIRE FOR EACH WICKET IN THE BENSON AND HEDGES CUP, 1972–1988

1st	164 A. Kennedy and D. Lloyd v Nottinghamshire at Old Trafford	1980
2nd	146 G. Fowler and F.C. Hayes v Northamptonshire at Old Trafford	1983
3rd	227 D. Lloyd and F.C. Hayes v Minor Counties North at Old Trafford	1973
4th	184* D. Lloyd and B.W. Reidy v Derbyshire at Chesterfield	1980
5th	106* J. Abrahams and N.H. Fairbrother v Minor Counties at Bowdon	1984
6th	93 I. Cockbain and J. Simmons v Worcestershire at Old Trafford	1980
7th	58 J. Simmons and J. Lyon v Derbyshire at Old Trafford	1978
8th	61 J. Simmons and C. Maynard v Warwickshire at Birmingham	1985
9th	34* I. Folley and C.E.H. Croft v Scotland at Old Trafford	1982
10th	69 J. Simmons and C.D. Mathews v Leicestershire at Leicester	1988

RECORD PARTNERSHIPS FOR LANCASHIRE FOR EACH WICKET IN THE GILLETTE CUP & NATWEST BANK TROPHY 1963–1988

1st	129 D. Lloyd and B. Wood v Bedfordshire at Luton	1973
2nd	110 G. Fowler and D. Lloyd v Northamptonshire at Northampton	1981
3rd	160 B. Wood and F.C. Hayes v Warwickshire at Birmingham	1976
4th	234* D. Lloyd and C.H. Lloyd v Gloucestershire at Old Trafford	1978
5th	114 C.H. Lloyd and D.P. Hughes v Surrey at Old Trafford	1977
6th	104 C.H. Lloyd and M. Watkinson v Worcestershire at Old Trafford	1985
7th	91 C.H. Lloyd and J. Simmons v Essex at Chelmsford	1971
8th	45* J. Simmons and D.P. Hughes v Kent at Lord's	1971
9th	46 J. Dyson and P. Lever v Essex at Old Trafford	1963
10th	37* D.P. Hughes and P.G. Lee v Middlesex at Lord's	1974

WICKET-KEEPING RECORDS

SIX DISMISSALS IN AN INNINGS

7	W. Farrimond	(St1, Ct6)	v Kent (Old Trafford)	1930
6	H.G. Garnett	(St0, Ct6)	v Warwickshire (Birmingham)	1914
6	G. Duckworth	(St1, Ct5)	v Kent (Dover)	1926
6	G. Duckworth	(St1, Ct5)	v Worcestershire (Worcester)	1936
6	F.M. Engineer	(St0, Ct6)	v Northamptonshire (Liverpool)	1970
6	F.M. Engineer	(St0, Ct6)	v Surrey (Oval)	1970
6	C. Maynard	(St0, Ct6)	v Glamorgan (Swansea)	1983

EIGHT DISMISSALS IN A MATCH

9	G. Clayton	(St1, Ct8)	v Gloucestershire (Gloucester)	1959
9	C. Maynard	(St1, Ct8)	v Somerset (Taunton)	1982
8	G. Duckworth	(St3, Ct5)	v Kent (Maidstone)	1928
8	G. Duckworth	(St5, Ct3)	v Warwickshire (Old Trafford)	1936
8	A. Wilson	(St0, Ct8)	v Hampshire (Portsmouth)	1955
8	G. Clayton	(St1, Ct7)	v Cambridge Univ. (Cambridge)	1964
8	F.M. Engineer	(St0, Ct8)	v Somerset (Taunton)	1969
8	F.M. Engineer	(St0, Ct8)	v Northamptonshire (Liverpool)	1970
8	F.M. Engineer	(St0, Ct8)	v Middlesex (Lord's)	1970
8	F.M. Engineer	(St0, Ct8)	v Nottinghamshire (Old Trafford)	1973
8	C. Maynard	(St0, Ct8)	v Glamorgan (Swansea)	1983

SEVENTY DISMISSALS IN A SEASON (70 OR MORE)

		For Lancashire			All First-Class Matches		
		St.	Ct.	Total	St.	Ct.	Total
G. Duckworth	1928	28	69	97	30	77	107
G. Duckworth	1929	26	44	70	37	58	95
G. Clayton	1962	6	86	92	6	86	92
F.M. Engineer	1970	4	78	82	5	86	91
G. Clayton	1960	7	76	83	7	82	89
G. Duckworth	1934	25	54	79	26	60	86
W. Farrimond	1938	15	69	84	15	70	85
G. Duckworth	1936	21	48	69	26	57	83
G. Duckworth	1930	23	37	60	28	53	81
C. Smith	1895	25	51	76	25	51	76
K. Goodwin	1967	7	66	73	7	66	73
F.M. Engineer	1975	3	69	72	3	69	72
W. Farrimond	1939	10	62	72	10	62	72
G. Clayton	1963	4	67	71	4	67	71

WICKET-KEEPING IN ALL FIRST-CLASS LANCASHIRE MATCHES, 1865–1988

	Played	Matches	Caught	Stumped	Total
G. Duckworth	1923–1938	424	634	288	922
R. Pilling	1877–1889	177	333	153	486
F.M. Engineer	1968–1976	175	429	35	464
C. Smith	1893–1902	167	312	119	431
G. Clayton	1959–1964	183	390	32	422

FIELDING RECORDS

FIVE OR MORE CATCHES IN AN INNINGS

No.	Player	Opponents	Venue	Year
6	R.K. Tyldesley	Hampshire	Liverpool	1921
6	K.J. Grieves	Sussex	Old Trafford	1951
5	A.G. Paul	Derbyshire	Derby	1897
5	K.J. Grieves	Glamorgan	Blackpool	1950
5	K.J. Grieves	Gloucestershire	Bristol	1954

SEVEN OR MORE CATCHES IN A MATCH

No.	Player	Opponents	Venue	Year
8	K.J. Grieves	Sussex	Old Trafford	1951
7	L.O.S. Poidevin	Yorkshire	Old Trafford	1906

45 OR MORE CATCHES IN A SEASON

No.	Player	Year	No.	Player	Year
63	K.J. Grieves	1950	45	J.T. Ikin	1946
54	K.J. Grieves	1953			

MOST CATCHES IN A CAREER

No.	Player	Years
555	K.J. Grieves	1949–64

LANCASHIRE PLAYERS IN TEST CRICKET

	Played	Mtchs	Runs	H.S.	Aver.	100's	Wkts	Aver.
P.J.W. Allott	1981–1985	13	213	*52	14.20	—	26	41.69
R.W. Barber	1960–1968	28	1495	185	35.59	1	42	43.00
R.G. Barlow	1881–1887	17	591	62	22.73	—	35	21.91
S.F. Barnes	1901–1914	27	242	38	8.06	—	189	16.43
R. Berry	1950	2	6	*4	3.00	—	9	25.33
W. Brearley	1905–1912	4	21	*11	7.00	—	17	21.11
J. Briggs	1884–1899	33	815	121	18.11	1	118	17.74
K. Cranston	1947–1948	8	209	45	14.92	—	18	25.61
W.R. Cuttell	1899	2	65	21	16.25	—	6	12.16
C.E.H. Croft (West Indies)	1977–1982	27	158	33	10.53	—	125	23.30
H. Dean	1912	3	10	8	5.00	—	11	13.90
G. Duckworth	1924–1936	24	234	*39	14.62	—	(St. 15, Ct. 44, T. 59)	
F.M. Engineer (India)	1961–1975	46	2611	121	31.08	2	(St. 16, Ct. 66, T. 82)	
N.H. Fairbrother	1987–1988	4	5	3	1.25	—	—	—
W. Farrimond	1931–1935	4	116	35	16.57	—	(St. 2, Ct. 7, T. 9)	
G. Fowler	1982–1985	21	1307	201	35.32	3	0	—
T. Greenhough	1959–1960	4	4	2	1.33	—	16	22.31
C. Hallows	1921–1928	2	42	26	42.00	—	—	—
F.C. Hayes	1973–1976	9	244	*106	15.25	1	—	—
K. Higgs	1965–1968	15	185	63	11.56	—	71	20.74
M.J. Hilton	1950–1952	4	37	15	7.40	—	15	33.64
J.L. Hopwood	1934	2	12	8	6.00	—	0	—

A.N. Hornby	1879–1884	3	21	9	3.50	—	0	—
N.D. Howard	1951–1952	4	86	25	17.20	—	—	—
J. Iddon	1935	5	170	72	28.33	—	0	—
J.T. Ikin	1946–1955	18	606	60	20.89	—	3	118.00
P. Lever	1970–1975	17	350	★88	21.87	—	41	36.80
C.H. Lloyd (West Indies)	1966–1985	110	7515	★242	46.67	19	10	62.20
D. Lloyd	1974–1975	9	552	★214	42.46	1	0	—
A.C. MacLaren	1894–1909	35	1931	140	33.87	5	—	—
H. Makepeace	1920–1921	4	279	117	34.87	1	—	—
A.W. Mold	1893	3	0	★0	0.00	—	7	33.42
N. Oldfield	1939	1	99	80	49.50	—	—	—
C.H. Parkin	1920–1924	10	160	36	12.30	—	32	35.25
B.P. Patterson (West Indies)	1986–1988	13	56	★21	8.00	—	47	28.80
E. Paynter	1931–1939	20	1540	243	59.23	4	—	—
R. Pilling	1881–1888	8	91	23	7.58	—	(St. 4, Ct. 10, T. 14)	
W. Place	1948	3	144	107	28.80	1	—	—
R. Pollard	1946–1948	4	13	★10	13.00	—	15	25.20
G. Pullar	1959–1963	28	1974	175	43.86	4	1	37.00
V.P.F.A. Royle	1879	1	21	18	10.50	—	—	—
S.S. Schultz	1879	1	20	20	20.00	—	1	26.00
J. Sharp	1909	3	188	105	47.00	1	3	37.00
K. Shuttleworth	1970–1971	5	46	28	7.66	—	12	35.38
R.H. Spooner	1905–1912	10	481	119	32.06	1	—	—
J.B. Statham	1951–1965	70	765	38	11.44	—	252	24.84
A.G. Steel	1880–1888	13	600	148	35.29	2	29	20.86
F.H. Sugg	1888	2	55	31	27.50	—	—	—
R. Tattersall	1951–1954	16	50	★10	5.00	—	58	26.18
G.E. Tyldesley	1921–1929	14	990	122	55.00	3	0	—
J.T. Tyldesley	1899–1909	31	1661	138	30.75	4	—	—
R. Tyldesley	1924–1930	7	47	29	7.83	—	19	32.57
A. Ward	1893–1895	7	487	117	37.46	1	—	—
C. Washbrook	1937–1956	37	2569	195	42.81	6	1	33.00
Wasim Akram (Pakistan)	1984–1988	25	410	66	16.40	—	76	27.60
A. Wharton	1949	1	20	13	10.00	—	—	—
L.L. Wilkinson	1938–1939	3	3	2	3.00	—	7	38.71
B. Wood	1972–1978	12	454	90	21.61	—	0	—
R. Wood	1887	1	6	6	3.00	—	—	—

(This list includes players who played Test cricket while playing for Lancashire)

LANCASHIRE CAPTAINS

1866–79	E.B. Rowley	1946	J.A. Fallows
1880–91	A.N. Hornby	1947–48	K. Cranston
1892–93	A.N. Hornby and S.M. Crosfield	1949–53	N.D. Howard
		1954–59	C. Washbrook
1894–96	A.C. MacLaren	1960–61	R.W. Barber
1897–98	A.N. Hornby	1962	J.F. Blackledge
1899	A.C. MacLaren and G.R. Bardswell	1963–64	K.J. Grieves
		1965–67	J.B. Statham
1900–07	A.C. MacLaren	1968–72	J.D. Bond
1908–14	A.H. Hornby	1973–77	D. Lloyd
1919–22	M.N. Kenyon	1978–80	F.C. Hayes
1923–25	J. Sharp	1981–83	C.H. Lloyd
1926–28	Colonel L. Green	1984–85	J. Abrahams
1929–35	P.T. Eckersley	1986	C.H. Lloyd
1936–39	W.H.L. Lister	1987–88	D.P. Hughes

LANCASHIRE CRICKETERS TO BE AWARDED A BLUE AT OXFORD

G.R. Bardswell	1894, 1896, 1897	Rev L.D. Hildyard	1884, 1885, 1886
R.V. Bardsley	1911, 1912, 1913	Sir F.H. Hollins	1901
E.A. Barlow	1932, 1933, 1934	C.C. Pilkington	1896
R. Bowman	1957	Rev V.P.F.A. Royle	1875, 1876
A. Eccles	1897, 1898, 1899	T.J. Taylor	1981, 1982
W. Findlay	1901, 1902, 1903	D.R. Worsley	1961, 1962, 1963, 1964
D.M. Green	1959, 1960, 1961	E.L. Wright	1905, 1906, 1907, 1908
K.A. Hayes	1981, 1982, 1983, 1984	Rev F.W. Wright	1863, 1864, 1865

LANCASHIRE CRICKETERS TO BE AWARDED A BLUE AT CAMBRIDGE

M.A. Atherton	1987, 1988	K.G. MacLeod	1908, 1909
R.W. Barber	1956, 1957	F.H. Mugliston	1907, 1908
Sir J.M.B. Brocklebank	1936	W.S. Patterson	1875, 1876, 1877
H.R.W. Butterworth	1929	S.S. Schultz	1877
E.J. Craig	1961, 1962, 1963	G.O. Shelmerdine	1922
F.D. Gaddum	1882	C.S. Smith	1954, 1955, 1956, 1957
Sir G.M. Kemp	1885, 1886, 1888	J. Stanning	1900
O.P. Lancashire	1880	A.G. Steel	1878, 1879, 1880, 1881
J. Makinson	1856, 1857, 1858	D.Q. Steel	1876, 1877, 1878, 1879
C.S. Marriott	1920, 1921	D.W. Varey	1982, 1983

BROTHERS WHO HAVE REPRESENTED LANCASHIRE

L.W. Cook, W. Cook
C. Coward, F. Coward
G.A. Edrich, E.H. Edrich
S. Ellis, W. Ellis
A. Hartley, C.R. Hartley
P. Higson, T.A. Higson
J. Hilton, M.J. Hilton
J.C.H.L. Hollins, Sir F.H. Hollins
C.L. Hornby, A.N. Hornby
N.D. Howard, B.J. Howard
R. Iddison, W.H. Iddison
J. Jackson, E. Jackson
J. Leach, H. Leach, R. Leach, R.C. Leach
E. Leese, J.F. Leese
J.A. MacLaren, A.C. MacLaren,
  G. MacLaren

W. Pilling, R. Pilling
W.H. Potter, T.O. Potter
E.B. Rowley, A.B. Rowley
D.J. Smith, C.S. Smith
R.H. Spooner, A.F. Spooner
J. Stanning, H.D. Stanning
A.G. Steel, H.B. Steel, E.E. Steel,
  D.Q. Steel
W.M. Tennent, H.N. Tennent
H.J. Tinsley, A. Tinsley
J.T. Tyldesley, G.E. Tyldesley
J.D. Tyldesley, R.K. Tyldesley,
  W.K. Tyldesley, H. Tyldesley
T. Wall, W. Wall, H. Wall

FATHERS AND SONS WHO HAVE REPRESENTED LANCASHIRE

Father   Son(s)
G. Bird — M.C. Bird
J. Ellis — S. Ellis
— W. Ellis
S. Haggas — W. Haggas
G. Hartley — A. Hartley
— C.R. Hartley
T.A. Higson — T.A. Higson
— P. Higson
A.N. Hornby — A.H. Hornby
R. Howard — B.J. Howard
— N.D. Howard
E. Leese — C.P. Leese
G.W. Littlewood — G.H. Littlewood
D. Lloyd — G.D. Lloyd
C.H. Parkin — R. Parkin
E.B. Rowley — E.B. Rowley

BIBLIOGRAPHY

V. Addison & B. Bearshaw: *Lancashire cricket at the Top* (S. Paul, 1971)
D. Foster: *Lancashire* (Findon, 1949)
A.W. Ledbrooke: *Lancashire County Cricket* (Phoenix House, 1954)
J. Kay: *Lancashire* (Arthur Barker, 1972)
Rex Pogson: *Lancashire County Cricket* (1952)
T.C.F. Prittie: *Lancashire Hot Pot* (Hutchinson, 1949)
F.R. Reynolds: *Lancashire County Cricket* (Heywood, 1881)
Lancashire CCC: *Annual Handbook* from 1930 to date
J.B. Statham: *Cricket Merry-Go-Round* (S. Paul, 1956)
J.B. Statham: *A Spell at the Top* (Souvenir, 1969)
W.A. Bettesworth: *Chats on the Cricket Field* (Merritt & Hatcher, 1910)
R.G. Barlow: *Forty Seasons of First-class Cricket* (Heywood, 1908)
L. Duckworth: *S.F. Barnes, Master Bowler* (Hutchinson, 1968)
N. Cardus: *Autobiography* (Collins, 1948)
N. Cardus: *A Cricketer's Book* (Grant Richards, 1922)
N. Cardus: *Days in the Sun* (Cape, 1929)
N. Cardus: *The Summer Game* (Cape, 1935)
N. Cardus: *Good Days* (Cape, 1937)
N. Cardus: *Cricket All The Year* (Collins, 1952)
N. Cardus: *The Playfair Cardus* (Playfair, 1963)
J.A.H. Catton: *Wickets and Goals* (Chapman & Hall, 1926)
W. Caffyn: *Seventy One Not Out* (Blackwood, 1899)
W.E. Howard: *Fifty Years of Cricket Reminiscences* (The Author, 1928)
M. Down: *Archie – A.C. MacLaren* (1981)
C.H. Parkin: *Cricket Reminiscences* (Hodder & Stoughton, 1923)
C.H. Parkin: *Cricket Triumphs and Troubles* (Nicholls, 1936)
E. Roper: *A Sportsman's Memories* (Tinling, 1921)
C. Washbrook: *Cricket – The Silver Lining* (Sportsguide, 1950)
P. Bailey, P. Thorn, P. Wynne-Thomas *Who's Who of Cricketers* (Newnes, 1985)
Cricket – A Weekly Record of The Game 1882 to 1913
The Cricketer 1921 to date
Wisden Cricket Monthly 1979 to date
The Cricket Field 1892 to 1895
The Cricket Statistician 1973 to date
The Cricket Quarterly 1963 to 1970
Wisden Cricketers' Almanack 1870 to date
MCC Scores & Biographies Vols I to XV

ACKNOWLEDGEMENTS

The author acknowledges with grateful thanks the advice and co-operation given to him by the Reverend Malcolm Lorimer, Honorary Librarian to Lancashire County Cricket Club. Mr Lorimer has also compiled the whole of the Record Section for this work. Mr Bob Warburton was kind enough to read through the manuscript and his comments were invaluable, enabling the author to avoid a number of pitfalls.

The publishers would like to thank the following for permission to reproduce photographs in this work: Lancashire CCC, Nottingham-shire CCC, Patrick Eagar, Allsport, and Bill Smith.

Where relevant, the statistics and records shown in this book comply with the various Guides to First-Class Cricket issued by the Association of Cricket Statisticians and the details of players' biographies were compiled in conjunction with the Association.

INDEX